Floyd County

A History
Of Its People
And Places

FLOYD COUNTY

A History
Of Its People
And Places

By:
Dr. Amos D. Wood

Edited By:
Ann Scott Swain Bailey

SOUTHERN PRINTING CO., INC.
501 Industrial Park Road
Blacksburg, Virginia   24060

FLOYD COUNTY: A HISTORY OF ITS
PEOPLE AND PLACES
by
Dr. Amos D. Wood

LIBRARY OF CONGRESS CATALOG CARD NUMBER: 81-69054
ISBN NO. 0-89227-040-3

PRINTED IN THE UNITED STATES OF AMERICA

Amos D. Wood

Taken at the WOOD REUNION in 1935. Left to right: Jefferson P. Wood - 76; Daniel Hillsman Wood - 74; Greenville D. Wood - 68; Amos D. Wood - 66; Sparrel Asa Wood - 61; and D. Robertson Wood - 58.

FROM THE EDITOR . . . .

Many of my forebears settled on the land that became Floyd County. The Wood's manuscript has provided missing links in my family tree. Interesting sidelights appear with each family sketch, and a desire to visit Floyd County is always present.

Dr. Amos D. Wood acquired a voluminous collection. He was a prodigious researcher--questionnaires were sent out and returned to him--some filled with family names, dates and traditional stories. As Mrs. Eula Willis Carter once wrote him, "There's the story of the *three* brothers again!"

Individual family members did not always agree on an identical name for a relative. Therefore the reader may find ambiguous and repetitious information. As editor of an eighteen month duration, I was unable to authenticate what Dr. Wood assembled over a ten-year period. Neither was there an attempt to revise his material |except where these brackets are evident|, or it is so stated. Time did not permit the actual rechecking of each family's genealogical data.

Miss Marguerite Tise, a native of Floyd, was the best co-worker one could ask for. She knew a great number of the families, facts and faces. She retyped the manuscript from an often confusing network of editorial changes and addenda. I am deeply grateful for her expertise in genealogical research.

The editorial difficulties were magnified by the fact that when Dr. Wood revised a page, it was retained but not dated.

Perhaps **FLOYD COUNTY: A HISTORY of ITS PEOPLE and PLACES** will prove genealogically useful in future generations. I welcome corrections and addenda. The original manuscript and material not included for publication will be filed at a later date by the New River Historical Society at the Wilderness Road Regional Museum, Newbern, VA 24126.

Ann Scott Swain Bailey

VII

DEDICATION

My wife Elizabeth Pritchett Wood and I, Richard Johnston Wood, wish to dedicate this book to our children, the grandchildren of the author.

Dr. Diana Pearis Wood, a Dentist in Birmingham, Alabama.

David Johnston Wood, a Presbyterian Minister in Pascagoula, Mississippi.

Hugh Chapman Wood, a law student at the University of Alabama.

PREFACE

Tracing the foregoing family sketches has occupied a period of more than ten years. Many relatives have been consulted personally or through letters. The records of many of the clerk's offices of the Virginia counties have been searched and many other sources of information resorted to including the Virginia historical magazines, the various Virginia county histories, Saffell's **Records of the Revolutionary War**, McAllister's **Virginia Militia in the Revolutionary War**, **Douglas Register**, Captain D. Lee Ross' Muster Roll, Records of the Confederate Veterans of Floyd County, Virginia, and The Huguenot Society's records.

Mrs. Jesse S. Carter, now Mrs. John M. Bell of Chester, South Carolina, has done most of the searching of the court records as well as other valuable work on the sketches. Miss Mary B. Statham, of Pasadena, California, has worked on the Wood sketch with considerable success. Others aiding in the search include:

Prof. Charles Benton Cannaday, Morgantown, W. Va.
Dr. Albert A. Cannaday, Roanoke, Va.
John P. Short, Parsons, Kansas.
Lucinda Mary Short, Floyd, Va.
Jefferson P. Wood, Floyd, Va.
William Wilson Wood, Bluefield, W. Va.
Sparrel H. Wood, Woolwine, Va.
Mrs. Rachel Turner, Floyd, Va.
Daniel Hillsman Wood, Dodson, Va.
Mrs. Deborah C. Smith, Floyd, Va.
Asa S. Smith, Floyd, Va.
D. Robertson Wood, Pulaski, Va.
Mrs. Leah Slusher, Floyd, Va.
George W. Slusher, Floyd, Va.
George B. Wood, Floyd, Va.
Sparrel A. Wood, Washington, D. C.
Mrs. Martha Ellen Rakes, Woolwine, Va.

Isaac Lemon, Endicott, Va.
James D. Cockram, Stuart, Va.
Larkin Cockram, Stuart, Va.
Greenville D. Wood, Floyd, Va.
Hughes D. Cannaday, Endicott, Va.
Mrs. Hughes D. Cannaday, Endicott, Va.
Mrs. Lucinda Thomas, Bluefield, W. Va.
Dr. Rufus M. DeHart, Floyd, Va.
Lemuel C. Radford, Ridgeway, Va.
Mrs. Lemuel C. Radford, Ridgeway, Va.
Mrs. George W. Slusher, Floyd, Va.
Mrs. Minerva Rakes, Floyd, Va.
Mrs. William Ingram, Floyd, Va.
Walter L. Robertson, Floyd, Va.
Richard F. Cannaday, Richlands, Va.
John Dinwiddie, Franklin Co., Va.
Walter L. Turner, Bluefield, W. Va.

In the poem "Now and Then," an effort was made to bring out or emphasize the old and quaint names and incidents found in the records through which these sketches ran. The compiler gratefully acknowledges the assistance mentioned above.

Bluefield, West Virginia, February 8, 1932.

Amos DeRussia Wood

Acknowledgments

Having carried the manuscript for this book around since my father's death in September of 1942, it is with great pleasure that I see it in print at last. As Dr. Amos DeRussia Wood's only child, I could never have been free of his literary effort until the book was published. It seemed at times that those yellowed pages already curling with age cried out for a hearing. I do not claim perfection for my father's work, only that it was a labor of love. Yet there is incalulable worth in this effort, for it captures a long forgotten time and unforgettable people whose descendants yet populate Floyd and other counties of Virginia and other places.

My father's book could never have been published without the enlightened and generous aid of others. In this regard I should like to acknowledge the help of Ann Scott Swain Bailey, Archivist of Radford University, who served as general editor, and Miss Marguerite Tise, who did the finished typing and retyping—work so vital and at times, so meticulous—in order that the manuscript could be presented to the printer in acceptable form. Last, but not least, to my good friend Jess Carr, without whose enthusiasm and encouragement this book might never have become a reality, I would like to express my deepest gratitude.

Richard J. Wood
Bluefield, W. Va.

1981

CONTENTS

Floyd County

A History
Of Its People
And Places

CHAPTER I

The Agee Family

The Agee family came from Patrick County, where they had lived for a number of years.

Joshua Agee (1799-1883) married Sallie Brammer (1796-18?), of Patrick County, and, about the year 1825, moved to the top of the Blue Ridge Mountains about three miles east of the Haycock Mountain. They were the parents of James Agee, who married Judith Thomas, daughter of Joseph Thomas, of Patrick County. James and Judith Agee lived in the original Joshua Agee homestead where they reared a large family. Judith Agee lived to be over 100 years old. One daughter married Floyd Dickerson, son of Morrel and Naomi.

William Agee, second son of Joshua, married Nancy Robertson, daughter of John Robertson, and they lived on a part of the Joshua Agee homeplace. Monroe Agee, son of William, is a well-known farmer of the Pine Creek neighborhood. Frances Agee, daughter of William, married Curtis Wickham, son of Nathaniel, and lives on Little River.

After the death of his first wife, Joshua Agee the settler married Mary J. Via of Patrick County in 1865, by whom he had two children: Cora Lee married Rev. Everett Lancaster, a Baptist minister; and Marion Agee married a granddaughter of James P. Martin and lives on the old Martin Place (formerly the old John Snuffer place), on the Floyd-Cannaday's Gap Road.

Samuel Agnew

Samuel W. Agnew settled in the present county of Floyd in the year 1820. He was born in Rockbridge County, Virginia, January 1, 1780, and died in Floyd County, November 17, 1868. He married Susan Preston (June 26, 1785-April 25, 1854) of Bedford County, Virginia, in 1803, and lived in Bedford County until 1820. He came to the present county of Floyd and settled 2½ miles south of where the county seat is now located. The two Bedford County families who came with him were Francis Hogan, who settled south of the courthouse on lands adjoining Samuel Agnew; and Thomas Lancaster, Sr., who settled three miles east of the courthouse. Samuel Agnew was a prominent farmer and member of the Primitive Baptist Church. He was largely instrumental in founding and building West Fork Church. He served there as deacon from its organization to the time of his death. When he moved to Floyd County, most of the land was original forest. Reputedly, he purchased about one thousand acres, the greater part of which he cleared and cultivated. When the county was organized in 1831, he was one of the largest landowners, as shown by the State Land Tax Books.

Samuel and Susan Agnew had 16 children, three of whom died in infancy, and 12 were married and raised 80 children. Their children were:

1. Malinda Agnew, died in infancy. 2. Easter Agnew (Feb. 25, 1804 - Jan. 21, 1854). 3. William B. Agnew (June 5, 1807 - June 19, 1854) married Elizabeth Carter June 14, 1827. 4. Malinda Agnew (July 20, 1808 - Nov. 9, 1875), named for the first Malinda who died in infancy, married Henry Carter August 31, 1826. 5. Charlotte Agnew (Jan. 16, 1810 - ?) married James Cannaday Jan. 12, 1832. 6. Irena Agnew (Oct. 3, 1811 - Dec. 1893) married Ezekiel McPeak Sept. 22, 1830. 7. Parthena Agnew (July 17, 1813 - ?) married David Owens May 4, 1837. 8. Booker P. Agnew (Mar. 16, 1815 - Dec. 8, 1897). 9. Joel R. Agnew (Jan. 1, 1817 - Jan. 13, 1897) married Luvenia McAlexander. 10. Nancy Jane Agnew (Aug. 15, 1818 - Dec. 12, 1894) married George Young Jan. 23, 1835. 11. Samuel W., Jr. (Mar. 18, 1820 - April 1, 1888) married Eliza Smith June 5, 1843. 12. Frank Agnew (May 4, 1822 - June 13, 1828). 13. Leah Agnew (Dec. 23, 1823 - Feb. 26, 1907) married James U. Graham Nov. 8, 1845. 14. Mariah Adaline Agnew (Nov. 23, 1825 - ?) married German Lee April 4, 1847. 15. Mary Ann Agnew (Feb. 5, 1827 - May 17, 1827). 16. Rachel Agnew (July 22, 1829 - July 1866) married Otey T. Simmons Jan. 2, 1850, son of Thomas W. Simmons and grandson of Charles Simmons the settler.

9. Joel R. Agnew, son of Samuel, Sr., was born in Bedford County in the year 1817. He married Luvenia McAlexander and lived in Floyd County. Their children were: (a) Mariah Elizabeth (b. 1843); (b) N. Johnson (b. Sept. 16, 1845); (c) Flemon Saunders (b. 1851) and (d) Pence Anna (b. 1857), deceased.

(b) N. Johnson Agnew, son of Joel R. and Luvenia, married Sarah Jane Williams, daughter of James R. Williams. Johnson

Agnew was a lifelong resident of Floyd County. He served nineteen months in the Confederate army as a member of Company G, 21st Virginia Cavalry, under Captain A. O. Dobyns; he was captured Sept. 22, 1864, and imprisoned five months at Point Lookout, Maryland. The children of Johnson Agnew are: James R. who married Cassa DeHart; Charles H., who married Ella DeHart; George W., a lawyer, who married Mallie I. Dickerson; Fred J., who married Maud Williams; and Stella E.

George W. Agnew (b. June 16, 1872), third son of Johnson and Sarah Jane Agnew, was educated in the free Public Schools of Floyd County. In 1890 he obtained a certificate to teach school and taught five terms. He was licensed to practice law in 1894, and practiced his profession in Floyd and adjoining counties. On Feb. 23, 1899, he married Mallie I. Dickerson (b. Aug. 22, 1871), daughter of Harvey and Octavia (Simmons) Dickerson. Harvey Dickerson was the son of Moral (Morrel?) and Naomi (Morricle) Dickerson. Naomi was the daughter of William Morricle. Children of George W. and Mallie I. Agnew: B. Winfield (b. Dec. 31, 1899); Harvey J. (b. Sept. 19, 1901); Stella Mae (b. Nov. 7, 1903); Winnie Apenta (b. Jan. 24, 1905); Sarah Octava (b. Feb. 29, 1908); George Martin (b. April 28, 1911); and Rachel Eleanor (b. Dec. 11, 1913 - d. Oct. 11, 1914).

The Akers Family

The name "Akers" is thought to be of English origin. The coat of arms and crescent of the English family go back to the Crusaders. The name was originally "Acres." The story goes that King Richard gave to one of his courtiers named John the town of "Acre" and thereafter he was known as "John De Acre." After a while the "De" was dropped and the name became "Acres." Finally it became "Akers."

William Akers purchased land in West Jersey prior to 1698, at which time 100 acres were granted to him and others by The West Jersey Company for a meetinghouse, burial ground and schoolhouse in the Maiden township above the falls of the Delaware. In all probability, Simon Akers was his son. Simon died intestate in Hunterdon County, New Jersey, 1722. Letters of administration were granted to Simon Akers, who was probably his oldest son. He had a son John, who bought land in Amwell township in Hunterdon County, N. J. His children were: William, Obadiah, Thomas, Susannah and Elsie. Another son of Simon was Robert (b. 1703) who married Sarah _____ (b. 1706). There is a tradition that an Akers ancestor, probably Sarah, his wife, was kidnapped in Wales as a child and brought to America. Robert and Sarah had a son William (1730-1810), who married Elizabeth Martye (or Marte) from Pennsylvania, of Holland-Dutch extraction, probably the daughter of Heinrich Martye (or Marte), who patented 175 acres in Nelson County, Va., in 1751, and later moved to Campbell County, Va. William Akers was a farmer of Campbell County. The children of William and Elizabeth were: Sarah, William, Mary, Catherine, Peter, Simon, John, Ruth, Elizabeth and Anne.

William Akers married Dolly Blackburn from Campbell County and reared the following children: James, Samuel, Daniel, John, Blackburn and Nathaniel. The daughters of the family are unknown.

Blackburn married Elizabeth LeSueur and lived on Little River in the northern section of the county. Of his children only two are known: George and James. George was the father of Professor Tazewell Akers, a noted educator of Richmond, Kentucky. Tazewell married Clara Harris, oldest daughter of Rev. John Kellogg Harris, of Oxford Academy, Floyd, Virginia. The daughters of Blackburn and Elizabeth are unknown.

Nathaniel Akers, sixth son of William and Dolly, married Elizabeth Akers, daughter of John. Their children were: Stephen, Celia, Sally, John, Letitia, "Fed" [Fred], Wesley, Samuel, Martha, Burwell, Nathaniel Clayborn, Elizabeth, Mary Ann, Caroline and Nancy. Stephen married Esther Snead; Celia married Nottly P. Adams; Sally married Peter Thomas, son of Charles, Jr., and was the mother of twenty-one children; John married Elizabeth Adams, and was probably the father of Major W. T. Akers of Buffalo Ridge, Patrick County, Virginia; Letitia married Anderson Crum; "Fed" married Elizabeth Eads; Wesley married Jane Steele; Samuel never married; Martha married Alex. Ingram; Burwell married Ellen Akers and was the Captain of Company I, 54th Virginia Infantry; Nathaniel Clayborn married Exonly Nolen; Elizabeth married Percy M. Arthur; Mary Ann married Hardin Ingram; Caroline married Jesse

Epperly; and Nancy married Elijah Via.

William J. Akers was the father of Andrew who married Susannah Duncan and lived in the Alum Ridge district of Floyd County in 1837. Lewis Akers, son of Andrew, married Mary Chaffin and was the father of a large family of children, the eldest of whom was Dr. Roley Tasville Akers, a well-known physician and minister of the Church of the Brethren. Dr. Akers married Lucy Reed and they had five sons, the eldest being Dr. W. C. Akers of Stuart, Virginia.

Adam Akers was the father of several sons, one of whom was Michael who married Louise Beldon, daughter of John Beldon of New Jersey. Their sons were Wallace and C. W. Akers. Wallace was the father of Dr. Silas Akers who married Lura A. Conduff (who later married John Phlegar) and they had two sons: John Wallace and Hunter Holmes. Dr. Silas Akers died c. 1900 of typhoid fever.

William Aldridge The Settler

In the very early days of the county, William Aldridge came from North Carolina and settled at Copper Hill, where one of his daughters married Andrew Conner, Sr., son of Daniel Conner the settler. Three of the Aldridge sons were: 1. Samuel, who returned to North Carolina; 2. Ezekiel; and 3. Leonard.

Ezekiel Aldridge (whose wife is unknown) was the father of the following children: 1. John (m. a Miss Mills) and their children were: William, John, and Elizabeth who married Dred Gearheart. 2. Anderson married Elizabeth Smith, daughter of Humphrey Smith the settler. 3. William M. (Oct. 8, 1826 - July 16, 1916) married Lucy Aldridge, daughter of Leonard. 4. Sallie. 5. Malinda.

The children of Anderson and Elizabeth were: (a) William H., who married Sallie Conner, daughter of John O. Conner (John O. Conner lived to the age of 96 years). (b) Sallie Ann, wife of David Link. (c) James P. married Elizabeth Aldridge. (d) John Taylor married first and secondly two daughters of Hiram Walters (Hiram was known as "Man High"). (e) Samuel H. married Vina J. Walters, their children were: George W.;

Florence, who married T. B. McNeil; Carrie J., who married J. W. Sloan of Dillon's Mill; Esther V.; Maude, who married S. W. Tabor of Simmons, W. Va.; Belva, of Simmons, W. Va.; C. M. of Bedford, Va., who married a Miss Byrd; Henry Howard of Thaxton, Va., married a Miss Byrd; Herman W. married Miss Lucas of Simpsons, Va.; Grace E.; Nellie Mae married J. B. King of W. Va., they had a son named Willard A.; and Ferrell McKinley; the last three live at Simpsons, Virginia. [Correspondence shows that M. E. Aldridge, daughter of Anderson, first married John Earls of East View, Floyd County, and then married Henry Mason of Callaway, Va.]

Leonard Aldridge, third son of William the settler, was one of the early members of the county court of justices of the peace, being elected by the Court and commissioned by the Governor of Virginia in the year 1833. The name of his wife is unknown. Their children were: 1. John F. moved to California. 2. Martin moved West. 3. Sanford married a Wimmer and moved to Missouri. 4. Green moved West. 5. Joseph married a Swebster and lived at Copper Hill, their children were: Milton J., Pinkney B., and Mary Jane. 6. Stanton married Mary J. Williams, their children were: John, George, William, James Thomas, Charles and Mary Lee. Stanton Aldridge was a member of Stuart's Horse Artillery in Pelham's Battery in the Confederate army. 7. Mary married a Redman. 8. Martha married a Redman. 9. Lucy married William M. Aldridge, son of Ezekiel, their children were: Joanna, who married Sam Hayes; Asa H., who married a Miss Taylor; Isaac, who married a Miss Aldridge of Missouri; John H., who married Alice Naff, daughter of Rev. William Naff; Jane, who married James R. Hall; Laura, who married Lincoln Whitlock of Roanoke; Octava, who married John William Hall; Mary, who married Asa Cannaday of Radford; Ballie, who married David Rutrough; Trudy, who married a Mr. Altizer.

Mary J. Aldridge, widow of Stanton, married John O. Jack of Pennsylvania and lived at Copper Hill. Two of their children were George and Harry Jack, both of whom are well-known newspapermen, the former lives in Roanoke and is connected with the *Roanoke Times*, and the latter lives in Huntington, West Virginia.

John Aldridge was a soldier of the line in Col. John Gibson's Detachment of the Virginia soldiers in the Revolutionary War.

In the Confederate army were William Aldridge, who was a member of Company I, 54th Virginia Infantry, under Captain Burwell Akers, and J. L. Aldridge, a member of Company G, 21st Virginia Cavalry, under Captain A. O. Dobyns.

Henry Willard Aldridge was a soldier in the World War.

The Altizer Family

The Altizer family is of German extraction and doubtless came to this country with that vast throng of Germans who sought asylum in America. William Penn's founding of Pennsylvania for the Quakers and other persecuted religious sects made Philadelphia the port of entry through which came the Altizers, along with the Slushers, the Harmans, the Smiths, the Goodykoontzes, the Weavers, and many other of Floyd County's early settlers. After the close of the Revolutionary period and the opening up of the Shenandoah Valley of Virginia and other portions of the state to the southwest, they came south, settling along Little River in Montgomery and Floyd counties, all of which was Montgomery at that early date.

The first of the family definitely known to their Floyd descendants was John Altizer, the settler, who had a son John born in what is known as the Broad Shoals section of the county. He married Elizabeth Elkins and lived all his life in Floyd County. To this union were born: Elias, Elisha, John Elkins, Cornelius, Jesse, Susan (m. Tobias Burk), and Ebbie (m. Anderson Ally).

John Elkins Altizer (1817-1894), son of John and Elizabeth (Elkins) Altizer, married Sarah, daughter of Jacob and Annie (Tuggle) Shelor, and lived in the Broad Shoals area where he was a well-known farmer. They raised the following children: William Hiley (m. Angeline Graham), James Harvey (m. Martha Riner), Mary Ellen (m. Stilman Thompson), John Lafayette (m. Catherine Peterman), and Sarah Anne (m. William Thomas Riner).

James Harvey Altizer, born July 22, 1847, the son of John and Sarah, married Martha, daughter of David Riner of Montgomery County, was a lawyer in Mineral Wells, Texas, where he was judge of the courts for some years. He removed to Fayetteville, Arkansas, in 1919, and lived the last two years of his life there, dying on May 7, 1921. His children were: Frances May (m. V. W. Moore), Riner Gayther, Marion Harrison (deceased), Alice Bertha (m. L. H. Hubbard) lived in Belton, Texas.

Sarah Anne Altizer, daughter of John and Sarah, married William Thomas Riner, son of David Riner of Montgomery County, lives at Simpsons, Floyd County, where Mr. Riner is proprietor of "Rest Cottage Ranch." Their children are: Mary Folk (m. William Thompson), Esther Flagg (m. a Riner), Vivian Edith (m. Thomas Roudabush), lived in Cambria, Va., Iva Lena (m. Andrew Hall), lived at Ethel, W. Va., Frank Marvin (deceased), Martha Ellen (deceased).

The Banks Family

The Banks family is of English descent and there are several branches of the family in Virginia and Kentucky.

There was a prominent branch of the Banks family in Eastern Virginia, beginning with Adam Banks, who owned land in Stafford County, Virginia, in 1674, and from whom was descended Henry Banks, a merchant of Richmond, who located grants in the counties of Giles, Bland and Buchanan of something over 200,000 acres in the years 1783 and 1784. Records can be found in the Clerk's Office of Montgomery County which covered the territory of present Giles, Bland and Buchanan counties. Most of this land, however, reverted to the government of Virginia from non-payment of taxes and was later covered by land warrants.

There is a Scottish line of the Banks family in Kentucky, having its origin in America in the person of General James Banks, who emigrated to America from Ayrshire, Scotland. I have been deterred from tracing back this family from the experiences of one of the family, who wrote of his misfortune along this line, as follows:

"We have known for some time of the existance

[sic] of the English branch of the Banks family, which we understand was established in America at an early period in its history, but we have no information that would seem to connect that branch with our own.

"I sympathize with your interest in the family genealogy, and trust that your indulgence of it may be free from any such discouraging experience as I recently had.

"Not long ago I picked up a copy of the "Louisville Courier Journal," and was shocked to learn from a front page article that I had the day before just broken out of the State Penitentiary at Frankfort and in a very sensational manner. At leased [sic] the article named 'David Banks' as the principal among a group of escaped convicts, and I am the only David Banks ever heard of before in Kentucky, except my father and grandfather who are both dead. That incident seems to make applicable for me, at least, Speaker Tom Reed's conclusions regarding researches into his own family history. 'I went back as far as my grandfather,' he said, 'and then, finding that no member of the family had ever been in jail, I thought it wise not to pursue the subject any further.'

"Only I reversed that, and stopped my investigations at the beginning of my own generation. Sincerely yours, David Banks."

The Floyd county branch of the Banks family is not connected with either of the other branches mentioned, as this branch came from England and was for some time domiciled in the State of New Jersey before coming to Virginia.

John Banks (b. 1757), who had lived in New Jersey, from which state he enlisted in the American army of the revolution, and was with General Washington's army at the crossing of the Delaware River on Christmas night, December 25, 1776, and assisted in gaining the victory at the Battle of Trenton the following day, married Deborah Cassell and their children were: William, Cassell, James, Deborah, Ruth (b. 1783), Mary and Thomas (b. 1803).

After the close of the war, and after the birth of his daughter Ruth, born in the City of Philadelphia in the year 1783, he moved with his rather large family to Virginia, settling in Floyd County, some six miles east of the present town of Floyd on the north side of the Blue Ridge Mountains, and some two and a half miles south of Major Thomas Goodson, who was his nearest neighbor. Here he took up a large body of land and soon his children grew up, married and settled on his lands close around him.

William Banks, the eldest son of John, married Polly (Mary) Martin, and lived awhile just north of his father's homestead, at William Brammer's place, now the home of Mr. Cameron Turner and family. He later moved, about 1833, with his family to Carroll County, Virginia, where he and family took a foremost place in the affairs of the county. Joseph Banks, son of William, lived in Carroll County, where he married Mary Scott, and raised a large family, of whom were: Thomas, Cassell, John, Anna, Rosabelle, Harriet, Polly Ann, and Sarah. Thomas Banks, the eldest of Joseph's children, was Sheriff of Carroll and was a member of the Virginia Legislature. He married Louemma Mullen, daughter of William (Gum) Mullen and Clementine Mullen, and their children were: Kirby, Mollie, Laura Lummie, Tilden, Florence, Willie, James, Mullen (deceased), Fred and Flora. Cassell married a Miss Martin and they live in Carroll County. John married Mary Horton. Anna married Dell Turner. Rosabelle married Thomas Quesenberry and had a daughter, Harriet Ada. Harriet never married. Polly Anne married Jeff Webb and had the following children: Dianna, Henry, Cassell, Joseph, Harriet Lizzie, Mary, Nancy, and William. Sarah married Thomas J. Jennings and moved to Greenwood, Missouri.

Isaac Banks (Feb. 22, 1826-Oct. 6, 1906), another son of William, married Lucy Webb and raised a large family, of whom were: James, Abigail, Hetty, Caroline, Elizabeth, Mary, Louisa, Joanna and Virginia. Abigail married Joseph Martin (first marriage) and their children were: Rush, James Lee and Lucy. She married, secondly, Barnett Jennings and their children were Dora, Emma, Charles, Roscoe and Cora. Hetty married William Haynes. Caroline married Rev. James Matt Jennings and their children were: John Daniel, Walter, James, Oscar, Maude and Eva. Elizabeth married Thomas Gardner and some of their children were: Caroline, Herbert, Jessie, Grace, Lucy, Berta, Flora, Posie, Charlie, Andrew and Bruce. Mary never married.

Louisa married Isaac Branscome and had one child, Lula. Joanna and Virginia both died in girlhood. James Banks, son of Isaac, married Dianna Clementine Satterfield, daughter of Andrew Jackson Satterfield of Surry County, N. C. He was a member of the Virginia Legislature and was a very large man, weighing 460 pounds. He lived on Snake Creek in Carroll County and was a prominent and well-known citizen. He was the father of Ella Dora, George Oscar and Robert Jackson. Ella Dora married Joseph William (Joe Bill) Johnson, Mt. Airy, N. C., and their children were: Foy Mae, Mary, Frank, Marjorie, Rush, Joseph, Wade, Arline, Loraine; George Oscar married Lettie Salome Webb, daughter of Louis F. and Nancy Elizabeth Webb, and their children are: Nellie Rae, Johnnie Hugh and Virginia Lois, and they live at Radford, Virginia; Robert Jackson married Daisy Lee Pulliam, daughter of David Pulliam, and they had a son named Clarence. This branch of the Banks family intermarried with the Quesenberry, Jennings, Webb and other well-known families of the west end of Floyd County.

William and Polly (Mary) Banks had three daughters: Nancy, Abigail (Abby) and Louisa. Nancy married Frederick Quesinberry; Abigail married Andrew Quesinberry and Louisa married Oliver Bowman.

Cassell Banks, the second son of John the settler, married and lived for a number of years at the John Snuffer place on Cannaday's Gap Road in Floyd County, and later moved to one of the midwestern states and of whom we have lost trace.

James Banks, third son of John the settler, married Lydia Shortt, daughter of Reuben Shortt and Lydia Clark, and lived for a number of years at the Rev. Asa D. Shortt place, and later moved west.

Deborah Banks, daughter of John the settler, married Henry, son of John and Susan (Nix) Clark, and lived for a number of years at the James Barton place. Here their four oldest children, Frances, John, Jefferson and James, were born. They also moved west, and we have been unable to trace them further.

Mary (Polly) Banks, another daughter of John the settler, married William, son of Major Thomas Goodson of Turtle Rock and lived later in the old Major Goodson home which was for years the residence of the late Captain Bennett Headen. Their children were in part: John, Caroline, Virginia and Sarah; Sarah married Ballard P. Shelor of Salem, Virginia. William Goodson was one of Floyd County's foremost citizens, and was the first clerk of the court.

Ruth Banks (1783-1875), daughter of John the settler, born in the City of Philadelphia just at the close of the Revolutionary War, came as an infant in arms with her father and family when they settled in Virginia. She married George, son of Captain Daniel Shelor, who also fought in the American army of the revolution, from the State of Maryland, but later moved to the present county of Floyd and settled on Little River. Squire George Shelor, as he was familiarly called, was one of the substantial farmers of the east end of the county. Their children were: Harriet, who married George Kitterman; Mary (1815-1891), who married Captain Isaac Cannaday of Franklin County; William B. (1820-1914), who married Elizabeth Helms, daughter of "River" John Helms; he lived on Little River and later at the river crossing of the Bent Mountain Pike, and was one of the early clerks of the county; and Sarah J., who married William A. Cannaday, son of James Cannaday of Turtle Rock, and was the mother of Thomas B., John H., Samuel A. J., William Edward, and Richard F., and is now living in Salem, Virginia, at the great age of 97 years.

Major Thomas Banks (b. 1803), the youngest son of John Banks the settler, married, first, Elizabeth Howard, daughter of Peter and Sarah (Strickland) Howard, and lived all of his life in Floyd County where he was one of the large farmers, inherited a large body of land from his father and owned slaves. He was one of the prominent early citizens, and was a member of the Legislature of Virginia. He built a fine residence, just a few hundred yards east of the old John Banks home, which is now the property and home of Mr. Jefferson P. Wood and family. Later he moved to Turtle Rock, just two and a half miles north of his former home, and here he built that fine residence which after him was long the home of William A. Cannaday and family. The children of Maj. Banks and Betsy Howard were: Peter, Sarah, Maria and Mary.

Peter Banks, only son of Major Tom Banks, married Elizabeth Leftwich. He was educated at the Gannaway School of

Floyd and Emory and Henry College, was a lawyer, and was Commonwealth's Attorney of Floyd County. He later moved to Texas, where he raised the following children: Florence, Minnie, Thomas, Harvey, Laura and Lizzie. Sarah Banks, eldest daughter of Major Tom, married John Tredwell Cannaday of Franklin County, son of James and Sara (Young) Cannaday, and lived in Franklin County on Smith's River. Their children were: Hughes Dillard, Hattie, and Mary Elizabeth. Hattie died as a young lady, unmarried. Mary Elizabeth also died as a young lady, unmarried. Hughes D. Cannaday married Linnie Mary Shelor, daughter of Marion Shelor and Nannie L. Jefferson. (Nannie Jefferson was a lineal descendant of Peter Field Jefferson, father of President Thomas Jefferson.) Their daughter, Sallie, married Leroy Ross. Maria Banks, second daughter of Major Banks, died while a young lady, unmarried. Mary Banks, youngest daughter of Major Thomas Banks, married Watt Huff, son of John Huff and Orina Livesay, and was the mother of: Ferdinand, Oscar, Fulton, Frank and Eliza. Mary lived all of her life at High Peak, on the county line of Floyd and Franklin. Ferdinand married Ardella Woolwine of Patrick County, daughter of Thomas Woolwine; Oscar married Ruth Woolwine, sister of Ardella; Fulton married a Miss Huff and lived in Floyd; Frank married Alice Shelor, daughter of Ballard Shelor of Floyd; Eliza married Scott Norris and moved to Florida.

Isham Barnard

Isham (Isram) Barnard of Patrick County, Virginia, presumably was born in the year 1785, and married Sarah Burch. Their ten children were: I. Tyee. II. James. III. Charles. IV. William. V. Mahala, wife of Richard Thompson. VI. Malinda, wife of James Stanley. VII. Sally, wife of James Thompson. VIII. Mina, wife of James Jennings, IX. Annie, wife of Samuel Adams. X. Mary (Polly), wife of Thomas B. Shelor, son of Daniel and Mary Goodson Shelor.

II. James Barnard was born in the year 1814, and married Elizabeth Thompson, daughter of Nathaniel Thompson of Carroll County. He lived in Patrick County where he raised a large family of children who were: 1. Sally Ann. 2. Susan. 3. Martha. 4. Jane. 5. Elijah and 6. Elisha, twins, who were well-known ministers of the Baptist Church. Elijah (1855-1918) married, first, Emma Joyce daughter of Perion Joyce, and, secondly, Elizabeth Lackey, daughter of Henry Lackey. Elijah had one child, Maggie, by first wife, and apparently no children by second wife. Elisha (1855-1913) married Louisa Webb, daughter of Anderson Webb. 7. John Conner, born 1857. 8. Jathina was born in the year 1859 and married John Turner, son of Samuel F. Turner. Their children were: Peter, Madison, John, Henry, Hattie, Annie, Minnie, Fannie, Effie and Rachel. They moved some years ago to the State of Washington.

7. John Conner Barnard was born in the year 1857 and died in 1925. He lived most of his life in Floyd County, and was Treasurer of the county. He married Mary Elizabeth Turner, daughter of Samuel F. Turner. Their chidren were: Howard, Lillie, Rachel, Samuel, Lura, Adaline, Maude and Myrtle. Howard married Blanche, daughter of W. G. Turner, and their children were: Oscar, Gordon, Robert, Lawrence, Earnest, Carl and Ruth. Daughter Lillie married Greenville D. Wood, son of Richard Wood, and their son, Dr. Richard Hugh Wood, became a prominent young physician in Richmond, Virginia. The other children born to Lillie and Greenville Wood were Greenville, John, Sudie Lee, and Elizabeth. Rachel married Tazewell Lancaster, son of Robert Lancaster, and their children were: Attaway, Grace, Maude, Mary, Annie, Albert, Virginia, Helen and Robert. Samuel married Annie Kelly, daughter of John Kelly, and they had one son, Samuel Kelly. Lura never married. Adaline married Thomas Easter, and they adopted one son, David. Maude married Walter Simpson, and they had three daughters: Frances Elizabeth, Dorothy Louise, and Margaret Anne. Myrtle married Arthur Halstead and they had one child, Arthur, Jr.

X. Mary (Polly) and Thomas B. Shelor's children were: Ballard P., James F., William Marion, Sarah Ann, Isham Barnard, Mary Jane, Thomas G., Daniel M., and Elizabeth. James F. and William Marion Shelor were members of Stuart's Horse Artillery in Pelham's Battery. Thomas G. Shelor was a member of Company G, 21st Virginia Cavalry under Captain A. O. Dobyns, and was captured June 4, 1864, and imprisoned at Point Lookout.

William Barton The Settler

The Floyd County family is derived from William Barton of Bedford County, Virginia, who married and settled in the present county of Floyd where he was one of the early schoolteachers of the Turtle Rock neighborhood, teaching in the Mary Pugh cabin about 1845. Among his pupils were many of the best young men of the county, including: Col. William B. Shelor, Dr. Aris B. Cox, Peter L. and Dr. Thomas Henry Howard, Jonathan L. Brammer and Samuel Sweeney.

Among the children of William Barton were the following: I. Thomas married Annie Terry, daughter of Jonathan Terry, and settled on the Cannaday's Gap road, six miles east of the courthouse. Their children were: Jonathan, Sarah, Darius, Rufus, Jane, Nancy, and Delia Ellen. Jonathan married Sallie Spangler; Sarah married William Howell, son of Hundley Howell; Darius married Hybernia Janney, daughter of Fleming Janney; Rufus married Quillie Rakes, daughter of Charles Rakes; Jane married Sampson Jones; Nancy Barton married Daniel Barton, son of John Barton; Delia Ellen (Tiny) married Daniel Boyd, son of Samuel Boyd. II. John J. (d. 1915) married Frances Robertson, daughter of John Robertson, and lived near County Line Church. He was a member of Company G, 21st Virginia Cavalry under Captain A. O. Dobyns in the Confederate army. Their children were: Daniel, Dennis, Jesse, Thomas, Amos, Demaris, Nettie and Theresa. Daniel married Nancy Barton, daughter of Thomas Barton; Dennis married Jennie Ingram, daughter of George Ingram; Jesse married Ella Thomas, daughter of Martin Thomas; Thomas married John Boyd's daughter; Nettie married Bob Weeks first and, secondly, married Waitman Nolen, son of William Nolen of Franklin County; Amos married someone in Illinois; Demaris married Ballard Underwood; Theresa married Tom Trail, son of Van Trail of Franklin County. III. William married _____ Griffith of Patrick County and later moved to West Virginia where he raised a family, one of whom was John Quincy Barton, who returned to Floyd County and married Cora Lancaster, daughter of Phillip Lancaster of Pine Creek. Other children of William Barton were Georgie, who married William Strickler; Vaske (?), who married Bob Huff, son of Peter Huff. IV. Mary

(Polly) married Hiram Boyd of Franklin County and lived on Shooting Creek in Floyd County. Their children were: John, who married a Miss Brown; Ellen, a daughter who married Tazewell Janney, son of John Janney and brother of Flemen Janney. V. A daughter who married Harvey Proffit. Two of their sons were Joseph P. and John Proffit of Floyd County. Joseph P. Proffit was a lifelong resident of Floyd and one of her most influential citizens. He was for many years treasurer of the county, hotel proprietor, merchant and businessman. VI. Nancy never married.

Moscoe John Barton was in service in the World War from Floyd County.

The Bishop Family

John Bishop, who was born in Holland, emigrated from that country to America and settled at the mouth of Indian Creek in the present county of Floyd in about the year 1777. He came with his wife Mary, and their four children. His wife was drowned while attempting to cross the New River on horseback. After the tragedy he married a Miss Simpkins. From this John Bishop all of the family of Bishops of Floyd County are descended. Four of the Bishop children were: Dr. John, Jr., Henry, Jacob and Mary. Henry Bishop married Nancy Quesenberry and was a Methodist minister. Jacob Bishop married Melvina Kinser and was also a Methodist minister. Mary Bishop married Mathew Cox, Jr., and one member of their large family was Dr. Aris B. Cox, a physician and Methodist minister.

Dr. John Bishop, Jr., the son of the settler, married Dicey Cox, daughter of Ambrose and Sallie (Reed) Cox, and lived on Indian Creek. Dr. Bishop was an herb doctor or a "Thompsonian doctor," and had a neighborhood practice of medicine. He was a wealthy man, owning a large boundary of land and many slaves who were freed before his death. His children were: Asa, Jacob, John, Nancy, Peggy (Margaret), Mary, Lucy and Mahala.

Asa Bishop, the eldest son of John and Dicey, married Elizabeth Dodd, daughter of Benjamin Dodd. They lived one mile west of the courthouse, on the Dodd homestead, one of the finest farms in the county. Their son, Burdine Bishop (b. Oct. 9,

1845) resided on the farm and was one of Floyd's foremost citizens. He was a member of the Legislature of Virginia in 1883 and 1884. He married Mary Scott, youngest daughter of Mathew and Mary Ann (Strickler) Scott, and their only child was Allie, who married a Mr. Munsey of Big Stone Gap. Birdine Bishop died Nov. 26, 1927, at age 82 years and is buried in the Dodd family burying ground on his farm. Other chlidren of Asa and Elizabeth were: Angeline, who married Samuel Harter; Catherine, who married Bethuel Hylton; Emeline, who died in infancy; Wesley, who married Lydia Caldwell; Julia, who married Harvey Slusher; Mary, who married Reed Kitterman; Harvey, who married Julia Clay; and Emily, who married Thompson Harman.

Dr. Jacob Bishop, second son of John and Dicey, married Lucy Cox, and was a well-known physician of Floyd County. John Bishop, third son of John, married Sarah Goad and lived in Floyd. Nancy Bishop, eldest daughter of John, married Thomas W. Williamson, son of George Williamson, and lived for many years in Indian Valley, where he was one of the first men to open a store and haul goods from Lynchburg, Virginia, in wagons, the first wagons to cross the mountains into Indian Valley. He later moved to Floyd Court House, and for many years kept a tavern.

Mary Bishop, daughter of Dr. John Bishop, married John Harman (1814-1893), son of Solomon and Elizabeth (Slusher) Harman. They lived at the old Harman homestead which they inherited together with the old mill on West Fork, one of the oldest mills in that part of the county. Their children were: James M., Malinda, Margaret, Nancy, Mary and Sarah, of whom Dr. James M. Harman, a prominent physician, was long located at Willis, Virginia.

Lucy Bishop, another daughter of John and Dicey (Cox) Bishop, married Charles Simmons, and lived in Floyd County. Peggy (Margaret) Bishop, fourth daughter of John, married Sparrel Slusher, son of David Slusher, and lived in the county of Floyd. Mahala Bishop, youngest daughter of John, married John Wade and lived in the west end of the county.

Moses Blackwell The Settler

Moses Blackwell of Halifax County, Virginia, married, first, Mary Williamson and settled in the present county of Floyd near Stonewall Schoolhouse. His nearest neighbor was Jacob Hoback. Moses was a prosperous farmer who married, secondly, Rebecca Walter, daughter of Rev. Martin Walter, who was the first resident Lutheran minister of the old Lutheran Church near Floyd.

The first set of children of Moses Blackwell were: John, Robert, Mary, Susan and Martin.

The second set were: 1. Thomas, 2. William, both of whom lost their lives while serving in the Confederate army: 3. Abraham G. (b. 1843) married Elizabeth Holt, daughter of Smith [Smithen] Holt. 4. Eli married Sarah Lawrence, daughter of Jacob; they lived on a farm 10 miles northeast of the town of Floyd and had the following children: William I., Bertie, Luther R., Dena, Ella, Chlo, Fred, Arthur and Noah. 5. Isaac married Sally Holt, daughter of Smith Holt, and had the following children: John O., Kate, Smith, Taylor, Flossie, William H., Samuel, Walter and Hattie. 6. Lewis married Martha Holt, daughter of Smith Holt and sister of Elizabeth and Sally; they had the following children: Laura, Cora, Ollie and Robert. 7. Austin married Ann Montgomery and lived at Callaway, Franklin County, Virginia; they had the following children: Alice, Archie, Albert, James, Nannie, William, Pearl, and Fannie. 8. Christina married Isaac Newton Overstreet and lived on Pine Creek, 5 miles southeast of Floyd. Their children were: Martha, Mary E., Emmer (Emma) and Hez. 9. Charlotte married George Whitlock, son of Henry and Elizabeth (Graham) Whitlock. Their children were: William, Mintie, Christian, Otho, Mary, Joseph and Eugenia.

George Booth The Settler

George Booth, the first of the family in America, was born in England about the year 1745, the son of an English earl. The tradition in the family is that he was secreted on board a ship and sent to America as a teenage boy to save his life. When still at home, he and some neighbor boys were trying their strength, lifting a stone on the bank of a creek in which they had been bathing. George Booth moved the stone. It was learned later that this stone was a cornerstone to a plot of land. At that time in England it was a capital offense to move a "corner to land." He was often heard to say that he was born with a "silver spoon in his mouth," but it would never do him any good.

He was a man of great energy, often making the trip on horseback from his home on Little River to the old home in the State of New York, bringing back many droves of horses, which he turned out on the "range." He lived in the present county of Floyd many years and is buried on the land he took up.

The names of only three of his children are known. They were: I. Obediah [this has not been verified]. II. Isaac. III. Daniel.

I. Obediah Booth married Clarissa Howard, born about the year 1770, daughter of William Howard of Montgomery County, Virginia, and a sister of Peter Howard of Little River. They were the parents of Delilah Booth [the parents of Delilah Booth were Abijah Booth and Rhoda Howard], who married Thomas W. Simmons, and was the mother of Otey T. Simmons (b. 1818), Matilda (b. 1820), Dr. William B. Simmons, and Roley M. Simmons, the latter the father of a prominent family of children, among whom is Dr. John W. Simmons of Martinsville, Virginia. Mary Simmons, another child of Delilah, married William T. Lester and was the mother of Posey G. Lester, who was a Member of Congress for the years 1889 to 1893, and who is a widely known minister of the Primitive Baptist Church and editor of "Zion's Landmark," a Baptist Church paper.

II. Isaac Booth, another son of George the settler, lived near the present Floyd and Montgomery county line, on Laurel Ridge, and near the mouth of Brush Creek.

III. Daniel Booth, the third son of George, lived on Beaver Creek at a place later known as "Bonsack's Machine," the home and property of David L. Eller.

The Booths were prominent farmers and large landowners, as evidenced by the names of five of the family being among a list (Land Tax Book) of the largest landowners in the county when it was organized in the year 1831. They were George, Abner, Joseph, Daniel and Isaac.

In the Confederate army, four of the names were among the veterans of Stuart's Horse Artillery - they were: Lewis Boothe, Noah R. Boothe, J. W. Boothe, and Thomas Boothe. Cornelius Boothe was a member of Company B, 42nd Virginia Infantry, under Captains Henry Lane and Abner Dobyns, captured at Chancellorsville, May 1863, and died in prison at Elmira, New York, in 1864. Wright Boothe was Orderly Sergeant under Captain Sparrel Griffith in Company H, 54th Infantry. William Boothe was a member of Company G, 21st Virginia Cavalry, under Captain A. O. Dobyns, captured and died in prison at Camp Chase. Abner Boothe was a member of Col. Robert L. Preston's Reserves, under Captain Andrew J. Graham.

Christopher Bower The Settler

Christopher Bower and Catherine Walter Bower came from Botetourt County, Virginia, and settled near Pine Creek Church, some six miles northeast of the courthouse. Their family of sons were:

1. Christopher, Jr., married Susan Snuffer, daughter of Peter, and lived one mile south of Pine Creek Church. Their children were: John, William and Tabitha. John Bower was born about 1850 and married a sister to Jim Black: their children were: Liza who married Rufus DeHart, another daughter who married Will Phlegar, Minnie who married W. H. Graham, and Christopher H. C. who married Kittie Epperly. William Bower was born about 1852 and married Dealy Sweeney; their children were: William Wallace who married a Miss Martin, Clyde who married J. W. Thomas, and several others. Tabitha Bower married Andrew J. Hall and their children were: Palmer who married a Gillenwater, Memmis, Gay who married a son of Alice and Thomas Hatcher. Christopher Bower was a short, stout man and was known as "Stuffle Bower." He was a millwright and in 1870 built for Major Howard a very tall flour mill near Turtle Rock that was for many years a landmark for that section of the country, being remarkable for its great height. This was in later years owned by Jeff Lancaster and after him by the late

Robert O. Harvey and was for years known as "Lancaster's Mill."

2. Martin married Maria Huff and moved to the State of West Virginia.

3. Philip married Catherine Snuffer.

4. Jacob (1828-1881) married Susan Smith, daughter of Luke Smith the settler, and lived eight miles east of the court-house, near Cannaday's Gap. His children were Josiah, Abraham, George, Isaac, Marion, Amanda, Ellen, Rosa, Anne (?), and others. Josiah married May Lee and they both died early from tuberculosis; Abraham married a Sowers and moved to Texas; Marion married a daughter of John Strickler; Amanda married John Gillenwater; Rosa married Will Rutrough; and Ellen married her first cousin, Joseph Bower.

5. Daniel married Elizabeth Smith, daughter of Luke, and lived near his father-in-law, six miles east of the county seat; his children were: Ann, Mary, Sarah Jane, Luke, Joseph, Eliza, Martin, Homer and Florence.

In the Confederate army: Second Corporal Luther W. Bower died at home during the service, and Fourth Corporal Robert H. Bower and David Bower were in Company A, 24th Virginia Infantry. W. R. Bowers was color bearer for General B. T. Johnson, in Company G, 21st Virginia Cavalry. Daniel Bower was with Clark's Battalion, 30th Virginia, and Christopher, Jr., John, Philip and Lewis Bower were with Captain James B. Headen in Col. Robert L. Preston's Reserves.

In the World War were William Wallace, Jabe Letcher and Posey Bower from Floyd County, of whom William Wallace Bower died in camp.

Peter Bowman

The original spelling of the name was **Beauman,** or **Beaumann.** A large number of Baumans were among the Pennsylvania German emigrants who came to America between the years of 1727 and 1776.

The Floyd County family had its origin in John Bowman, who was born in Germany and emigrated to America. He settled in Pennsylvania where he died in the year 1804.

His son Christian Bowman was born in Pennsylvania, April 17, 1791, and married Hannah Rineheart on May 18, 1815. He settled in Virginia in the present county of Roanoke, about where the N&W railroad station is now located. He was a minister of the Church of the Brethren, and was well known to a large circle of friends. Hannah Bowman died January 2, 1886, at a great old age. Christian Bowman died on July 24, 1867. Their ten children were: Nancy, Elizabeth, Magdaline, Frances, Mary, Susannah, Hannah, Lydia, Peter and Christian.

Peter Bowman, son of Christian, was born in the year 1822, and married Mary Spangler, daughter of David Spangler, and settled in Floyd County on Terry's Creek in the east end of the county about 1838. Their children were: 1. David. 2. Joseph, both of whom died in infancy. 3. John married Elizabeth Bower. 4. Samuel, a well-known minister of the Brethren Church, married, first, Emma Lesueur and, secondly, Ella Hylton. 5. Darius married Lavina Keith and moved to Colorado. 6. Asa, a minister of the Brethren Church, married Martha Yearout and lived for a number of years in Floyd County. He now resides at Christiansburg, Virginia. 7. Margaret, wife of David Slusher, son of Ananias, lives in Floyd County. David Slusher was Sheriff of Floyd County for twelve years. They raised a large family of children, one of whom is Dr. William Clarie Slusher of Bluefield, West Virginia. 8. Amanda, wife of Abraham Spangler. 9. Isabel, unmarried. 10. Lydia, died in infancy.

Peter C., William Henry, Carlie D. and William F. Bowman were soldiers in the World War.

The Brammer Family

The Brammers lere longtime residents of Patrick County, Virginia, where they were farmers and good citizens. William Brammer (1803-1879), the son of John Brammer who married a Miss Lee, the sister of "Preacher Billy Lee" of Patrick County, married Belinda Lancaster, daughter of Dr. Lewis (Washington) Lancaster, who married a Miss Wheeler and was an old time herb or "Thompsonian doctor." Wm. also was one of the early schoolteachers of the Turtle Rock neighborhood, and lived two miles south of Turtle Rock. He was a practical farmer who raised a large family of three sons and three daughters:

I. Jonathan L. Brammer (1833-1908), married Miss Juliana Burnett about 1856, daughter of Jeremiah ("Sweeper") Burnett of Patrick County, and they lived one mile west of Cannaday's Gap in the Blue Ridge Mountains. Their children were: Stanton B. (1857-1889), who married Sallie Elizabeth Cannaday and was the father of Dr. Frank Brammer, a prominent young physician of Callaway, Franklin County, who had a son Arthur B. and daughter Effie; Sarah B. Brammer (b. 1860), who married Jefferson P. Wood, son of Richard J. Wood. They had six children, included in Wood family sketch; Elizabeth Brammer, who married George B. Wood, brother of Jefferson P. Wood; William J. Brammer, who married Miss May E. Crockett, daughter of James W., their children were: Burks, Crockett, Lena and Annie; and John W. Brammer (b. 1873), who married Miss Laura Lester, daughter of John, who lives in Floyd where he is Sheriff of the county.

II. Tazewell C. Brammer (1841-1914) married Normanda Graham, daughter of Perry, and lived at the old William Brammer homestead which was the original home of William Banks. Their children were: Helen, Elzora, Nina and William J. Helen was unmarried; Elzora married Samuel Brammer, son of Jeff Brammer; Nina married Gilley Thomas; and William J. married an Atkins.

III. Madison L. Brammer (1845-1903), the youngest son of William, married Miss Amanda E. Shortt, daughter of Naaman J. Shortt, and was the father of Naaman and Wilton Brammer, who live on Little River where they own and reside in the Col. John Williams homestead. Other children of Madison L. Brammer were: Etta, who married a Cobler; Nannie, who married David Stockwell; Willie, who married Willis Peters; Sallie, who married James Williamson; and Fannie. Madison was killed by a runaway team near Martinsville, Va., in 1903.

IV. Penina Brammer (1830-1907), eldest daughter of William, married Peter Turner, son of Francis Turner, and was the mother of William F. Turner. William F. first married Eliza Smith, daughter of Josiah Smith, and, secondly, Fannie Hoback, daughter of James Hoback. They had one son, J. P., who married Annie Huff. William F. Turner lives five miles east of the courthouse on the Franklin Pike.

V. Lucinda Brammer (1835-1920), married William J. Pedigo, who was a prominent justice of the peace in the Little River District.

VI. Elizabeth A. Brammer (1839-1912), youngest daughter of William, married Addison Epperly, son of Jacob Epperly, a prominent farmer, who lived on the Bent Mountain Pike, four miles from the county seat. Among their children were: Brethard; Dove, wife of Aaron Williams, son of David Williams; and Leona.

Apparently William Brammer had a brother named John, a sister who married Joshua Agee and lived near County Line Baptist Church, a sister who married a Moran, and a sister named Bethina who married Alexander Wood, son of Richard Wood of Wood's Gap.

Burnett

The Floyd County Burnett descendants came into the county across the Blue Ridge from the county of Patrick, where they had lived for many years. William Burnett (1766?) lived in Patrick County where he was a farmer, among whose children were: Jeremiah and Elizabeth.

Jeremiah Burnett (1791-1869), known as "Sweeper," married Sarah Campbell, whose mother was a Hale, of Franklin County, Virginia, and lived all his life at the foot of Wood's Gap in Patrick County. He was a farmer and a slave owner. His children were: Juliana, Sarah and John A. Juliana (b. 1833) married Jonathan L. Brammer (see Brammer sketch for children); Sarah (1828?-1900) married Capt. Thomas Hall (Mar. 1, 1822-1914) and lived five miles east of the courthouse; John A. (1830?-1897), a well-known surveyor and farmer at the foot of the mountain section of Patrick County, married Elizabeth, daughter of Pleasant Thomas, and their children were: Augustus, J. Pleasant, Fannie, Mintory, Thomas, Abram, Charles, Cora, Morrel, Minnie and Hallie.

Elizabeth Burnett, daughter of William, married John Tuggle and was the mother of Elder Green Tuggle, a widely known minister of the Primitive Baptist Church; a second son, Henry, was a prominent farmer and Sheriff of Henry County, whose children were: Robert, William, Thomas, Walter, A. L., and a daughter who married a Scales; other children of Elizabeth and John were John, Elizabeth who married a Joyce, and one other.

Austin Burnett, son of Valentine of Patrick County, married a Miss Slaughter, lived for some time in the county of Patrick, and later moved to Floyd, settling in the west end of the county where he engaged in farming and raising cattle. His children were: Abraham D., George, William, Martha, Nannie and Mahala. George married Lorena Branscome; William married a Miss Williams, had two sons, Gilbert and Willie, and lived in the State of Missouri; Martha married John T. Phillips and had a son by the name of John Emmett; Nannie married Phillip W. Guthrie and they had one son, Charlie; Mahala married James Hylton and their children were: Walter, Abe, Cabbell, Laura and Loula; Abraham Dandridge (d. 1907) married Julina, daughter of Aris R. Cox and Irene Maberry, and lived and owned the old Judge Fleming Saunders farm, known in earlier days as the "Quarters." He was a succesful farmer and large cattle raiser. He carried his "Badge of Frazier's Farm," an empty sleeve (lost his arm in Confederate battle), but never uttered a word of complaint. He went to work after the conflict was over to make a home for his family, who were: Walter Roscoe, Dr. Charles K., a well-known physician of Willis, Henry Prince, Eddie Samuel, Rosa I., Laura and Hattie.

Josiah Burnett (d. 1850), a first cousin of Jeremiah and Austin, on Feb. 26, 1824, married Jemimah (d. 1902), daughter of Moses and Nancy (Reed) Dickerson, lived in the Indian Valley section where he was a well-known farmer. Their large family of seven daughters and four sons were: Nancy, who married Benjamin Duncan and they were the parents of four sons and ten daughters; Early went to the state of Iowa, married Martha Doud, and had two children; William Austin married Sarah Wright and lived in Indiana; Asa married Orlena Morricle and died in the Civil War; Elizabeth married Ballard Bowlen; Sophia married a Mr. Smith; Susan married Henry Bond; Drusilla married William Quesenberry and they had two sons and two daughters; Sarah and Jemimah never married; and Josiah D. (July 25, 1838-May 18, 1922) married Elizabeth, daughter of

George Duncan, and lived all of his life in Indian Valley, where he raised a family of ten children, all of whom lived to their majority.

Elisha Burnett, brother of Josiah, Sr., married Fannie Sumpter, and their daughter married Crocket Reed.

The Burwell Family

The first Burwell in America was Lewis, who came to this country from England in 1640. Major Lewis first settled on Carter's Creek in Gloucester County. Nothing is definitely known of his English ancestry. There were eight of the name down through successive generations, and the fourth Lewis was the father of William Meade and John Edward Burwell's great-great-grandfather, Nathaniel Burwell.

Major Nathaniel Burwell was an officer in the American Revolution under General Washington, and present at the surrender of Lord Cornwallis at Yorktown. After the close of the war he married Martha, daughter of Sir Dudley Digges of Williamsburg. Their seven children were: Nathaniel, Frances Thacker, Thomas Nelson, Martha Digges, Lewis, Lucy, and one other daughter whose name is not recalled. Major Nathaniel Burwell died about the year 1800, and soon after that his widow and seven children moved from Eastern Virginia to Botetourt County (Rustic Lodge, about three miles west of Fincastle), where Mrs. Burwell died at the age of 91.

Her oldest son, Nathaniel (William Meade and John Edward's grandfather), married Lucy Carter of Shirley in 1809, with whose patrimony he purchased Dropmore, near Salem, Virginia. There he raised a family of five children: Anne Carter, Nathaniel, Martha Digges, Lewis and Charles William. Nathaniel died there in 1866.

The marriage of Nathaniel Burwell to Lucy Carter of Shirley (whose sister Anne Carter was the mother of General Robert E. Lee), united the family with a very large connection in Virginia. The family tree of the Carters begins with the first of the name in America, Robert Carter, about 1620, and contains 2700 names of his descendants. Many of the most notable people in Virginia, including the late Bishop A. M. Randolph of the

Episcopal Church, are on the Carter tree.

Frances Thacker, daughter of Major Nathaniel Burwell, married Lewis Harvey of Speedwell, near Cave Springs in Roanoke County. Among her numerous descendants were Mrs. Marshall G. McClung, of Salem, Virginia.

Thomas Nelson, second son of Major Nathaniel Burwell, married Miss Nicholson of Eastern Virginia, and lived at Rustic Lodge, the original home of the family in Botetourt County. His grandson, William P. Trent, is a Professor at Columbia University, New York.

Martha Digges never married, nor did Lewis. Lucy married a Mr. Bowyer, and lived in Salem all her days, dying there during the Civil War in the house where the Episcopal Church now stands. She had one son, of whom nothing is known.

William Meade and John Edward's father, Nathaniel Burwell, was born at Rustic Lodge near Fincastle, and reared at Salem, Virginia. In 1865 he married Nancy Pendleton of Patrick County, Virginia, and in that year they moved to Spring Camp, Willis, Floyd County, Virginia, and reared the following children: William Meade; Mary Ahava, who married J. T. Helms and lives in Danville, Virginia; John Edward of Floyd, Virginia; Nathaniel (deceased); Annie L., a trained nurse in Norfolk, Virginia; Curtis A. (deceased); Lettitia married John E. Pickett and lives in Danville, Virginia; and Arthur H. Burwell, Spring Camp, Willis, Virginia.

Spring Camp, the home of the Burwell Family of Floyd County is a part of an original tract (nineteen thousand and more acres in Floyd, Patrick and Carroll counties) granted by the State of Virginia to General Henry ("Light Horse Harry") Lee for services rendered by him to the colonies during the American Revolution. After his death his three sons, Charles Carter, Sidney Smith and Robert Edward Lee, became the owners.

During their ownership Charles Carter Lee, a talented alumnus of Harvard University, spent much time at Spring Camp, and there wrote a book of poems entitled **The Maid of the Doe**, a copy of which he left at Spring Camp which he wished to remain there always. Also while residing at Spring Camp Charles Carter Lee, a lawyer, was a candidate for the Virginia

House of Delegates (from Montgomery County) but was defeated for the office. The three Lee brothers sold their lands to Nathaniel Burwell of Salem.

Dr. Aris B. Cox, in his book, **Footprints on the Sands of Time,** writes of this home as follows, "Spring Camp farm, at the foot of Buffalo mountain on the south side, is one of the most valuable farms in the county. It was owned by Hon. Charles C. Lee, a distinguished lawyer and statesman, whose patriotic love of country reflected credit on himself and country. This valuable farm was afterward owned by Nathaniel Burwell and brothers."

The Cannaday Family

This family reputedly came to America from Buckinghamshire, England, some years before the American Revolution. Family tradition says the immigrant and his wife, whose names are unknown, had three sons: James; John, said to have immigrated to Wayne Co., Kentucky; and one other who died in the war. This family history begins with James:

I. James Cannaday fought under General Greene in the Revolution, and lived in the western part of Franklin County. He married Elizabeth Raikes (who lived to be 105); their children were:

A. Mary Cannaday (1770-1847), married March 6, 1800, Pleasant Thomas, son of Charles, the settler, and lived on Poplar Camp Creek, a tributary of Smiths River, in Patrick County. Their eight children:

1. Charles; 2. Pleasant; 3. Richard;

4. Judith married John Young Shortt, son of Reuben; their children were: (a) Lydia; (b) Naaman J.; (c) Susan; (d) Judith A. (1834-1899) m. Richard J. Wood (1828-1917), son of John R. Wood; their children: Emeline, Susan E., Jefferson P., Daniel H., George B., Greenville D., Amos D., Sparrel A., and D. Robertson; (e) Martha; (f) John P., (g) Elizabeth; (h) Lucinda, and six others.

5. James; 6. Susan; 7. Elizabeth; and 8. Mary (Polly) (Jan. 10, 1803-June 18, 1902).

B. William Cannaday (1772-1874), known as "Patrick Billy," lived just east of old Charity Primitive Baptist Church in

Patrick County. He married Patsy Wright; William and Patsy Cannaday had 24 children:

1. James; 2. Ferdinand; 3. Fleming; 4. Delilah; 5. Burwell; 6. Constant; 7. John 8. Pleasant; 9. Stephen m. Elizabeth Lemon, daughter of Isaac, their children: Tazewell, Isaac, Stuart, Nancy, Emmazetta, Laura and Eliza; 10. Randall; 11. William; 12. Marshall; 13. Joshua; and eleven others. William married, secondly, Nancy Hill.

C. James N. Cannaday, Jr. (b. 1786) lived at the Mat Spencer place on Runnet Bag Creek. He owned all the land on both sides of the creek for five square miles, on down the creek where it joined Otter Creek and to the junction with Smiths River. He built the road up the Blue Ridge Mountain which bears the name, "Cannaday's Gap," in his honor. He owned fifty slaves. On Feb. 22, 1813, he married Sarah Young, daughter of Peter; they had seven sons and five daughters:

1. Peter married Annie Turner; their children were: (a) Martha m. James Prillaman; (b) Carolina m. Dr. Hickman; (c) Eliza m. Andrew Turner; (d) Emiline m. Huff; (e) George m. Amanda Teel; (f) Tazewell; and (g) Madison.

2. James (1815) married Martha Turner; they moved from Franklin to Pittsylvania County, and later to Missouri; their children: Sarah; Louisa; Anne; Lurinda; Greene; Abigail; Creed (physician in Texas); James; Alice; Lee.

3. Isaac (1817-61), lived at old Long Branch Primitive Baptist Church in Franklin County. He was in the Virginia Legislature, 1856-57; organized a company at beginning of Civil War but died before entering service; married Mary (1815-1891), daughter of George and Ruth (Banks) Shelor; their children:

(a) Harriet (d. 1891) m. 1859, Floyd W. Edwards, Sheriff of Floyd County: their children: Mary m. Judge Charles P. Latham; Eugenia m. Frank P. Harman; Nell, never married (d. 1920); Susan E. m. Valentine M. Sowder; India m. Roscoe F. Tompkins; Ashby G. m. Allie Mullins of Martinsville; and Joseph m. a Redd. Other children died in infancy.

(b) Ruth (d. 1913) m. Jacob Spickard.

(c) Sarah (1846-1894), married Giles L. Cannaday in 1866, and they had the following children: Charles Benton, married Mary Foster, and is at present Professor of Latin at West Virginia University; Laura, died in 1894; George B., in business at New Orleans, La.; Frederick, married Lilly Spindle and resides at Roanoke, Virginia; Isaac, married Helen Chandler and lives at Ranchi, India, as a missionary; Mary, died in 1896; Carl H., in business at Danville, Va.; Robert Wythe, married Nena Hale and is a practicing physician at Spring Valley, Grayson County, Virginia.

      (d)   George (1849-1913) m. Alice Wall.

      (e)   Caroline m. James Duncan.

      (f)   Isabella m. Dr. P. F. Whiting.

      (g)   Virginia m. Parker Wingo.

    4. William A. (1819-1900) married Sarah J. (Nov. 9, 1825-June 22, 1922), daughter of George and Ruth Shelor; and lived on a ridge one mile east of Pine Creek and three miles west of Turtle Rock, later at Turtle Rock on the Thomas Banks homestead; their children:

      (a)   Thomas Banks m. (1) Melinda Helms, and (2) Gertrude McCaulay; children: Henry Marks m. Hallie Wingfield; Sallie m. Bruce Webb; India m. Gilbert C. Walker Francis; Thadius A., unmarried.

      (b)   Malinda m. Jacob T. Helms; they had one son, Frank m. Corrie, daughter of Judge Z. T. Dobyns.

      (c)   John H. m. Minerva Williams, daughter of Col. John Williams; their children: Samuel Richard m. Annie Williams, daughter of Tazewell; Ada m. Capt. Whipple of New London, Conn.; Dr. Dexter Peter m. Bessie Vermillion, daughter of Dr. Vermillion of Giles County; and Fannie May, unmarried.

      (d)   Samuel, died while a student at Roanoke College.

      (e)   Nannie, never married.

      (f)   Richard Fox m. Emma Huff, daughter of Robert; Dr. Royal Cannaday of New York City is a son.

      (g)   Elizabeth, never married.

      (h)   Emma m. Ballard P. Shelor; their children: Frederick L. m. Weeta Proffit, daughter of John; Katharine; Richard B. m. daughter of Rev. Dr. Gilmer of Wythe County; Charles Edward; Nancy; Fitzhugh; Annie.

      (i)   William Jr., never married.

at Marion, Va.

    Harvey D. (1840-1920) married Nannie Howell in 1867. Their children were: Bell (m. Charles Dickerson) in Bluefield,

(j) Edward m. Cora Payne, daughter of Col. John B. Payne.

(k), (1), and (m) Julia, Sallie, and a son, died when small.

5. Caroline married Andrew J. Simms; their children: (a) Julia m. Turner Griffith; (b) James m. Elizabeth Cannaday; (c) Mary; (d) Virginia m. Lewis Hancock; (e) Harriet m. John Mitchell; (f) Andrew J. m. Blanche Shelton.

6. Elizabeth married Major Thomas Banks; no children.

7. Stephen (d. 1871), Sheriff of Franklin County; never married.

8. David (1830-1859), never married.

9. Mary m. Wiley Menefee; no children.

10. Sarah (d. 1855) m. Harrison Byrd; their children: James and others.

11. Harriet married Captain Thomas Moseley of Lynchburg; their child: Walker m. Miss Menefee.

12. John Treadwell m. (1) Sarah Banks, daughter of Thomas and Elizabeth (Howard) Banks; he married (2) Miss Prillaman, no children. Son of the first marriage:

(a) Hughes Dillard m. Linnie Mary Shelor (b. May 14, 1868), daughter of Marion and Nannie Louvenie (Jefferson); their child was: Sallie m. Mr. Ross. Their fine old homestead is at the mouth of Otter and Runnet Bag creeks in Franklin County.

D. John Cannaday married Susan Winfrey, daughter of Stephen; their children:

1. Bailey (1822-1912) m. Mary Ruff, and lived in the Head of the River section; their children: (a) John m. Susan Thurman; (b) Martha m. James Howery; (c) James m. Miss Kelley; (d) Asa m. Mary Aldrich; (e) Peter m. Nannie Woolwine; (f) Otho m. Miss Shively; (g) Katharine m. Joseph Howery; (h) Amanda m. John Kelley.

2. Pleasant, never married.

3. Elizabeth (b. 1824) married Preston Howery; they lived on Little River near the bridge; their children: Pleasant, and others.

4. James m. Martha Huff; no children.

E. David Cannaday married Virginia Walker; most of

this branch moved to Raleigh County, West Va.; their children:

    1. Adaline m. James Ingram.

    2. Ferdinand.

    3. George (d. 1861), a prominent physician; never married.

    4. Fleming m. Miss Toney.

    5. Crockett.

    F. Charles Cannaday (1794-1853) married Mary Ingram; their children:

    1. James (1827-1899) m. Sarah Turner; their children, most of whom moved to Texas; Hairston; John; James B.; Charles; Eugene; Creed; Octavia; Matilda; and others.

    2. Charles Cannaday, physician.

    3. John B. Cannaday (1833-1897) married Virginia Ingram; their children:

      (a) John (Charles?) E., physician, m. Margaret Roller.

      (b) Chloe m. Thomas Lester.

    4. Asa Cannaday (1836-1907), physician and member of the Virginia Legislature m. Demaris Graham (d. Apr. 23, 1925), daughter of Alvin; their children: (a) Walter (b. 1859), name of wife unknown; (b) Charles G. (1850-1908), physician, m. Emma Chrisman, no children: (c) Albert A. (b. 1863), physician m. (1) Della Poff, and (2) Ruth Eliason; (d) Minnie (b. 1866) m. W. J. Poff; (e) George m. Miss Poff.

    5. Giles W. (1839-1908) married (1) Sarah Cannaday, daughter of Isaac and Mary Shelor Cannaday, and (2) Lucy Angell; children:

      (a) Charles Benton (b. 1867), professor in West Virginia University, m. Mary Foster, daughter of William; no children.

      (b) Laura (1869-1894).

      (c) George R. (b. 1871), moved to New Orleans.

      (d) Frederick (b. 1873) m. Lily Spindle.

      (e) Isaac (b. 1876), Lutheran missionary in India, m. Helen Chandler.

      (f) Mary (1878-1896).

      (g) Carl H. (b. 1881), lives in Danville, Va., never married.

      (h) Robert Wythe (b. 1883), physician, m. Nena Hale

of Grayson County.

G. Pleasant Cannaday married Elizabeth Young (d. at age of about 100), daughter of Joshua and Nancy Young, and niece of Sarah Young (m. James Cannaday), they had one son:

    1. Isaac m. Mary Raikes; their children:

    (a) Peter, County Supervisor, m. Adaline Turner, daughter of Charles; they had three children: Amos, member of Virginia Legislature, and a Supervisor, m. Antonia Hall; Ezra, died while attending William & Mary College; Sallie E. m. Stanton Brammer, one son was Dr. Frank Brammer of Callaway, Va.

    (b) Elizabeth m. James Simms.

    (c) German.

    (d) Mitchell.

    (e) Richard.

    (f) Charles.

The Carter Family

The Floyd County family of the name is derived from Henry Carter and the following brothers and sisters who settled in the present county around the Revolutionary period: Jesse, Bailey, John, Nancy (m. David Howell), and Fannie (m. Andy Howell).

Henry Carter married Malinda Agnew, August 31, 1826, and they had the following children: Lewis, John, Samuel, Henry Calvin, Jacob T., Madison, Isaac N., Harvey D., James, David V., Susan (m. Calvin Simmons), Ann (m. John Gardner), Letha Jane, Mary Adaline (m. Col. P. T. Howell). Lewis moved to Kentucky. John and Samuel moved to California. Henry Calvin moved to Kentucky. Isaac N. was wounded in the battle of Williamsburg in the Civil War and died of his wounds. Ann's husband, John Gardner, was also wounded at Williamsburg and died. James was in the army and died of fever at Manassas, Va. Jacob T. and David V. moved to Texas and died there. Susan Simmons died in Missouri. Madison died at Pulaski, Va. Ann Gardner died at Salem, Va. Adaline Howell died in Floyd County. Harvey D. died at Bluefield, W. Va. Letha Jane lived at Marion, Va.

Harvey D. (1840-1920) married Nannie Howell in 1867. Their children were: Bell (m. Charles Dickerson) in Bluefield,

W. Va.; Emma (m. Henry Quessenberry); Lillian in Bluefield, W. Va.; Homer (m. Eve Slusher) in Radford, Va.; Edith (m. Robert Ritter); Otho (m. Ada Dillard) in Bluefield, W. Va.; Ella Mae; Velma Clyde (m. Charles K. Burnett) in Willis, Va.

Clarke

According to court records in Chesterfield County, a John Clarke's estate was being settled December 10, 1838. This was Maj. John Clarke, likely a nephew of the John Clarke who came to Floyd County in 1804.

President Thomas Jefferson came from this section; his parents were Peter Jefferson and Jane Randolph. Peter Jefferson was the son of Thomas Jefferson (will dated March 15, 1723, proved in Henrico County, April 1731), who married, November 20, 1697, Mary Field, daughter of Major Peter Field, of New Kent County. The above is mentioned to show the similarity of the family names of the Jeffersons and the Clarkes. Thomas Jefferson's father had a brother Field Jefferson. President Thomas Jefferson had a brother Peter Field Jefferson, and later there were many in the Jefferson family named Peter and Field and Peterfield. Allison Clarke II had a son, Allison III, another, Field Clarke, and another, Peter Clarke.

```
                     (Allison II (died before his father)—   (Allison III
                     (wife Blanche                            (Field
                     (Will Feb. 10, 1766                      (Peter
                     (                                        (Shadrack
Allison Clarke       (                                        (Amelia
wife Martha          (                                        (Frances
Will dated           (
Feb. 18, 1769        (William—      (John  (died)
                     (wife Phebe    (Isham  (Probably John & James were
                     (              (Joseph  full brothers and Joseph and Isham
                     (              (James   full brothers)
                     (John
                     (1st wife Obedience
                     (2d wife Susan (Nix)—   John and Susan Nix came to
                     (                        Floyd County in 1804 with their
                     (                        daughter Lydia Clarke Shortt,
                     (Mary Rowlett            wife of Reuben Shortt.  The
                     (Sarah Fowler            children of John Clarke were:
                     (
                     (Edy Hatcher        1.  Martha, m., Joshua Russell
                     (Martha Clarke (unmar.) 2.  Frances, m. Thomas
                     (                        Bartlett (or Bartley)
                     (Jesse Clarke       3.  Lydia, m. Reuben Shortt
                     (George Clarke      4.  Henry, m. Deborah Banks
```

The children of John Clarke (first wife, Obedience, second wife Susan Nix), were: 1. Martha Clarke, married Joshua Russell, was the mother of Jeremiah Russell and grandmother of John Russell of Floyd County; 2. Frances Clarke, married Thomas Bartlett (or Bartley), was the mother of two daughters, Nancy and Annie, both of whom married in the Carter family of Floyd County, and later moved West; 3. Lydia Clarke, daughter of John Clarke and his second wife, Susan Nix, married Reuben Shortt, son of Young Shortt, of Chesterfield County, Virginia, and came with him and their young family to the present county of Floyd in 1804. She was the mother and grandmother of all the Shortts of Floyd County; 4. Henry Clarke, only son of John, came with his father and mother to Floyd County as a young man. He married Deborah Banks, daughter of John Banks the settler, and lived at the Thomas Barton homestead, six or seven miles east of the present courthouse. County Line Baptist Church is on this farm and stands only a few hundred yards east of the Henry Clarke residence. Here they lived until their four oldest children were born, who were: Frances, John, Jefferson and James, and then they moved West.

The Russells, the Bartletts, the Robertsons, the Shortts, and the LeSueurs came with the Clarkes to the present county of Floyd from Chesterfield County, Virginia, about 1804, all of whom were connected by marriage.

Cockram originally Cockerham

Harry (Henry) Cockerham, planter, made a deed in Bedford County to John Phelps, a bill of sale of cattle and furniture (Book A, page 8), in the year 1754. William Cockram was a taxpayer in the same county in 1784.

From the marriage records of Franklin County: Letty Cochram to William Lane, Jan. 7, 1799. This Letty Cochram must have been the granddaughter of the widow Lettuce Cockerham of Mecklenburg County, who was living there between the years 1782 and 1790. William Cockram to Lucy Milem (?), Dec. 12, 1803. John Cockram to Susannah Lumsden, daughter of John Lumsden, Jan. 21, 1786, all married by Rev.

John Wyatt. Henry Pedigo to Leah Cockram, Nov. 17, 1790, by Rev. Randolph Hall.

Franklin County Order Book, August 1787, Samuel Cockram is allowed 4 days attendance as a witness for Wm. Cockram in suit of Holley vs Cockram; John Cockram allowed 3 days for the same. Order Book, July 1788, Samuel Cockram appointed an ensign for the militia of this county.

Franklin County Records: Deed to Edward Cockram from Wm. Edwards, July 18, 1788, for 50 pounds, a tract of land of 200 acres, a part of a 400-acre tract patented by Edwards in 1753, on the dividing ridge between Shooting Creek and Turkey Cock Creek, and lying partly in Franklin County and partly in Henry (now Patrick); part of the line runs with line of Charles Rakes and with the line of Edward Cockram. Oct. 3, 1824, deed from Isham Cockram to Edward Cockram (son of above Edward) for $178.50, 100 acres, being in Franklin and Patrick counties on the branches of Turkey Cock Creek, land is on Rakes' line and crosses Raccoon Branch. Deed, May 1787, from Abner Cockram to Townshend.

Edward Cockram, Sr., lived on the lower waters of Shooting Creek near where the creek enters Smiths River. The old home was on the east slopes of Renfro Ridge. He made his will May 26, 1816, which was recorded in Franklin County:

"In the name of God Amen, I, Edward Cockram, Senr, of the county of Franklin and State of Virginia being weak of body but of perfect memory and calling to mind the mortality of my body and that it is appd onst for all men to die, have made this my last will and testament. First of all I resign my Soul into the hands of Almighty God who give it me, and my body to be Buried in Christian-like Manner at the discretion of my Executors, nothing doubting but I shall receive the same again by the mighty power of God at the General Reseraction at the last Day. And as touching my worldly estate whare with it has bin Please to Bless me with, I give and bequeath it in following manner that is to say, I give and Bequeath my whole Estate real and personal to my Beloved wife Mary so long as she lives and after her Disseas the whole that is left Land and other Property of every kind to be sold at publick auction on a Credit of twelve months by giving

Bond and approved Security and the money arising from such Sale to be Equally divided between my ten Children namely: Leah Pedigo, Nathan, Isham, Rachel Wood, wife of Richard Wood, Lydia, Preston, Mary, Edward, Charlotte, Sarah Proffitt. Also, I appoint my wife Executrix Nathan my son, Executor of this my last Will and Testament, Signed, Sealed and Acknowledged this twenty sixth day of May in the Year of Our Lord one thousand eight hundred and sixteen. (Signed) Edward Cockram. Teste: Thomas Hale, Brice Edwards, John Wood." Proved July 1, 1816.

Isham Cockram, Sr., son of the above Edward Cockram, Sr., married a daughter of Samuel Rakes from Franklin County, and they had a son, David Cockram, who married his first cousin, Annie Wood, daughter of Richard and Rachel (Cockram) Wood. David and Annie Cockram had the following children: 1. Alexander Cockram, married a daughter of Jeremiah Wood, children: Larkin, Gabriel and Jefferson. 2. Richard Cockram, also married a daughter of Jeremiah Wood, children: Malinda and Jackson. 3. Isham Cockram, Jr., married Elizabeth Salmons, children: Rufus, Janey, Robert, Buren, and Alice. 4. Jackson Cockram, married Martha Salmons, no children. 5. Harvey Cockram, married Milly Jane DeHart, daughter of Wilson DeHart, children: James D. Cockram (Primitive Baptist Minister), Asa, Amos, Joseph, Green, Mathew, Rebecca Ann, Lilly and Allie. 6. David Cockram, married Ellen Cannaday, and after her death, married Iowa Griffith, no children. 7. Peter Cockram married Mahala Cannaday, children: John Wm., David. 8. German Cockram, married Mary Wood, daughter of Jeremiah Wood, no children. 9. Leah Cockram, married John Ashworth, children: Green Ashworth, Sarah Ashworth, Lelia Ashworth and Tazewell Ashworth. 10. Nancy Cockram, married Jonathan Salmons, children: John M. Salmons, Waller C. Salmons, Sarah Salmons, and Martha Ann Salmons. 11. Sarah Cockram, married Mark Salmons, children: Rena Salmons and others.

Edward Cockram, Jr., son of Edward, Sr., and Mary, married Bashie Rakes, daughter of Charles Rakes, and lived near the mouth of Shooting Creek, and near Renfro Ridge in Franklin County. Their children were: 1. Nathan, who married Rachel Via, daughter of Samuel Via; Nathan was killed by a body of details while sitting on a fence eating his dinner. 2. Rhoda, who married Anderson Vest, their children: Nancy, Mary, John and Edward. 3. Martha, who married Isaac Via, their children: Rev. Wily (Willy?) A. Via, and Polly Proffit, wife of Joseph P. Proffit of Floyd. 4. Harding, who married Mary A. Griffith, one daughter: Rhoda, who married Mart Bowers. 5. Bryce, who married and moved West. 6. Artie M., who married William Riley Radford, a well-known minister of the Baptist Church who was pastor of Union Church on Smiths River for about forty years, their children: (see Radford sketch). 7. Charles, who married Ruth Radford, daughter of Robert Radford, their children: Jackson, who married Ellen Shiveley; Michael, who married Lina Vest; Martha and Robert. 8. Anna, who married Riley Whitlock, one son: Harden Whitlock, who married Ella Boyd, daughter of Samuel Boyd; Samuel Boyd was cruelly killed or murdered by the details in the time of the Civil War.

In 1831, Nathan Cockram of Floyd County was living on a farm of 420 acres situated on headwaters of Pine Creek and Shooting Creek, near the crest of the Blue Ridge Mountains; and in 1833 William B. Cockram was nominated for Justice of the Peace for the County Court, along with Thomas McCabe, Peter Slusher, Solomon Slusher, and Archibald Goodykoontz.

Joseph Cole

The Floyd County family is descended from Joseph Cole, a Revolutionary soldier, who married a Miss Cooper and settled near Laurel Ridge about 1805 in the present county of Floyd. His great-grandson, Elder H. Valentine Cole, has in his possession a cypress-wood canteen which Joseph Cole carried as a soldier in the Revolutionary War. The children of Joseph Cole were: I. Byrd. II. Joseph, Jr. III. Lydia, wife of John Thrash of "Thrash's Mountain."

I. Byrd Cole married first and secondly women of the Underwood family. The last wife was Sarah Underwood. His first set of children were: Lucinda, wife of William A. Conner - they moved to West Virginia; and James, who married a Miss Underwood and also moved to West Virginia. The second set of children were four sons and five daughters: 1. Harvey married Cynthia Winifred and lived near the "Head of the River" Primitive Baptist Church where he raised a family of four sons and four daughters: Juliana, Pleasant, Harvey, Jr., Bailey, Valentine, Kyle, Sarah and Caroline. 2. Fleming married Abigail Vest, daughter of Charles - they had one son, Elder H. Valentine Cole, who is a well-known minister of the Baptist Church. 3. Byrd, Jr., married Sarah Iddings - their children were: Lloyd, Rosetta and Eliza. 4. Pleasant married Sarah Lawrence. 5. Mary, wife of John F. Hall. 6. Lydia, wife of James Wilson. 7. Eliza, wife of Charles M. Hall. 8. Eveline, wife of William Martin. 9. Nancy, wife of Henry Light.

Pleasant and Byrd Cole were members of Company H, 54th Virginia Infantry, under Captain Sparrel H. Griffith in the Confederate army. Byrd Cole died at White Sulphur Springs, Montgomery County, date of which is unknown. Pleasant Cole was a member of Company I, 54th Virginia Infantry under Captain Burwell Akers. Harvey Cole served in the Confederate army but his command is unknown. Fleming Cole was in McCauley's Corps.

The Conner Family

The Conner family of Floyd County is of Scots-Irish descent. The name is sometimes spelled **Conner, Connor,** and **O'Connor.** Daniel Conner, the emigrant ancestor, settled near the "head of the river" in the east end of the county about 1773, and his descendants are numerous in the county today. Daniel Conner's deed to 300 acres shows that he gave a valuable shotgun for the land. In 1784 he acquired a land grant which was written on a deerskin and signed by Robert Brooks, Governor of Virginia (probably as acting Governor). Soon after this he founded a church in the neighborhood. Daniel Conner deeded a plot of ground on which the Salem Primitive Baptist Church is built, "to be for the use of a church forever" - this deed was also written on a skin. Andrew, son of Daniel Conner, acquired land near his father's grant. Andrew's grant bears the date of September 1799, and is signed by James Monroe, Governor of Virginia. This deed is written on a skin, and these parchments are in the possession of the Conner relatives in

Floyd County.

Daniel Conner signed his will March 15, 1810, in the presence of Humphrey Smith, John Smith, Olivia Smith, Elizabeth Smith, and Henry Iddings. A codicil was added to the will on April 12, 1812, after the death of his wife Mary. This will was probated at the January term of Montgomery County Court in 1815. His death probably occurred in the latter part of 1814, his wife Mary preceding him by three years. The children of Daniel Conner and wife Mary were: Andrew, Jonathan, William, Zadock, Daniel, Jacob, Barbara (m. Shields), Mary (m. Hill), Rebecca (m. Reed), Sarah and Christina.

The children of Andrew Conner were in part: William A.; Aaron (1811-1867); Daniel O. (Sept. 7, 1813 - Jan. 14, 1897); John O. (Dec. 8, 1814 - Dec. 17, 1910); Nancy (m. Samuel Otey); Bethania (m. Gordon Hall, Sr.); Mary (m. Jackson Light).

The children of Daniel O. Conner, the son of Andrew, were: James P. (b. March 22, 1864); Mary (b. Nov. 24, 1856) married James W. Walton; Bethania (b. Nov. 14, 1858) married W. T. Simpson; Nancy (April 22, 1855 - April 25, 1921) married Elijah Furrow; Drusilla (b. June 21, 1869) married William N. Poff; Susan Elvira (b. Nov. 28, 1853, d. Feb. 11, 1883) married Walton.

Jonathan Conner, Sr., second son of Daniel the settler, was one of the very early justices of the peace, and was executor of his father's will. He was the father of William Conner, known as "Billy Strong," who was the father of Jonathan Conner (1831-1914), a well-known citizen of the head of the river section, whose farm joined the Old Ogle Farm. Jonathan Conner, Sr., married a Miss Iddings; his son William Conner married Elizabeth, daughter of Henry Poff; Jonathan Conner, Jr., married Mahala, daughter of Valentine and Harriet (Gray) Thrash. The children of Jonathan Conner, Jr., were: Valentine Thrash; Shelton L.; Robert Lee; and Harriet E., who married S. Homer Strickler.

As mentioned earlier, the will of Daniel Conner the settler gave the plot of land on which the Salem Primitive Baptist Church now stands.

"In the name of God Amen, I, Daniel Conner of the County of Montgomery being of sound mind, memory and understanding, calling to mind the mortality of my body and that it is appointed unto all men once to die do therefore make, ordain this my last will and testament in manner and form following . . . Item 4, I give and bequeath unto the Baptist Society the land enclosed within the fence around the meeting house entering the front square of the fence down to where the Bent mountain road crosses the branch to them and their successors for ever . . . I nominate, appoint and make my two sons Jonathan and Andrew Conner my true and legal executors of this my last will and testament March 15, 1810. Daniel Conner, L. S."

Copper Hill, Va.
May the 12th, 1922?

Dr. A. D. Wood
Bluefield, West Va.

Daniel O'Conner lived ¼ mile from Salem Church on the main road running from Floyd C. H. to Roanoke City. The farm is known as the Albert Conner Farm. The land grant or title to Daniel Conner is written on a deer skin, signed by Robert Brooks, Governor of Virginia, dated April 1784. Another grant to Andrew Conner on a skin also dated September 1799, signed by James Monroe, Governor of Virginia. Salem Church grounds was deeded to the church by said Daniel Conner to be church property forever, also written on same sort of a skin. This was known as Botetourt County and embraced Floyd, Montgomery and other lands. I have tried to count up the Conner families. There are over forty families of Conners living in Locust Grove District at this time. The Conners are of English and Irish descent, are large and well built, a very industrious people and strictly honest and truthful.

Dr. Wood, I do not know of anything that I can write at this time. I am, Sincerely your friend,

Noah Wilson

The Corn Family - a border family

The Corn family of Franklin and Patrick counties is of German extraction, emigrating to America some time just after the close of the American Revolution, and settling in what is now Patrick County on Smith's River in the vicinity of Elamsville.

Major Corn (b. 1765?) married Nancy Hancock of Virginia and lived near Elamsville, where he raised a family who were in part: John, William, Samuel, Jesse, Polly, Mary and Permelia, all of whom moved to Kentucky, near Winchester, excepting Jesse, who married and raised a family in Patrick County.

Jesse Corn (b. 1798?), son of Major Corn, married Elizabeth Burnett of Patrick County and lived all of his life in Patrick. He was a large farmer and was for many years presiding justice of the courts.

The children of Jesse were: John B. (m. Elizabeth Ann Cutler), a Methodist minister; Nancy (m. William Witcher); William H. married Mary Koger; Malinda; Judith married Peyton Ross, Sr.; Elizabeth married William Copeland; Susan married Burwell Moles; Mary (Pollie) married Flemon Via; Jane married Joseph Wimbish; Permelia married Joseph M. Stovall, and they had the following children: Elizabeth J., Nancy M., Susan S., Mary H., Virginia, Martha L., Permelia R., Fannie J. who married Daniel Hillsman Wood (his second wife), George W., Jesse T., Joseph P., and John T. (unmarried); Dicey married Peyton Ross, Jr.; Peter; Jesse, Jr., died in infancy.

Peter Corn (1835-1919), youngest son of Jesse, married Clementine Turner (b. 1836), daughter of Shadrach Turner, and lived in the west end of Franklin County where he was a well-known minister of the Primitive Baptist Church for more than forty years. He was a soldier in the Confederate army, a member of Company D, 51st Regiment of Virginia Infantry.

The children of Rev. Peter Corn were: Elizabeth (m. James Helms), Ruth (m. D. Hillsman Wood), Clementine (m. George W. Slusher), Mary (m. J. P. Miles), Silas E. (m. Lelia Philpott).

The Cox Family

The Cox family is of English descent, the Floyd County branch having its origin in Mathew Cox, Sr., who was a soldier in the French and Indian War and was with Colonel George Washington at Braddock's Defeat in 1755. Mathew lived for many years in Halifax County, Virginia, and later moved with his family to the west end of Floyd County. He married a Mrs. Spencer, who formerly was a Miss Dickinson [Dickerson?]. They had seven children: Carter, Mastin, Aris, Mathew, Jr., Ambrose, Braxton and Delphine.

Carter Cox, the son of Mathew, Sr., married Nancy Reed, and they had ten children: Mathew Cox (1786-1860), who married Mary Bishop (1791-1880) daughter of John Bishop, the settler, and they were the parents of Dr. Aris B. Cox (Jan. 1, 1816-Jan. 30, 1907) who married Phebe Edwards (1825-1893), and others. After the death of his first wife, Mathew, Jr., married Drusilla, daughter of William and Polly Gilham, and they had the following children: Ann Eliza, Amanda Ellen, Leah Jane, Noah G., and Mary. Ross Cox, second son of Carter Cox, married Annie Wade; George W. Cox; Carter Cox (1805-1898) married Naomi Gilham, daughter of William Gilham (1775-1831) and Polly Goodykoontz (1771-1867), and they were the parents of nine children: Mary S., Giles A., William G., Drusilla A., Hamilton L., Fleming L., Wesley D., Melvin B., and Lydia L. Lucy Cox, daughter of Carter and Nancy Cox, married Robert Jones; Elizabeth Cox, daughter of Carter and Nancy, married Anderson Wade; Sallie Cox, daughter of Carter and Nancy, married Mathew Thurman; Nancy Cox married David Slusher; Susan Cox married John W. Helms of Burke's Fork; and Charlotte Cox married Milton Clay.

Ambrose Cox, son of Mathew Cox, Sr., married Sallie Reed, daughter of George Reed, and lived in Indian Valley on Little Indian Creek where he had a very large farm, was a slave owner and a wealthy man. Late in life he freed all his slaves who would accept freedom. He was the father of thirteen children: Luke (b. 1791); Dicey (b. 1792); who married Dr. John Bishop, the "herb doctor"; Ambrose (b. 1793); Lucy (b. 1794), who married Tobias Phillips; Nancy (b. 1798), who married Samuel Lester; Sarah (b. 1800), who married George Quesenberry; Eliza (b. 1802), who married Henry Wade (1799), son of John the settler, and was the mother of Jacob, John and others; Mary (b. 1804), who married Randolph Phillips; Paul (b. 1808), who died young; Eunice (b. 1810), who married John Wilson; Mastin (1813-1913), who lived in Illinois; and Aris R. (1817-1860), who married Irene Maberry (1824-1907). [Note: one name is missing to complete list of 13 children.]

Braxton Cox, the son of Mathew Cox, Sr., married Nancy Ellison and their four children were: William, who lived in Indiana; Dr. James, who lived in Kentucky; Jerry, who lived in Charleston, West Virginia and was killed by a falling tree; and Ambrose, who died young.

Concerning the other children of Mathew Cox, Sr., Mastin moved to Georgia; Aris moved to Kentucky; Mathew Jr., moved to North Carolina, and reared the following children: Aris B. (mentioned earlier); Cloyd (b. 1820) married Cynthia Reeves; Ross (1824-1842), died of diphtheria; Jordan (1829-1905) married Emaline Evans; James (1835-1878) married Letitia Neal; Elizabeth (1813-1872) married James Hill; and Sarah (b. 1818) married Carter Wade. Delphine, daughter of Mathew Sr., married William (Billie) Roberts and lived in Burke County, North Carolina.

Aris R. Cox (1817-1860), son of Ambrose and Sallie (Reed) Cox, married Irene Maberry (1824-1907) and lived in Indian Valley, where he was a well-known farmer, constable and tax collector. He lost his life in 1860 by a falling tree. He was the father of the following: Julina, who married Abraham D. Burnett (son of Austin) of Indian Valley; Winfield; Bluford; Franklin; Warren; Fulton; Melvina and Louanna.

DeHart

Aaron DeHart appears in the early settlement of Patrick County, Virginia. There are records of family connections and descendants of the following children: Elijah, James, Gabriel and Susan. It is recorded that Aaron DeHart was living in Amherst County, Virginia, in 1780, with a family of nine. Probably all of his children did not come to Patrick County. The compiler's |A. D. Wood| grandmother was Lucinda DeHart, daughter of James, and granddaughter of Aaron DeHart the settler. She married John R. Wood, son of Richard Wood of "Wood's Gap," in Patrick County. She was authority for the information that her father, James DeHart, married Ellen (or Elinda) Dennis, her mother, of Franklin County. Tradition does not supply the name of Aaron DeHart's wife. An account, as far as known, of the four children of Aaron DeHart is given:

I. Elijah DeHart married Mary Ellyson Jordan, and their family of twelve children were:

A. Aaron DeHart, Jr., m. Dollie Cruise; he was in Company D, 51st Virginia Infantry in the Confederate army under Captain D. Lee Ross.

B. Thomas DeHart m. Patsy Via; he was in Company A, 24th Virginia Infantry under Captain C. M. Stigleman.

C. Jackson DeHart m. Liddie Bell.

D. Jesse DeHart m. Deborah (Debby) Thomas; he served in Company A, 24th Virginia Infantry under Captain Stigleman.

E. Charles DeHart m. Nancy Conner.

F. Elijah DeHart, Jr., m. Rebecca McAlexander.

G. Dennis DeHart, never married.

H. Mary Jordan DeHart m. James Via.

I. Susan DeHart m. Wilson Vaughan.

J. Rebecca DeHart m. Carroll Thomas.

K. Malinda DeHart m. David Taylor.

L. Nancy DeHart m. Fountain Howell.

II. Gabriel DeHart married Charity (Hannah?) Hubbard: their children:

A. Thomas DeHart m., first, Millie Conner and, secondly, Mary Pendleton; no children. He was in Co. A, 24th Va. Infantry under Captain Stigleman; he was a miller and, according to family tradition, invented the turbine water wheel.

B. Jesse H. m. Mintory Ayers; their children: Clinton, Perceval, John Milton, Alice; he was in Co. A, 24th Va. Infantry, and was killed in battle at Chafin's Farm, 1862.

C. Polly m. Jeremiah Wood, son of old man Dickey Wood; their children: Richard, Isaac, Stephen, Charity, Judith, Sally, Nancy, Polly, Mahala.

D. Lucinda m. Saul DeHart; their children: John, William, Aaron, Paul, Thomas, Lucinda.

E. Sallie m. Chesley Rakes; their children: Thomas,

Chesley, Aaron, Isaac, Jack, Ziny, Lucinda, Malinda.

F. Susan m. William Blackard; their children: Jesse D., Willoughby, Stephen, Thomas, Lucinda and Susannah.

G. John m. Sally Palmer; their children: Daniel, Martha, Mahala, Lucinda, Preston, Claibe, Jesse D., and Thomas.

H. Hannah m. a Johnson; their children: Robert, Rhoda.

I. Gabriel m. Patsy Gates; their children: Stephen, Henry, Will, Green, John, Nat, Sally, Lucinda and Puss.

J. Stephen married Susan Pickle Elgin, sister of John Elgin. Their thirteen children were:

1. America m. Willoughby Blackard; their children: John Claibe, Susan Alice, Virginia Ellen, Joseph Bishop and Lucinda Victoria.

2. Claibe m. Milly Burnette; their children: George Rufus, Alice Josephine, Susan, Dock, Alvis, Ella, Rosa.

3. Jonathan m. Mahala Shelor, daughter of Randolph; their children: Charles Davis, of Danville, Virginia; and John William (deceased) of Louisville, Kentucky.

4. Isham, never married.

5. Benjamin, never married.

6. David, never married.

7. Daniel m. the daughter of Kentucky John DeHart, her name may have been Martha; their children: Nannie; the others were known by nicknames only: "Big Boy"; "Little Boy"; "High Child"; and "Baby."

8. Stephen disappeared during the Civil War and was never heard of again.

9. Thomas Madison (Mat) married in Kentucky.

10. Lucinda m. William Davis Brammer; their children: Susan Adaline, Nancy Emmaline, Sarah, America Ann, John Stephen, and Benjamin Franklin.

11. Sally m. Samuel Turner; their children: Nannie O., Alice and Ellis.

12. Elizabeth m. Jack Robertson; one daughter, Ella, married a Howard.

13. Milly m. James Hubbard; their children were: Victoria, died in infancy; George Dallas; Susan; Lucinda; Tyler;

and Lucy Alberta.

III. James DeHart married Ellen (or Elinda) Dennis of Franklin County, Va.; their five children of record were:

1. James Wilson DeHart m. Rebecca Martin; their children:

(a) William F., Co. A, 24th Va. Infantry under Dr. C. M. Stigleman, killed in battle at Drewry's Bluff, near Richmond, May 16, 1864.

(b) James A., Sheriff of Floyd County; Co. A, 24th Va. Infantry under Captain C. M. Stigleman.

(c) Joseph, went West.

(d) Reed, never married.

(e) Millie Jane, now (1932) living nearly 100 years old, married William Harvey Cockram; their children: James David Cockram, who has assisted considerably in collecting data for the DeHart family sketch: Rebecca Ann; William Green; Lillie E.; Samuel A.; Asa A.; Joseph A.; Amos C.; and Virginia Alice.

(f) Lucinda, no record.

(g) Addie m. Jerry A. Trusler.

(h) Ellen m. Alexander Howell.

2. Thomas T. DeHart m. Margaret Boyd; he was in Co. H, 51st Va. Infantry, under Capt. D. Lee Ross.

3. Lucinda DeHart (1797-1853) m. John Richard Wood; their children: Annie, Stephen, Delilah, Mary, Richard Johnson, Leah and Rachel, twins.

4. Elijah DeHart; his children were: John, Eli, Joseph, all three of whom were in Co. D, 51st Va. Infantry under Captain Daniel Lee Ross.

5. Thomas T. DeHart, Co. D, 51st Va. Infantry under Captain D. Lee Ross.

IV. Susan DeHart, came to Patrick County and married Stephen Hubbard, a Baptist preacher; one child is recalled, Annie.

Deskins

Harvey Deskins, the son of Steven and Ann Deskins of Tazewell County, Virginia, was one of the prominent men in the early days of Floyd County. He was one of the early justices of the peace - a member of the County Court - also a promoter of the "Brick Academy" in 1847. He was a merchant by occupation and his store was on the north side of Main Street, adjoining the first residence occupied by Dr. Samuel A. J. Evans before he moved to his farm on Little River. Later the Evans' house became the home of Harvey Deskins.

Harvey was twice married, with no children by his first wife. His second wife was Sally Duke of Charlottesville, by whom he had one daughter, Nannie Howe Deskins, who married a Presbyterian minister by the name of Robinson. The Deskins family belonged to the Jacksonville Presbyterian Church, and are buried in the old cemetery in the Town of Floyd. He was a promoter and member of the Jacksonville Savings Bank.

Harvey Deskins was one of eight children, another of whom was Ellen Deskins (b. 1826), who married Captain Jackson Godbey. Harvey was born in the year 1804 and died in 1868. He was a member of the Legislature of Virginia, and was also elected a member of the Convention in 1860 to decide the question of secession. He was opposed to seceding from the Union, but when Virginia adopted secession by an overwhelming majority, he was loyal to his state.

The DeWitt Family

The DeWitt family is of French extraction and had its origin in America in Jeremiah DeWitt. He came direct from France to America and settled at Charlemont or Dan's Mill, Bedford County, Virginia, about 1750-60. DeWitt was a soldier under General Lafayette in the Revolutionary War. Jeremiah had at least two sons, Jeremiah and James, Sr.

James, Sr., was the father of James DeWitt, Jr. (b. May 19, 1780, d. June 9, 1859) who married Dorcas Worley (b. Nov. 23, 1788) of Bedford County, Virginia, on Feb. 25, 1806, and possibly served in the War of 1812. It is said that there were two Worley sons - Manson who manufactured the best flax spinning wheels known; and William of "a different turn," who was a violinist and taught music and dancing "schools" in Marion or

Abingdon.

To James, Jr., and Dorcas were born nine children: Nelson
C. (b. 1807), a clergyman; Alanson C. (b. 1809), a clergyman;
Elisha D. (b. 1811), also a clergyman; William H. (b. 1813);
Bennett M. (b. 1815), newspaper editor, owner and founder of
the *Richmond Enquirer*, and at the time of his death editor of
the *Virginia Index* - he died at his home in Nelson County on
March 13, 1863; Zachariah Worley (b. 1817); Catherine M. (b.
1820); Mary F. (b. 1823); and Permelia A. (b. 1825).

Zachariah W. DeWitt married Mary Ann Keen (d. July 27,
1857), daughter of Thomas S. Keen of Franklin County, Virginia, on January 27, 1846. They were the parents of Thomas
Keen DeWitt (b. Dec. 31, 1846) who came to Floyd County on
April 16, 1868. He married Sarah Rosabelle Strickler, daughter
of Samuel and Nancy Ann (Helms) Strickler, and they live at
Copper Hill, Floyd County, Virginia. Thomas Keen DeWitt is
a well-known farmer and justice of the peace.

Amelia Ann Eliza (b. Oct. 1, 1854), daughter of Zachariah
and Mary, married Sydney E. Payne of Floyd, later moved to
Bluefield, W. Va. Sarah Frances (b. Oct. 30, 1852), another
daughter of Zachariah and Mary, married Dr. John T. Bishop
of Stuart, Virginia. James Henry, son of Zachariah and Mary,
was born July 10, 1848. Martha Elizabeth Catharine, daughter
of Zachariah and Mary, was born Oct. 1, 1850. William Elisha,
son of Zachariah and Mary, died in infancy.

The children of Thomas and Sarah DeWitt are: Samuel
Zachariah (b. Oct. 8, 1875); James Strickler (b. Oct. 9, 1886).
Samuel married a Miss Vest and James married a Miss Furrow.

Dickerson

The Dickerson family came from Pittsylvania County and
settled on West Fork of Little River, three miles north of present Floyd Court House.

Moses Dickerson, Sr., (1746? - Mar. 23, 1834), married
Jemima Sullivan (1756 - May 26, 1846); both are buried in Pine
Creek Cemetery. Their children were: I. Frances (b. March 20,
1778); II. Anna (b. Feb. 13, 1780); III. Moses, Jr. (b. Oct. 10,

1783); IV. John (b. Nov. 8, 1785); V. Elizabeth (b. May 9, 1888); VI. Morrel (b. Sept. 13, 1790). Family tradition says that one of the girls married a Martin and settled where Pulaski City is now. Moses and Morrel married sisters, Nancy and Elizabeth Reed, and settled on the home place.

III. Moses Dickerson, Jr., eldest son of Moses, Sr., pioneer settler, married, first, Nancy Reed on Sept. 28, 1802, and their children were:

1. Polly (Mary) Dickerson (b. Nov. 8, 1803);

2. Jemima Dickerson (b. March 11, 1806) married Josiah Burnett and settled near Copper Valley, Floyd County; some of their children: Early moved to Iowa, Asa married a Morricle and died in the Civil War, Josiah, Jr., married a Duncan;

3. Andrew Dickerson (b. May 9, 1807) moved to North Salem, Indiana; two of his sons, Floyd and Calvin, were in the Union Army in the Civil War and were captured by some of their cousins on the Confederate side;

4. Sarah Dickerson (b. Feb. 28, 1809) married a Duncan and settled in Carroll County, Va.;

5. Morrel Dickerson (b. Mar. 20, 1811) married a Morricle; their children: William, who served as a Confederate soldier through the Civil War; Harvey married a Miss Simmons and lived near Floyd; Eli married a Jones; Floyd married an Agee and had ten children; Emeline married a Hylton; Callahill married a Hylton and lives near Floyd;

6. Humphrey (b. Oct. 9, 1813) died when he was young;

7. George (b. May 25, 1816) died on his way to the Mexican War;

8. Elizabeth (b. Sept. 24, 1818) married Powhatan Williams and lives on Pine Creek; they had five boys and two girls: William T. (m. Albina Young) lives in Floyd; Henry (m. Florence Young) moved to St. Louis, Missouri; David (m. Lina Spangler); Thomas (m. Anna Saunders) settled near Salem, Va.; George M. D. (m. Sarah Epperly) lives in Texas; Demaris (m. Isaac Epperly); and Manerva (m. Captain Darius W. Sowers) had four sons: Trig and Walter live in Illinois, Aaron, editor of the *Floyd Press*, lives in Floyd, and Robert R., a minister of the Lutheran Church, lives in South Carolina.

9. Early Dickerson (b. Aug. 17, 1822) served through the Civil War, 2nd Lieut., Co. A, 54th Regiment, married Susan Williams; they had nine children:

(a) Nancy married a Slusher;

(b) Lafayette W. married a Raines from Pulaski Co., Va.; they had five children: Adrian, died when he was 21 years old; W. H. married Agnes Kersey, they have three children: Beatrice, Nell and Howard, and live near Willis, Va.; Eulalia married P. H. Dickerson, son of Elder James M. Dickerson, and lives in Richmond, Va.; Lillian married C. H. Sutphin, son of Hon. J.A.L. Sutphin, and lives in Richmond; Alma married Burnett Kersey and has one girl, Ruth Evelyn, and lives near Willis;

(c) J. K. Dickerson never married and died in Jacksonville, Florida;

(d) Mathew C. Dickerson was judge of County Court of Floyd, married Frances Dobyns, daughter of Samuel Dobyns, and moved to Bluefield, W. Va., where he was engaged with the N. & W. Railway; they had six children: Willie, Samuel, Frank, Mary, Annie, Mattie;

(e) H. M. Dickerson married Alice Slusher and lives in Powhatan, W. Va.; they have one son who lives at Elk Horn, W. Va.;

(f) W. H. Dickerson married a Miss Hale and lives in Colorado;

(g) H. A. Dickerson married a Godbey and lives in Limestone, Tenn.; they have two children, Walter and Freddie;

(h) C. L. Dickerson married a Carter and lives in Bluefièld, W. Va.;

(i) Julina married E. L. Albright and lives at Elk Horn, W. Va.

After the death of his first wife Nancy (d. July 16, 1823), Moses Dickerson, Jr., would not remarry until Early, the youngest child "could outrun his stepmother"; his second wife was Elizabeth Wickham and the children of that marriage were:

10. Amos Dickerson (b. May 16, 1832) married Polly Slusher; he was a minister of the Primitive Baptist Church, served through the Civil War, and represented the county for 2 terms in the Virginia Legislature; he had six children:

(a) Landon married a Kitterman and lives in Carroll County, Va., has one son and one daughter;

(b) George W. married a Jenkins and lives near Floyd, had one daughter who married a Hylton;

(c) D. M. Dickerson married a Harman, had one son and two daughters;

(d) Rosabell (m. Wade Thompson) had three boys;

(e) Adaline (m. Jackson Graham) had five children;

(f) Lydia married Monroe Simmons.

11. Coffee Dickerson, sixth son of Moses, Jr. married a Graham and had a large family, among whom Peter, the second son, represented Floyd County for 2 terms in the Virginia Legislature, Walter married a Hylton, Posey died in France in the World War, Julius lives near Floyd;

12. Diana Dickerson married James Simmons and lives in Alum Ridge;

13. Moses Dickerson died when he was young.

VI. Morrel Dickerson, youngest son of Moses, Sr. and Jemima, married Elizabeth Reed (who lived to be 105 years old) ; their children were:

1. Moses Dickerson (b. Oct. 21, 1810) lived in the east end of Floyd County;

2. Polly (Mary) Dickerson (b. Sept. 12, 1812) married Wigington Dickerson, had several children and was grandmother of Elder James (Jimmy) M. Dickerson, Minister of the Primitive Baptist Church, and State Senator from Floyd County;

3. Michael Dickerson (b. Feb. 20, 1815) married Catherine Craig, daughter of Joseph and Mary (Townsly) Craig; they had 12 children:

Charles married a Miss Silver and moved to Tennessee;

Burdine (b. Nov. 17, 1838) became Commissioner of Revenue following his uncle, John Dickerson, and married Nancy Sowers, daughter of David and Margaret (Spangler) Sowers; they had 11 children, some were: Dr. Leonidas Cameron Dickerson (b. 1869) of Stuart, Va., Nora, Vada, George, Charles,

Ashby, James B., Nannie and Vance;

John died in Confederate army;

Andrew died in Confederate army;

George Riley married Elizabeth Winter, daughter of David Winter, some of their children: Amos, Grant, Alma Lindy;

Emmazetta died in infancy;

Elizabeth;

Ellen died in infancy;

Sarah never married and moved to Kentucky;

Catherine married a McPeak and lived in Pulaski County; Isabelle;

Mary lived in Montgomery County.

4. John Dickerson (b. April 21, 1817) held the office of Commissioner of Revenue for twenty years and was well known to the people of the county; he married Frances Dick, and had ten children, some were: William, Abner, Joseph, Alma, and Moses, a prominent minister of the Brethren Church.

5. Andrew Dickerson (b. Sept. 7, 1819), Captain of Co. A, 54th Va. Regiment in Civil War, married Mrs. Elizabeth Williams, they had one son, Morel, and two daughters, one of whom married a Methodist preacher;

6. Riley (b. Dec. 14, 1822) married Sarah Rutrough;

7. Morrel Dickerson (b. March 1, 1824) married Charlotte Jones and had two sons and three daughters, he died in Missouri;

8. Jemima (b. Sept. 30, 1826) married Asa Sumpter, some of their children were: Richard, Morrell, B.P., Early and Elizabeth;

9. Elijah Dickerson (b. Jan. 11, 1828) married Demaris Williams, was killed in the Campaign for Chattanooga in the Civil War, and left 3 sons and 2 daughters.

The Dobyns Family

A will made Nov. 7, 1817, and probated on Dec. 27, 1819, for Griffin Dobyns at the courthouse in Bedford County left his estate to Mary Ann, his wife, and nine children, namely: Sarah

Bond, Elizabeth Martin, Catherine Johnson, Thomas Dobyns, Griffin Dobyns, Jr., Joseph Dobyns, Jonah Dobyns, John Dobyns, and Abner Dobyns. Son Abner was named executor with Nicholas Johnson (probably Catherine's husband) and Abner received the homeland.

Abner Dobyns and Elizabeth, his wife, were of English extraction and lived in Bedford County, Virginia, near Liberty - now Bedford City. Two of their sons, Thomas M. and Samuel Dobyns came to Jacksonville about 1840, and entered into the mercantile business.

Samuel Dobyns first married a Miss Otey of Lynchburg, Virginia, and they lived on Main Street where Dr. John W. Simmons later lived. They were the parents of six sons, five of whom were in the Confederate army. Thomas P. (Tom), a member of the drygoods firm of "Dobyns and Shields" of Christiansburg, Virginia, was the first to volunteer, became a captain and was killed in battle in 1863 at Blackwater, Virginia. Abner Dobyns was a member of Dr. Callahill M. Stigleman's Company - Company A, 54th Regiment of Virginia Infantry - was captured, exchanged and promoted to captain. After the conflict be became a member of the firm of "Samuel Dobyns and Son." He married Miss Olivia (Ollie) Price of Franklin County, and later moved to that county, engaging in the tobacco business at Callaway, Virginia (Olivia, widowed, married Col. George Helms, and they had a daughter, Olivia, who married a Mr. Churchfield and lived in Richmond, Va.). Frazier O. Dobyns, a member of Dr. Stigleman's Company, was twice wounded. After the war he married Miss Ellie Cecil, his first wife, of Carroll County. Dr. Benjamin S. Dobyns of Fries, Virginia, is a son. Frazier Dobyns was engaged in the mercantile business and after the death of his father he purchased the home property, moved back and continued the business in Floyd. After the death of his first wife, he married Miss Carrie Howard, a daughter of Col. Joseph L. Howard, also of Floyd. He was Treasurer of Floyd County and a well-known citizen of the county.

Captain Armstead O. Dobyns, another son, organized a cavalry company of Floyd men and was assigned to service in

Northern Virginia. After the war he married Miss Reta Howell of Floyd and was a cattle dealer. He, too, was one of Floyd County's Treasurers.

Judge Zachary T. Dobyns, another son, married Miss Lula Pendleton, a sister to Wm. and Walter Pendleton. He was a distinguished lawyer, Commonwealth's Attorney of the county, and judge of the court. Corrie, daughter of Judge Dobyns, married Frank Helms and lived in Bristol, Virginia; daughter Ethel lived in Bristol, Va., and another daughter married J. D. Meador of Roanoke.

Jennie, daughter of Samuel Dobyns, married John L. Jett, son of Joseph Jett, and was the mother of Dr. Cabell Jett and others; Fannie, another daughter, married Matthew C. Dickerson, son of Early Dickerson; Nettie died young.

Thomas M. Dobyns, brother of Samuel, came to Floyd from Bedford, went in business in Floyd with his brother Samuel in 1848. He married Miss Lurinda Conner of Patrick County and went to housekeeping in the house now occupied [1922] by Mr. Wm. Russell on Locust Street. Their son, Samuel G. Dobyns, was born (1851) there, and after the mother died, Samuel G. Dobyns was left to his mother's only sister, Mrs. Charles De-Hart. After Thomas' second marriage to Miss Permelia Lemon of Franklin County, he moved to Wolf Glade, Carroll County, and sold goods as "S. and T. M. Dobyns." His second wife died, leaving one child, a daughter, Henrietta. Thomas' third wife was Miss Kate Gannaway of Wythe County, Virginia (a sister of Professor William T. Gannaway, head of the Male Academy at Jacksonville for some years). There were six children born to Thomas and Kate Dobyns.

Samuel G. Dobyns, eldest son of Thomas M. Dobyns, married Miss Ruth Lawson, daughter of Elder William M. Lawson, a gifted Primitive Baptist minister, who was widely known in Patrick, Floyd and adjoining counties. Samuel and Ruth Dobyns celebrated their golden wedding anniversary on February 6, 1922.

Benjamin Dodd

Benjamin Dodd, the ancestor of the Floyd County family, was born in Franklin County, Virginia, July 18, 1780. He married Mary Prosize of Franklin County, who was born December 30, 1780. The Prosize family like that of the Dodds' were few in number in Colonial Virginia.

Soon after his marriage, Benjamin Dodd moved over the Blue Ridge into the county of Montgomery, now Floyd, settling on a creek which has since borne his name - Dodds Creek. The property he acquired is one of the finest farms in Floyd County, and is now the home and property of his grandson, the Hon. Burdine Bishop. This property, according to a statement made by the late Dr. C. M. Stigleman, was first owned by a Mr. Price and Joshua Howell, who were among the very early settlers of this section of the county. The Dodds had as neighbors: the Phlegars, the Kittermans, the Tices, the Goodykoontzes, the Weavers and others later. This fine farm is one mile west of the present town of Floyd on Dodds Creek or South Fork of Little River. Here Benjamin Dodd died September 8, 1856; his wife preceded him, dying June 23, 1844, and both are buried in the family burying ground along with many of their descendants and neighbors. Their eight children were: William, Fleming, Cynthia, Sebrina, Caleb, Susan, Alfred and Elizabeth.

William (b. Jan. 18, 1802) married Elizabeth Tice, lived three miles west of the county seat on a part of his father's original farm, where he was a farmer. Their children were: Calvin, Claiborne and Wilson Henderson. Calvin married Phoebe Rigney, their children were: Caleb, Martha and Roena. Claiborne married Susan Tice, they had two daughters: Laura and Lelia. Wilson Henderson (d. 1886), a widely known minister of the Primitive Baptist Church, lived all of his life in Floyd County, married Mary Rigney and was the father of six sons and two daughters: Noah, Callahill, Walker, Lena (who died young), Aaron, Hathaway, John and Malena. Noah married Dollie Adams, lives at Cloverdale in Botetourt County, has but one child, Lelia. Callahill married Mary Shelor and their children were: Kent, Harold, Otis, Shelor, Clement and Golden. Walker married, first, Minnie Basham, had one son Basil Thomas; his second wife was Nellie Charlton, no children. They live at Pilot in Montgomery County. Lena died in infancy. Aaron married Olivia Maberry, lives at Springwood, Botetourt County, and he too has but one child, Gladys. Hathaway married Ocie Moomaw, moved to Crawford, Nebraska, where he now lives. His children were: Mary, Harold and Ellen. John married Mary Bowling, and he too moved to Crawford, Nebraska; his children were: William and John, Jr. Malena married Tobias Hylton of Floyd County; one child's name was Beulah and others unknown.

Fleming (b. 1803) died young. Cynthia (b. 1805) married Manasseh Tice. Sebrina (b. 1810) married Solomon Weaver. Caleb (b. Dec. 10, 1812) died in infancy. Susan (b. 1815) married Joseph Harter. Alfred (b. Feb. 10, 1820) no record. Elizabeth (b. June 4, 1823) married Asa Bishop, son of Dr. John and Dicey (Cox) Bishop, and lived all of her life on her old parental homestead. Elizabeth and Asa were the parents of Burdine Bishop (b. Oct. 9, 1845), a member of the Virginia Legislature 1883-84, who married Mary L., youngest daughter of Mathew and Mary Ann (Strickler) Scott, and they were the parents of one daughter, Allie Bishop. Other children of Elizabeth were: Angeline (b. Feb. 10, 1844) married Samuel Harter; Catherine (b. March 31, 1847) married Bethuel Hylton of Burks Fork Creek; Emeline (b. Dec. 19, 1848) died in infancy; Wesley (b. Oct. 1, 1860) married Lydia Caldwell; Julia (b. June 16, 1854) married Harvey Slusher; Mary (b. April 5, 1856) married Reed Kitterman; Harvey (b. April 4, 1858) married Julia Clay; and Emily (b. Jan. 10, 1861) married Thompson Harman.

The Duncan Family

The Duncan family in Floyd County is derived from Blanch, Thomas and John Duncan, three brothers who emigrated to America from Scotland about the year 1775 and first located in the Indian Valley section.

Blanch Duncan married Nancy Reed and raised a family of seven sons and one daughter: Henry (m. Elizabeth Weddle, daughter of David Weddle), Reed (m. Sarah Dickerson), Spencer (m. Sally Byrd), John (m. Annie Reed), Peter (m. Viola Cox), George (m. Elizabeth Morricle), Blanch, Jr. (m., first, Mary Morricle, secondly, Catherine Phillips), Sally (m. Peter Reed, and moved to Tennessee).

George Duncan, son of Blanch, the emigrant, married Elizabeth Morricle and lived in the Indian Valley section. George died in 1858; Elizabeth, his wife, died in 1886. They were the parents of the following ten children: Fleming (m. first, Evelyn Cox, secondly, Catherine Spangler), Timanda (m. Esau Reed), Lucinda (m. Allen Howell), Beauford (m. Elizabeth Simmons), Rhoda (m. Jubal Reed), Chrisley (m. Malinda Lester), Nancy (m. Samuel Palmer), Samuel (m. Ellen Hylton), Elizabeth (m. Josiah Burnett (1838-1922), Margaret (m. John Quesenberry).

Thomas Duncan, the settler, brother of Blanch, had the following ten children: Lewis (m. Susan Akers), Riley (m. Mahala Akers), Humphrey (m. Lucy Boothe), Crockett (m. _____ Wray), Thomas (m. Unis Akers), Lynch (m. Betsy Akers), Lucy (m. Jacob Akers), Polly (m. Luke Grimes), Nancy (m. Andrew Reed), Susie (m. Andrew Akers).

From John Duncan, the settler, brother of Blanch and Thomas, are derived: Benjamin Duncan, who married Nancy Burnett, daughter of Josiah Burnett, Sr., and raised a large family of children: four sons and ten daughters. Tommy Duncan was a brother of Benjamin. Rhoda, sister of Benjamin and Tommy, married Stephen Hughett.

Dr. Aris B. Cox, in his book entitled **Footprints on the Sands of Time,** speaks as follows of Blanch Duncan the settler, "One other we will refer to is known as Old Uncle Blanch Duncan, a natural genius in woodwork, and iron; a carpenter, millwright and blacksmith; a good neighbour and worthy citizen, who lived on Indian Creek."

Epperly

This family is of German descent and the name was formerly spelled **Eberle.** Three brothers, Christian, George and Jacob, were the first to come to Floyd County.

Children, in part, of Christian Epperly and wife Elizabeth: Salome (b. April 2, 1792); Elizabeth (b. March 20, 1794); William (b. Aug. 12, 1798); Jacob (b. June 1, 1801); Margaret (b. Nov. 21, 1803); Rhoda (b. March 8, 1808); Mathas (b. April 5, 1810); Joseph (b. May 20, 1812); Levina (b. Jan. 20, 1815).

All were born in present Floyd County and baptized at Zion Lutheran Church.

George Epperly and family moved West.

Children, in part, of Jacob Epperly and wife Catherine, born in present Floyd County and baptized in Zion Lutheran Church: Solomon (b. May 14, 1797); Maria (b. Feb. 12, 1799); Philip (b. Jan. 24, 1801); Margaret (b. Dec. 9, 1803); Sarah (b. July 27, 1806); Daniel (b. Nov. 4, 1808).

Jacob Epperly (1801-1883), son of Christian and Elizabeth Epperly, married Eliza Phlegar (1801-1877), daughter of Abraham and Margaret (Goodykoontz) Phlegar. They lived three miles east of the town of Jacksonville, now Floyd, where he was a well-known farmer. They raised eleven children:

    1.   Canaan (b. Nov. 29, 1825-d. 1873), lived at home.

    2.   Calvin (b. Feb. 26, 1827), married and moved to Bonne Terre, Missouri,

    3.   Eva (b. May 21, 1828), married a Mr. Trout and lived in Roanoke, Va.

    4.   Rachel (b. Oct. 3, 1829), married a Mr. Palmer and lived in Missouri.

    5.   Mary Ann (b. Apr. 24, 1831), married a Mr. Phlegar and lived in Roanoke, Virginia.

    6.   Addison (b. Oct. 6, 1832-d. 1914), married Elizabeth (b. 1839), daughter of William and Alice (Lancaster) Brammer, and they lived four miles east of the town of Floyd on the Bent Mountain Pike, where he was a well-known, practical farmer.

    7.   Akin (b. Apr. 7, 1834), married Ann Eliza, daughter of Samuel and Nancy (Helms) Strickler.

    8.   William Haden (b. Feb. 25, 1837), married Malinda Lemon, daughter of Isaac, and lived on Pine Creek.

    9.   Lucinda Margaret (b. Nov. 23, 1838), married a Mr. Franklin.

    10.   Elizabeth (b. Aug. 15, 1840), married a Mr. Brammer.

    11.   Clementine (b. Feb. 9, 1844), married a Mr. Young.

Eden Epperly (1814-1876), son of John and Nancy (Farris) Epperly, married Leah, daughter of William and Polly (Goodykoontz) Gilham, and lived in Floyd County on Dodds Creek. Their children, who lived to adulthood, were:

1. Mary married J. T. Agee and lived near Meadows of Dan.

2. John William married May 16, 1875, Nancy A. Cannaday, and lives in Floyd County; their children: Arthur E. (b. 1876) ; Levi G. (b. 1877) ; Isaac L. (b. 1879) ; Etta (b. 1880) ; Callahill M. (b. 1882) ; Laura (b. 1884); Fitzhugh L. (b. 1885); Giles M. (b. 1887); Leah Elizabeth (b. 1890) ; Julia (b. 1891) ; and Florence (b. 1897).

3. Rosetta married John S. Allison and lived in Pulaski County.

The Evans Family

Dr. Samuel A. J. Evans and Sallie (Jackson) Evans, his wife, came from the vicinity of Alexandria to Floyd County when they were comparatively a young couple. They lived first at Jacksonville and later on a farm near Spangler's Mill on Little River. Here Dr. Samuel Evans engaged in the general practice of medicine, and was a neighbor and friend of Job Wells who lived some two miles north, near the Little River bridge. Dr. Evans later sold the farm to James Graham and moved back to Jacksonville where he continued his extensive practice in the town and county. They lived in the brick residence which was later the home of Dr. William Pendleton, Floyd's well-known druggist. At a previous time, Dr. Evans resided in a frame house just west of the present Floyd County Bank building.

Dr. Evans was an Elder in the Jacksonville Presbyterian Church when it was organized and continued to serve the church in the same capacity until his death. He was a member of the Legislature of Virginia and one of Floyd's prominent citizens. His children were: Sallie M. Evans, one of Floyd County's popular and efficient schoolteachers (teaching at the LeSueur tanyard four miles above town), who married Dr. Brainard W. Hines on April 25, 1986, prominent physician of the Huffville neighborhood; Rear Admiral Robley D. Evans (1846-1912) of the United States Navy; Dr. Samuel Evans, a prominent physician of Tennessee; and William M. Evans, who was a prominent lawyer of Portland, Oregon.

Soon after the death of Dr. Evans, the family moved from Floyd Court House to Fairfax County, Virginia, near Alexandria. His widow later married Captain Joel Pepper, an ardent Southern supporter, and lived during the Civil War at the top of Laurel Ridge on the Floyd-Christiansburg pike.

In Dr. George Milton Wells' "Autobiography" we find that Dr. Samuel A. J. Evans had a mercantile business with Thomas G. Shelor at Jacksonville about 1854.

"In the meantime, my uncle Thomas G. Shelor (who had been associated with Dr. Samuel A. J. Evans, father of the late Admiral Robley D. Evans, in the mercantile business) induced my father (Job Wells) to join him in opening a general merchandising business in the village and take me in for business training. A stock of goods was purchased by my uncle in Baltimore, and in due time the store was opened for business. We had daily mails, connecting with the Virginia and Tennessee Railroad at Christiansburg, twenty-one miles away, and my uncle secured the appointment as Postmaster, which added to the importance of our business.

"There was a copper mine in operation some miles from the village and much prospecting for other minerals. The country was flush with Tennessee money ("Shin-plasters" as they were commonly called), which was of doubtful value and greatly obstructed business. In the meantime the copper mine was closed and everything sold out at auction or forced sale. In as much as our store had done a large credit business, it was necessary to either increase the capital stock or discontinue the business, and my father decided on the latter course. During the time of my employment in the store, the Virginia and Tennessee Railroad was extended from Lynchburg, Virginia, to Bristol, Tenn."

Soon after closing the mercantile business between Thomas G. Shelor and himself, Dr. Evans' death occurred. The above quotation from the writings of Dr. Wells helps to present a view of the town of Jacksonville just prior to the Civil War.

Gilham

William Gilham, born in 1775 in Pennsylvania, died in Floyd County in the year of its organization, 1831. He had lived for some years in the vicinity of Winchester, Virginia, prior to settling on Dodds Creek on a farm now owned by Mr. John F. Smith. Before the organization of Floyd County, William Gilham was a member of the Virginia Legislature from the county of Montgomery.

He married Polly (Maria) Goodykoontz, fourth daughter of Hans Georg Goodykoontz, who was born in 1779. They had eight children:

1. Isaac Gilham married Polly Slusher - children: William M. and Hugh M.

2. Ezekiel Gilham married Bianna Wade - children: John W. and Eliza.

3. Drusilla Gilham married Mathew Cox - children: Ann Eliza, Amanda Ellen, Leah Jane, Noah G. and Mary.

4. Naomi Gilham (March 17, 1809 - Jan. 10, 1890) married Carter Cox (July 20, 1805 - July 2, 1898) - children: Mary S., wife of D. C. Meredith; Giles A.; William G.; Drusilla A.; Fleming L.; Hamilton L.; Wesley D.; Melville B.; and Lydia L.

5. David Gilham married Mary Howell - children: Wesley, George and Drusilla.

6. Levi Gilham.

7. Lydia Gilham married Fleming Jones - children: Emanuel L., William A., Mary, Leah Ann, and Naomi.

8. Leah Gilham married Eden Epperly, son of John Epperly- children: Mary, John W., Rosetta, Lafayette, Madison, Elizabeth Adaline, and Drusilla.

The Gillenwater Family

The Gillenwater family is of German descent, the name originally being spelled in German, **Gillenvater.**

The Gillenwater family had its origin in America in Hugo and Rosa Gillenwater, who emigrated from Baden, Germany, in 1814. They first made their home near Troy, New York, then moved to the State of Pennsylvania near Scranton. Some of their children were five sons: Elijah, Joshua, Riley, Sparrel, and James.

Sparrel lived with his parents in Pennsylvania until he was about 20 years old, then moved to Rockbridge County, where he worked on a farm. The other four sons of Hugo and Rosa probably remained in Pennsylvania. Sparrel Gillenwater was born in 1822, married Eliza Anne Hutchinson of Campbell County, Virginia, who was born in 1836 near Lynchburg; their marriage was solemnized in 1856.

After their marriage they moved to Franklin County, Virginia; and from there to Floyd County, settling on Little River on a tract of land commonly known as the "Burnt House Place." This was near Pine Creek Primitive Baptist Cemetery, where they are buried. They had been married 51 years when Eliza Anne died in 1907 at the age of 71. She had been a member of the Methodist Episcopal Church, South. Sparrel died the next year, 1908, at age 86. His church connection was with the Christian Church, commonly called the Campbellites or Disciples of Christ. During the Civil War, Sparrel Gillenwater was on detail work in Floyd County for the Confederate army.

The children of Sparrel and Eliza Anne Gillenwater were seven sons and three daughters: John B., who owns a farm and resides in Floyd County; Henry W. who now lives in Raleigh County, West Virginia; Robert O., who lives in McDowell County, West Virginia; Samuel F., in the logging business but now retired, lives in Nicholas County, West Virginia; Andrew J. lived in Floyd and died from diphtheria; Gus D., a miner by occupation, lives in McDowell County, West Virginia; Burdine D. lives in Virginia; Elizabeth A. lives in Virginia; Sarah F. (m. Reed), died from typhoid fever; and Artrian S., deceased.

Godbey

George Godbey owned a grist and sawmill on Indian Creek in the Indian Valley section of the county in 1831. He was appointed a member of the first court of justices of the county upon its organization by Governor John Floyd. Godbey held the important position of Justice of the Peace for many years, and just before the Civil War went to live with one of his daughters at Lenoir, Tenn. He is buried at Cleveland, Tennessee. He was born in 1796 and died in 1874.

George Godbey married Nancy Elswick of Montgomery County. Their children were: 1. Maria Godbey married Asa Crandall of Floyd County; 2. Rachel Godbey never married; 3. Jackson Godbey married Ellen Deskins (b. 1826), daughter of Steven and Ann Deskins of Tazewell County, a sister of Harvey Deskins and youngest of eight children: 4. Crockett Godbey, a Methodist minister, died in 1911; and 5. Julia Godbey married William C. Daily, a Methodist minister.

Jackson Godbey and his wife, Ellen, lived on the north side of Main Street, where he had a store adjoining his residence. He was a prominent member of the Methodist Church, and, together with other members of the Godbey family and Rev. Abraham Hogan, did much toward establishing Methodism in Floyd County. When the Civil War began, he organized a company and entered the service as its captain, which was Company B, 54th Virginia Infantry. He was also one of the active promoters of the Jacksonville Brick Academy, where his children were educated. They were: 1. Nannie P. Godbey, who married Robert G. Latimer of Montgomery County, had one son Warren Latimer; Nannie Latimer, after the death of her husband, lived many years in Portland, Oregon; she was born July 1, 1845, and was still living in 1926; 2. Alice Godbey married Dr. John T. Wells, son of Job Wells, and moved to the Pacific Coast; 3. Julia Godbey married Rice D. Montague of Christiansburg; 4. Josephine Godbey, no record; 5. Walter H. Godbey married Lillian Hall of Memphis, Tenn., and later moved to Miami, Florida.

The Goodson Family

This family of English descent was one of the first to settle in the county. Major Thomas Goodson located at Turtle Rock (Pizarro) before the Revolutionary War. When the war broke out he closed his cabin, containing his bed and cooking utensils, and went to fight for his country. After the war he married a Miss Poage from Roanoke County, Virginia. Some of their children:

Robert Goodson was one of the first justices of the county after it was organized in 1831.

Annie Goodson married Daniel Shelor, son of Captain Daniel Shelor, and their children were: Jane, Elizabeth, Ruth, Mary Ann, Thomas B. and Floyd. Thomas B. Shelor married Mary Barnard, daughter of Isham, and their children were: Ballard P., James F., William Marion, Sarah Ann, Isham B., Daniel M., Mary Jane, Thomas G., and Elizabeth.

William Goodson, first Clerk of the Floyd Court, married, first, Mary (Polly) Banks, daughter of John Banks, and they had four children: John, Caroline, Virginia and Sarah (m. Ballard Shelor). After the death of his first wife, William married America Sandifer, daughter of Mathew Sandifer of Turtle Rock, and they had one daughter, Abigail (Abby), who married Captain Bennett Headen, and they had a son, William. (Captain Headen's first wife was a daughter of Col. Jacob Helms.) Captain Bennett Headen lived in the Major Thomas and William Goodson home after the death of William Goodson.

Mary Goodson married William Shelor (son of Captain Daniel Shelor) and they were parents of six children: Rhoda, Sarah, Mary, Thomas G., George and Elizabeth.

Wells Goodykoontz, U. S. Congressman
5th District, West Virginia, 1922

The Goodykoontz Family In America

The Virginia branch of this family sprang from Hans Georg Gutekunst, a German, who landed at the port of Philadelphia in 1750, took the oath of allegiance, entered and surveyed land upon which he settled in Northhampton County, Pennsylvania, now Lehigh County. Hans Georg was a soldier in the War of the Revolution. He was first in Company 5 of the 2nd Battalion, Northhampton County militia, of which Peter Trexel was captain. In 1779 he bought land near Middletown in Frederick County, Virginia, and settled his family there. Hans Georg died in Frederick County in 1784, intestate, leaving a widow, Margaret (Anna Margaretha), and nine children. Margaret was one of the administrators of her husband's personal estate in Frederick County. She moved with the rest of the family to southwestern Virginia where she died in 1819 and is buried in Zion Lutheran Cemetery, one mile north of the Floyd courthouse.

The children of Hans Georg and Margaret Goodykoontz (the spelling of the name changed), in the order of birth, are as follows:

I. Maria Magdalena Goodykoontz (1769-July 7, 1850) was married to George Phlegar (1762-July 25, 1839) on May 6, 1788, in Frederick County, Virginia, by the Rev. Simon Harr. They were buried in Zion Lutheran Church Cemetery, Floyd, Va. Their children:

A. Elizabeth Phlegar (1789-1850), never married,

B. Lydia Phlegar (1792-18?), never married,

C. Joseph Phlegar (1794-18?) married, and had children: 1. Isaac Phlegar; 2. John Phlegar; 3. Margaret Phlegar married Slusher; 4. Calvin Phlegar; 5. Eliza Phlegar married Simmons, and 6. Sarah Phlegar married Lesueur.

D. Isaac Phlegar (1796-1859) married, first, Sophia Kitterman and, secondly, Sarah Catherine Rutherford, and had the following children: (first marriage) 1. Jacob Phlegar; 2. David Phlegar; (second marriage) 3. Joseph Phlegar; 4. Magdaline Phlegar; 5. Rufus Phlegar; 6. Harvey Phlegar, and 7. George Phlegar.

E. David Phlegar (1806-1869), who moved to Lafayette County, Missouri.

F. Rhoda Phlegar (1806-1891), never married.

G. Benjamin Phlegar (1812-1892), whose first wife was Mary Weddle, his second wife was Sarah Surface, and his children numbered nineteen: (first marriage) 1. George Phlegar, who was a Confederate soldier and lost his life in the Battle of Gettysburg in 1863; 2. Andrew Phlegar (1839-19?), never married; 3. Simon P. Phlegar (1840-1905), married Rebecca _____, and moved to Lexington, Missouri; 4. Ellen Phlegar, married David Willis, and lived at Floyd Court House, Virginia; 5. Gideon Phlegar, never married; 6. Mary Phlegar, married Judge Merritt; 7. Adaline Phlegar, never married;

8. Thomas Phlegar, never married; 9. Abraham Phlegar, died in infancy; 10. Henrietta Phlegar, married Rev. Summers; 11. John Phlegar 12. Lillie Phlegar, never married; 13. Nancy Phlegar, married Rev. John Smith; 14. Benjamin Phlegar, died in infancy; 15. Dora Phlegar, married Irving Roney and lived in New York City 16. Estella Phlegar, married Dr. Josiah Smith and lives at East Radford, Virginia; 17. William Phlegar, married Emma Smith; 18. Mattie Phlegar, married Dr. Brown and lives in North Carolina; and 19. Jessie Phlegar, died in infancy.

II.   Jacob Goodykoontz (1771-1835), the eldest son, married Margaret (Peggy), daughter of George Beaver of Strasburg, Virginia.   In 1802, Jacob moved his family to present Floyd County and bought land from Guy Smith on West Fork of Little River known as "The Mills," which he sold in 1809 to Solomon Harman.   Jacob and his family moved to Madison County, Indiana.   They had two children: A. Eli B., whose children were: 1. Story, and 2. Bessie; B. Daniel.   Jacob and Margaret are buried one mile north of Anderson, Indiana.

III.   George Goodykoontz (April 23, 1773-Sept. 13, 1824), baptized at Strasburg, Shenandoah County, Va., on Nov. 2, 1790; married Mary Beaver (July 16, 1784-June 14, 1847) on Sept. 4, 1800 in Strasburg.   She was the daughter of George Beaver. George Goodykoontz sold his lands in Frederick County and, with his widowed mother, moved to Montgomery (now Floyd County), Va., and settled on West Fork, five miles west of the present county seat.   George and Mary are buried in the Goodykoontz graveyard, within sight of their home.   George and Mary Goodykoontz had 12 children:

A.   Catherine Goodykoontz (Sept. 19, 1801-1888), married Moseby Lesueur Feb. 16, 1819, and lived on Camp Creek, about six miles from the town of Floyd; their children; 1. Martel Lesueur (May 16, 1821-Nov. 28, 1904) married Sarah Phlegar, daughter of Joseph, and had three children: Elbert J. moved to South Dakota; Alice married Howery; Flora A. married Van Fleet and lives in Missouri; 2. James W. Lesueur (1823-1884) married Nancy C. Yearout; their children: (a) Ellen married Turner of Riner, Va.; (b) Eliza A. married J. A. Sowers of Floyd; (c) Charles W., of Johnson City, Tenn.; (d) John R.; (e) Catherine married Shell; (f) Jennie V. married

West; (g) James Thomas, of Riner, Va.; (h) Crockett; (i) Foster; (j) Lucy C. married Weaver; (k) Richard; (1) Mary; and (m) Edwin F.

B.   Rebecca Goodykoontz (May 3, 1803-Dec. 25, 1891) married James Lesueur of Henry, Va.; their children: 1. George W.; 2. Mary E. married Prillaman; 3. Elizabeth; 4. Catherine; and 5. Dollie.

C.   David Goodykoontz (Dec. 8, 1805-Mar. 15, 1871) married Ruth Harter in 1830; they had 12 children:

1.   Henry M. (1832-1876) married Amanda Wade; they had six children: Winton (1859-1879) lived in Antonio, Texas; Lou Ella (1861-19?); Webster (1864-19?), Sweet Springs, W. Va.; Edward; Flora; Ida H. married Arthur B. Allison, Allison, Va.

2.   Mary F. (1835-19?) married Rev. B. F. Nuckolis of Old Town, Va. (the author of **Pioneer Settlers of Grayson County, Virginia**); their children: William David; Rosa Ellen; Ruth Francis and Isaac Clark.

3.   Elizabeth (1834-1842)

4.   Julia (1838-1879) married Rev. Benjamin W. S. Bishop, Emory College, Va.; their children; Charles M.; Lucy; Mattie married John Price of the M. E. Publishing House, Nashville, Tenn.; and David.

5.   George W. (1847-1897) married Mary Williamson and lived in East Radford, Va.; he was a Confederate soldier and was wounded at Drewry's Bluff, May 16, 1864; they had eight children: (a) Nancy; (b) William married _____ Pope of Mason City, Iowa, and they had one child, Ruth Evelyn; (c) Alfred married Sadie Bosang, of Pulaski, Va., and they live in East Radford; (d) John T. married Nellie Williams of Roanoke, Va., and their children are: Harry G., William, John T. Jr.; (e) Ida married Charles Caldwell of East Radford, Va., where they live: (f) Charles H. married Silene F. Rhea, daughter of Judge William F. Rhea of Richmond, Va., and their children are: Mary Chester, Charles H., Jr., and William; (g) Lena married and lives in East Radford; (h) Harry married Blanche Witten, daughter of Maxey Witten, and lives in Bluefield, W. Va.

6.   William M. (1842-1910) married Lucinda Woolwine of

Patrick County, and lived at the old Goodykoontz homestead on West Fork until about 1900, when they sold out and moved to Roanoke, Virginia. He was a Confederate soldier, being wounded at Williamsburg, May 5, 1863, and at Gettysburg, July 5, 1863, carrying a minnie ball in his arm to the day of his death. They had seven children: (a) Horace Wells, married Irene Hooper of New Orleans, and they have no children; Wells, as he is called, is a lawyer and businessman of Williamson, West Va., and a Member of Congress (1918-1922) from the Fifth District of W. Va. (See page 67) ; (b) Arthur Emmett; (c) Oscar Wilmer; (d) Oakey B.; (e) Robert I.; (f) William C.; and (g) Lake E. m. Samuel Fishburn Woody and lives in Roanoke, Va.

7. Alfred (1844-1872) married Ellen Cecil in 1870; they lived at Center Mills, Va., and had two sons: John ((1871-1897) ; and Alfred, who died at the age of 2 years.

8. Adaline J. (1846-1856).

9. Nancy Rosetta (1851-1856).

10. Ellen (1849-19?) married S. E. Cecil and lived at Newbern, Va. They had six children: (a) Ruth H. married Isaac Walton McClure, and their children were: Wanda Virginia, Flora May, Lee Cecil, Ellen Winifred, Malinda Anne, Jesse Samuel, and Albert Grayson; (b) Samuel married Mary T. Wallace; (c) Malinda, never married; (d) Mary married D. B. Southern, and they have two sons: Gerard and David E.; (e) Julia married L. E. Boothe, and they have one son, Garland C.; (f) Esthill H., never married.

11. David (1853-1853).

12. Millard (1855-19?) married, first, Mary Howery, and, after her death, secondly, Lizzie McCauley. They lived at Graham, Va. He had eleven children: (a) Julia May married J. D. Williams of Roanoke; (b) Mattie Myrtle married W. D. Bower of Camp Creek, Va.; (c) Minnie Ruth married L. Snead and lives at Carlover, Bath Co., Va.; (d) Glenn P. of Portsmouth, Ohio; (second marriage) (e) Clarence E.; (f) Robert E.; (g) Harry L.; (h) Roy F.; (i) Nannie A.; (j) William D.; and (k) Bernard Ellis.

D. Archibald Goodykoontz (Jan. 24, 1807-Oct. 4, 1849) married Letitia Robinson (1809-1854), and they had 7 children:

1. Hamilton Wade, married, first, Margaret Hopkins and,

secondly, Mrs. Jane Cloud; and had nine children: (first marriage) Madge married W. C. Chamberlin; (second marriage) Letitia married A. F. Chamberlin; Horace; Joseph married Ethel Stropp; Louis married Martha Yeoman; Walter H.; Norval; Lucia; and Jennie. This family lives in Kansas and Oklahoma.

    2. Carrosa (1837-1837)

    3. David R. (1838-1845)

    4. Alfred Eli (1840-   )

    5. Norval W. (1842-   ) was a Union soldier from 1861-1865.

    6. John (1845-1884) married Minerva Spalding, and had two children: Carrie B. and John R.

    7. Archibald, Jr., married Amanda Blythe, and had two children: Frank and Ethel.

    E. Isaac Goodykoontz (1809-1884) married Amanda Cecil, they had no children. Isaac was a membr of the Virginia House of Delegates in 1859-1861 and 1863-1865.

    F. George Goodykoontz (1812-1888) married Sarah, daughter of George Williamson, and moved to Missouri; their children: 1. Redmond; 2. Letitia married _____ Bland; 3. Clark; 4. Mary married _____ Bland; 5. Thomas.

    G. Alfred M. Goodykoontz (1813-1857) married Mary A. Kirkpatrick. Alfred was one of the early traveling or itinerant ministers of the Methodist Church, and on his father's home place was held the first camp meeting of the Methodists in Floyd County in 1833 or 1834. Alfred and Mary had two children: 1. Mary E., not married; 2. George E. married Sarah J. Loning, and they had eight children: Minnie A.; Charles Franklin; Edgar Marion; William Lewis; Thomas K. B.; James Richard; Joseph Wiley; and Mary Margaret. This family lived in Prosise, Tennessee.

    H. Rachel Goodykoontz (1815-1818), was drowned.

    I. Nancy Goodykoontz (1817-1842) married Pascal Baber; their children:

    1. Arabella Baber married William Hall of Christiansburg, Va., and their children are: Washington C.; Mae Adda married Crockett Lesueur; Nannie L. and William Rush; 2. John W.

Baber (1840-1861) ; and 3. Clementine Baber, never married.

J. Adeline Goodykoontz (1820-19?) married Jonathan Hall of Riner, Va.; they had no children.

K. Washington Goodyknootz (1822-1895), never married. He lived near Floyd and was a soldier in the Confederate army from 1861 to 1865.

L. Polly Goodyknootz (1824 - died when a little girl).

IV. Margaretha Goodykoontz (Jan. 25, 1775-1851), evidently named for her mother, was confirmed at the age of 15 on Nov. 21, 1790. On Dec. 12, 1797, she was married to Abraham Phlegar (Jan. 25, 1776-Sept. 14, 1865) by Rev. Christian Streit, in Frederick County, Va. They moved to present Floyd County, and had 9 children:

A. Leah Phlegar (1798-1880) married Francis Hogan; they had two children:

1. Mary Hogan, married Nathaniel Lancaster, and they were the parents of Rev. Davis G. Lancaster; Leah S.; Hester A.; Abigail; Ruth; and Clinton F.

2. Abraham Hogan, long a prominent Methodist preacher of Floyd, married Sarah C. Organ; their children: Mary E. married Martin Penn; Sarah Francis married Joseph Whitlock; Minnie L. married Taz Draper; Callahill A.; and Rosa Virginia.

B. Rachel Phlegar (1800-1851), never married.

C. Eliza Phlegar (1801-1877), married Jacob Epperly (1801-1883) ; they had eleven children:

1. Canaan (1825-1873), never married;
2. Calvin moved to Bonne Terre, Missouri;
3. Eva married Wm. Trout and lived in Roanoke;
4. Rachel married _____ Palmer and lived in Missouri;
5. Ann married Calvin Phlegar;
6. Addison married Elizabeth, daughter of William Brammer;
7. Akin married Ann Eliza, daughter of Samuel Strickler;
8. Haden;
9. Lucinda married _____ Franklin;
10. Lizzie married _____ Brammer;
11. Clementine married _____ Young.

D. Maza Phlegar (1802-1881), never married.

E. Delilah Phlegar (1804-1884), never married.

F. Eli Phlegar (1808-1864), married Ann C. Trigg, and they were the parents of two children:

1. Judge Archer A. Phlegar (1846-1913), known as one of Virginia's most able lawyers, married Susan Shanks of Salem, Virginia; their children: Ella; David S.; Mary; Archer, and Hunter;

2. Ellen Phlegar, married _____ Johnson and their children are: Anna married _____ Campbell; Susan, married _____ Price; Richard; Lettie; and Archer.

G. Arabella Phlegar (1809-1865), married Jonathan Willis (1806-1889), and their 12 children are: 1. Margaret married _____ Williamson; 2. David married Ellen Phlegar; 3. Hamilton; 4. Bennet; 5. Lavinia married Jonas Harman; 6. Thomas; 7. Peter; 8. James; 9. Martha married _____ Harman; 10. John; 11. George; and 12. Henry.

H. Lavinia Phlegar (1813-1890), married Owen Wade, and lived on Burks Fork. They had twelve children:

1. William B. Wade married Eliza J. Summers and lived at Higginsville, Missouri; their children: (a) Kate Cora married A. F. Harvey; (b) Ida Stella married W. S. Dornblaser; (c) Emmett Lee, never married; (d) Lelia Levina married Joseph A. Hawkins, and (e) Charles A., never married.

2. Abraham Wade (1834-18?); married M. E. Allen; they had one daughter, Ann Levina.

3. Eli Wade (1837?), married E. F. Allen, lived in Missouri; their children: Laura married Lawrence Lewis; Herbert; and Robert Lee.

4. Amanda W. Wade (1839-?), married Henry M. Goodykoontz, and they had five children.

5. Hannah Wade (1840-19?), married J. B. Albright and lived on Burks Fork; they were the parents of: (a) Amanda H. married H. A. Dickerson and lives at Radford, Va.; (b) David R. married Belle Rader and lives at Christiansburg, Va.; (c) Charles B. married Ali Ann Slusher; (d) Nannie L. married A. J. Knowles and lives at Willis, Va.; (e) Lillie A. married S. M. Keith and lives at Radford, Va.; (f) Emett L.; (g) Henry E. married Lizena Hylton and lives at Duncan, Va.; (h) Lucy

F., Burks Fork, Va.; (i) Mark A.; and (j) Ellen N., Burks Fork, Va.

6. Sarah Wade (1844-19?) married C. C. Weeks, they live on Burks Fork, and have three children: Stella F.; Esper R.; and Kyle M. Weeks.

7. Julia A. Wade (1843-19?), married William L. Bird, and they live on Burks Fork; they have two children: Nannie L., married S. E. Hylton; and Eli, of Burks Fork.

8. Rev. Peyton Wade (1847-19?) married Sue P. Hylton; they have three children: Edward W.; William A.; and Lena E. Wade.

9. Eliza A. Wade (1849-19?) married L. D. Weddle of Burks Fork, and they are the parents of one son: William Weddle, married Dollie DeHart.

10. Joseph Wade (1851-1892) married Ann Fisher; they have two children: Charles B.; and William O. Wade of Woltz, Va.

11. Mary Wade (1853-19?) married Isaac Taylor and lives at Willis; they have one daughter, Clara Taylor.

12. David B. Wade (1856-1862).

I. Lucinda Phlegar (1815-1867), never married.

V. Elizabeth Goodykoontz (1776-1858), never married.

VI. Maria (Polly) Goodykoontz (ca. 1779-?) married William Gilham (1775-1831); they had eight children:

A. Isaac Gilham, married Polly Slusher; their children: 1. William W.; 2. Hugh M.

B. Ezekiel Gilham married Bianna Wade; their children: 1. John W.; 2. Eliza, married Wolhford Scott.

C. Drusilla Gilham, married Mathew Cox; their children: Ann Eliza; Amanda Ellen; Leah Jane; Noah G.; and Mary.

D. Naomi Gilham (March 17, 1809-Jan. 10, 1890) married Carter Cox (July 20, 1805-July 2, 1898) in September 1830; they had nine children:

1. Mary S. Cox (1831-?) married D. C. Meredith and had four children: Giles M.; Julia A.; Sarah L.; and Wesley T.;

2. Giles A. Cox (1832-March 11, 1862);

3. William G. Cox (1834-19?) married Sarah A. Carnahan, and had five children: Edney W.; Bettie M. married Dr.

J. C. Hurst; Hamilton C.; Keener W. who married Bartie L. Harris; and Pearl (1879-19?);

    4. Drusilla A. Cox (1835-?);

    5. Fleming L. Cox (1837-?);

    6. Hamilton L. Cox (1839-?);

    7. Wesley D. Cox (1841-?);

    8. Melville B. Cox (1843-?);

    9. Lydia L. Cox (1846-?).

    E. David Gilham married Polly Howell; they had three children:

    1. Wesley, whose children were Bessie, and McF. Gilham;

    2. George; and 3. Drusilla

    F. Levi Gilham, never married.

    G. Lydia Gilham, married Fleming Jones; they had five children: Emanuel L.; William A.; Mary; Leah Ann; and Naomi.

    H. Leah Gilham married Eden Epperly on Sept. 11, 1845; their children: Mary; John W.; and Rosetta Epperly.

    VII. Eva Goodykoontz (1781-1867), never married.

    VIII. Catherine Goodykoontz (1783-?) married Christian Stipe in 1803 in Frederick County, Va.

    IX. Daniel Goodykoontz (1784-Sept. 16, 1843) married Hannah, daughter of George Beaver, and sister of Margaret and Mary Beaver. They moved to Indiana and had four children:

    A. Jacob Goodykoontz (1809-1888) married, first, Mary Ward and they had twelve children: 1. Rebecca; 2. Thomas Jefferson; 3. Daniel Franklin; 4. Caroline B. married Wilson Spencer; 5. Naomi McClure married Egbert Robbins; 6. Elizabeth W. married John Tovey; 7. Ansel Espa married Jane Hall; 8. Floyd Madison; 9. Noble Jacob; 10. Mary Emma married Henry Wilson; 11. Sarah Ermina; 12. Dora Virginia married Thomas Dooley.

Jacob married, secondly, Sarah Reynolds and they had two children: Dollie May, and Lola France.

    B. Simon Goodykoontz (1810-18?).

    C. Leah Goodykoontz (1811-1892) married Zedic Craycraft of Anderson, Indiana; they had one son, Daniel Craycraft who married, first, Eliza Willitts; their children were: Jessie, and Maude; he married, secondly, Mary Ross, and their children were: Mabel; George; Fred; Edith and Albert.

D. Harvey Goodykoontz (1813-1882) married Elizabeth Wood, and lived at Atlanta, Indiana; they had children:

1. Joseph T.;
2. Columbus;
3. David married, first, Martha J. Murry; their eight children: John H.; Izora B.; Eliza Ellen; James V.; Catherine; Asher; Josephine and Lucinda and, by his second marriage: Newton.

George Beaver, father of Margaret, Mary and Hannah Beaver who married three Goodykoontz brothers, fought through the American Revolution. The father of George and Abraham Phlegar was likewise a Revolutionary soldier.

Graham

The Graham family is of Scots-Irish descent. Jacob Graham, who married a Miss Terry, came with his family to America from North Ireland. At the time of the Revolution they were living in the colony of Maryland. Three of the sons of Jacob Graham were: Jonathan, Jacob, Jr., and John or "Jack." Family tradition is that "Jack" Graham was a soldier in the Revolutionary War.

The Grahams and Shelors were neighbors in Maryland. Jonathan Graham (b. 1750?) married Mary (Polly) Shelor, daughter of Lawrence Shelor (Lorents Shuler), the emigrant ancestor of the Floyd County family of Shelors, and they lived for some years in Maryland. Soon after the close of the war for independence, three Maryland families, the Grahams, the Shelors and the Banks, moved to Virginia and settled near each other in the present county of Floyd. Jonathan Graham and John Banks settled on adjoining plantations on the north side of the Blue Ridge Mountains, some six or seven miles due east of the present county seat. The Shelors settled about five miles north of the other two families, and about eight miles northeast of the county seat on Little River. The old Shelor home and mill were the property in later years of the late William H. Harman.

Jonathan Graham acquired a large body of land on which he later settled most of his sons near the homestead. Jonathan and Polly Graham had seven sons and five daughters:

I. Silas, never married.

II. Lawrence (1804-1902) married Mary Simmons, daughter of William Simmons, and lived in Floyd County. Their children were: William, Calvin, Joseph, Lafayette, Catherine and Angeline.

III. Alexander (1808-1886) married Lucinda Hall, daughter of Thomas, of Patrick County, and lived all of his life at the old Jonathan Graham homestead. Their children were: (1) Andrew J., who was captain at the close of the Civil War of a company of "Virginia Reserves" under Col. Robert L. Preston. He was a progressive farmer, one of the first to adopt the use of modern machinery in farming. He married Senora Turner, daughter of Stephen, of Patrick County, and they had the following children: Melissa m. Greenville D. Wood, son of Richard; Stephen m. Lillian Phlegar; Bunyan m. Dollie Martin; Loula [Lucinda?] m. Samuel Walker; Cleophas m. Cora Mitchell; Lester m. Pearle Yeatts, and Dr. James m. Carrie Conduff and they had a daughter, Ruth. (2) Viola, married David Hall. Their children were: Antonia, Della, Alexander and Amos. (3) Sally, married Rev. Asa D. Shortt (1842-1917), son of Joseph N. Shortt, who was a well-known minister of the Primitive Baptist Church. They lived near the old Jonathan Graham home. Their children were Albert, Iowa, Lucinda Mary, George, Lydia, Amos, Senora, Cleo and Rena.

IV. Alvin (1810-1882) married Sarah Simmons, daughter of William, and lived in the town of Jacksonville on lower Main Street. The home was later the home and property of Burdine and Mary Bishop. Alvin Graham was one of Floyd's best known citizens. They had three sons and two daughters: (1) Tazewell Graham (1832-1884) m. Permelia Underwood, daughter of Joshua, and they had one son, Walter, who died young, unmarried. Tazewell's widow married Isaac Martin. (2) McDowell Graham moved to Kentucky and married there. They had a son and a daughter. (3) Erasmus Graham, never married. He was Commonwealth's Attorney of Floyd County. (4) Demaris Graham (1842-1925), married Dr. Asa H. Cannaday, son of James, of Franklin County. They were the parents of: Walter, Dr. Charles G., Dr. Albert A. (both physicians in Roanoke City), Minnie and George. Dr. Asa H. Cannaday was a prominent physician of the Copper Hill section of the county and was a member of the Legislature of Virginia. (5) Lina Graham married Benjamin Dobyns and lived in Carroll County before moving West. They had a son and a daughter.

V. Perry (b. April 2, 1812 - d. April 2, 1869) married, first, Sarah Reynolds of Patrick County, and lived all of his life near the parental homestead. Their children were: Monroe, Millie, Jane (m. Peter Huff), and Normanda (m. Tazewell C. Brammer). Perry Graham's second wife was Sally Lee and their two sons were: William and Caswell.

VI. Harrison married Judith Creasy and they lived in West Virginia. Their children were: Susan, Jonathan, David and Winfield.

VII. Jacob married Elizabeth Radford and lived on Pine Creek. Their children: Amos, Joseph, Perry, Octavia, Sarah and Mary. Octavia married Elder John C. Hall. Mary married Thomas Hall, John's brother.

VIII. Martha, eldest daughter, married John Stephens of North Carolina, and moved to Indiana.

IV. Elizabeth married Henry Whitlock (b. 1805) and lived on Little River. Their children were: John, Babe [Alvin?], Mahlon, Isaac, Linus, Hyatt, George, and Mary.

X. Mary married Mahlon Smith and moved to Indiana.

XI. Celia married Zebedee Whitlock and they lived in Floyd County. They were the parents of Asa Whitlock.

XII. Catherine married George Sowers and had two daughters: Octavia and Ellen, both of whom lived in Minnesota.

The Gray Family

William, Joseph and Edward Gray came to America from England just prior to the American Revolution, according to records in the Congressional Library in Washington, D. C.

Tradition holds that Edward Gray enlisted as a sailor from London and when his people learned that he had enlisted just to get to America, they sent him a lot of money. He fiddled and danced on the ship and ignored the money, which was returned to his people in England. When he landed in America he was a very poor man.

Edward's son Cairy (Cary?) married Rebecca Sowder and raised the following children:

1. William Riley, who married Elizabeth Prillaman, daughter of Abraham Prillaman of Franklin County. They lived in the east end of the county, near the present post office of Graysville. He was a prosperous farmer, merchant and cattleman, and owned one of the finest farms in the county. Later in life, William Riley moved first to Texas and finally to Oklahoma in 1878, where he and his wife died. The names of their children were: Abraham C., J. R., Tarlton, George William, Catherine, A_____, and Charity.

II. James, married _____, and lived in the east end of the county. His children were: A. William Benjamin, married _____ and lives in Floyd County; B. John W. lives in Salem; C. George lives in Kentucky; D. Cairy Lewis, a well-known railroad conductor on the Norfolk and Western, lives at Bell Springs; and Mary Lizzie, who married John Harvey (now deceased) lives at Riner.

III. Harvey, married Nancy E. Moore, oldest daughter of Noah B. Moore, and lives at Salem.

IV. Mary, married John Weaver of Brush Creek.

V. Martha, youngest daughter, married Jacob Prillaman, son of Abraham Prillaman of Franklin County.

Joseph Gray, the emigrant brother of Edward, married Mary Howard and lived in the east end of Floyd County. He came to this area from Rockbridge County, Virginia, about 1810. One of his sons, James Howard Gray, married Rhoda Wilson, daughter of Peter Wilson, the settler, and they lived near Graysville. James Howard Gray built the first old-fashioned water wheel mill in that part of the county and he was interested in the smelting of iron. His children were:

A. Osburn Gray, moved to Raleigh County, West Va.

B. James Madison (Mathew?) Gray (1849-1889), married Nannie Ellen Lester, daughter of Abner Lester, Jr., and lived near Graysville; their children were: Byron A., Bunyan E., Eliza A., Odessa, James M., Jr., and Providence.

C. Joseph M. Gray (1842-1915), married Mrs. Mary Moore, widow of Captain Jack Moore, who was Mary Walton before her first marriage. They were the parents of Howard, Ernest, Hampton, Walter, Genevra, and Oscar.

D. Rhoda Gray (1842-1885), married Henry Custer of Floyd County and lived near Graysville; they were the parents of: Homer, a prominent lawyer of Danville, Va.; Prince m. daughter of Leland Gray; Joseph m. Sallie —————; Miriam m. Charles Aldridge; Eliza m. Cox; and Tony m. Philip Siner.

James and Harvey Gray, sons of Cary, were both noble Confederate soldiers. Harvey served in the Cavalry. James belonged to Stuart's Light Horse Artillery. He rode the lead horse of eight to a piece of artillery around McClellan's Army. They were three days and nights in making this round - without food or water except while on their horses. He was then transferred to drive a team of four mules to a commissary wagon. He did this until April 8, 1865, the evening before the surrender, when he was captured by the Northern army. James Gray was one of the prominent men when Floyd County was organized in 1831. William Riley Gray was an early justice of the peace in the Locust Grove district.

Jehu Griffith The Settler

Daniel Griffith lived in the west end of Franklin County near Long Branch Baptist Church. His son, Jehu Griffith, moved with his wife (the widow Campbell) and family of children over the Blue Ridge Mountains and settled in the east end of the present county of Floyd near Cannaday's Gap, on the Floyd-Cannaday's Gap Road. His aged father, Daniel Griffith, made his home with him. The farm has since been the home of John Young Shortt, the Snuffers, Francis Snead, James Martin, and at present is the home of Marion Agee.

The children of Jehu Griffith: 1. Sparrel H. (m. a Miss [Mary] Campbell) at the outbreak of the Civil War organized Company H, 54th Regiment of Virginia Infantry, composed of Floyd County men, and entered the service of the Confederacy as its captain; 2. Turner; 3. Elkanah, with a cousin, Daniel A. Griffith, was a member of Company A, 54th Virginia Infantry, under Captain C. M. Stigleman; 4. Tyler; and 5. James married Harriet Jones, and with Jefferson and W. A. Griffith was a member of Company F, 14th Virginia Infantry. After the war, James was a well-known minister of the Baptist Church. He lived for some years in the Middle West but returned to spend his old age in Floyd County.

Ann Griffith of Franklin County, Virginia, married Charles Rakes, son of Samuel, and grandson of Charles Rakes, the settler.

Guthrie

William Guthrey moved from Pennsylvania to Augusta County in 1777, and bought land from Alexander Stuart, ten miles below Staunton. His children were: Adam, John, Daniel, Nancy and Ann. Adam married a daughter of Gilbert Christian. Nancy married Isaac Roberts on January 11, 1794. Ann was married to Isaac Blain by Rev. John McCue on April 9, 1795. On December 21, 1779, Adam Guthery and James Brown were granted certificates as nephews and heirs-at-law of James Dunlap, deceased, who was a lieutenant in Captain Hog's Company of Rangers which was destroyed by the enemy at the fort in the upper tract on the South Branch of the Potomac in 1758. Adam and James became the only legal heirs in the state. These certificates called for grants of land for military service rendered the Colony of Virginia by the said James Dunlap. The name was variously spelled by members of the same family at different dates: Gutherie, Guthery and Guthrey.

Captain George Guthrie was an officer in Lt. Col. Henry (Light Horse Harry) Lee's Legion of Cavalry. This same Captain George Guthrie was listed as receiving land warrants prior to Dec. 31, 1784, for Revolutionary War services.

Benjamin Guthrie and wife, Sarah, lived near Boones Mill in Franklin County until soon after the birth of their son, William, which occurred May 21, 1809. They moved to Montgomery County, now Floyd, settling on Pine Creek near the home of Phillip Williams, the settler. Here William Guthrie grew up and on January 21, 1834, married Isabella (b. Aug. 21, 1809), daughter of Phillip and Jane (Poag) Williams, sister to Col. John Williams. They moved to the west end of the county, locating on a farm on Burks Fork Creek, where they resided until William's death on September 10, 1892. Isabella died February 5, 1892, in her eighty-third year.

Benjamin Guthrie died January 16, 1853, his wife, Sarah, following him to the grave on Nov. 13, 1853.

William and Isabelle Guthrie had ten children:

1. Elizabeth Jane (Aug. 22, 1834-Nov. 10, 1862).

2. Phillip William (June 6, 1836-Nov. 13, 1906) married on Jan. 26, 1860, Nannie Susan (Aug. 26, 1837-Sept. 8, 1904), daughter of Beverly Austin Burnett (Sept. 11, 1811-Oct. 31, 1890) and his wife, Juda Slaughter Burnett (Aug. 19, 1816- Nov. 5, 1886), and lived on Burks Fork where he was a well-known farmer. Their children were: Laura Isabel (Oct. 1, 1863-Sept. 21, 1879) Ella Rosabel (Feb. 21, 1869-Mar. 14, 1877); George William Austin (Aug. 22, 1875-Mar. 21, 1877); and Charles Luther (July 7, 1879-?). Laura married William Henry Willis, son of Jonathan Willis, on May 30, 1878, and was the mother of one son, Edward Bennett Willis (b. Sept. 10, 1879), who lives at Floyd Court House where he is associated with and part owner of the Farmer's Supply Company. He married Lelia Goodson of Shawsville, Va. Charles Luther married, first, Annie Rebecca Morris on Oct. 8, 1912, daughter of James T. and Priscilla Lee Morris. After her death on July 5, 1913, he married on Oct. 14, 1916, Ethel Mabel (b. Apr. 24, 1890), daughter of Isaac Bonaparte and Etta Wilburn (Hardy) Bell of Lunenburg County, Va. They have two children: Charles Luther, Jr. (b. July 5, 1917) and William Bell (b. July 9, 1922), Charles Luther Guthrie is a prominent druggist of Petersburg, Va.

3. Sarah Amanda (Feb. 22, 1838-?).

4. Martha Ann (Dec. 27, 1840-Nov. 26, 1862).

5. James Henry (Dec. 6, 1842-Jan. 15, 1917) married Martha A., daughter of S. G. Conduff, Sr., and lives in Burks Fork district. Their children are: A. Lee, a farmer and teacher in the public schools of Floyd County for thirty years, married Ocie Weeks; L. Mary married John Lee Altizer of Copper Valley; J. K. Guthrie lives in Franklin County; J. M. Guthrie lives

in Illinois; O. Dyer Guthrie lives in Iowa; Fannie married H. S. Johnston and lives at Bluff City, Tennessee; William S. Guthrie married Hattie A. Simmons, lives at Forest Depot in Bedford County where he owns a large farm and is engaged in raising purebred livestock.

6. John H. (April 21, 1845-Nov. 1, 1862).
7. Thomas T. (Nov. 27, 1847-Dec. 10, 1862).
8. Mary Emily (Feb. 1, 1850-Nov. 22, 1862).
9. Benjamin Joseph (July 1, 1852-?).
10. David (July 18, 1854-Jan. 17, 1855).

Wiley Guthrie, a member of Captain Henry Lane's Company, Company B, 42nd Virginia Infantry, was wounded, captured and imprisoned at Elmira, New York. He was color bearer of a brigade of skirmishers and scouts.

Phillip Guthrie was third sergeant and James H. Guthrie was private in Company D, 54th Virginia Infantry under Captain Henry Slusher. Phillip Guthrie was a member of Company E, 27th Battalion, which was afterwards changed to the 25th Virginia Infantry in the Confederate army.

The Hall Family

There are several branches of the Hall Family in Floyd County; some came from Patrick and Franklin counties.

Thomas Hall, who lived in Patrick County, was a well-known farmer; some of his children were:

1. Thomas Hall, Jr., married Sarah, daughter of Jeremiah Burnett of Patrick County. They lived to a great old age six miles east of the courthouse on the Cannaday's Gap road; they had no children. Thomas was a soldier in the Civil War.

2. Violet Hall married Charles Turner, son of Francis Turner of Patrick County. They lived on the summit of the Blue Ridge Mountains, some eight miles southeast of the courthouse. A widow for many years, Violet reared eight children: Caroline, married Francis Snead; Adaline, married Peter Cannaday, and was the mother of Amos L. Cannaday, a member of the Virginia Legislature; Onie, married Ira Hatcher, and was the mother of Peter Hatcher and others; Amanda, married William Houchins; Serrepta, married Alexander Nolen; Abigail,

married Joseph Sowers; Victoria, married Ira Thomas; and S. Tyler, married Flora, daughter of Walter Thomas of Patrick County.

3. Lucinda married Alexander Graham, son of Jonathan and Polly (Shelor) Graham, and lived at the old Jonathan Graham homestead, some five miles east of the courthouse. She was the mother of two daughters and a son, Captain Andrew J. Graham of the Turtle Rock section.

David Hall, Peter P. Hall and Andrew Hall were all descendants of the Patrick County Halls.

The Harman Family

In the early part of the eighteenth century, seven brothers by the name of Herman, according to tradition, came from Germany to Pennsylvania. One of the brothers, Jacob Harman (spelling of name changed), settled in Bucks County, Pa., where he died in 1741, leaving four children, the youngest of whom, Matthias, saw service in the Revolutionary War. Matthias and his wife Elizabeth sold their farm and home in Bucks County in 1783 and moved with their family to Frederick County, Virginia, where he lived until his death in 1812. Two of his sons, Jacob and Solomon, moved to Montgomery County (now Floyd), Virginia, and are the ancestors of the Harman family in Floyd County.

JACOB HARMAN

Jacob Harman (Aug. 11, 1769-1829) married Christina Mock (Jan. 26, 1769-1839) daughter of George and Sophia Mock of Frederick County, Va., on Oct. 29, 1797. They lived in Frederick County until 1802 when they moved to present Floyd County. He bought 326 acres of land on West Fork of Little River from John Vancill, Jr., two miles south of the Floyd-Carroll Pike, where they lived until his death. Later, Dr. Will Hylton built a house on the old homestead. Jacob and Christina were members of Zion Lutheran Church near the courthouse, where some of their children were baptized. They had ten children:

I. Catherine (b. Oct. 10, 1798) was baptized Nov. 18,

1798, at St. Paul's Lutheran Church, Strasburg, Va.; married Henry Smith of Floyd Co.

II. Susanna (b. Jan. 3, 1800) was baptized April 6, 1800, at St. Paul's Lutheran Church, Strasburg; married Christopher Sutphin of Floyd.

III. Solomon (b. Sept. 23, 1801), christened Dec. 25, 1801.

IV. Elizabeth (b. Sept. 11, 1803), baptized July 14, 1805, at Zion Church, Floyd County.

V. Benjamin (b. Jan. 29, 1805), married Martha (Patsy) Hylton, daughter of Archelaus Hylton; they had five children:

A. George Harman married Mary J. Radford; their children: Owen, Jeremiah, Martha Ann, Stewart Samuel, Dennis, and Ellen, all of whom married and have families.

B. Lanan married first, a Miss Sutphin, secondly, Harriet Radford, and, thirdly, Mary Simmons.

C. Charlotte, never married.

D. Elizabeth married Preston Quesenberry.

E. Christopher (March 14, 1834-Sept. 11, 1914) married Nancy J. Hylton on October 25, 1855. Their children:

1. Lydia married J. H. M. Terry; they had one child, Almeda, who married O. L. Hendricks.

2. Liona married Henry Quesenberry; their children: Mastin, Owen (dec'd), and Liona, who married Oscar Webb.

3. Jabez married Marcella Elgin; their children: Christopher, William and Dorothy. Dr. Jabez M. Harman received his early education in the public schools, graduated from the medical college at Louisville, Kentucky, at an early age, and took postgraduate courses from time to time in New York and Baltimore. He has practiced his profession most successfully in his native county.

4. Martha Ann, dec'd.

5. Gordon married Margaret Thompson; their children: Nova; Arlie; John married Lelia Akers and they had one child, Marjorie Hope; Ray; Nancy; Annie; and Norma.

VI. Jacob (Jan. 30, 1807-1872) married Anna Hylton (May

18, 1812-Nov. 1, 1895), daughter of Archelaus Hylton. They had eleven children:

A. Jabez (Jan. 1, 1832-Mar. 2, 1862), never married. killed in the Civil War.

B. Abraham (July 6, 1833-Sept. 2, 1855), never married, killed by a thrashing machine.

C. Julia Ann (1834-Nov. 30, 1902), never married.

D. Jonas (Feb. 23, 1837-Nov. 12, 1918) married first, Martha Willis (1849-1875), daughter of Jonathan and Arabella (Phlegar) Willis, on March 28, 1867; their children: Arabella, married William Sowers; Naomi, died in infancy; Dora, married William Weeks; Jennie, married Isaac Belton; Lavinia, married Harry Potter; and Thomas H., an attorney in Pikeville, Ky., married Marjory McMartin. After the death of his first wife, Jonas Harman married Lavinia Willis (d. 1916), daughter of Jonathan and Arabella, on Oct. 19, 1879; their children: Martha, died in infancy; Della, married Van Buren Dickerson; and Jonathan, died in infancy. Jonas Harman served throughout the Civil War, with the exception of one month, first in Company D, 54th Virginia Infantry, and then as 2nd Lieut. in Co. E, 25th Virginia Cavalry; at the end of the war he was in command of his company.

E. Serena (May 3, 1839-Nov. 24, 1912), married Caleb Weddle.

F. Naomi (b. 1841), never married.

G. Henry (Nov. 28, 1843- July 29, 1914), married Bettie Gardner.

H. Bethlehem (Apr. 15, 1845?), married Nannie Hylton.

I. Barbara (1847-1888), never married.

J. Eliza (1849-Dec. 28, 1913), never married.

K. Dennis (Dec. 25, 1852-?), married Julia Burgess; their children: Edna; Austin; Arthur T., married Minnie L. Hylton; and Caleb W., married Alice Hylton.

VII. Daniel Harman (b. Nov. 13, 1809).

VIII. John Harman (April 4, 1811-Jan. 25, 1896), married Celia Hylton, daughter of Archelaus Hylton; they had nine children:

A. Austin, married Sarah Harter, their children: France, Alice, Flora, Florence, Henry and Margaret, all married and have families.

B.   Mary (Polly) (b. Jan. 10, 1839), married Isaac Phlegar on Sept. 8, 1863; their children: Henry, dec'd; John Calvin, married first, Stella Weeks, their children: McClure, Rhea and Stella; married secondly, Lura A. Akers.

C.   Margaret B. (b. April 21, 1841), married Elder Harvey Weddle on Sept. 13, 1884, their children: Noah, Mary and Celia.

D.   Daniel T. (Oct. 23, 1851-June 28, 1924), married Florence O. Carter; their children: Hattie, married Samuel Spangler; Claud; Perna, married Daniel Crenshaw; Dayton, married Kate Sutphin; Henry; Leta, married John R. Weddle; and Lavera; all have families except Dayton.

E.   Elijah Harman (b. Nov. 10, 1852), married Senora Young on Oct. 26, 1882; their children: Emma, married Esper R. Weeks, children: Moir and Renia; Edgar A., married Mary Slusher, children: Pauline, Senora, Lucile, Richard and Marvin.

F.   Christina (Dec. 5, 1843-Nov. 1910) married John Calvin Weddle on March 12, 1866; their children: Martin, Joanna, Emmet, Harvey, Daniel, Emezetta and John William, all married and have large families except Emezetta.

G.   Annie (b. Jan. 1846), married Andrew Weddle on March 19, 1888; their children: Naomi, Elza, Joseph, Ebby and Haden.

H.   Catherine (b. March 16, 1849), married Samuel P. Weddle on Aug. 12, 1869; their children: Levi, Austin, Mordecai, Garfield, Ellie A., Virginia, Addie and Delilah.

I.   Emerzetta, married Henry B. Dillon, first, and their children were: Margaret, Maude and Henry B.; she married, secondly, Thomas Shelor, and they had one son, Harman.

IX.   Christina Harman (b. Dec. 25, 1812), baptized Nov. 5, 1814 at Zion Lutheran Church.

X.   Anna Maria (Mary) (b. Apr. 9, 1815), married George Hylton, son of Archelaus.

SOLOMON HARMAN

Solomon Harman (Oct. 24, 1779-1842) moved from Frederick County, Va., to present Floyd County, and in 1809 bought "The Mills" on West Fork of Little River, seven miles west of the present town of Floyd.   On March 7, 1810, he married

Elizabeth Slusher, daughter of Solomon and Eva Slusher of Floyd Co. They had nine children:

I. Jacob S. Harman (Oct. 1, 1811-1880) married Sophia Weddle (1811-1880) and lived at the Christopher Slusher place, five miles northwest of the courthouse, where he was Postmaster for many years and a successful farmer. Their children were:

A. Ala Ann (1836-1900) married Rev. John B. Hylton (his second wife), no children.

B. Mahala (1838-1861); children: 1. Millard (1854-1861); 2. Amon P. (1860-1924), married Sarah Hylton; their children: Walter married Lucy Dickerson, one son, Elbert; Addie married J. H. Sumpter; Etta married Elbert Weddle and moved to the state of Washington; Russell married Nancy L. Howard; Alma married Paris Sutphin; Kate married Shields Jett; Lydia married Oscar Duncan; and Grace.

C. Nancy (1841-1880), was the second wife of Daniel Bowman, no children.

D. Eli W. (1843-?), was a member of Company D, 54th Virginia Infantry, in the Confederate army, under Captain Henry Slusher, and was killed at Missionary Ridge, Nov. 25, 1863.

E. Ananias (1845-1919), married Mary Hylton on August 22, 1867; their children: 1. Emmet J. (Oct. 28, 1868-Oct. 11, 1887), never married; 2. Luther E., married Dicie Bishop, three children; 3. Absalom G., married Maude Wagoner and lives in Indianapolis, three children; 4. Amanda E., married David Dickerson, three children; and 5. Ida S., married Noah Hylton, three children.

F. Emazetta Harman (1848-1884), was first wife of Daniel Bowman; their children: 1. Salena, married G. W. Hylton, children: Emazetta Gay, Clarice, John B., Effie A., Jabe, Essie, Ila and Ira, twins, Julian, and Maynard; 2. Eli A., married Carrie Hickman, first, and Elizabeth Spangler, secondly, no children; 3. Jonas E., married Pearl Vaniman of Illinois.

G. Asa W. (b. 1853), married Julia Slusher, no children.

II. John Harman (March 30, 1814-1893), married Mary (Polly) Bishop, daughter of John and Dicie Bishop; their six children:

A. Dr. James M. Harman (b. 1844), married Fannie Scott,

of Texas, they now live at Galax, Virginia; their children: 1. Floyd, married and lives in the State of Washington; 2. Mary; 3. Joel, married and lives at Galax, Va., six children.

B. Malinda Harman (1846-1883), married John T. Conduff on Feb. 10, 1867, their children: 1. Laura, married Joseph Bones; 2. Lucy, dec'd; 3. Dr. Samuel I., married Myrta Preston, one child, Preston Harman; 4. Lura, married first, Dr. Silas E. Akers, their children: Hunter Holmes, and John Wallace; second husband, John Phlegar; 5. Dr. Charles Edward, married Annie Childress, their children: Vincent C., and Charles E., Jr.; 6. Daniel, married Lillian Richardson, their children: Linda, John Ray, Robert, Pauline and Jesse.

C. Margaret Harman (July 10, 1848-Sept. 5, 1921), married Jacob Hylton on August 10, 1868; their children: 1. Mary M., married William Lee Jennings; 2. Alice, married C. W. Harman; 3. Minnie, married Arthur T. Harman, their children: Olin, married Harriet Alderman; Edna O.; Elree B.; Freeda L.; Jacob M.; and Beulah M.; 4. John J., married Lydia Bowman of Illinois, on December 17, 1903, their children: Harman and Mawyer Dale; 5. Lucy F., married A. C. Boone, their children: Treva, married Newton Weddle, their children: Eveline and Joseph; Irvine, married Haston Haster; Raymond; Oneida; Ruth; and Moir.

D. Nancy Harman (b. Jan. 24, 1851), married S. G. Conduff on March 16, 1871; their children: 1. James Harvey; 2. Dr. Simon, married Gertrude Alexander, their children: Boyd, Ellen, Susan and Gertrude; 3. Lydia, married Eldred Bones, their children: Mary, Eva, Charles, Joseph, William, Lena, Hilda and Dorothy; 4. Dr. Thomas; 5. Dr. Miles Glenn, married Elizabeth Howard, their children: Miles Glenn, Jr., Joseph Howard, Betty; 6. Dr. Asa, married Belle Webb, one child: Duke; 7. Ora, married William C. Buck, their children: Helen, Mildred and Virginia; and 8. Wren, married Lydia Weddle.

E. Mary Ann Harman.

F. Sarah Harman.

III. Margaret Harman (Nov. 19, 1818-May 12, 1870), married Isaac Phlegar, their children:

A. Harvey, and B. Elza, both of whom died in young

manhood.

C. Lafayette, married Virginia Peterman, their children: 1. Arthur, dec'd; 2. Lillian, married Stephen Graham, first, and Ward Lovell, secondly, one child, Kenneth Graham; 3. Ethel, married Edd Dooley, their children: Virginia, Irene and Donald; and 4. Kate, married Eli Wade.

IV. Benjamin Harman (b. June 13, 1816), married Susie Huff; their children: Esaias, Nicholas, Rowland, Levi, Elizabeth, Johnson and Hannah, all of whom married and had large families.

V. Mary (Polly) Harman (b. April 7, 1821), married John Phlegar; they had one son, Callahill, who married Della Carter, their children: Charles, dec'd.; and Lizzie, married Abe Hylton.

VI. Stephen (b. Jan. 1, 1824).

VII. Peter S. Harman (July 31, 1826-April 29, 1914), married Sarah McGrady, first wife, their children: A. Noah, married Minnie Wade; B. Joseph Crockett, married and lives in Kansas City, Missouri; C. Thompson, married Emaline Bishop, their children: Ernest, Charles, Lola, Edgar, John, Harry, Opal, Minnesota and Beulah Lawton; D. Church; E. Solomon, married Mariba A. Harman, one child: Ora, married Ennis Shelor; F. Simon, married Annie Hylton; G. Isaac, died unmarried; H. Elzy M., married and lives in Illinois; I. James, married Lizzie Bishop and lives in Illinois; J. Louis Hamilton, married Clara Slusher; K. Catherine, married Noah Smith, their children: Walker, Stanton, Leonard, Ida and Roscoe; and L. Virginia, married Simon Hylton, and they had a large family.

VIII. David Harman (May 8, 1831-January 21, 1907), married Orlena Southern (1841-Feb. 25, 1902), on Nov. 24, 1858; their children:

A. Leander, married Nannie E. Hurst in Jan. 1882; he died Aug. 27, 1883.

B. Dr. Uriah (b. April 9, 1865), married Clara Augusta Dickman on June 11, 1905, no children. Dr. Uriah Harman attended the public schools, taught school in the county, attended William and Mary College, and graduated from the Medical College of Virginia in 1895 with the highest honors of the first class in Dentistry. He was the first registered dentist in Floyd

County, and practiced as an itinerant dentist in Floyd, Carroll and Patrick counties. In 1897 he moved to Richmond where he is conducting a successful practice, and is a leading citizen of that city.

C. India, married Jefferson D. Smith on June 18, 1888; died Sept. 9, 1907.

D. Albert (b. Oct. 6, 1869), married Ida L. Thompson on May 22, 1901; their children: Roy David, Ava Lee, Vera Alta who married Thomas F. Convey, and Mary India.

E. Samaria, died young.

IX. Mathias Harman, died in infancy.

Floyd County Harmans in the Confederate army:

Martin Harman was a member of Company A, 24th Virginia Infantry, under Captain C. M. Stigleman; he died in 1862 at Richmond.

In Company D, 54th Virginia Infantry, under Captain Henry Slusher, were Major Austin Harman, wounded at Mount Zion Church, June 25, 1864; 2nd Lieutenant Jonas Harman; 1st Sergeant Jabez Harman; Privates George W. Harman, Lanan Harman and Eli W. Harman, the latter lost his life at Missionary Ridge, Nov. 25, 1863; Christopher Harman; and Peter Harman.

In Company G, 21st Virginia Cavalry, under Captain A. O. Dobyns, were James Harman, Third Corporal, who was captured and imprisoned at Fort Douglas; E. S. Harman, wounded Nov. 12, 1864, and left on the battlefield.

Benjamin and Bethlehem Harman were members of Col. Robert L. Preston's Reserves.

Madison Harman was a member of Stuart's Horse Artillery and was captured and taken to prison at Fort Delaware, May 6, 1865.

In Company E, 27th Battalion were Henry Harman, wounded; Bethuel Harman; 2nd Lieut. Jonas Harman and David Harman.

The Headen Family

Three brothers, John W. Headen, James Bennett Headen and Tazewell Headen, came from Bedford County to settle in Floyd County.

Dr. John W. Headen married Ellen Helms, daughter of Col. Jacob Helms of "Rose Hill"; they were the parents of John W. Headen and Rosabelle Headen. Captain John W. Headen married Addie, daughter of Bryant Hylton (who ran the hotel later known as Lee's Hotel at Floyd Court House). Captain Headen taught school at Falling Branch, and was an active worker in the Temperance Worker's Organization. Rosabelle Headen married Major Henry Lane, and their children were: Dr. G. Cook Lane, and Kittie Lane, who married Rev. G. W. Thompson. After the death of Dr. John Headen, Ellen married Asa L. Howard, son of Ira Howard. See Howard sketch for children.

Captain James Bennett Headen served as Deputy Clerk of the county court. He commanded a company of Reserves in the Civil War, under Colonel Robert L. Preston. He was twice married, first to Malinda Helms, and, secondly, to Abigail, daughter of William and America (Sandifer) Goodson of Turtle Rock. They had one son, William, a newspaperman with the *Roanoke Times* for many years. The home of the Goodsons and Headens at Turtle Rock is still standing, more than one hundred years old.

Dr. Tazewell Headen was a member of the court of justices in 1847, and was one of the early physicians of the county. He married a daughter of Archibald Stuart of Patrick County; she was a sister of Gen. J. E. B. Stuart and of Dr. John D. Stuart of Floyd.

Dr. Tazewell Headen and James Bennett Headen were both trustees of the "Brick Academy" when it was organized in 1847.

The Helms Family

The Helms family lived in Franklin and Patrick counties before coming to what is now Floyd. The name was probably spelled "Helm" originally. Johan Nicklaus Helm arrived at Philadelphia, Aug. 24, 1750, from Rotterdam; Johan Jacob Helm arrived at Philadelphia, Sept. 19, 1752, from Amsterdam; Joh.

Jacob Helm and John Jacob Helm arrived at Philadelphia, Oct. 26, 1754, from Amsterdam; John Frederick Helm arrived at Philadelphia, Sept. 23, 1766, from Rotterdam; J. Frantz Helm arrived at Philadelphia, Oct. 3, 1768, from London.

Meredith Helm was a major in the Colonial wars, residing in Frederick County from 1755 to 1761. Thomas Helm, with his two sons, Meredith and William J., and one daughter, Margaret (who married Ambrose Barnet, June 8, 1791) were living within the limits of Augusta County, according to Chalkley's **Abstracts of Augusta County, Virginia.**

The Helms family of Floyd is derived from Thomas Helms, who lived at the foot of Daniel's Run in Franklin County, and Adam Helms, a brother, who lived on Goblintown Creek in Patrick County.

Thomas Helms became a very wealthy man before his death, owning over a hundred slaves and large tracts of land in Floyd County on both sides of the Bent Mountain Pike, and large tracts in Franklin County.

The children of Thomas Helms were: Barbara, Nancy, Sallie, Lucy, Mary (Polly), Lavina J., Eliza, Fleming, James, John, Daniel, Thomas and Samuel, most of whom lived in Franklin County. Four of the children married and lived in Floyd County:

Nancy Helms married James Litterell of Franklin County and lived on Bent Mountain at the top of the Blue Ridge, twelve miles northeast of the present county seat. She was living there in 1831 when the county line was drawn. Nancy and James had but one child, Polly, who married Samuel Helm. Their children were: Biah married James C. Martin; Capt. James William Helm, a gallant officer in the Confederate army; Alie Ann married James Sublett; and George, killed in the Civil War. Samuel Helm undoubtedly belonged to that family of emigrants who had not changed the original spelling of the name.

Lavina (Larina?) J. Helms married, first, Lewis Harvey, and was the mother of Robert O. Harvey; after the death of Lewis she married Ira W. Hurt and was the mother of another family of children. She died leaving her husband and a large family of small children.

Eliza Helms married Ira W. Hurt, the second husband and widower of her sister Lavina.

John Helms, called "River John" to distinguish him from John Helms of Burks Fork, son of Adam, married Sally, daughter of Peter Livesay, the settler, and lived on Little River at the crossing of the Bent Mountain Pike, six miles east of the county seat. The children of John and Sally Helms were: Elizabeth, Nancy and Ellen. Elizabeth married Col. William B. Shelor, Clerk of Floyd County, and Lieutenant Colonel of the 54th Regiment of Virginia Infantry, C.S.A. They lived at the John Helms homestead at the crossing of Little River where they raised the following children: Emma, Eliza. George W., Henry C., Sallie and Nannie.

Nancy, second daughter of John, married Samuel Strickler, son of Jacob, the settler, and lived five or six miles east of the county seat on Little River. They had ten children: Ann Eliza, Sarah, John B., Jacob, Josephine, Samuel Homer, Flournoy, Biah, William and Nora D.

Ellen, third daughter of John, married James W. Crockett and lived on Little River; they had three daughters: May, Gay and Daisy.

Adam Helms lived on Goblintown Creek in Patrick County. Two of his sons, Jacob and John, moved to what is now Floyd County. Jacob settled on land two miles west of the present town of Floyd. John settled on Burks Fork Creek.

Col. Jacob Helms (b. 1791), whose home, "Rose Hill," was two miles west of the present county seat, was a member of the Legislature of Virginia from Montgomery County in 1831 when the bill for forming the County of Floyd out of Montgomery was passed and became law. He was aided by Hon. William B. Preston, State Senator for this section at the time. Col. Helms was a member of the first Court of Justices of Floyd County. He owned much land and more slaves than any man in the county in 1831.

Col. Jacob Helms married Elizabeth Smith; they had four children: Madison S., Ellen, Harriet and Malinda.

1. Madison S. Helms married Sarah Howard and lived on Little River, some eight miles east of the county seat, at the

Conner Barnard place near Pizarro.

2. Ellen Helms married, first, Dr. John Headen, and was the mother of John W., and Rosabelle Headen, who married Henry Lane, a lawyer. After the death of Dr. Headen, Ellen married Asa L. Howard, son of Ira, by whom she had Laura, Charles A., and Adaline.

3. Harriet A. Helms married Henry Dillon; they had eight children.

4. Malinda Helms married James Bennett Headen, brother of Dr. John Headen.

As a citizen, Col Jacob Helms contributed much to the good of society. He was a public spirited man whose home, "Rose Hill," was a preaching place for the itinerant Methodist preacher, and a hospitable house for way-worn ministers of the gospel. The family contributed much toward the first Methodist camp meeting, located near their home. Copied from the tombstone of Col. Jacob Helms and his wife, who remarried after his death, is the inscription: "Colonel Jacob Helms died May 22, 1835, in his 44th year. Eliza Helms, late Eliza Kennerly, died Dec. 23, 1855, in her 63d year."

Jacob T. Helms, oldest son of Madison Helms, married Malinda Cannaday; they had one son, Frank, who married Corrie Dobyns; they live in Bristol. Jacob Helms was a member of Dr. C. M. Stigleman's company, Company A, 54th Regiment of Virginia Infantry. He called on the author in 1922, carrying his Drewry's Bluff badge, an empty sleeve, in his seventy-sixth year, looking fit.

Col. John W. Helms (Jan. 31, 1797-Sept. 24, 1862), second son of Adam, known as "Burks Fork John," lived on Burks Fork Creek, a tributary of Reed Island Creek, on the Dugspur Road, some four miles southwest of Buffalo Mountain. Here he owned a valuable farm. He was a member of the Virginia Legislature (1844-1845) and served as sheriff of the county. He married Susannah Cox (1803-1845), daughter of Carter and Nancy (Reed) Cox, of Floyd County, and they had eleven children: Hamilton (b. 1822), Addison (b. 1826), Floyd (b. 1828), Susannah, Malinda Nancy (1832-1913), Adaline, Jacob, George

W., Elizabeth, John and Tazewell.

Hamilton, Addison and Floyd moved to Oregon many years ago. Susannah married Joseph P. Turman of Floyd. Malinda Nancy married Roley M. Simmons of Floyd. Adaline married Jacob Helms, a distant relative, and moved to Collin County, Texas. Jacob also moved to Texas. George W. married, first, Olivia Helms Bush; secondly, Ollie Price Dobyns (widow of Capt. Abner Dobyns of Franklin County); and, thirdly, Mary Reese. He was Superintendent of the Virginia Penitentiary for several years. Elizabeth married Fleming Howery, a hotel proprietor of Floyd. John moved to Texas. Tazewell married Mrs. Eliza Hurt Menefee, widow of Addison Menefee, and lived in Franklin County; they were parents of: Col. Willis Helms, graduate of West Point (1892) and Commander of Camp Meade; Stella Helms (m. Willis); Clyde Helms (m. Anglin); and Margaret Helms (m. Norwood Carper).

Names on the roll of Floyd County soldiers in the Confederate army:

George W. Helms, 3rd Lieutenant, Co. A, 24th Va. Infantry, wounded at Drewry's Bluff.

Jacob T. Helms, lost an arm at Drewry's Bluff.

John W. Helms, wounded at Plymouth, N. C.

James F. Helms, 3rd Sergeant, elected Captain and transferred to Co. F.

Peter Helms, died in Lexington, Ky., 1862.

Tazewell Helms, 3rd Lieut., wounded at Berryville.

Joseph Helms, George W. Helms, M. S. Helms, Samuel M. Helms, Benjamin Helms.

Brainard W. Hines

Dr. Brainard W. Hines was born in Rockbridge County, son of Michael N. and Agnes V. (Mathews) Hines who came to Montgomery County in 1858. He was one of five brothers who served in the Confederate army: Robert was in the 11th Virginia Infantry and was killed at Seven Pines, May 31, 1862; George was in Edgar's Battalion and was twice wounded; John served in Morgan's command and was killed at Cynthiana, Kentucky; William served two years; and Brainard W. was twice wounded, July 3, 1863, and again at Drewry's Bluff, May 16, 1864. Brainard W. Hines was postmaster at Newport, Giles County, in 1853, and in 1865 settled in practice in Montgomery County. On April 25, 1866, in Floyd County, he was united in marriage with Sallie M. Evans, and they are the parents of three daughters and seven sons: Sally, Edmonia, Robby, Norris, Oscar, Brainard, Richard, Edward and William (twins), and Charlotte, a bright, beautiful child who died in her seventh month.

Samuel A. J. and Sallie (Jackson) Evans settled in Floyd County about 1843, and were the parents of Sallie M. Evans Hines. She was born in Floyd County in January 1844. Mrs. Hines is a sister to Robley D. Evans, Rear Admiral of the U.S. Navy; to Dr. Samuel T. Evans, a prominent physician of Tennessee; and to William M. Evans, a member of the bar at Portland, Oregon.

Dr. Hines had many warm friends among his patrons and acquaintances. His residence and post office address were at Pilot, Montgomery County, Virginia.

The Hoback Family

Jacob Hoback (Nov. 15, 1797-Sept. 30, 1886) and his wife Cynthia (Shaver) (April 5, 1800-May 8, 1891) of Wythe County, moved to Floyd County where he was one of the early men of prominence. He was nominated and elected a member of the court of justices when they were commissioned by the Governor of Virginia. Jacob owned a fine farm on Little River in the east end of the county (near Friendship Church and schoolhouse), just north of the home of the late William H. Harman. Here on this farm, he and his wife are buried, along with Solomon Rutrough and wife, Dr. Andrew J. Hoback and his first wife, and many of their neighbors. The children of Jacob Hoback were:

1. William Hoback (1820-1851), married Magdaline, daughter of Christian and Hannah Bowman of Roanoke County. Their children were: C. M. Hoback and James A. Hoback. C. M. Hoback served through the Civil War; afterward he married

Christina, daughter of Luke Smith, the settler; they had four sons. James A. Hoback (b. March 2, 1850) is a minister of the Church of the Brethren and a farmer of the east end of the county; he married Hannah, daughter of Luke Smith, and they had two children: Fannie and Maggie. Fannie married William Turner and Maggie married Andrew Mohler of Ohio.

2. Eveline Hoback (April 21, 1823-Dec. 23, 1903), only daughter of Jacob, married Solomon Rutrough (Nov. 19, 1813-July 10, 1894), and they were the parents of seven sons and three daughters: Jacob (married, first, Sarah Naff, secondly, Hannah ————, and, thirdly, Alice Black) ; James (m. Martha Mitchell) ; John ; Haden (m. Miss Woody) ; David (married, first, Theotis Epperly, secondly, Miss Aldridge) ; Samuel (m. Miss Sowers) ; Frank (m. Miss Kefauver) ; Cynthia ; Julia ; and Maggie.

3. Dr. Andrew J. Hoback (January 27, 1832-Aug. 19, 1912), for many years head of the Jacksonville Academy, known as the Male Academy, was one of the well-known physicians of the Little River Township. His home for many years was near Friendship Church and schoolhouse. He was twice married, first to Julia Taylor of Franklin County, and, secondly, to Molly Woody of Richmond. He enlisted as a private in Company I, 54th Virginia Infantry, under Captain Burwell Akers, and was promoted to sergeant. His children were: Eugenia, Frederick, Julia and Joseph.

The Howard Family

The ancestor of this Virginia family was Sir William Howard, born in 1732 in Yorkshire, England. In 1757 he married Hannah Psalter (1738-1810) and was disinherited by his father because she was not of noble birth. Their first two children were born in England, Ezekiel (1759) and Peter (1762), before they immigrated to America in 1763.

Sir William settled in the Shenandoah Valley in Virginia where he was engaged in the manufacture of iron and made guns and ammunition for the Continental Army. In the war years he was auditor of accounts in Richmond, Virginia. After

Dr. Thomas H. Howard
(1834-1910)

the war he moved to Montgomery County, Virginia, and settled on Mill Creek where he lived until his death in 1815. He became a preacher of the Baptist Church and was the first pastor of the Salem Primitive Baptist Church in Floyd County. Sir William and his wife Hannah had thirteen children; they are buried near Riner in Montgomery County.

Peter Howard (April 4, 1762-May 9, 1827), second son of

Sir William Howard, was also a preacher of the Baptist Church and for years was pastor of the Pine Creek Church, Floyd County. He was a devout Christian and a great believer in prayer. An interesting incident illustrates this belief. About the year 1800, a severe and prolonged drought occurred in the county. Peter Howard asked that all the people of the surrounding country gather at his church to pray for rain. When they met at the appointed hour, their preacher arrived with an umbrella under his arm. The meeting began and there was a lengthy prayer, being a supplication for God to send rain down upon the parched earth. Shortly afterward there was a flash of lightning, a clap of thunder, and the rain began to pour down, the like of which had not been seen for many years. The benediction was pronounced and Rev. Howard stepped to the door and raised his umbrella, but before departing he turned to the people and said, "I expected to get what we came to pray for, and so I came prepared."

He was a soldier in the Revolutionary War, serving in the 5th Virginia Regiment and later in the 3rd Virginia Regiment in Col. Buford's Detachment. His home was near the Little River ford on the old Christiansburg Pike.

Peter Howard was married twice, the name of his first wife unknown. There were two children of this marriage: Peter, Jr., who settled in New Orleans, Louisiana; and William Ziba, died 1797, and buried in Pine Creek Cemetery, Floyd County.

Peter Howard married, secondly, Sarah Strickland (March 12, 1761-Nov. 23, 1846) of Amherst County, Virginia. Peter and Sarah Howard are buried in Pine Creek Cemetery. They had seven children; the three sons of Peter Howard were prominent men in the first years of the new County of Floyd:

I. Joseph Howard (Jan. 6, 1794-July 27, 1865) was a member of the first Court of Justices of Floyd County, appointed by Governor John Floyd, a position which he held for many years; he was a public spirited businessman. He lived at the old Peter Howard homestead at Little River bridge. He married, first, Mary Hylton; they had one son, Darius, who married Lizzie

Goodwin and lived in Portland, Oregon. Joseph married, secondly, Jane Shelor, daughter of Daniel Shelor; their children:

A. Sarah (Sakes) ; B. James Madison m. Amelia Howard; C. Elizabeth; D. Ira; E. Mary m. Christopher Fiege; F. John.

Judge Waller Lane Howard
(1854-1910)

II. Major Howard (Sept. 8, 1795-July 26, 1869) held public offices of the county and was one of the trustees of the Jacksonville Academy; he lived for many years near Turtle Rock where he owned a tall flouring mill (constructed by Christopher Bower), which was long a landmark in the Little River Township; it was later owned by Jeff Lancaster and was then known as Lancaster's Mill. Major married, first, Sarah (Sally) Shelor, daughter of William and granddaughter of Captain Daniel Shelor; they had one daughter, Sarah Amanda, who married Madison (Mat) Helms. Major Howard married, secondly, Caroline Amanda Latham; both are buried in Pine Creek Cemetery; their children were:

A. Dr. Tazewell M.; B. Emeline (never married) ; C. Peter L. (1832-1893), a prominent merchant of the county seat; D. Dr. Thomas H. (1834-1910), one of the well-known and prominent physicians of Floyd County (See page 100) ; E. Malinda (never married); F. Dr. Monroe.

III. Ira Howard (Oct. 6, 1797-May 21, 1865) was one of the first merchants to locate at the new county seat. His home and store were on the northwest corner of Main and Locust Streets, which later became the home and property of his son, Col. Joseph L. Howard. Ira Howard was also a promoter and trustee of the Jacksonville Academy. He married, first, Permelia Lester (1798-1815); their children were:

A. Asa married Ellen Headen, widow of Dr. John Headen, and lived at the Jacob Helms homestead; their children were:

1. Laura m. Captain Peter F. Shelton; 2. Charles A.; 3. Adelaide m. Judge William Dennis Vaughan.

B. Col. Joseph L. married Ann Amanda Smith of Pittsylvania County; their children:

1. Homer married Mattie Clements.

2. Belle married Peter L. Howard; their children: (a) Horatio S.; (b) Peter T.; (c) Gertrude C. Howard Wood; (d) Dr. Grover L.; (e) Maidai Howard Tronor; (f) Ola Howard Briggs; (g) Anna Belle Howard Carr.

3. Judge Waller L., lawyer and judge of Floyd Co., married Nannie Harman, daughter of William H. (See page 102); their children: (a) Virginia (Jennie) married Dr. Samuel Griggs Jett; (b) Lottie married Fred Hoback; (c) Mary married Green Proffit; (d) Waller, Jr., married Lucy Stump; (e) William, unmarried; (f) Nan married Russell Harman; (g) Katherine married H. G. Shores; (h) Elizabeth married Dr. M.

Glenn Conduff; and (i) Sue married Patterson Proffit.

4. Lilly D. married Wilson Lawson; their children: (a) Lena; (b) Harry L.; (c) Lottye; (d) Nettie; (e) Annie Howard.

5. Asa F. married Beulah Spencer, daughter of Howard; their children: (a) Allie; (b) Seldon.

6. Albert Tap married Minnie Simmons; their children: (a) Claude S.; (b) Joseph; (c) Glenn; (d) Mary; (e) Kent.

7. Maude L. married Dr. Thomas Henry Howard; their children: (a) Hunter C.; (b) Thomas H., Jr.; (c) Gretchen.

8. Carrie married Frazier Dobyns; their children: (a) Maude; (b) Joseph; (c) Alice.

9. Brown G., lawyer of Floyd, married Katherine Sutherland; their children: (a) Brown G., Jr., married Alice Smith; (b) Leo.

10. Pattie married Walter Tipton, lawyer of Hillsville.

11. India married Edward W. Early of Hillsville.

III. (cont.) Ira Howard married, secondly, Emaline O'Bryan; their children:

A. Sarah Jane (never married).

B. Amelia Ann married James Madison Howard.

C. Emmazetta married Dr. William E. Campbell of West Virginia.

D. Abigail married Captain Luke Tompkins.

E. Rhoda married John W. (Watt) Shelton.

F. William Ira.

G. Elizabeth (never married).

H. Hathaway (never married).

IV. Sarah Howard married Capt. Job Wells.

V. Nancy Howard married Isaac Moore.

VI. Elizabeth (Betsy) Howard married Thomas Banks.

VII. Abigail Howard married William Howard.

In the Confederate army:

Peter L. Howard, First Lieutenant in Co. H, 54th Virginia Infantry, under Captain Sparrel H. Griffith.

Dr. Thomas Henry Howard, 1st Sergeant, Co. I, 54th Virginia Infantry under Captain Burwell Akers.

Darius W. Howard, Stuart's Horse Artillery.

Dr. Monroe Howard, Co. A, 24th Va. Infantry, with Dr.

C. M. Stigleman.

James M. Howard, discharged at Manassas, Sept. 16, 1862, on account of disability; was killed by Stoneman's men April 2, 1865, in Floyd County.

Howell

The Howells were from Loudoun County. Between 1775 and 1780, David Howell and a Mr. Price settled one mile from the present town of Floyd. "Three David Howells settled near Floyd Court House in an early day: David Howell, my grand-father, and David N. Howell, a prominent member of the Primitive Baptist Church, and David Howell, called 'Little David,' to distinguish him from the other two," according to Burdine Tolliver Howell of Girard, Kansas.

Dr. C. M. Stigleman says: "A Mr. Price and Joshua Howell were among the very earliest to settle in what is now Floyd County. They with their wives settled on the farm one mile west of the town of Floyd on what was later known as the Ben Dodd farm. They are buried on this farm. These families settled here in this wilderness of timber, the ground all covered over with the wild entanglement of pea vines, and the sound of the chopping ax was heard felling the forest of giant oaks, and building log cabins, from early dawn until late at night."

In the year 1835, Daniel Howell, Sr., aged 75, was living in Floyd County, as listed in McAllister's **Virginia Militia in the Revolutionary War.**

The first David Howell mentioned married a Miss Hylton and they had the following children:

1. Isaac married Miss Thomas and their children were: Lorenzo Dow, Rutherford, Dillard, Caroline and Octavia.

2. Andrew married Miss Carter, and some of their children were: William, Jefferson, Jackson, and others.

3. Nancy married David Rigney.

4. Alexander (b. May 5, 1809) married Timandra Dobyns, daughter of John (John was uncle of Samuel Dobyns), and their children were:

(a) Melvina married Caleb Howell and moved to Carroll County in 1855 where Caleb joined Civil War forces in Carroll.

Caleb died in 1894 leaving his wife and ten children. Melvina died in 1912.

(b) Elizabeth married Isaac Carter.

(c) Minerva married Burwell Akers.

(d) Burdine Tolliver married Mary Jane Lawrence, and their children were: Edgar P., Florence, Effie, Charles, Ira, Grace, Frances and Inez. They moved to Girard, Kansas, where they celebrated their fiftieth wedding anniversary.

(e) Perrydine Tillman, known as Col. Tip Howell, married Adaline Carter, their children were George Forrest, India, Pannel, Mazarine, Julia, Timandra and Florence. Col. Tip Howell was lieutenant in Company B, 54th Virginia Infantry in the Confederate army. He was treasurer of Floyd County, and one of the justices of the peace, also mayor of the town of Floyd.

(f) Mazarine Charman, never married; he was wounded in second battle of Manassas Junction, taken prisoner, and never heard from.

(g) Virgil Augustus married Sarah Lawrence, and their children were: Josephine, Alvin and Bert; his second wife was Nora Fanatia, and their children were: Willma, Velma, Rodger and Allen.

(h) George Palestine died at age eleven.

5. Jinsy Howell.

6. Beauford Howell married Susan Link, daughter of Henry, and their children were: Isabell, Elmer D., Chaplin D., Winfield, David, Langley, Lemuel and Emetta.

Benjamin Howell was one of the early justices of the peace when the county was first formed. He was the father of Pleasant, Annie and Andrew. Pleasant Howell was sheriff of Floyd.

David N. Howell, known as "Big Davy," was of another branch of the family. He married Nancy Carter and their children were: Samantha, wife of Wolhford Scott; Joseph married Mollie, daughter of Thomas Nixon; Harriet, wife of John Harter; Caleb married Melvina Howell, daughter of Alexander. "Big Davy" was one of the early justices of the peace.

The Howery Family

The Howery family, of German descent, lived for a time in Botetourt County, where there is still a neighborhood known as "Howry Town."

Between the years 1835 and 1840, three brothers, Daniel, Jonathan and Michael Howery, came from Montgomery and settled in the east end of Floyd County. All of the Howery family of the county are descended from these three brothers.

I. Daniel Howery (1789?-1869), married Mary Fellers (1792?-1872), and their children were: Lewis, Peter and Nancy. About 1840, Daniel bought the "Old Ogle Farm" (owned by Thomas Ogle) on the head of the river, at the junction of Payne's Creek, Pipestem Branch and Booth's Creek. This was one of the best farms in the east end of the county.

A. Lewis Howery (1815?-1873) married Sarah Pate and they had the following children: Allen, George, Hamilton, Mary, Nancy, Lou (Lon?) and Jane.

B. Peter Howery (1813-1882?) moved with his father to the Old Ogle Farm and married Frances Pate (1812-1861), their children:

1. Wilson J., never married, died in the Civil War.

2. William Edward, married Elizabeth Jane Williams, daughter of Joseph, and lived in Salem; they had no children.

3. James P., married Martha E. Cannaday (dau of Bailey) they had one son: Arthur (m. Bell Wray), and they had the following children: Edward, Warren, Etoil, Flora, Chlora, Ethel, Pearle, Doris, and Edith.

4. Joseph L. married Rina Cannaday; their children: Millie, never married; Mary (m. Schuyler Cole); Minnie (m. John H. Pickle).

5. Olivia married John Gibson, their children: Alice (m. Joseph Hall); Annie (m. A. G. Winter); Mary and Leonard.

6. Martha married George Winter, and after his death, married Isaac Moore. Her daughter Willie Winter married Purse Williams; children of her second marriage: Frank and Ella, both unmarried.

7. Mary married Millard Goodykoontz, their children: May (m. Jesse Williams); Myrtle (m. Walter Bower); Minnie.

8. Elmira (m. John Wright), their children: William;

Frank (m. Sallie Shelor) ; and Lillie.

9. John H. married Mary E. Gray; he is a farmer in Floyd County; their children: Dr. George G. Howery, married Nell Sharitz, and is a prominent physician of Radford; James R. (d. Oct. 6, 1917) married Ardella Turner, their children: Anabel (d. Oct. 15, 1917), Evelyn, Marie; Rufus (died at early age) ; Eliza G. (m. Henry C. Prillaman) ; Fannie (m. Charles W. Prillaman) ; Ella (m. Noah Spangler) ; Ida Belle; and Annie Gray (died when small).

C. Nancy Howery (1827-1902) married Hamilton Graham; no children.

II. Jonathan Howery (1791) was the father of five sons: Preston, Fleming, George, Jehu and William; and a daughter.

Preston Howery (1822-1918) married Elizabeth, daughter of John and Susan (Winfrey) Cannaday of Franklin County, and lived on Little River, near the covered bridge. He was a prosperous farmer and a member of the Virginia Legislature (about 1857). Their children: Pleasant, John, William, Martha (m. Thomas Mitchell), Roena (m. Isaac Naff), Ellen (unmarried), Eliza (m. Tazewell Naff), Alice (m. Osborn Sowers).

Fleming Howery married Eliza Helms, daughter of Col. John Helms of Burks Fork, and lived at Jacksonville. He was a hotel proprietor and was sheriff of the county during the Civil War.

III. Michael Howery (Oct. 5, 1795-Aug. 15, 1873), youngest of the brothers, married Elenor Sheridan, and lived near Pine Creek Primitive Baptist Church. He was a prominent minister of the Primitive Baptist denomination. He raised a family of eight: 1. Wilson married Miss Bradshaw of Rogersville, Tennessee; 2. Michael, Jr., a soldier in the Confederacy; 3. Dennis married a Miss Six of Tazewell County, their children: Michael, William, Reece, Anda (?), Dennis, Jr., Edward, Samuel, James, Clinton, Ellen and Eliza; 4. Isaac married Virginia, daughter of Lewis Payne, the settler, and they were the parents of Hughes Howery who married Sarah Shelor, daughter of Col. William B. Shelor; and Elvira married James A. Huff, son of Sparrel Huff, their children: Walter (married Mary Earls, daughter of Henry) Horatio (m. Miss Weeks), Forest (m. Emma Ware), Grover (m. Ruby King), Howard, Ethel (m. a Mr.

Wright), Marsula (m. Archa Pugh), Carmon (m. Clarence Walker), Roberta (m. Jacob F. Spangler); 5. Caleb (m. Catherine Dameron); 6. Alice (m. Riley Bower); 7. Jane (m. Thomas Iddings), and 8. Sallie, never married.

The Huff Family

There are two branches of the Huff family in Floyd County.

HENRY HUFF LINE

Henry Huff (b. Jan. 15, 1786), came from Pittsylvania County about the year 1807 and settled in the northeastern part of the county while it was part of Montgomery. Henry Huff's ancestors came from Holland and he was called "the spotted Dutchman," so named because of large freckles all over his face. He married Rachel Jackson, and died at the great age of ninety-one on March 20, 1877. Their nine children were:

I. Esom Huff married, first, a Miss Barnett (later divorced) of Montgomery County; they had two sons: Robert, married Mary Kinsey; and Charles H., married a Miss Joyce; Esom's second wife was Kitty Wilson; after Esom Huff's death, Kitty married Thomas Jennings. Esom Huff was one of the early justices of the Locust Grove District.

II. Wilson Huff married Mary (Polly), daughter of John Lawrence, and lived at Copper Hill; their children: Byrd, Jr., married Melitie Kinsey; Giles, married Nellie, daughter of Robert Huff; and Callie, married Ira Poff.

III. Jackson Huff married Elizabeth Sowder, and lived in Copper Hill; they had but one child who died in infancy.

IV. Byrd Huff married Emily Lavender; no children; his tombstone in the Salem Baptist Churchyard shows that he was born May 23, 1820, died March 14, 1890.

V. Robert Huff lived on the Floyd-Bent Mountain Pike; he was a prominent farmer, and married Mary, daughter of Peter Kefauver of Roanoke County; their children were: John J., never married; Nellie (b. 1848), married Giles, son of Wilson Huff, and after his death, H. T. Fowler; Emma, married Richard

F. Cannaday (son of William A.), one of the well-known drum-mers of Southwest Virginia; one of their sons was Dr. Royal Cannaday of New York City; Waller, married Lucy Taylor.

VI. Ann Huff married George, son of Peter Kefauver and lived at Copper Hill; their children were: Peter, married Susan Snuffer, and after her death married Eliza Price; Isaac, married a Miss Garnand; Henrietta, married William Tice; and Susan, married Riley Poff.

VII. Lydia Huff (b. March 23, 1827), married William Riley Sowder, son of Daniel, no children.

VIII. Jane Huff married John, son of Peter Kefauver of Roanoke County; their children: Virginia, married Ed Loyd; S. H. (Dick), married Mrs. Annie Harding; and Goggins.

IX. Isaac Henry Huff (1829-1908), married Lucinda, daughter of Peter Kefauver, lived for some years at Copper Hill in Floyd County, later moved to Roanoke, their children:

A. Ballard P., married Florence Thomas, daughter of Charles M. and Jane (Crawford) Thomas of Big Lick;

B. Phillip W., married first, Eva Snyder, and after her death, Georgia Kirk Robinson;

C. George C., married Blanche Vinyard;

D. Atwood J., married Nannie Meade;

E. Eva Anne, married Frank P. Rutrough;

F. Peter C., married Nora Vinyard;

G. Essie Virginia, married Ross Cook;

H. William W., married Edna Hoskins; and

I. Alice Peyton, married Harry Girvin.

All of the children of Isaac Henry Huff settled in the city of Roanoke where they were businessmen and were foremost in the development of the Magic City. Ballard P. Huff was presi-dent of the wholesale firm of Huff, Andrews and Thomas.

In 1835, John Huff, aged 71, of Franklin County, Virginia, was pensioned for services in the Virginia Militia during the Revolutionary War, as shown in McAllister's **Virginia Militia in the Revolutionary War**.

Henry Huff is mentioned as among the largest landowners in the year 1831, when the county of Floyd was organized as found in the **Land Tax Book** in the Virginia State Library.

Wilson Huff was a member of Captain John W. Headen's

Company in the 54th Regiment of Virginia Infantry. John J. Huff was First Sergeant in Captain Andrew Graham's Company in Col. Robert L. Preston's Reserves. Robert Huff was a member of Stuart's Horse Artillery. John Huff served in the Confederate army, command unknown. Ferdinand A. Huff was a member of Company A, 54th Virginia Infantry. J. H. Huff and F. Huff were members of Captain Sparrell Griffith's Company, Co. H, 54th Virginia Infantry. Peter and Isaac Huff were members of Captain Burwell Akers' Company; the latter was captured and taken prisoner to Rock Island, Illinois.

JOHN HUFF LINE

Family tradition is that John Huff, who settled at High Peak on the crest of the Blue Ridge (later the Watt Huff place on the Franklin-Floyd Pike in Franklin County), was the emigrant ancestor of this branch of the family. John Huff and wife, Elizabeth (Mary?) Tony came from Wales to this country reputedly in the middle or latter part of the 18th century. Their children were in part: Peter, Jacob, Isaac, Susan and John. They were buried on a little knoll near the Amos Cannaday place near Little River; some of their children were buried near Pigg River Church.

I. Peter (1793-1834) moved to Carroll County. At the time of his death he was reputed to be the wealthiest man in that county.

II. Jacob married a Miss Cannaday, and had the following children: Isaac, George and Samuel.

III. Isaac (1797-1874) married Elizabeth Snuffer, lived for some years on Otter Creek in Franklin County, later moving to Floyd and settling first at the Evans place one mile east of the county seat and later in the Pine Creek neighborhood; their eight children were:

A. Mary, married Sparrel Livesay, son of Peter, and lived near New Haven Baptist Church; they had two daughters: Susan, married John Lee; and Sallie, married William Lee, county surveyor for many years.

B. John married Martha Moore; they had no children.

C. Susan married Joseph Williams (1813-1875), son of Philip and Jane (Poag) Williams, the settler, lived on Pine

Creek, and they had five sons and three daughters.

D. Jacob (b. 1827), married Ann Graham, lived on the Floyd-Franklin Pike some five miles east of the courthouse; their two sons were: Jackson, married Sakes Bower; and Monroe, married Adaway Nolen, daughter of Alexander.

E. Peter (b. 1829), married Millie Jane, daughter of Perry Graham, lived on Pine Creek where he was a prosperous farmer, and had two sons and four daughters: Robert, married Nevada Lancaster; William; Lula, married Jefferson D. Shortt.

F. Nancy (1830-1906), married, first, Jackson Hall, who was killed in the Civil War, and their children were: Isaac T.; Peter P.; Mary Susan; and Adeline; in 1867 Nancy married, secondly, John I. Brame; and they had two sons: John Robert Lee Brame and Samuel Roffe Brame.

G. Isaac (b. 1834), married Adeline, daughter of George Kitterman, and lived on Pine Creek; they had four sons and four daughters, some of whom were: George, Isaac, Thomas, Peter, Elizabeth, Sallie, Florence. Dr. Isaac Eldridge Huff, second son of Isaac and Adeline, was born in Floyd County in 1866; attended Oxford Academy; received his medical education in colleges in Baltimore and New York City, graduating in 1892; began practicing medicine at Simpson, Floyd County, in 1892, where he continued until 1904 when he moved to Roanoke, and is one of the leading physicians of that city; in 1893 he married Flora McIver Francis, daughter of Capt. Wm. H. Francis of Montgomery County; they had three children: W. Banks, physician; Doris, married Robert Hunt; and Francis Eldridge (National Grocery Co.).

H. Elizabeth, married Isaac, son of John Robertson, the settler, and lived three miles east of the town of Floyd; their two children: Thomas, married Rosa Smith, now living at the old homestead; and Mary, married Zera Shortt, son of Naaman.

IV. Susan Huff married John Snuffer of Franklin County, and lived near Copper Hill, Floyd County.

V. John Huff (b. 1803), married Orina, daughter of Peter and Savannah (McGhee) Livesay, and lived on Little River, about nine miles northeast of the county seat. Their children were in part:

A. Martha, married James Cannaday.

B. Ferdinand, died in 1865 in the Civil War.

C. Peter.

D. George Washington, known as "Watt," (1827-1903) married Ann (Oct. 24, 1828-April 1865), daughter of Major Thomas and Elizabeth (Howard) Banks, and lived at the old Huff place at High Peak; their six children were:

1. Peter Ferdinand, married Ardella, daughter of Thomas Woolwine of Patrick County, and was long a prominent merchant of the Turtle Rock section; he later moved to Patrick County; their children: Walter, Mary, Eliza, Katherine (died when ten years old), Alice, John, and George. Peter Ferdinand's second wife was a Smith.

2. Oscar A. (d. 1920), married Ruth, daughter of Thomas Woolwine of Patrick County, and lived all of his life at the High Peak home place where he was a well-known merchant; their only child, Sallie, now resides there.

3. John Franklin married Alice, daughter of Ballard P. and Mary (Barnard) Shelor, and lived at Turtle Rock; they had no children.

4. Thomas Howard Fulton (b. 1854), "Fult," married Elizabeth, daughter of Isaac and Adeline (Kitterman) Huff, and lives at the old John Huff homestead on Little River; their children are: Thomas F., Adaline, Elizabeth, Alice, George (who died early).

5. Eliza married Scott Norris (d. 1922) of Baltimore, Maryland; no children were born to them; she now resides at High Peak.

6. Laurie, died at age three.

The Hylton Family

Some time prior to the American Revolution two brothers, George and Elijah Hylton, settled in Virginia: George in Amherst County, where he became a wealthy man but left no children; Elijah in Montgomery County (now Floyd), reputedly about 1772, by land grant, on a farm now owned by Rev. Abram N. Hylton, a descendant of the settler. Both George and Elijah were soldiers in the Revolution and fought under George Washington. The children of Elijah Hylton were in part: George, John, Archelaus, Betsy (Elizabeth), Katie (Katherine), Lucy and Jeremiah.

I. George Hylton, first son of Elijah, married Tabitha Arter, and their eight children were:

A. Elijah married, first, a Miss Smith, secondly, Emily Massey; their children were: Ira, John, Eli, Henry, Frederick, Frances and Tilda.

B. Nathaniel.

C. Simeon married a Miss Harbour.

D. Archelaus married Lavinia Stegall.

E. James married Susan Stegall; their children were: Asa, Tobias and Letitia who married Vaughan.

F. George B. (d. 1888), buried in Willis Cemetery, married Sally DeLong; their children: Clayborn Ampie, William, Noah, John, Armsted, Samuel, Andrew, Rosanna, Ann, Adaline, Charlotte.

G. Nancy married John Quesenberry; some of their nineteen children: William, John, Elijah, Nathaniel, Lewis, James, Patsy, Rena and Katherine.

H. Betsy.

II. John Hylton married Nancy Howell, daughter of Dave Howell of Floyd County; their children were in part:

A. Burwell (1801-1883) married Polly Slusher, daughter of Stuf Slusher; they had a family of twelve sons and four daughters, and eight of the sons fought in the Confederate army; they were in part: Riley, Nathan, Ira, Ananias, John, Madison, Henderson, Lorenzo, Levi, Julia, Nancy, Lizzie, and Lucretia who married Weeks.

B. Bryant (1807-1882), buried at Indian Valley, married Nancy Wade, daughter of Anderson, of Floyd County, and was one of the first justices of the county; their children were: Lewis, William, Preston, James, Benjamin, Addie, Headen, Allie, Elliott and Lizzie. Hylton's Tavern was run by Bryant Hylton and was located on the southwest corner of Main and Locust streets, before and after "the surrender."

C. Gordon (d. Aug. 11, 1858) married Lydia Stegall; their children were in part: John, Maston, Frances, and Nancy

(m. Harman).

D. Tabithia (Tilda) married Jacob Slusher, son of Stephen, the settler; their children: John, Jeremiah (a minister of the Brethren Church), Marion, Oliver Perry, George and Mary M.

E. Mary (1800-Feb. 15, 1825) married Joseph Howard (1794-1865), son of Peter, the settler; they had one son, Darius, who moved to Portland, Oregon.

III. Archelaus Hylton (1779-Dec. 10, 1865) married Catherine Weddle in 1804, daughter of Benjamin and Mary; he is buried in the Hylton Cemetery on Hylton farm in Floyd: they had five sons and seven daughters:

A. Henry (1808-1901), buried at Topeco Cemetery, married, first, Peggy Hylton, secondly, Mary Harter; their children Katherine (m. Pratt), John and Lizzie.

B. George (1809-1865), buried on his farm, married Polly Harman; their children: John, William, Andrew, Solomon, Celia (m. Sowers), Martha (m. Weddle), Sarah (m. Weeks), and Eliza (m. Vaughan).

C. John (1815-1896), buried on farm, married Peggy Harter; their children: Marion, Jacob, Cain, Beth, Albert, Samuel, Catherine, Amanda, Lizena and Adaline.

D. Elijah (1830-1908), buried at Topeco, married, first. Hannah Bowman, secondly, Mary Bowman Phillips; his first set of children were: Darius, Daniel, Granville, Joseph, Abraham, Isabell (m. Marshall), Roena (m. Marshall), Eliza (m. Sutphin), Cassie (m. Aldridge); the second set were: Clovis, Lala (m. Bowers), and Tempie.

E. Jonas (b. 1819—died in infancy).

F. Charlotte (1804-1894), buried in Harris burial ground, married, first, Stephen Slusher, secondly, Jackson Harris; her first set of children were: Henry, Samuel, Eva (m. Quesenberry), Polly (m. Quesenberry), Susan (m. Hylton), Lizzie (m. Martin), and Katherine, died when a young woman; second set of children were: Jackson, Elijah, Sarah and Martha.

G. Susan (1805-1879), buried in Dickerson Cemetery at Indian Ridge, married Leonard Dickerson, son of Len Dickerson; their children: Eli, Archibald, Ira, Charlotte, Martha and

Hulda (m. Martin).

H. Patsy (1807-1847), buried in Hylton Cemetery, married Benjamin Harman, son of Jacob; their children: Christopher, George, Lanan, Charlotte and Elizabeth.

I. Anna (1812-1895), buried in Hylton Cemetery, married Jacob Harman, son of Jacob, the settler; their children: Jabez, Henry, Abram, Beth, Jonas, Dennis, Rena, Julian, Barbara, Naamah and Eliza.

J. Celia (1814-1898), buried in Hylton Cemetery, married John Harman, son of Jacob, the settler; their children: Austin, Elijah, Daniel, Polly (m. Phlegar), Margaret, Tena, Ann, Catherine (m. Weddle), and Emmazetta (m. Dillon).

K. Eliza (1823-1865), buried in Hylton Cemetery, married William Cannaday, son of Tom; their children: Zachary T., George, William, Hester, Martha (m. Hylton), Louisa (m. Weddle), Catherine (m. Hill), Elizabeth (m. Keith), and Charlotte (m. Duncan).

L. Julia (June 29, 1821-1836), buried in Hylton Cemetery.

IV. Elizabeth (Betsy) Hylton, married Henry Hylton; this set of Hyltons was related to the Elijah Hylton line and had settled in Floyd prior to the date of Elijah's settlement; Henry was a brother to Elisha, a soldier in the Revolutionary War; James; and Obedience, married James Pratt, a soldier in the War of 1812, he died at Norfolk, leaving his wife and seven small children. Children of Betsy and Henry Hylton were four sons and five daughters: [one daughter's name is missing].

A. Austin (1794-1879), married Rachel Booth, daughter of George; their children: Hardin P. (Nov. 11, 1822-Dec. 24, 1905), Solomon, Asa, Rheta, Susanna, Anna (m. Bowman), Millie (m. Hylton), and Martha (m. Castle); Austin married, secondly, Widow Bowman, mother of Elder George C. Bowman. Austin Hylton was one of the pioneer preachers of the Brethren Church in southwestern Virginia. He was called to the ministry in 1829 and ordained eight years later. About 1850, he moved to east Tennessee and located on Boones Creek in the Knob Creek congregation. All of his children went with him to Tennessee except his oldest son, Hardin P., who remained in Floyd. Elder Austin Hylton lived an exemplary life.

1. Hardin P. Hylton married Frances Bowman (d. Feb. 15,

1898) in 1844; they had nine children, of whom three, John W. B., Chrisley D., and Solomon P., are elders in the church; Hardin married, secondly, Sarah Carter. Hardin was ordained elder of the Brethren Church in 1850 and was active in the ministry for about fifty years. Elder Chrisley D. Hylton, son of Hardin, married Mattie E. Bowman, of Tennessee. He was ordained to the eldership of the church on October 2, 1892, and was sent by the church to Louisiana and Florida, as well as in Virginia. He did evangelistic work in Virginia, North Carolina, Tennessee, West Virginia, Maryland and Pennsylvania. He is now located in Botetourt County. The Hyltons played an important part in the history of the Brick Church of Floyd County.

B. Tinie, son of Betsy and Henry, married Rebecca Arter; their children: Richard, Henry, Betsy (m. Cruise), Ruth (m. Helms), Ara (m. Radford), and Zilpha (m. Starr).

C. Hiram (1804-1880), buried in Pratt graveyard, (Black Ridge), married Millie Booth, daughter of George; their children: Zachariah, Isaac, Archibald, Ira, Ananias, Chesley, Rachel (m. Harris), Lizzie (m. Burnett), Almira (m. Burnett).

D. Solomon, married Celia Edens; their children: Joseph, Erastus, Levi, Austin, Rachel (m. Keith), and Margaret (m. Woods).

E. Susan, married Leonard Dickerson; their children: Henry and Ura.

F. Delilah, married Richard Hungate; their children: Jacob, Naptilla and Lethia, all of whom died without descendants.

G. Juda (Judith), married Isaac Spence; their children: Isaiah, and "a set of twin boys."

H. Celia, married John Sutphin, son of Henderson; their children: Jordan Fleming, Julia and Anna (m. Bolt).

V. Lucy Hylton, married Charles Turman.

VI. Katie (Katherine) Hylton (b. 1791), married Luke (b. 1791), son of Ambrose and Sally (Reed) Cox.

VII. Jeremiah Hylton settled in Patrick County.

[Editor's Note: Found in the Wood's papers were these names: James Hylton married Mahala Burnett and they had seven children: Lara, Emma, Alice, Lula L., Abram W., J. Walter and Posey Caffle].

The Janney (Janie) Family
(a border family)

Moses Janie (original spelling of name) was born in Virginia and moved to what is now Franklin County where he settled at the foot of the Blue Ridge Mountains on the headwaters of Otter Creek. He married a Miss Swinney; they had six children:

A. Isaac Janney married Mary Radford, daughter of James, and lived at the James Goode Hash place on Runnet Bag Creek in the west end of Franklin County: Their children:

1. Flemon Janney married Mary Ann Boyd, daughter of Samuel (Samuel Boyd was cruelly slain by the "details" in the time of the Civil War); they and their several children moved to Missouri in 1876.

2. Elizabeth Janney married Wiley A. Via, a well-known Primitive Baptist preacher; their children: (a) Thomas, (b) Martha, (c) Ellen, (d) Flemon. Elder Via died on the headwaters of Pig River in Franklin County and was buried in the Radford burial ground about one mile east of S. T. Turner's store.

3. Sarah Janney married Tazewell Radford; their daughter: Sarah Ann.

4. Adline Janney married John Griffith; their (known) child: (a) Eb Griffith married Burney Dixon, daughter of William, and died of fever soon afterwards.

5. Malinda Janney married Wid Rakes; their child: Seifus.

6. Isaac Janney died when a youth.

7. Martha Janney married Edmund Dixon; their children: (a) Washington Dixon married Tiney Martin; their children: William, Rufus, Isaac, Martha, Lucinda, Sallie Jane and Statirie; (b) Burwell Dixon died of epilepsy when a young man; (c) Sarah Dixon married John Right.

B. Nat Janney married and moved to Tennessee when a young man.

C. John Janney (b. about 1816) married Elizabeth Underwood, daughter of Earsley; their children:

1. Flemon Janney, born August 21, 1842, at the foot of Barton's Spur on the headwaters of Otter Creek in Franklin

County, was a Confederate soldier in Company A, 54th Virginia Infantry, from 1861 to May 15, 1864, when he lost an arm at Resaca, Georgia. After the war he married Mrs. Martha Jane Shortt Lemons, widow of William Lemons who was killed in the Civil War; their children: Aaron, Hibirnie, William S., and Malinda Susan.

2. Nancy; 3. Ann; 4. Burwell; 5. Martha; 6. Ellen; 7. John; and 8. Taswell Janney.

D. Sarah Janney married Calvin Shortt, son of Reuben, and moved to Wythe County, Virginia, where they lived in a large log house near the railroad about one mile from Wytheville. Calvin Shortt was a Confederate soldier and one of their sons was killed at the battle of Cloyd's Mountain. Their children: 1. Columbus; 2. Americus; 3. Demarcus; 4. Benjamin; 5. Henrietta; and 6. Chancellor.

E. Burwell Janney married Polly Radford, daughter of Robert, they lived in Floyd County, near Silverleaf, where their children were born:

1. Robert married in Zanesville, Ohio.

2. Peter married Linda Via; their children: Lida, Albert, Homer, and others.

3. Jesse died at Boones Mill, Franklin County.

4. Moses married and had a family.

5. Mary died early.

6. Ellen married John Vest.

7. Charlie (no information).

8. Ruth married John Janney; their children: Seifus, Tazewell, Allie.

F. Flemon Janney married in Franklin County and, with his brother Nat, moved to Tennessee when a young man.

Those serving in the Confederate army:

Company A, 54th Virginia Infantry: Flemon Janney, lost an arm at Resaca, Georgia, May 15, 1864.

Company B, 54th Infantry: Jesse D. Janney.

Company H, 54th Infantry: Burwell, Flemon, Sr., John W., Moses N., Jesse and Robert P. Janney. Moses N. Janney was wounded at Missionary Ridge, Nov. 25, 1863.

Company I, 54th Infantry: John Janney.

Company G, 21st Virginia Cavalry: Burwell Janney (died,

time and place unknown).

Capt. James Bennet Headen's Company of Reserves: John and Burwell Janney.

Jett

The Jett family of Virginia has been very small in number.

Dr. Jett, an old-time herb doctor, or "Thompsonian doctor," lived near the Buffalo Knob in the west end of the county. One of his sons was Joseph T. Jett, who lived many years in the Head of the River section in the east end of Floyd County. He was a farmer and justice of the peace. His first family of children were in part: John L., Joseph T., Jr. and Annie. John L. married Jennie Dobyns (dau. of Samuel) and lived in Floyd where he raised a large family; one of whom was Dr. Cabell Jett of West Virginia. Joseph T., Jr., married Olivia, daughter of Edward Evans of Floyd County, and was a popular hotel keeper, along with his father; they had no children. Annie married Claude, son of Andrew Stephens, a well-known saddle and harness maker of Floyd. Their children were: Harry L., Percy, Clyde and Joseph.

The second wife of Joseph T. Jett, Sr., was Eliza, a sister of Dr. William Pendleton of Patrick County; their children were: Samuel C., Edgar, Walter and Lula. Dr. Samuel C. Jett, a prominent physician of North Carolina, married Jennie, daughter of Judge Waller L. Howard of Floyd.

Joseph T. Jett spent the greater part of his life in the town of Floyd where he was a merchant, farmer and popular hotel proprietor (Jett Hotel).

Another son of Dr. Jett was Peter, unmarried.

Kelley

Alexander, Benjamin, Garrett, James and William Kelley were Colonial soldiers prior to the Revolutionary War in Virginia. Alexander Kelley was a Captain in the Virginia Militia in Greenbrier County, Virginia, during the Revolutionary War. James, Jesse, John, Gordon, Patrick, Thaddy, Timothy, Thomas and William Kelly were soldiers in the Continental

Army during the Revolutionary War.

Rev. George W. Kelley, a Primitive Baptist minister, who served in the War of 1812 and participated in the Battle of New Orleans, married Sarah Webster of Franklin County, and moved with his family in 1840 to the east end of Floyd County at the top of Daniel's Run. Their children were: 1. Elizabeth married Nathan Conner; 2. James married, first, Sallie Lester, and their children were: Nancy, Sary and George; and, secondly, Sallie Sowder; 3. Benjamin (unmarried) moved to Kentucky; 4. Joseph Pedigo married Sarah Katherine, daughter of Lewis Payne, the settler; 5. Annie married James Gray, their children were: Mary Elizabeth, Benjamin, John, George, Moses and Cary Louis; 6. George, married in Kentucky; 7. William married Charlotte Powell, their children were: Mary Catherine, John, Samuel, James, Hall and Amos; and 8. Moses married Catherine Conner, their children were: George Nathan, Emma, Silas, James, Thomas, Lucy, Eliza and Prudence.

The children of Joseph Pedigo Kelley and Sarah Payne were: Sarah Elizabeth, George Louis, John Benj., Jefferson Lafayette, Homer Hansford and James Marion. Sarah Elizabeth married James M. Cannaday; George L. married Nancy Walters; Homer H. married Leonora Ingram; John B. married Amanda S. Cannaday and they now live in Salem; Jefferson L. married, first, Emma Kelley, secondly, Miranda Martin; James M. married Mary Vest.

Joseph P. Kelley, a member of Company A, 54th Virginia Infantry, lost his life at the Battle of Seven Pines, June 1862. In Company H, 54th Virginia Infantry, were First Corporal James L. Kelley, Moses and William D. Kelley; the latter two were captured at Franklin, Tenn., date unknown.

John Kitterman

John Kitterman (1767-1833) was one of the largest land-owners and taxpayers when the county of Floyd was organized in 1831. He, with Abraham Phlegar and Manassah Tice, lived on and owned the present site of the town of Floyd. His line joined Main Street and his lands extended south including all the southern portion of the town and the historic Storker's Knob.

His home stood near the present Primitive Baptist Church, and the home of his son, David, was just east of the late Judge Waller L. Howard's residence.

The Kittermans, or Kattermans, as they originally spelled their name, along with many other German families, came from Pennsylvania. Three emigrants of the name came through the port of Philadelphia:

Hans Jacob Kattermann, Oct. 27, 1738
Hans Ulrich Katerman, Oct. 27, 1738
Johannes Katterman, Sept. 26, 1743

John Kitterman married Juliana _____, and settled in Floyd County about the year 1800. Four of his sons moved West; Philip was born Sept. 11, 1974; Solomon married Tabitha Slusher. David Kitterman, another son, married Sally Sowers and lived all his life in the town of Floyd; their children were: 1. Aaron married, first, Rosabel Sowers, and their children were: William D., George T., James F., Charles W. and Missie O.; and, secondly, Maggie J. Dickerson; they had one daughter, Okey; 2. John married Ellen Agnew, their children: Abigail (m. Jack Martin), Loula (m. Abner Earles), Mittie (never married), Alice (m. M. Howell), Georgia (m. F. M. Harman), and Samuel; 3. William Reed married, first, Mary Bishop (b. 1856), daughter of Asa, and they raised a family of twelve children; and, secondly, Mrs. C. A. Quesenberry; 4. George married Mary Elizabeth Kirby; their children: Alberta, Nannie B., Dolly T., Sallie Ann, Ada B., and Peter D. 5. Peter; 6. Joseph never married; 7. Mary married Nelson B. Stimpson; 8. Julia married J. M. Stigleman; 9. Nancy married, first, Peyton J. Richardson, and, secondly, J. Tazewell Agnew; 10. Elizabeth married Landon Dickerson; 11. Malinda married Benjamin Thomas.

George W. Kitterman, Third Lieutenant in Company A, 24th Virginia Infantry, under Captain C. M. Stigleman, was wounded at Gettysburg, July 3, 1863, and imprisoned at Fort Delaware.

In Company I, 54th Virginia Infantry were Joseph Kitterman, killed in battle at Lynchburg, June 17, 1864; and John A. Kitterman, captured at Resaca, Georgia, May 15, 1864.

Aaron Kitterman was Second Lieutenant in Company G,

21st Virginia Cavalry, under Captain A. O. Dobyns, wounded and captured Nov. 12, 1864, and imprisoned at Fort Delaware.

The Lancasters

There were only a few families by the name of Lancaster in Colonial Virginia. John, Richard, Robert, Robert, Jr., and William Lancaster lived in Orange County, Nathaniel in Prince Edward, Henry in Isle of Wight, and Jeremiah in Frederick County.

William Lancaster was a soldier in the Virginia Militia in the Revolutionary War, according to McAllister's **Virginia Militia in the Revolutionary War.**

John Lancaster was born about the year 1768. He came from England to Virginia, and is said to be the emigrant ancestor of the Floyd County family. He married Susan Parrot. Two of their sons, (Lewis) Washington and Thomas, moved with their families from Bedford County and settled in Floyd County. (Lewis) Washington settled eight miles east of the county seat near Cannaday's Gap; and Thomas settled on a farm three miles southeast of the courthouse. Here, from the family of Thomas Lancaster, Sr., was the start of the Missionary Baptist Church in Floyd County.

I. (Lewis) Washington Lancaster (1791-1854), married Nancy Wheeler of Bedford County. He was a man of education and was one of the early schoolteachers. He was an "herb doctor," or "Thompsonian doctor," who did some local practice with roots and herbs. Although his name was Washington, he was usually called "Dr. Lewis Lancaster." Nancy Wheeler Lancaster's brother, Roland Wheeler, was captured by the Indians and carried a prisoner to the Kanawha River section when a young man, but he escaped and returned to his home. The story goes that about the same time the Indians captured a colored woman belonging to Roland's father, but she never returned. (Lewis) Washington and Nancy had the following children:

A. Belinda, married William Brammer, son of John of Patrick County. She lived to a great old age, near the parental home, and they were the parents of three sons and three daughters:

1. Jonathan L. Brammer married Juliana Burnett, daughter of Jeremiah, and their children were: Stanton, William, John, Belinda and Elizabeth.

2. Tazewell C. married Normanda Graham, daughter of Perry, and their children were: Helen, Nina, William B. and Elizabeth (m. Sam Bowman).

3. Madison L. married Amanda Shortt, daughter of Naaman, and their children were: Naaman, Wilton (Bub), Etta, Nannie, Willie, Sallie, Fannie, James and Jefferson.

4. Lucinda married William Pedigo.

5. Elizabeth married Addison Epperly, son of Jacob, and their children were: Leonia, Fannie, Dove, Calvin, Peter, Theotis, Brethard, William.

6. Pernina married Peter Turner, son of Francis, and they had one son, William F., who married, first, Eliza Smith, daughter of Josiah, and secondly, Fannie Hoback, daughter of James.

B. Thomas Lancaster (1811-1884), married Sarah Williams, daughter of Philip, the settler, and lived near the Williams' home four or five miles east of the courthouse on Pine Creek. Thomas, like his father, was an "herb doctor" and was known as Dr. Tom Lancaster. Children of Thomas and Sarah:

1. Anderson W. (1834-1890), married Teresa Haynes, and their children were: Victoria and Marion.

2. Mary Jane (b. 1836) married James Walton, and their children were: Jasper, Jesse, Virginia, Bier, Cora and Hallie.

3. Philip (b. 1838), a gallant soldier in the Confederate army, married Mary Sue Corbin, daughter of Benjamin, and their children were: Musco, Cora, Georgia and Vada.

4. Sallie (1841-1892) married Landon Stone, and their children were: Sallie, Elizabeth and others.

5. Rosabelle E. (b. 1843), married Quincy Haynes, and their children were: Luther and Maude.

6. Nancy (b. 1846), married Jonathan Lee, and their children were: Abner, Abigail, Arabella, and others.

7. Lucinda A. (b. 1854) never married.

8. Eliza (b. 1856), married Darias Young, and their

children were: Gertrude, Trum and others.

C. Lucinda Lancaster, married William Lee; they lived in Patrick County at the foot of Rock Castle Gap.

D. Washington Lancaster, Jr., known as Jeff, (b. 1814), married Lausie Underwood, daughter of Joshua, and they lived at Turtle Rock (Pizarro) in the old John West home. They had one daughter, Delilah (b. 1860) who married Robert O. Harvey, and their children were: Lala, Effie, Fannie, Dr. Lewis, Robert, Angie, Amelia, Irvin and Isaac. Jeff Lancaster, a man of considerable means, owned a very fine farm, on which was the old Major Howard flouring mill, one of the landmarks of the county. This was long known as Lancaster's Mill. The four-story flouring mill was built by Christopher Bower, Jr., and was located on a branch of Meadow Creek.

E. John Lancaster, married Ellen Greer, and their children were: William, Joseph, Lewis, Green, Lucinda and Belinda (m. Thompson).

II. Thomas Lancaster, Sr. (1793-1854), married Susan Chapman; their children were:

A. Eliza (1817-1887), married Samuel Phlegar and had nine children: Judson, James, Thomas, Lee, Henry, Catherine, Ann, Mary and Alberta.

B. James (b. 1819), married Mary Evans, and their children were: Bruce (a lawyer); John (a physician); William and Pauline. James Lancaster moved to Ohio.

C. Nancy (b. 1820) married David Shewey; their children were: William, James, George, Elizabeth, Mary, Lettie.

D. Lewis (1822-1895), married Elizabeth Beamer, and their children were: James, William, Thomas (m. a Miss Purdy), John and Mary (m. Norman Young and moved to Kansas).

E. Nathaniel (b. 1825), married Mary Hogan, daughter of Francis, the settler; their children were:

1. Rev. Davis G. Lancaster (b. 1855), a well-known minister of the Baptist Church who was pastor of New Haven Church, married Katherine Henley; their only child: Maynard H.

2. Clinton, died unmarried.

3. Leah, never married.

4. Hester, never married.

5. Ruth, married James P. Phlegar; they had no children.

6. Abigail, married Edward A. Williams; their children were: Eric C., Charles, Ida B., Gervassa A., Frank N. and Mary Thelma.

F. John, married Annie Taylor, daughter of Rev. Daniel; he was a minister of the Baptist denomination, and moved to North Carolina; their children were: Robert, Emma, John, George and Elizabeth.

G. Robert (1828-1906), married Octavia Underwood, daughter of Joshua and Delilah (West) Underwood, and their children were:

1. Elma (b. 1864), married Judson Phlegar, son of Samuel, and their children were: Robert (a physician), and Walter (a lawyer).

2. Attaway (1867-1889), first wife of Dr. J. Wilton Thurman, son of David; Attaway died quite young, leaving one daughter, Lena, who married John Edgar Wood, son of Jefferson P. and Belinda (Brammer) Wood; their children were: Margaret and Mary.

3. Tazewell (b. 1872) married Rachel Barnard, daughter of Conner and Mary Elizabeth (Turner) Barnard, and their children were: Attaway, Grace, Albert, Maude, Robert, Mary, Annie, Virginia, Helen, John.

4. Albert C. (b. 1875), a physician, who never married.

5. Caroline, died when about 18 years old.

H. Susan (b. 1830) married Ira Weddle; their children: Oscar, Elza, Simon, Maggie and Florentine.

I. Jefferson (b. 1832), married Mahala Beamer, and moved to Ohio; they had two children: Gustavus and Emma.

J. Whitfield (b. 1836), married Mrs. Dosia Wilson Atkins; their children were: Everett (a clergyman), Lilly, Dayton, Ernest, Barnard, Lynwood, Jeter and Ulysses. Everett (b. 1863) married Cora Lee Agee, daughter of Joshua, and lived in North Carolina where he was a Baptist minister; their children: Benjamin, Dayton, Breman, Alvin, Irvin, Linda, Lilly, Bell, Cassie and Doris.

K. Florentine (b. 1837), married Lafayette Ferguson;

their children: Charley, Josy, Sallie.

L. Sarah (b. 1839), married Asa Keith; their children: Charley, Alice, Bell, Minnie.

M. Elizabeth (b. 1844), died young.

The Lawrence Family

John Lawrence was born in Pennsylvania about the year 1775. He married a Miss Peden in 1797(?), who was of Welsh descent, and soon thereafter moved to Virginia. They settled on Brush Creek in Montgomery County, where he lived to be 83 years old. They had nine sons and four daughters:

1. Elizabeth (b. about 1798) married Daniel Epperly.

2. Briggs (b. 1800) married a Miss Wickham; their family of five sons all died young of diphtheria. The oldest was named Calvin.

3. James (b.1801) married (wife unknown); their children were in part: Jackson moved to Ohio; Caanan married a Miss Weaver; Jacob married Molly Dobbins; and James married Elizabeth Stuart and had a family of four sons, one of whom is Dr. E. L. Lawrence of Roanoke.

4. Sarah (b. 1802) married a Mr. Cassady.

5. William (b. 1804) married a Miss Booth; their children were: William B., Zan, John, Isaac and others.

6. Nancy (b. 1806) married William Sowers, and they were the parents of Caleb and William T. Sowers, and others.

7. Polly (b. 1807) married Wilson Huff; their children were Giles, Byrd and Callie, wife of Ira Poff.

8. Benjamin (b. 1810) moved to Tennessee.

9. John (b. Dec. 16, 1811) was twice married; two sons and one daughter by first wife, and four sons and two daughters by the second marriage. Most of these children moved to Illinois.

10. Peden (no information).

11. Jacob (b. 1814) married Nancy Rutrough, and their children were: Gideon; Thomas (killed in the Civil War); Luther M. married Miss Hancock; Darius married a Miss Hall;

Solomon married a Miss Board; James married a Miss Martin; Elizabeth married Byrd Light; Sarah married Eli Blackwell, son of Moses; Lena married Washington Light; Laura married James Basham; and Martha married George Martin.

12. Silas (b. 1821) married a Miss Wilson; their children were: Noah, Asa, Frank, Julia and Emeline.

13. Thomas (b. 1824) married Susan F. Obryan; they had six daughters and three sons; the sons were: (a) Luther (dec'd); (b) William P. married Eliza, daughter of George Young, and raised a family of nine; he has been one of Floyd County's prominent and well-known schoolteachers, having taught thirty-five terms in the counties of Floyd and Pulaski; he is the present Postmaster in the town of Floyd; (c) Henry A. married Adaline, daughter of George Young, and raised a family of four sons and nine daughters; like his brother, Henry Lawrence has been one of Floyd County's foremost schoolteachers.

In Company A, 54th Virginia Infantry under Captain C. M. Stigleman, was Gideon L. Lawrence, captured at Stony Creek, March 3, 1865. W. T. Lawrence was a member of Company H, 54th Virginia Infantry under Captain Sparrel H. Griffith. In Company I, 54th Virginia Infantry under Captain Burwell Akers were Caanan, William B. (died at Mount Sterling, Ky.), James E. and Isaac B. Lawrence. Jacob B., William and Silas B. Lawrence were members of Col. Robert L. Preston's Reserves. Jacob B. Lawrence was a member of Stuart's Horse Artillery.

The Lee Family

William Lee lived in Floyd County near the Floyd-Patrick County line, some six miles south of the town of Floyd. He married a Miss Alexander, and their children were (in part):

John W. Lee married Susan Livesay, daughter of Sparrel who was the son of Peter Livesay, and they lived in Floyd

County. They were the parents of Robert Lee, W. Turner Lee, and others.

William Lee, Jr., married Sallie Livesay, daughter of Sparrel, and was a county surveyor for about twenty years. He lived south of the courthouse.

The Lemon Family

Isaac Lemon, Sr. (1753-1833), lived on Pigg River in the west end of Franklin County, and the court records of that county show the following land transaction: "This indenture made this 13th day of November 1786 between Elijah Jones, for and in consideration of the sum of eighty pounds paid him in hand by the sd. Isaac Lemon, the receipt whereof he doth acknowledge, have bargained and sold to the sd. Isaac Lemon one certain tract or parcel of land . . . lying and being in the County of Franklin on the head waters of Pig River and bounded as follows . . ." At the time of this deal, Isaac Lemon, Sr., was thirty-three years old. Here he raised a family, two of whom were Isaac, Jr., and Benjamin. The late Dr. Rufus Lemon of Callaway and Creed Lemon of the west end of Franklin County were descendants of Isaac Lemon, Sr.

Isaac Lemon, Jr. (1806-1896), son of Isaac, married Sally Young (1811-1862), daughter of Joshua, and settled in the east end of Floyd County near Joshua Young's home, where he was a well-known farmer, blacksmith, wagonmaker and a mechanic of considerable skill. Isaac and Sally Lemon had twelve children:

1. Nancy (1832-1906) married Naaman J. Shortt and lived at the old Reuben Shortt place; their children were: Amanda, John W., Prince E., Zera H., Jefferson D., Everett T., Callahill and Thomas.

2. Amanda (1830-1906) married Col. John Williams and lived at the Philip Williams place on Pine Creek; they had one child, Minerva.

3. Elizabeth (1833-1886) married Stephen, son of

William and Patty (Wright) Cannaday of Patrick County (Stephen was one of 24 children); they raised a large family, most of whom moved to Ohio; one of their sons is Tazewell Cannaday of Floyd.

4. William (1841-1864) married Martha Jane Shortt, daughter of John Y. Shortt, and their children were: Isaac, Lucinda, Thomas and Sallie. William Lemon lost his life in the Civil War. He was a member of Company H, 54th Virginia Infantry, under Captain Sparrel H. Griffith. After his death his widow married Flemon Janney, a Confederate soldier who lost an arm at Resaca, Georgia, May 15, 1864; he was a member of Co. A, 54th Virginia Infantry, under Captain Andrew Dickerson; they had one child, William.

5. Crawford (1846-19—?) married Sally Albright. He was third sergeant in Captain Andrew J. Graham's Company of Reserves under Col. Robert L. Preston in the Confederate army.

6. and 7. Thomas (1844-1863, killed in war) and John (1849-1876) never married.

8. America (1837-1896) married Burwell Young.

9. Malinda (1843-1863) married Haden Epperly, son of Jacob, and lived on Pine Creek.

10. Eliza (1845-1886) married Andrew Weddle.

11. Emmeline (1842-1906) married Caleb Tice, son of Manassah, and lived at Floyd.

12. James (1851-19 ?) married Margaret Moore, daughter of Noah B. and lived on Little River.

After the death of his wife, Isaac Lemon, Jr., married, secondly, Mrs. Susan Turner (nee Shortt), widow of Jefferson Turner who lost his life in the Civil War. They were the parents of one daughter, Minerva, who married Samuel Rakes, and lived for many years at the old homestead, five miles southeast of the Court House. Mrs. Rakes and family now live at Floyd.

Elder Posey G. Lester
(1850-1929)

The Lester Family

The Lester family is of English stock and lived first in Bucks County, Pennsylvania. Later three brothers came to Virginia. Of these, John Lester settled at the mouth of Brush Creek on Little River in what is now Montgomery County. John Lester (1752-1825) married Miss Plick and was the founder of the family in Montgomery and Floyd counties. Their children: John, James, William, Abner, Samuel, Hulen, Catherine (Katie), Susan and Rhoda.

I. John Lester, oldest son of John, married Mary Ann Terry

and settled five miles northwest of the town of Jacksonville. He was a successful farmer and prominent citizen, a large taxpayer with some social distinction as an owner of slaves, as was accorded in his day. He served his community as justice of the peace; as such was a member of the county court, commissioned by the Governor of Virginia. Men in that day dignified the office of justice of the peace and made its service one of honor and distinction. He had six sons and two daughters: Hulen, Amos, Byrd, John, William T., Hiley, Malinda and Catherine. Of these, Hulen, Amos and Byrd settled in Illinois, Indiana and West Virginia respectively.

A. John Lester, III, was a leading justice of the peace of the county court until by virtue of seniority he became High Sheriff of the county, which was the rule in his day. He died in the midst of his usefulness. He married Mary Gardner of Montgomery County and their children were:

1. James G. married Mary Semones and was the father of Dr. D. D. Lester, a dentist of Charlotte Courthouse, who is the father of Dr. James B. Lester, a dentist of Richmond.

2. Dudley, and 3. John were killed in the Civil War.

4. Elmira, wife of A. P. Dobbins, was the mother of Giles G. Dobbins of Beaver Creek in Floyd County.

5. Virginia, wife of George Shelor, was the grandmother of George D. Shelor, Clerk of Floyd County.

6. Octavia, wife of Gordon Dobbins, was the mother of Rice A. and Millard Dobbins, businessmen of Radford.

7. Mary, wife of C. E. Elder of Kentucky, whose daughter married Judge Ledru Guthrie of Oklahoma.

8. Rhodabell, wife of George Williamson of Riner, is the mother of five sons and three daughters: Len, Harvey, Sydney, Thurman, John, Mary, Florence and Zora, all of whom are citizens of Montgomery County.

B. William T. Lester, a man of prominence locally, served as Captain of Militia prior to the Civil War, and was 2nd Lieutenant in the Forty-Second Reserves, under Col. Robert L. Preston in the Confederate army. He married Mary Amanda Simmons, daughter of Thomas W. She was an attractive brunette and was locally known as "pretty Polly Simmons." They were the parents of six sons and three daughters:

1. Serena Matilda, wife of Charles C. Weeks, moved to Warren County, Iowa.

2. John Thomas married Mary Simmons, daughter of James, and moved to Warren County, Iowa.

3. Hiley Washington married Mary Starbuck of Iowa.

4. Asa Willivan married, first, Mary Hunt of Iowa, and secondly, Mrs. Mary Ridinger (nee Sowers) of Floyd County.

*5. Posey Greene, see below.

6. Arabella Emily m. Asa L. Boothe (settled in Indianola, Iowa).

7. Charles Hugh Dillard m. Mary Dobbins, daughter of A. P. Dobbins (settled in Indianola, Iowa).

8. Cary Houston m. Laura M. Whitlock and settled at the old home place. Their children were: Verbena, Casper and Mary.

9. Jennie m. Albert Whitlock. Their children were: Winnie, Lester, Merle, Blanche and Vernon. Lester moved to Gordon, Neb, after the World War.

*Posey Green married Emmette Harris of Reidsville, North Carolina, and settled in the town of Floyd. He is the father of two sons and one daughter: Posey Green, Jr., Masten H. and Annie May. Posey G. Lester was perhaps the most noted of any of the Lesters in this part of the country. He was born March 12, 1850, and received a limited education in the common schools. At the age of twenty-three he entered the ministry of the Primitive Baptist Church and was one of the most extensively known of its ministers. He traveled and preached in about twenty-one states and in Ontario, Canada, covering as much as thirteen thousand miles in a single year. During these years he served as pastor in Kentucky and Virginia, and later was pastor of a large church in the city of Roanoke. There he resided during the last years of his life. He was Moderator of the New River District Primitive Baptist Association, which numbered twenty-six churches and twenty-two ministers, and about 2000 members. For forty years he was associate editor, and was editor-in-chief of *Zions Landmark,* a leading church paper for the Primitive Baptists, published at Wilson, North Carolina.

In 1888 he was elected to represent the Fifth District of

Virginia in the Congress of the United States. He was reelected for a second term, but refused a third nomination, preferring to devote himself to his church work. (See page 131).

In 1898 he married Emmette Harris, daughter of Elder J. M. and Annie E. Harris of Reidsville, N. C.

II. Hulen Lester (1795-1888), youngest son of John the settler, married Nellie Simmons, and their children were: Joshua, Ira, Floyd, Harve, Charles, Paradine, Aveline, Ellen and Catherine.

A. Joshua Lester (1821-1901) married Catherine Peterman, and they were the parents of six sons:

1. Giles married Mary Walter; and their children were: Earley, Earnest, Eustace and Elbert.

2. Harve married Hauze Baker, and their children were: Curtis, Hampton, Hunt, Mary, Nellie, Louis and Willie.

3. William married Florence Williamson, and their children were: Paul, Marvin, Cletus and Walter.

4. Sidney married Sarah Webster, and their children were: Daisy, Olivia (Ollie) and Tresia.

5. Oscar married Florence Charlton, and their children were: Edna, Leslie, and others.

6. Helm married Laura Basham, and had one child: Harry.

B. Ira Lester (1823-1878) married Amanda Guy, and they were the parents of seven sons and three daughters:

1. Monroe married Biddie Mitchell, and their children were: Cora, Milton and Newman.

2. George Henry married Millie Akers and their children were: Mattie, Jennie, Gay, Nannie, May, Myrtle, Georgia, Harley, Plockie and Oakley.

3. Charles married Arrena Simmons, and their children were: Augustus (Guss), James, Tamer and Angeline.

4. Albert married Susan Altizer, and their children were: German, Audrey, Ira, Allie and Mosby.

5. Floyd J. married a Simpkins.

6. Bunyan (Bun) married Dora Altizer.

7. Elmer married Bertie Underwood.

8. Alice married Edward Moore.

9. Elizabeth (Lizzie) married Samuel Cromer.

10. Adaline (Addie) married Jacob Altizer, and their children were: Agnes, Gertrude, Edith, Ivy, Lacy, Ray and Allen.

C. Floyd Lester (1828-1899) married Susan Chaffin, and they had six children:

1. Dudley married Ellen Bishop, and their children were: Rufus, Silas, Harvey, William, Pate, Hosey, Nannie, Vivian, Florence and Dora.

2. James married Sarah Cooper, and they were the parents of three daughters and two sons.

3. Hulen married Zilla Duncan, and their children were: Leonard, Wilmer, Icy, Gladys and Ora.

4. Harvey married Ida Scaggs, and their children were: Kyle, Obediah, Posey, Ervin, Bentley, Frederick, Gray, Virginia, Margie, Nellie and Olivia.

5. John married Parthena Scaggs, and their children were: Mont, Sherman, Dudley, Waitman, Sallie and Kittie.

6. Sallie married Crockett Howard, and their children were: Lillian, Mary, Annie, Loraine, Reuben, William, Franklin and Oakley.

D. Harve Lester moved to Idaho when a young man, and never married.

E. Charles Lester 1838-1911) married Mary Wright and had seven children:

1. Letcher married Abigail Howell, and their children were: Lancy, Lathy, Frederick and Iris.

2. Frank married Adaline (Addie) Argabright, and their children were: Randall and Huston.

3. Alma married Henry Earles, and they have no children.

4. Grace never married.

5. Posey married George Akers, and their children were: Reginald, Raymond, Audrey, Mary and Hazel.

6. Minnie married David Howell, and they are the parents

of a daughter, Mary.

7. Ida married David Bowlen, and they have no children.

F. Paradine Lester married Daniel Peterman, and their children were: William, Dudley, Giles, Harve, Octavia, Susan, Ellen, Jennie and Catherine.

G. Aveline Lester married John Peterman, and their children were: Crockett, John, Mary, Emma, Olivia, Belle and Callie.

H. Ellen Lester married an Akers.

I. Catherine Lester never married.

The Floyd County Lesters serving in the Confederate army in the Civil War were:

In Company A, 24th Virginia Infantry, under Captain C. M. Stigleman, were: George W. Lester, John W. Lester (captured at Williamsburg, May 5, 1862), and Dudley Lester (who died in a hospital).

In Company A, 54th Virginia Infantry, under Captain Andrew Dickerson, were Austin Lester and Hornbarger Lester.

In Company B, 54th Virginia Infantry, under Captain Jackson Godbey, were Abner Lester (who died in a hospital at Abingdon in 1862), Lindsay, Lewis, Harrison and Lynch S. Lester.

In Company I, 54th Virginia Infantry, under Captain Burwell Akers, were James G. Lester and William S. Lester.

In Col. Robert L. Preston's Reserves, under Captain James B. Headen, were Byrd Lester and William T. Lester, 2nd Lieut.

In the World War were: Lathie W., Zachariah T., and Casper Lester, all of whom enlisted from Floyd County.

LeSueur

The LeSueur family of Floyd County is of French extraction. Moseby and James L. LeSueur, sons of the emigrant, married sisters, daughters of John George and Mary (Beaver) Goodykoontz, and granddaughters of Hans Georg Gutekunst, of Frederick County, Virginia.

Moseby LeSueur married, February 16, 1819, Catherine

(Sept. 19, 1801-1888), oldest daughter of John George Goodykoontz, and they settled on Camp Creek in Floyd County. Their
children were, in part: Martel (May 16, 1821-1904), and James
W. (April 3, 1823-1884). Catherine, the mother, died in 1888.

Martel, older son of Moseby, married, March 3, 1853, Sarah
Phlegar, and they lived on Camp Creek. Their children were,
in part: Elbert J. (moved to S. Dak.); Alice (m. Howery, lived
on Camp Creek); and Flora A. (m. Van Fleet, lived in Mo.)

James W., younger son of Moseby, married, January 10,
1850, Nancy C. Yearout, daughter of Charles. Their children
were: Ellen (m. Turner, lived at Riner, Va.) ; Eliza (m. James
Asa Sowers, Floyd, their children: Joseph A., cashier of the
Floyd County Bank, Edwin F., M. Alma, and Ruby Lee) ; Char-
les W. (b. June 1854, lived in Johnson City, Tenn.) ; John R.
(lived at Wallace, Va.) ; Catherine C. (m. Shell) ; Jennie V. (m.
West, Soldiers Home, Tenn.) ; James Thomas (Riner, Va.) ; H.
Crockett (a wealthy farmer, died Aug. 30, 1922, aged 60, at his
home six miles north of Bristol, Tenn.); Foster (Bristol, Tenn.);
Lucy C. (m. Weaver, lived in Elizabethton, Tenn.); Richard
(Bristol, Tenn.) ; Mary and Edwin died in infancy. James W.
LeSueur died on June 29, 1884, at age 61.

James L. LeSueur, younger brother of Moseby, was born
Oct. 15, 1798. He married, March 16, 1826, Rebecca, daughter
of John George and Mary (Beaver) Goodykoontz, and lived in
Franklin County, Virginia, on Town Creek; their children were:
George W. (b. 1836), Mary F. (1827-1904, m. Prillaman), Eliz-
abeth (b. 1829), Catherine (b. 1845), Dollie (b. 1845). James
L. LeSueur died May 31, 1871; Rebecca, his wife, died Dec. 25,
1891.

Light

The Light family is derived from Dr. Lazarus Light, who
emigrated to America from England about the end of the American Revolution. He settled in New York City, where he engaged in the practice of medicine. He later moved to Philadelphia,
continued to practice his profession, in which he attained con-

siderable eminence. Some of his children settled in Virginia.

Samuel Jackson Light (b. 1795), grandson of Dr. Lazarus Light, the immigrant, lived in the southern part of Virginia. In 1812 he moved to the county of Patrick, where he died at an advanced age. His children were, in part: John, James, Lazarus, Henry, Samuel Jackson, Jr., and Lavina. Samuel Jackson, Jr. (Nov. 1, 1828-June 22, 1888) married Salina E., daughter of David Link, and lived near Simpsons in Floyd County. He was one of the early schoolteachers, who taught many years before the "free" or public school system was inaugurated. He also taught many subscription schools. Their children were: Scipio, Brownlow, Jasper, Stella, Aurora (deceased), Cleopatra and Augusta.

Samuel and Cannaday Light were members of Company B, 54th Regiment of Virginia Infantry. John W. Light was a member of Company B, 42nd Regiment of Virginia Infantry under Captain Henry Lane. In Company I, 54th Regiment of Virginia Infantry under Captain Burwell Akers, were James Light, Simon Light, and Wilson F. Light who died at Rocky Gap, Bland County, Virginia, date unknown.

James Litterell

The Litterell family was among the very early settlers of the east end of Floyd County. In 1831, the home of the Litterells was on the county line when the boundary of Floyd County was established by the Legislature, as follows: "Beginning at the Widow Litterell's; then a straight line to John Thrasher's; then a straight line to John Cooper's old place, . . ." The Widow Litterell, mentioned, was the widow of John Litterell, whose son, James Litterell married Nancy Helms, daughter of Thomas Helms of Calloway, Franklin County, Virginia. In 1831, at the April term of court, a license was granted to James Litterell to keep an orderly "House of Private Entertainment," at his home. The fee for this was two dollars. This was the first of its kind licensed and opened within the county of Floyd.

James and Nancy Litterell had only one child, a daughter,

Polly, who married Major Samuel Marks Helm of Franklin County and lived all of her life in the old Litterell home. Their children were: 1. Biah, married James C. Martin; 2. Capt. James William Helm, a gallant officer in the Confederate army; 3. Abigail Ann, married James Sublett; and 4. George Helm, who lost his life in the Civil War.

Peter Livesay The Settler

Peter Livesay, the first of the Floyd County family, married Susannah McGhee and moved in 1848 from Henrico County, Virginia, to Floyd County and settled on a farm eight miles east of the county seat. (His grandson, Dr. J. Wilton Thurman, owns and resides on the old Livesay farm.) Their children were:

1. Meriweather, never married. He lived for many years at the old homestead.

II. Sparrel, married Mary Huff, daughter of Isaac Huff, and lived near New Haven Baptist Church. Their two daughters were: Susan m. John Lee; and Sally m. William Lee: William and John Lee were brothers and members of the Rockcastle family of Lees. William Lee was Surveyor of Floyd County for many years.

III. Orina, married John Huff, son of John Huff, the settler. They lived in the east end of the county where they raised a family of children: 1. Martha m. James Cannaday; 2. Ferdinand, lost his life in the Civil War; 3. Peter; 4. George Washington, known as "Watt," who married Mary Ann Banks, daughter of Thomas and S. Araminta.

IV. Ann A. m. David Thurman, lived at the old Livesay home; their children are: Dr. J. Wilton Thurman, a well-known physician of the east end of the county; Robert; John; and Emma m. A. Lincoln Vest of the Pine Creek section of the county.

V. Sallie, married John Helms, son of Thomas of Calloway, Franklin County, and they lived at the river crossing on

the Bent Mountain Pike. Their children were: Elizabeth m. Col.
William B. Shelor; Nancy A. m. Samuel Strickler; and Ellen m
James W. Crockett.

The Lucas Family

The Lucases came to Virginia after the downfall and execu-
tion of Charles I in 1649. The Lucases claim to be direct descendants of Sir Charles Lucas of English history.

Charles D. Lucas, Esq., John Lucas, Captain Jack, Wilson
and Samuel were settlers of Montgomery County (before the
formation of Floyd County). Wilson Lucas married Mary Webb
of Franklin County; their twelve children: Nancy m. N. Bonaparte Wilson; Julia m. Reed Hall; Docia m. Harvey P. Wilson;
Catherine m. Obediah Bishop; Elizabeth m. William Flincham;
John m. (1) Rachel Scaggs and (2) Catherine Howard; Samuel
m. Elmira Shelor; Thomas m. Ellen Cromer; Jacob m. Celia
Akers; Harvey and Charles were killed in the Civil War;

Andrew J., youngest son of Wilson and Mary Lucas, married Priscilla Altizer in 1864 and moved to Floyd County in
1878, near Simpsons; they had ten boys and one girl:

1. Daniel Stuart (b. April 26, 1865) married Gay Hall;
they had seven girls and four boys. Daniel taught school twenty-
four years, carried a rural mail route twelve years, without the
loss of a day, and has been cashier of the State Bank of Check
since its organization in 1917.

2. Aquila (b. Feb. 5, 1867) married Alice D. Iddings and is
a farmer of Simpsons, Va.; they have three boys and three girls.

3. William Q. (b. March 5, 1869) married Minnie Craghead of Athens, W. Va., and is a farmer and miller of Simpsons,
Va.; they have three boys and two girls.

4. Andrew Wilson (b. 1871?) married Callie Clower and
is a farmer of Gower, Mo.; they have five boys and a girl.

5. Elias G. (b. Nov. 21, 1873) died in young manhood.

6. Jenny Lind (b. July 5, 1876) married Lee Shank and
lives near Bedford, Virginia, with a fine family of girls and
boys.

7. Emory Jackson (b. July 1878) married Willie O. Sisson

and is a farmer of Calvert, Md.; they have five boys and a girl.

8. Doctor Clark (b. August 1880) married Eugenia Basham and is a real estate broker of Rising Sun, Md.; they have two children.

9. Joseph A. (b. August 1882) married Pearl Howery and is a carpenter of Princeton, W. Va.; they have two daughters.

10. Blaine L. (b. June 1884) married Ione Light and is an architect and civil engineer of Raleigh, N. C.; they have two sons.

11. Trigg Mosby (b. Sept. 13, 1886) married Laura Conner of Floyd County and is farming on the old homestead; they have two children.

Maberry

The family tradition is that the Maberry ancestors came directly from England and settled in Carroll County, then Grayson County, Virginia.

Isaiah lived in Carroll County, married Susannah Dalton and, after her death, married Jennie Pratt. His family of children were: William, Martin, Joshua, Alfred, Jefferson (1830), Millie, Sally, Nellie and Elizabeth, all of whom lived in Carroll County except Jefferson who married Mary W., daughter of Jacob Barringer. They moved to Floyd County in 1851, settling on a farm three miles south of Willis. Isaiah volunteered at the outbreak of the Civil War but was rejected because of physical disability. He was later detailed as a shoemaker.

Jefferson Maberry's family of children were: Jackson, married Magdaline, daughter of Madison Palmer; Winfield, married Mollie, daughter of Burwell Robertson; Wilson P., married Malinda, daughter of Solomon Spangler, and lived near Willis; George Monroe, married Dove, daughter of William P. Lawrence; M. Augustus, married Zora, daughter of Benjamin Alderman; Julia A., married William Morris; and Laura L., married Frank, son of Alexander Weddle.

Isaac Moore The Settler

Isaac Moore was born in 1789 and died in Floyd County in 1875. He married Nancy Howard, daughter of Peter Howard and Sarah (Strickland) Howard. They located on a farm one-half mile west of the Little River covered bridge on land adjoining Peter Howard. Isaac was a good farmer, a prominent citizen and a leading member of the Baptist Church. Among his family of children were: Noah B., Peter, Jacob and Vashti.

Noah B. Moore (1821-1901) lived one-half mile east of the Little River crossing, on the Richard and Job Wells farm. He was prominent in county affairs and was a member of the Virginia Legislature in 1867-8. He married, first, Artieminsa Hall, daughter of Harden Hall of Patrick County, and their children were: 1. Emeline, married James Sowers; 2. Nancy, married Harvey Gray; 3. Isaac, married, first, Mallie Altizer and, secondly, Mattie Winters; 4. Martha, married John Williams, son of Joseph; 5. Margaret, married James Lemon, son of Isaac; 6. Clementine, married Jacob Og. Williams, son of Joseph; and 7. David, married Emily Winters.

Noah B. Moore married, secondly, Jane H. Prillaman, daughter of Samuel of Franklin County. Their children were: 1. Mary Ellen, married Alfred Nixon, son of Thomas; 2. Samuel, married Eliza Ellen Naff; 3. Permelia, married Andrew Martin; 4. Laura E., married George Simmons, son of Roley M., and lives five miles north of the courthouse; 5. Annabelle, married Luther Blackwell, son of Moses; 6. Eugenia, married Thomas Huff, for many years a merchant of Floyd; and 7. Dollie, married Luther Jones.

Nixon

Thomas L. Nixon was the son of Pattison and Elizabeth Nixon of Dufton, Westmoreland, England, who emigrated to this country in 1830. They left England on August 11 and landed in New York, October 27, 1830, with the entire family of five children: Mary, William, John, James and Thomas, who was the youngest of the family. They settled the same year in Wythe County near the lead mines of that district. The entire family was christened and registered in the church of their hometown in England. Pattison Nixon moved from Wythe to the county of Franklin where he made his permanent home. Thomas L. Nixon moved to Surry County, North Carolina, and still later settled in Floyd County.

Thomas L. Nixon was a prominent member of the Primitive Baptist Church in Floyd County, was long one of the supervisors of the county, and was a member of Co. I, 54th Virginia Infantry in the Confederate army; he died January 6, 1900, and is buried near his old home in Floyd County. He married Elizabeth Nixon, his first cousin, and their children were:

A. Jane married Jacob Smith of Floyd Court House, later of Indian Valley; their children: 1. Elizabeth m. E. L. Dickerson; 2. Thomas P. m. Bessie Wescott; 3. Alfred W. m. Carrie Tomer (Tower?) ; 4. Kittie m. Elijah Weeks; 5. Mary m. Harrison Caldwell; 6. Arthur m. Etta Reed; 7. Laura m. Walker Quesenberry; 8. Abner B. m. Ada Dickerson; 9. Luther M. m. Opal Harman; 10. Tazwell Jacob m. Minnesota Harman.

B. George W. married Wilmoth (Willie) J. Earles, daughter of John, Jan. 11, 1877; their children: 1. Mary Elizabeth m. Albert W. Simmons; 2. William Clifton m. Cela Clyde Harman; 3. Mattie Jane m. Amos Thompson; 4. Lucy E. m. Oliver W. Slusher; 5. John T. m. Bertha Summers; 6. George Grover; 7. General Patterson; 8. Wellington Lee (Wellie) m. Clara Richardson; 9. Effie Essie m. Oliver W. Slusher, 2nd wife.

C. Mollie married Joseph Howell of Floyd Court House, later of White Oak Grove; he was a Confederate soldier, wounded in battle; their children: 1. Abagail m. Joseph L. Lester; 2. Minnie m. Tilden H. Sowers, son of Cabell; 3. David Thomas m. Minnie Lester, daughter of Charles; 4. George P. m. Dora Simmons, daughter of Daniel; 5. May m. Walter Keith, son of Jacob; 6. Edward moved to Iowa and married there.

D. Albert P. (b. Dec. 19, 1849) married Mary Ellen Moore, daughter of Noah B., October 1878; their children: 1. Noah Thomas m. May Dickerson; 2. William A. m. Mary Akers; 3. Charles m. Agnes Altizer; 4. Asa Ward; 5. Posey G.

m. Bettie Downing; 6. Dollie; 7. Dr. Samuel m. Gertrude Altizer;
8. Maude; 9. Virginia.

E.   Emma married John W. Richardson, Sept. 1880; their
children: 1. Paton Thomas m. Pearl Cromer; 2. Lilly m. Daniel
Condiff; 3. Nancy m. Edward Childress; 4. William m. Olie
Akers; 5. Bessie m. William Greer; 6. Letcher; 7. Mallie; 8. Rice;
9. Mary; 10. Fred.

Lewis Payne The Settler

The Paynes were numerous in Colonial Virginia and accord-
ing to the tax records owned large bodies of land and many
slaves. Those of the name serving in the Colonial wars were:
John, John and William Payne. Augustine, Francis, George,
Henry, Josias, Jr., Nicholas and William Payne were in the
Virginia Militia in the Revolutionary War. (McAllister's
Virginia Militia in the Revolutionary War).

The Floyd County family is derived from Augustine Payne
(m. Katherine Young) of Fauquier County, Virginia, who was
the father of the following children: I. Lewis (d. 1860) II. James
and III. Lucinda.

Lewis Payne was born in Fauquier County where he married Elizabeth Bowen, daughter of Stephen and Elizabeth (Ball)
Bowen. About 1825 they moved to the present county of Floyd
with their family of twelve children. They settled in the east
end of the county on a creek which has since borne the name of
Paynes Creek. Lewis Payne was a member of the first court
of Justices of the Peace. He was senior member and was
presiding justice for some time, as well as sheriff of the county,
which then included the office of treasurer.

Lewis and Elizabeth Payne's children were: 1. Stephen
m. first, Mrs. Huff, secondly, Anna Aspinwall, 1882; 3. Lafayette; 4. Edwin m. Lucinda Lawson; 5. Marion; 6. James;
7. Jefferson; 8. William m. Susan Smith; 9. Elvira m. Alex Boyd;
10. Katherine m. Joseph Kelley; 11. Mildred m. Jackson Akers;
12. Virginia m. Isaac Howery.

2.   John Bowen Payne married Ellen Smith (1831) and
she was living in Roanoke in 1922 at the great age of 91 years.

Ellen was the daughter of Jabez and Elizabeth (Light) Smith and granddaughter of Humphrey Smith, the settler. John Bowen Payne resided at the old Lewis Payne homestead where he was a prominent farmer, mill owner, and a member of the Virginia Legislature in 1871-2. He was known as Col. John Payne. Their children were: (a) Horace, never married; (b) Virgil H. m. first, Adaline Dobyns and, secondly, Martha Mitchell; (c) Gideon m. Mollie Long of Pennsylvania; (d) Marcella m. Henry Shelor, son of Col. William B. Shelor; (e) Flora E. m. Captain John S. Woods; (f) Cora L. m. Edward Cannaday, son of William A. and Sarah J. (Shelor) Cannaday; (g) Dora A. m. George W. Jett; (h) Ada m. William Francis, son of Captain William Francis. One son, Howard, died in infancy.

Those serving in the Civil War were: Francis M. Payne, a member of Co. A, 24th Virginia Infantry under Captain C. M. Stigleman, and later transferred to the 21st Virginia Cavalry; James H. Payne, killed in the battle of Kernstown, May 23, 1862, and a member of Co. B, 42d Virginia Infantry under Captain Henry Lane; and F. M. Payne, Co. G, 21st Cavalry, killed at Moorefield, West Virginia, June 5, 1864.

Peterman

Michael Peterman emigrated from Pennsylvania to Montgomery County in the late eighteenth century. In 1860, Daniel Peterman, Jr., son of Daniel Peterman and grandson of Michael Peterman, moved from Montgomery County to Floyd County and settled near White Oak Grove.

Daniel Peterman, Jr., married Paradine Lester, daughter of Hulen Lester, in 1840; he died during the Civil War. Daniel and Paradine had ten children.

1. George, died in camp during the Civil War.

2. Octavia married, first, Michael Surface, and they had two children: George and Charles; after the death of her husband Octavia married J. Akers and moved to Kansas, where she died.

3. Ellen married Frank Horton; they had eleven children: Margaret, Lacy, Thomas, Dudley, John, William, Frank, Jeffer-

son, Sidney, Nellie and Katherine.

4.   William married in Ohio but moved to Ft. Worth, Texas.

5.   Dudley married Virginia Williams; they had three children: Ocie, Jessie and Alice.

6.   Susan married Tazewell Pugh; they had three children: Willard, Edwin and Cline.

7.   Giles married Alice Graham; they had four children: Clarence, Beulah, Gold and Doris.

8.   Virginia married Lafayette Phlegar; they had three children: Lillian, Ethel and Katherine.

9.   Harvey married Angeline Earles and settled in Washington County, Va.; they had five children: Roscoe, Stella, Ollie, Willie and Glenna.

10.   Kate married John Altizer and settled in Montgomery County; they had three children: Olya, Otho and Gray. Of the ten children of Daniel Peterman, Giles and Kate are the only ones living (1923).

George Peterman was a member of Andrew Dickerson's Co. A, 54th Virginia Infantry. He died in service at Christiansburg, Va., in 1861. Crockett Peterman was a member of the same company.

The Phillips Family

The Phillips family dates far back in Colonial Virginia.

Tobias Phillips is the ancestor of the Floyd County family. He came from the Valley of Virginia about the year 1780 with his young family and settled on Greasy Creek within the now county of Carroll and near the present Floyd County line. The Phillipses of the Valley of Virginia were from Wales and had been living in the valley only a few years when Tobias moved to Greasy Creek. His wife was a Miss Henson; their family of children numbered fourteen, seven sons and seven daughters. Two daughters married men by the name of Dalton; the seven known children:

I.   William (b. abt. 1765), wife's name unknown, their four children:

A.   Tobias (b. 1790) married Lucy Cox (b. 1794), daughter of Ambrose Cox, and lived in Indian Valley; their eight children:

1. William C. (b. 1814) married Martha Snow and moved to Henry County, Va.; their children: Dr. Frederick (Ferdinand?) S.; William; Dolphus; Peter; Elvira; and Jane. Of these, Peter Phillips lived in Carroll County, where he raised a large family and was prominent in politics. He was Sheriff and Constable for many years.

2. Nancy (1816-1878) married Robert W. Phillips, son of John and Sally (Worrell) Phillips; their children:

(a) Luke.

(b) John T. married Martha Burnett; their children: Albert, William, John E., Julina, Florence, Nancy.

(c) Robert W., Jr. (1841-1911) m. Allie Wade; their children: Nathan, Robert L., Terry, Delphine and Allie.

(d) Tobias married Elizabeth Quessenberry; their children: Andrew C., Robert T., Noah, Lee, Clarence, Dessie, Abigail, Elly, Nannie, Ruth, Hattie and Rosa.

(e) Noah married Victoria Quessenberry and moved to West Va.; their children: Ida, Norman, Foster and Gerushia.

(f) Mary married, first, Noah Duncan; their children: Martha and Alberta; Mary married, secondly, Maston Cox; their children: Noah, Ham, Shem, Joseph (Japheth?), Nannie, Minty and Sarah.

(g) Sarah married Randolph Phillips; their children: Embazetta, and others?

(h) Nannie married Beauford Cox; their children: Walter, Henry and Louis.

(i) Martha married Noah Wade; their children: James, Robert, Noah, Jr., Joseph, Charles, Saba, Delphia, Nannie and Sarah.

3. Ambrose C. (1818-1885) married Lucy Jennings; their twelve children:

(a) Polk, no issue.

(b) Ballard P. married Amanda Moore; their children: William N., Ballard P., Jr., Alfred T., Henderson, Katherine, Susanna, Louvena, and Victoria.

(c) Thomas J. married Sarah J. Cooper; their children: James, John, Lee, Mary, Elizabeth, Florence, Ann, Ellen, Alverta and Roena.

(d) Henderson married Emazetta Cox and moved to West Va.

(e) Ambrose, Jr., married Maranda Moore; their children, Homer, Walter, Ambrose, Liona, Larma, Alberta and Lillie.

(f) Martha married Jackson Wright and moved to Ohio.

(g) Sarah married Carter Good; their children: James, Ballard P., Ambrose, George, Belle and Lina.

(h) Nancy married Jacob Nester; they had one son, Preston.

(i) Louvena married Owen Quesenberry; no issue.

(j) Mary married Robert N. Quesenberry; their children: Benjamin, Albert, Victoria, Loula, Minty, Lucy, Mettie and Lillie.

(k) Adaline married Judson Quesenberry; their children: Dillard, Cazza, Millard, Tazza, Herman, Florida, Mary, Sarah and Lora.

(1) Elizabeth married Jacob Duncan; their children: Claybourn, Leburn, Harley, Jesse, Cordillia, Sis, Jane, Lucy, Pearl, Bessie, Woody and Mary.

4. Sarah (b. 1820) married Slate Cox and had one son, Frazier.

5. Anderson (b. 1822) married Sally Cox and moved West.

6. Henderson (1824-1891) married Mary Cole and settled in Henry County, Va.; he was a member of the firm of Headen, Phillips & Co., pioneer hog and cattle drovers, handling cattle and hogs of Floyd and Carroll counties and driving them to the Eastern markets. Their children: William W.; Walter H.; Charles; Mary; Fletcher; and Lucy. Of these, William W. Phillips married Lillian H. Draper and raised a family of eight sons and five daughters. He lived for some years in Henry County, then in Floyd County, later moved to Roanoke City where he was traveling agent for the *Roanoke Times*. Four of his sons were in the World War, three in service in France:

1st Lt. Tobias C. Phillips, now a lawyer of Bluefield, W. Va.; Roy D. Phillips, proprietor of Bluefield Shoe Co., Bluefield, W. Va.; Sgt. E. H. Phillips of Fort Dupont, Delaware; and Harry F. Phillips of Roanoke, Va.

      7. Preston (1826-1889) married Martha P. Cox; their children: Waller, Marsha, Florence, Daisy, Woody and Damis.

      8. Tobias (1828-1890), no children.

      B. William, Jr. (b. 1794) married and moved to South Bend, Indiana.

      C. Randolph (b. 1805) married Polly Cox; they had nine sons and two daughters:

      1. William (b. 1829) married Eliza J. Montgomery; their children: George W., James R., Elder John M., Allen T., Mary J., Columbia E., and Susan M.

      2. Mahlon (b. 1831) married, first, Rachel Montgomery; their children: Marion F., Robert J., Caswell and Elsie. After his first wife's death, Mahlon married Elizabeth Viperman, and their children were: Julina, Loula, Marsha, Onie and Virgie.

      3. John, no issue.

      4. Fleming (b. 1835) married, first, Lucy Phillips; their children: Rosanna and Vinesa. He married, secondly, Martha J. Quesenberry; their children: Grant, Jethero and Delia.

      5. Randolph (b. 1837) married Sarah Phillips [Nancy, Tobias, William].

      6. Bryant (1839-1916) married Allie Phillips; their children: John H., Mack, Walker, Sylvester, Jethero, Louisa, Luvina, Phoebe Jane, Polly, Orlena, and Alverta.

      7. Enoch (1840-1918) married Susan Quesenberry; their children: McNelia, William J., Albert E., Walker E., Cardle, Lelia and Virgie.

      8. Noah (b. 1843) married Elizabeth (Betsy) Quesenberry; their children: LeRoy, Leechman, Zebrum, Ulysses, Cornelius, Lanna, Sylvira and Leticia.

      9. Henderson (b. 1845) married Margaret M. Quesenberry; their children: Elkana, Crockett D., Hosa, Bennett G., Rosetta, Emma and Nora.

      10. Elsie (b. 1846) married Tobias D. Phillips; their children: Walker, Bryant P., Tobias, Fleming R., Mary, Phoebe,

Sally, Rosetta and Lucy.

    11. Millie, no issue.

    D. Nancy married Braxton Cox; their children: Lawyer, William, Armstead, Owen, Thimer, Millie, Sarah, Elsie, Lucy and Nancy.

    [End of William]

    II. Jehu Phillips (b. abt. 1770) married Phoebe J. Darnell; their children:

    A. Tobias D. married Elsie Phillips [Randolph, William].

    B. John married Polly Nester; their children: Jefferson D. and Caroline.

    C. Eliza married Ephram Dickens.

    D. Polly married Jackson Cox; their children: Thomas J., George V., Artamissie and Emeline.

    E. Allie married Bryant Phillips [Randolph, William].

    III. John Phillips (b. 1775) married Sally Worrell; their children:

    A. John C. (b. 1810) married and moved to Plymouth, Ill.; among his descendants was Elder Wyatt Phillips, an able and prominent minister of the Primitive Baptist Church.

    B. Robert W. (1813-1903) married Nancy Phillips [Tobias, William].

    C. Catherine (b. 1815) married Blanch Duncan; their children: Solomon, Blanch, Jr., John, Andrew, Reed, Robert, Iteemus, Green B., Beauford, Mary, Jane, Ruth and Susan.

    IV. Richard (b. 1778) married Catherine Good; their children:

    A. Aaron (b. 1800) married a Miss Smith; their children:

    1. Obediah married Sarah Duncan; their children: Ellis, Mary and Delphia.

    2. Richard, Jr., married Julia Turman; their children: Norman, Beecher, Corbet, Simmons, Dewey, Emazetta, Lora, Isora and Trulove.

    3. Julia married William C. Hollandsworth; their children: John C., Aaron R., William G., Sylvester P., Amanda,

Elizabeth, Victoria, Darthulia, Cordillia, Lina and Aldora.

4. Lina married Ballard Quesenberry; their children: Calvin, Joseph, Malachi, Lafayett, Perry, Susanna, Emazetta, Trifeena and Mary E.

5. Virginia married John Reece; their children: Joseph W., James E., Lee and Early E.

6. Patsy married James Marshall; no children.

B. Tobias (b. 1805) married Martha Hollandsworth; their children: Thomas, Joseph, John, Corrilda, Sarah J., Syreena and Eliza J.

C. Susan (b. 1807) married Amon Moore; their children: John N., Thomas, Malinda, Amanda, Maranda and Liona.

D. Sarah (b. 1809) married James Quesenberry; their children: Asa, Ballard, Jackson, Tobias, Walker, Milly, Betsy, Jane and Delilah.

E. Fannie (name of husband unknown), from whom were descended: Wesley, Sally and William B. Phillips.

V. Nancy (b. 1772) married Berry Duncan and settled on Berty's Creek in Carroll County; their children: Joshua, John, Noah, Tobias and Peggy.

VI. Thomas, moved to Tennessee.

VII. Joseph, moved to West Virginia.

Those serving in the Civil War: In Co. B, 54th Virginia Infantry, under Col. Robert C. Trigg, Lt. Col. Wm. B. Shelor and Captains Jackson Godbey and Armstead O. Dobyns were Enoch Phillips, captured at Bentonville, N. C.; Flemon Phillips, died in the service; Bryant, James, John, Preston, Mahlon, Robert, Tobias D., Noah, James P., and Randolph Phillips. In Company B, 42nd Virginia Infantry, was Aaron Phillips, wounded at Winchester, Va., May 25, 1862, and later captured at Spottsylvania C. H., May 3, 1864, taken to Point Lookout, and discharged after the surrender.

Nathan Phillips was a member of the Constitutional Convention after the close of the Civil War. He was killed at his home in Floyd by a kicking horse soon after returning from the Convention in Richmond, Virginia.

William and Randolph Phillips were two of the largest landowners in Floyd County at the time of its organization in

1831, as shown by the Land Tax Book.

(The author is indebted to Robert L. Phillips, son of Robert Phillips and Allie Wade, his wife, for much of the family data in this sketch, also to the assistance of Elder John M. Phillips and others.)

The Phlegar (Pfluger) Family

Hans Georg Frederick Pflüger and his family came to Philadelphia in 1731 on the ship "Samuel." At this time there were few settlements in Pennsylvania except in the vicinity of Philadelphia. Soon a few brave settlers began to venture to the west of the Susquehanna River to make their homes, though the Indians still held this territory. Among these pioneers was the Pflüger family. They cut down trees, built rude log houses and barns and cultivated the bits of land thus cleared. This area was later organized as York County. Most of the settlers brought with them a supply of household goods, seeds, and implements. By tilling the fertile soil with skill and industry, they were soon able to live comfortably. In 1733 the Lutherans west of the river began to hold religious services in barns and houses under the leadership of the famous John Casper Stoever. He went about preaching to the settlers, despite the perils of wilderness travel. He baptized George Frederick, the younger son of the Pflüger family, who was born in 1735. Stoever also officiated at the marriage of the daughter, Maria Catherine, to John Caussler in 1742.

Hans George Frederick Pflüger signed his will Dec. 10, 1753, and died before Feb. 4, 1754, when the will was probated. The original document is lost, but the quaint translation made by Bartholome Maule, the schoolmaster, is on record. He divided his property among his three surviving children after making provisions for his wife.

His two sons, Jacob and George Frederick, owned adjoining farms on the outskirts of the present city of York. Both, with several of their sons, served in the Revolutionary War. The late Rev. Abraham Hogan, of Floyd, wrote: "My grandfather, Abraham Phlegar, told me before he died that his father was in the memorable march without shoes over the frozen ground, and from that exposure was taken with a 'breast complaint' from which he died." That was George Frederick, born 1735, whose will was probated in 1791. His wife, Anna Maria Margaretha, lived until 1816.

Soon after the Revolution, five of the young Phlegars set out to make homes in Virginia. Two sons of Jacob are on record as having resided at "Fincastletown," Virginia, but have not been traced further. George, Abraham and Michael, sons of George Frederick, lived for a few years at Middletown, Frederick County, Virginia. Soon after 1800 they sold their land in Frederick County and moved further on, settling in Montgomery County, which was later organized as Floyd County. In 1802 Abraham bought 279 acres from Colonel Andrew Lewis, son of General Andrew Lewis, the great Indian fighter; George bought 365 acres from Colonel Lewis. Michael's land adjoined the farms of both his brothers, and they spent the remainder of their lives on these plantations.

In 1813 they and their neighbors organized the Zion Lutheran Congregation and used for worship a log schoolhouse near the spot where the present church stands.

Michael Phlegar's home, which stood next to the Zion churchyard, passed into other hands and is gone. William S. Phlegar, son of Benjamin, owns the house of George, his grandfather. This place, like Abraham's, has never been owned by anyone out of direct line of descent. At the death of Abraham Phlegar, his property was bought by his grandson, David Willis, who lived there until his death in 1925, having left the homestead to his children. The ancient trees, the century-old boxwood, the huge Dutch chimneys, the quaint staircases of those old homes speak eloquently of pioneer days in Floyd County. Abraham Phlegar's house was the third built in what is now the town of Floyd; however the present dwelling was not erected until 1822.

    I. George Phlegar (1762-1839) married (1788) Mary M. Goodykoontz (d. July 7, 1850, aged 81 yrs.), daughter of Hans Georg; their children:

    A. Elizabeth (1789-1850), never married.

    B. Lydia.

C. Joseph (b. 1794), married and had the following children: 1. Isaac; 2. John; 3. Margaret m. Slusher; 4. Calvin; 5. Eliza m. Simmons, and 6. Sarah m. LeSueur.

D. Isaac (1796-1859), married, first, Sophia _____, and secondly, Sarah _____, and had 7 children: 1. Jacob; 2. David; 3. Joseph; 4. Magdaline; 5. Rufus; 6. Harvey; and 7. George.

E. David (1806-1891) moved to Fayette County, Missouri.

F. Rhoda.

G. Benjamin (1812-1892), married, first, Mary _____; their children: 1. George; 2. Andrew, never married; 3. Simon P. m. Rebecca _____ and lived in Lexington, Mo.; 4. Ellen m. David Willis; 5. Gideon, never married; 6. Mary m. Judge Merritt; 7. Adaline, never married. Benjamin married a second time, after the death of his first wife; their children: 1. Henrietta m. Rev. George W. Summers; 2. John N., never married; 3. Lillie, never married; 4. Nancy m. John Smith; 5. Benjamin d. in infancy; 6. Dora, m. Irving Roney and lives in New York City; 7. Estella m. Dr. J. S. Smith; 8. William S. m. Emma Smith; 9. Mattie m. Brown; 10. Jessie d. in infancy.

Seven of George Phlegar's grandsons served in the Confederate army: George (killed in the Battle of Gettysburg, 1863), Andrew, Gideon (killed in battle), Simon, all sons of Benjamin; Calvin, son of Joseph; Joseph and George, sons of Isaac. At least seven of George Phlegar's descendants were in the World War. One, Hagan Phlegar, was with the Marines, first of the American forces sent into battle.

II. Abraham Phlegar (1776-1865) married Margaret Goodykoontz (1775-1851), daughter of Hans Georg; their nine children:

A. Leah (1798-1880) married Francis Hogan and they were the parents of:

1. Mary Hogan, married Nathaniel Lancaster; their children: Rev. Davis; Leah; Hester; Abigail; Ruth; and Clinton.

2. Rev. Abraham Hogan (b. 1837) married Sarah C. Organ; their children: Mary Elizabeth; Sarah F. m. Whitlock; Minnie L. m. Draper; Callahill Abraham; Rosa V.

B. Rachel (1800-1851).

C. Eliza (1801-1877) married Jacob Epperly (1801-

1883) ; they had eleven children: 1. Canaan; 2. Calvin, moved to Bonne Terre, Missouri; 3. Eva m. Trout of Roanoke; 4. Rachel m. Palmer and lives at Bonne Terre, Mo.; 5. Ann m. Phlegar and lived in Roanoke; 6. Addison (b. 1832) m. Alice Brammer; 7. Akin (b. 1834) m. Ann Eliza Strickler; 8. W. H. Epperly (b. 1837) lives in Salem; 9. Lucinda m. Franklin; 10. Lizzie m. Brammer; and 11. Clementine m. Young.

    D. Maza (1802-1881), never married.

    E. Delilah (1804-1884), never married.

    F. Eli (1808-1864) married Ann C. _____; their children: 1. Judge Archer A. m. Susan Shanks of Salem; their children: David S.; Mrs. E. B. Crosley; Mary; Hunter; and Archer. 2. Ella m. _____ Johnson; their children: Anna m. Campbell; Susan m. Price; Richard; Lettie; and Archer P.

    G. Arabella (1809-1865) married Jonathan Willis (1806-1889) ; they had eleven children: 1. James, of Washington, D. C.; 2. David; 3. Hamilton; 4. Bennet; 5. Peter; 6. John; 7. Henry; 8. George; 9. Margaret m. Williamson; 10. Lavina m. Harman; and 11. Martha m. Harman.

    H. Lavinia (1813-1890) married Owen Wade (1809-1884) and lived on Burks Fork; they had twelve children:

    1. William B. (b. 1833) married Eliza J. Summers; their children: Kate Cora m. A. F. Harvey; Ida Stella m. W. S. Dornbaser; Emmett Lee, never married; Lelia Lavina m. Joseph A. Hawkins; Charles A.

    2. Abraham m. M. E. Allen and they had one child, Ann Levina.

    3. Eli married E. F. Allen; their children: Laura m. Lawrence Lewis; Herbert, never married; Robert Lee.

    4. Amanda M. married Henry M. Goodykoontz; their children: Winton, never married; Lou Ella; Webster; Edward; Flora; and Ida m. Arthur B. Allison.

    5. Hannah married J. B. Albright; they had ten children: Amanda H. m. H. A. Dickerson; David H. m. Belle Rader; Charles B. m. Alia Ann Slusher; Nannie m. A. J. Knowles; Lillie A. m. S. H. Keith; Emmett L. m. _____; Henry E. m. Lizena Hylton; Lucy F., never married; Marks A.; and Ellen N.

    6. Sarah married Cornelius C. Weeks; their children:

Kyle M.; Esper R.; Stella F.

7. Julia A. married William L. Bird; their children: Nannie L. m. S. E. Hylton; Eli.

8. Peyton J. married Sue P. Hylton; their children: Edward W.; William A.; and Lena E.

9. Eliza A. married L. D. Weddle; they had one child, William, who married Dollie DeHart.

10. Joseph married Ann Fisher; they had two sons: Charles B. and William O.

11. Mary married Isaac Taylor; they had one daughter, Clara.

12. David B., died young.

I. Lucinda Phlegar (1815-1871), never married.

Abraham Phlegar gave to the county the acre of ground upon which the Court House stands. His son, Eli, who later settled at Christiansburg, was the first lawyer the county produced. Eli's son, Archer, became one of the foremost lawyers of the state.

The following grandsons of Abraham Phlegar served in the Confederate army: Archer A. Phlegar, Abraham Hogan, Akin, Addison and Headen Epperly; David, Bennet, Samuel, Thomas, James and Peter Willis. Five of Abraham Phlegar's great-grandsons were commissioned officers in the World War.

III. Michael Phlegar (1780-1850) married Eva Catherine _____ (d. July 4, 1858, aged 84 yrs. 9 mos. & 16 days), their children:

A. Sally m. Hamilton; B. Mary; C. Margaret (Peggy); D. Mahala m. Bishop; E. Samuel; F. John.

Michael's descendants are not numerous; among them are James and Harvey L. of Giles County, and Judson of Floyd County.

Poff (Pfaff)

The Poff family, of German descent, the name originally spelled **Pfaff**, is among the very early settlers of Floyd County. Henry Poff, with his five brothers: Anthony, Charles, Peter, Michael and Samuel, and John Poff (Johannes Pfaff), probably a cousin, settled in the east end of the county about 1805.

Anthony Poff married Sally Wilson; their children:

1. Peter;

2. Joshua married Rachel Jackson; their children: William Isaac; Jacob H. m. Elizabeth Poff, daughter of Fleming, Sr.; Sarah J.; Lydia Rosabelle m. Samuel Wilson of Willis, Va.; Daniel Headen moved to Idaho; James A.; Charles Lafayette; and John Floyd;

3. Isaac; 4. Andrew; 5. Katie; 6. Mary Jane; 7. Julia; 8. Emeline; 9. Doshia; 10. Eliza; and 11 Betsy.

Michael and Samuel Poff moved to Indiana.

From tombstones in Salem Baptist Churchyard:

"Henry Poff, born Feb. 13, 1792, died April 26, 1854"

"Sarah Poff, born March 25, 1794, died October 11, 1854"

Henry Poff, the settler, had five sons and seven daughters:

1. James married, first, Miss Gray; their children: Caroline m. Graham; Matilda m. Joseph Sumpter; Martha m. Samuel ("Slick") Conner; Amanda m. J. V. Carr; Rebecca m. Andrew Conner; Fleming H. m. Paradine Conner, daughter of Nathan, Sr.; William Riley moved to Missouri; second set of children: Mima m. Wesley Gardner; Lucinda m. William J. Sowder; Lyzena m. Noah Wilson; Ennis moved to Missouri.

2. Flemmon married, first, Barbara Ellen Furrow and, secondly, Martha F. Byrd.

3. Samuel married Matilda Dewese.

4. Adaline married Lewis Coswell.

5. Annie married Madison Shockey.

6. Margaret married John Weaver, moved to Indiana and died there.

7. Eliza married Adam Furrow.

8. Lucinda married John O. Conner; she died at the age of 92 years, and he at the age of 96.

9. Charity married Burwell Wimmer.

10. William H. (June 5, 1826-Jan. 12, 1903) married Mary Jane (1834-1904), daughter of Henry W. Carr; their children: Ira Wilson m. Callie, daughter of Wilson Huff; Johnson J. m. Miriam, daughter of Robert W. Kropff; Della J. m. Dr. Albert A. Cannaday, son of Dr. Asa H.; William Jackson m. Minnie, daughter of Dr. Asa H. Cannaday; Alfred m. Louisa, daughter

of Dr. Thee Greer of Callaway; Minnie E. m. George A. Cannaday, son of Dr. Asa H.

11. Joseph married, first, Miss Sumpter and, secondly, Miss Snuffer; his children: Alice m. W. J. Kropff of Check, Va.; and William of Smithfield, Missouri.

12. Lydia married Samuel R. Conner.

John Poff (b. 1790?), probably a cousin of Henry, the settler, married a Miss Wilson, and lived in the Poff and Wilson neighborhood in the east end of Floyd County. Their family of children were, in part:

1. Harvey.

2. Lewis (1828-1863) married Nancy, daughter of Daniel and Lizzie (Lawrence) Epperly; their children: Taylor m. Ellen Jackson; Eliza m. John Crump; Perry W. (b. 1853) m. Nellie Mullins, daughter of James, and lives in Bluefield, West Va., where he is a well-known photographer, they had four children: Hazel, Lewis, Perry and Dorothea; Lizzie m. Fleming Richards; Henry m. Emma Light; Rosa m. Callahill Vest.

The Radford Family

James Radford was born near Jamestown, Virginia [according to tradition]. He married and moved to Franklin County when his oldest child was only a few years old. He secured a title to all the lands lying between the waters of Runnet Bag and Otter creeks, bounded by the top of the Blue Ridge, and settled near the base of this mountain. James was a wealthy man; his near neighbor was James Cannaday who owned a similar tract of land just south of Radford's. Both Radford and Cannaday raised large quantities of corn which they sold to the early settlers in Floyd County. James Radford's seven known children:

I. Lewis Radford married a Miss Scruggs and settled on Black Ridge in Floyd County.

II. Mary Radford married Isaac Janney; their children, in part:

A. Fleming Janney married Mary Ann, daughter of Samuel Boyd; they moved to Texas in 1876.

B. Elizabeth Janney married Wiley A. Via, the Baptist

preacher; their children: Thomas, Martha Ellen, Flem and others.

C. Malinda Janney married Wid Rakes; they had one child, Seifus (Cephas?).

D. Sarah Janney married Tazewell Radford.

III. Elizabeth Radford—no information.

IV. Joshua Radford married Fannie Thompson; one (known) daughter:

A. Hulda Radford married James Underwood; their children:

1. W. (son) married Liza Underwood.

2. Puss married Fleming Janney (robbed of a quite a sum of money many years ago), son of P. Ike Janney; their children: Lucinda m. Jake Pate; Elkanah, never married.

3. Mary Jane married Henderson Duncan.

4. Ann married James Crew; their children: James, Samuel, others.

5. Octavia married James Trail (7 feet tall).

6. Sarah Frances Underwood married Jake, son of John and Bessie (Adkins) Brogan, grandson of James Adkins, a pioneer settler on Runnet Bag Creek.

7. James Sucker Underwood married a sister to Thomas Peters.

V. Samuel Radford married Minnie Underwood; their children:

A. Sintha married Alexander Underwood; their children: Samuel, William, Nellie, others.

B. James, died a young man.

VI. Rosanna Radford married (name unknown); their children:

A. Polly, never married.

B. Mildred (Milly) married James Glaspie; their children: Josie m. Martin Thomas; Lausie; Polly; James; Charlie and William.

C. Rosanna married Jacob West; their children: William; George; Matt; Jacob; Mary; Elizabeth and Washington.

D. Sealy, never married.

E. Franklin, never married.

F. James.

G. George.

VII. Robert Radford married Eleanor Underwood, daughter of Samuel, and lived two miles east of S. T. Turner's store near the Radford Burying Ground; their children:

A. Rosanna married Sparrel Janney; their children: Adline, Mahlon and Ellen.

B. Lewis married Elizabeth Via; they lived at Silver Leaf on the Floyd-Franklin pike; their children: Mary; Ellen Jane; Gabriel m. Elizabeth Nolen, and their children were: Ocea, Augusta and Eldee; Robert; Samuel; Octavia and Amos.

C. Wm. Riley (b. Aug. 3, 1825), a Primitive Baptist preacher, married Dec. 2, 1845, Artie M. (b. Sept. 14, 1818, Patrick Co.), daughter of Edward and Mary (Rakes) Cochran; they lived near Barton's Spur; their children:

1. Edward Americus (b. Oct. 26, 1846), married Addie Underwood; their children: Peachy m. a daughter of Clabron Thomas; Ophelia m. Stanton Lawrence; Beulah m. Kelly.

2. Robert Wingfield (b. March 29, 1849-d. 1908).

3. Mary A. Elender (b. Oct. 31, 1851), married Everett DeHart; their child: William Riley.

4. Elias (b. May 2, 1854), married Mary, daughter of Pleasant and Jane (Foster) Thomas; their children: Floyd, Martin, Thomas, Eura, Samuel and Alice.

5. Roda Rosanna (b. Oct. 4, 1856), married Jake West; their children: Wm. Riley, Roscoe, Mintie, Pearl, Winfield and Frasier.

6. Lemuel Cassell (b. July 24, 1860), married Lucinda Emeline (b. March 1856), daughter of William and Martha Jane (Shortt) Lemon; they are living at Ridgeway, Henry Co.; their children:

(a) Tula Artie (b. Aug. 19, 1883), m. John Cowen; their children: Clarence, Pauline, Gretchen, Mildred and Ty Cobb.

(b) Lula May (b. Oct. 3, 18—), m. Will Wilson; their children: Margaret, Hubbard, Charles, Mary, Lucinda, Eugene, Fred, one other.

(c) Maudie (b. May 24, 1896), died in infancy at Spray, N. C.

(d) Harvey Simmons (b. June 24, 1897), a soldier in the

World War.

D. Jesse Radford married Dollie Thomas (sister to Stephen) ; their children: Timandy, Ezra, Matt and Mike.

E. Polly Radford married Burwell Janney; their children:

1. Robert married in Zanesville, Ohio.

2. Peter married Linda Via; their children: Lida, Albert, Homer, others.

3. Jesse died at Boones Mill, Va., at the age of 45 years.

4. Ruth married John Janney; their children: Seifus, Taswell, and one girl.

5. Ellen Janney married John Vest.

6. Mary, died in infancy.

7. Charlie, no issue.

8. Moses.

The Rakes Family

The Rakes family lived in the Blue Ridge section, which is the boundary line between Floyd and Patrick.

The family claims to be of Irish descent, and some members have resided in Patrick and Franklin counties for many years.

Elizabeth Raikes (Rakes) who lived to be 105 years old, married James Cannaday who served under General Nathaniel Greene, and for whom a Virginia military land warrant was issued prior to December 21, 1784. James died in 1817. They were the parents of: Mary (1770-1847) m. Pleasant Thomas; William; James, Jr.; John; David; Charles; and Pleasant.

Charles Rakes (doubtless the Charles Rakes who carried the surveyor's chain in surveying the county line between Franklin and Henry counties in 1785 or 1786 and received his pay in tobacco: 144 pounds) was one of the Petitioners in the year 1797 who petitioned the General Assembly of Virginia for the establishment of the present town of South Boston. The petition is quoted, with some of its signers:

PETITION TO THE GENERAL ASSEMBLY 1797

Petition of the Inhabitants of Montgomery, Franklin and Pittsylvania counties for establishing a New Town, in Halifax County, Virginia, as Tobacco Market.

Thomas Goodson, Jr.	Jonathan Graham
Aaron Graham	Henry Helton
Wm. Cannaday, Sr.	Edward Helton
John Cannaday	Pleasant Thomas
Thomas Goodson	Charles Thomas, Jr.
Daniel Shelor	Charles Rakes
John Simmons	Rich'd Wood

Charles Rakes lived in Franklin County on the waters of Smiths River, near where the counties of Franklin and Patrick join, where he raised his family, one of whom was Samuel.

Samuel Rakes married Dec. 18, 1815, Lucinda, daughter of John Nowlin; they were the parents of:

1. Nancy Rakes, married Fleming Turner, son of Francis.

2. Richard Rakes, married Deborah, daughter of Francis Turner.

3. Alexander Rakes, married Annie, daughter of Francis Turner.

4. Columbus Rakes (b. Feb. 6, 1840) married Martha, daughter of Charles P. Nowlin; their children:

   (a) S. Tyler Rakes (b. Oct. 2, 1868) m. Ellen M., daughter of W. C. Hooker.

   (b) George C. Rakes (1870-1904) married Nannie D., daughter of G. S. Nolen.

5. German Rakes married Jan. 9, 1850, Mary Ann, daughter of William Allen.

6. Jennie Rakes, married David Hall.

7. Elizabeth (Betsy) Rakes, married James M. Spencer.

8. Malinda Rakes, married Isaac Snuffer.

9. Judith Rakes, married John Griffith, moved to Raleigh, County, W. Va.

10. Jackson Rakes, married Ruth Thomas.

11. Charles Rakes, married Mary Ann Griffith.

Many of the descendants of these families of Rakeses have settled in Floyd County.

George Reed The Settler

About 1770, George Reed, whose wife was a Miss Wigington, came with his brother-in-law from Franklin County across the Blue Ridge Mountains and settled on the north side of Wills Ridge. Wigington settled on the south side of this ridge and the two took up several thousand acres of land.

George Reed and his wife raised a family of four sons and three daughters, among whom were Humphrey, George, Jr., Peter and Michael. One daughter, Sarah, married Ambrose Cox, a wealthy slave owner, but after he joined the Brethren Church he freed all his slaves.

George Reed, the settler, is the ancestor of all of the name residing in present Floyd County. They are largely members of the Brethren, or Dunkards, and are men of industry and frugality who have helped subdue the wilderness of Floyd County and have built many beautiful homes.

Those serving in the Confederate army from Floyd were: Robert, William B., John, A. J., Sr., and John Reed with Stuart's Horse Artillery in Pelham's Battery. In Company B, 42nd Virginia Infantry under Captain Henry Lane, were Michael, John and Otey Reed, the latter was wounded at Kernstown, May 23, 1863. Charles and Humphrey Reed were members of Company I, 54th Virginia Infantry under Captain Burwell Akers. W. H. Reed was with Captain A. J. Graham's Company of Reserves under Col. Robert L. Preston; also M. M. Reed, whose command is unknown.

Enoch, Raymond R., William A., Homer M., Henry E., Oakley T., Roscoe Q. E., Archie, Oscar L., Walter S., Carl S., Griffith L., Vernon, William K., Dennis W., Jesse M., Daniel W. and Lonnie M. Reed were soldiers in the World War. Samuel Q. Reed enlisted in the Navy.

The Robertson Family

About 1804, Isaac Robertson and his wife Nancy (Shortt), daughter of Young and Mary (Bilbo) Shortt, moved from Chesterfield County, Virginia, to the Blue Ridge section of Virginia, now the border between Floyd, Franklin and Patrick counties. Other families moving West from Chesterfield and adjoining counties to this section about the same time were Reuben Shortt, Isaac Robertson's brother-in-law; Martel LeSueur; John Clarke (Reuben Shortt's father-in-law) and family, and Joshua Russell and family. Isaac and Nancy Robertson had at least two sons: John and Archibald.

I. John Robertson, son of Isaac Robertson and Nancy (Shortt), married Fannie Rosser of Campbell County, Virginia, and lived at the old Robertson homestead on the crest of the Blue Ridge Mountains, seven miles southwest of the courthouse. Here they raised their family:

1. Thomas L. Robertson (1825-1917) married Perminta Underwood, daughter of Joshua, and lived in the east end of the county where he was a well-known Baptist preacher; they had three children: John married a Prillaman and lived in Franklin County; Birtie married Isaac Williams, son of Joseph; and Walter married a Martin of Carroll County.

2. Frances Robertson married John Barton; they had a large family of children.

3. Nancy Robertson married William Agee, son of Joshua; large family.

4. A daughter married Pleasant Greer; they had a large family.

5. Isaac E. Robertson married Elizabeth Huff, daughter of Isaac the settler, and lived four miles east of the town of Floyd; their two children: Thomas, and Mary m. Zera Shortt.

6. Jesse Robertson, long a well-known hotel proprietor of Rocky Mount, Franklin County, married Ida Connally of Franklin County; they had three children: Bedford m. Louise Klotz of Washington, D. C.; Blanche m. George W. Gilberti; and Mary, never married.

7. Emeline Robertson married William Ingram.

Archibald Robertson visited his brother, John, at his home adjoining Reuben Shortt's farm, and while on this visit was taken ill and died. He was buried on the Reuben Shortt farm in the same cemetery with John Robertson, Reuben Shortt,

Joseph N. Shortt, and Naaman J. Shortt and wife, and many others of close kinship.

Isaac E. and Jesse Robertson were members of Stuart's Horse Artillery, in Pelham's Battery in the Confederate army.

I. Edward Robertson was a soldier in the World War.

The Ross Family
(a border family)

The Ross family came to America at the close of the American Revolution. John, Robert and Milton Ross came from Scotland to Virginia, "being three months in crossing the Atlantic."

John Ross settled in Bedford County near the "Shallow Ford" on the Roanoke River and married a Miss Boswell. Their children were, in part:

A. John Ross, settled in Monroe County, W. Va.

B. Robert Ross, settled in Bedford City (then Liberty).

C. Sutherland Ross married Docia, daughter of Richard Turner and granddaughter of Abednego Turner the settler. They lived in the west end of Franklin County, about twelve miles from the courthouse. Sutherland Ross was a soldier in the War of 1812. He was gored and killed by a bull at the age of 77. Their children were, in part:

1. Robert V. Ross, married March 28, 1846, Lucinda Turner, daughter of Meshach, granddaughter of William and great-granddaughter of Meshach Turner, the immigrant ancestor of a large branch of the Turner family living in the west end of Franklin County; they had six sons and three daughters. Elder Charles Lee Ross is one of the sons and lives on Town Creek in the west end of Franklin County, near his great-great-grandfather's home; he is a preacher of the Primitive Baptist Church. Two of his sons, William E. Ross, Attorney-at-law, and Virgel E. Ross, Commonwealth's Attorney for Mercer County, W. Va., live in Bluefield, West Va.

2. James H. Ross moved to North Carolina, where he died at the age of 70, leaving two sons and two daughters.

Milton Ross, the third immigrant brother, settled in Patrick County, then Henry; this family intermarried with the Coxes, the Prillamans, the Conners, the Kinnerlys, and the Jeffersons.

A. Daniel Ross, Sr., married a Miss Garst of Albemarle County; their children:

1. William; 2. Churchen; 3. David; 4. Nathaniel; 5. Jackson; 6. Sally m. Cox; 7. Susan m. Pedigo; and

8. Daniel, Jr., married Nancy Ingram and was a well-known farmer of Patrick County; their children: William m. Mahala Burnett and among their children was Hardin m. Martha Conner, and their children were: Alice m. Hooker, Ella m. Rakes, J.D., J.B., D.C., Dr. Wm. T., and Dr. C. H. of Bassett, Va.; Dicey m. Prillaman, two children's names were Gabriel and Flem; Onie m. Conner; Kizzy m. Conner; Charles; Burwell; Susan m. Turner; Malinda m. a Mr. Jefferson, a lineal descendant of Peter Jefferson, father of Thomas Jefferson; Martha m. Kinnerly; McD.; and Daniel Lee m. Bettie Alzyra Jamison of Franklin, their ten children: Fannie L. m. Jamison, Lula m. Tatum, C. Brewster, Kittie L., T. Lybrook, Cora m. Weaver, Nannie, T.F., Guy W. and Erie.

Captain Daniel Lee Ross, Co. D, 51st Virginia Infantry, commanded a company composed of men from the vicinity of Woods Gap and Charity Church in Patrick County.

Mathew Scott The Settler

Mathew Scott, the settler, was born in County Tyrone, Ireland, emigrating to America with his family, and settling on lands in the east end of what is now Floyd County. His home was near the present village of Graysville and was made "while its soil was yet disputed for by the savages and white invaders." The inscription on his tombstone in Salem Primitive Baptist Churchyard reads, "Matthew Scott, died 1818."

John Scott, son of Mathew, the settler, married China Evans, of German descent, who spoke only broken English; their children were:

1. Mathew Scott married Mary Ann, daughter of Jacob and Mary (Kagey) Strickler, and moved to the town of Jacksonville where he was a well-known watch and gunsmith; it was said he could make almost anything out of metal. He was also

Treasurer of Floyd County. Their children:

(a) Samuel, and (b) Winfield were prominent merchants in the town of Floyd. They were joined in business by J. M. Boyd, their brother-in-law, and the firm's name was "Scott and Boyd." Later Captain Boyd opened a mercantile store across the street and the firm's name changed to "S. & W. Scott."

(c) Martha married James Madison Boyd, known as Captain Mat; they had one daughter, Mrs. Etta Boyd Harless of Christiansburg. Captain Boyd, a leading citizen and merchant of the town of Floyd, was an elder in the Presbyterian Church. He entered the Confederate army as a Second Sergeant in Company B, 54th Regiment of Virginia Infantry in 1861 under Captain Jackson Godbey, and in 1862 was First Lieutenant under Captain A. O. Dobyns. He was promoted to Captain.

(d) James Scott married Nannie, daughter of Charles Hale of Mercer County, West Va., and has lived in Princeton and Bluefield.

(e) Alice Scott married James Stultz and lives in Martinsville, Va.

(f) Walter Scott, a farmer, never married.

(g) Mary Scott married Birdine, son of Asa Bishop, and lived in the town of Floyd. She was Postmistress of the town of Floyd before her marriage and was for a short while editor of the *Floyd Press*. Their only child, Allie, married a Mr. Muncey of Big Stone Gap.

2. Dr. John Doke Scott (b. Feb. 28, 1829) married, first, Almira P. Kipps (Nov. 5, 1837-Nov. 4, 1874) on March 3, 1853, in Mercer County, West, Va.; later he lived in Salem, Virginia, where he was a physician and a dentist, making dentistry his profession. He was also a local Methodist minister. Children of this marriage:

(a) Evan Brown (b. May 27, 1854) m. Jan. 1885.

(b) Rosanna (b. Sept. 24, 1856) m. June 25, 1883.

(c) Mathew Pendleton (Penn) (b. Jan. 4, 1860), he was for many years with the firm of Scott and Boyd, merchants, in Floyd, Virginia.

(d) Evelina (b. May 5, 1864) m. Sept. 1882.

(e) Salle Liou (b. June 30, 1866).

(f) John Wesley (b. June 27, 1869).

Dr. John Scott married, secondly, August 26, 1875, Margaret Virginia Lucas (b. Jan. 25, 1844); their children: Walter Lucas (b. Oct. 7, 1876); Robert Mayo (b. Jan. 15, 1878); China Agnes (b. May 5, 1879); Samuel Alexander (b. Feb. 26, 1881); Hercules James (b. May 7, 1883).

Dr. John Scott served as mayor of Christiansburg one year; he moved to Childress Store, Montgomery County, Virginia.

3. Mark Scott, served in the Confederate army in the home service.

4. Robert Scott, captain of a militia company in Confederate army.

5. Hercules Scott, known as "Captain Hack," was a familiar character in the town of Princeton, West Va., where he was a merchant and banker, living to a great old age in a log house encased in modern weatherboarding. He died only a few years ago, about 1915. He never married. This old house was torn down in 1925, and hidden away in the walls behind the modern ceiling were old account books showing the prices of country produce; butter was quoted at ten cents per pound. Captain Scott was the cashier of the bank in Princeton. It is said he would rise early, walk five miles to his farm, look after things there, and return on foot before the bank was opened for business in the morning. He would wear the same hat for years. It has been told that when he went to Baltimore on business connected with the bank, he was mistaken for a tramp at the hotel, until it was learned that he was a banker; then nothing was too good to be offered or done for him. He was Captain of Company G, 24th Virginia Infantry, and was twice wounded, at Manassas and at Gettysburg.

6. Charity Scott, never married; was housekeeper for her brother, Hercules.

7. Delilah, married William, son of John Poff, the settler, and they were parents of nine children [there is some doubt about this being a daughter of John Scott—Editor].

Mathew Scott was a member of Captain J. B. Headen's

Company of Col. Robert L. Preston's Reserves. Samuel Scott
was a member of Captain W. H. Price's Company, Company H,
51st Virginia Infantry; he was captured at Waynesboro Va.,
and taken to Fort Delaware and kept prisoner until June 1865.

The Shelor Family

NOTE: The following record is based on an article that
appeared some twenty-five years ago in a newspaper published
at Floyd, Va. The material for the article is said to have been
gathered by Dr. C. M. Stigleman, who was deeply interested in
the early history of Virginia and who himself had married into
the Shelor family. The changes in the article consist merely
of the addition of certain facts not given in the original [and by
the editor].

The Shelor family is of German descent. The name was
doubtless originally spelled **Schüler**, or possibly **Schiller**. Lawrence Shelor emigrated from Germany some twenty-five years
before the Revolutionary War with his wife and one child, a
son. His wife, however, died while crossing the Atlantic [ac-
cording to tradition]. He settled in Maryland or Pennsylvania
and later married an American lady, by whom he had five children. All of these removed to Virginia after the war except
the son by the first wife and the second daughter, who married
a gentleman by the name of Delaplane.

I. Mary (Polly) Shelor married Jonathan Graham, son of
Jacob, and they had twelve children: Martha, Silas, Elizabeth,
Lawrence (b. 1804 and lived to be over 90), Mary, Alexander (b.
1808), Alvin (b. 1810), Perry, Harrison, Jacob, Celia and Catharine. One of the daughters of Alvin Graham, Damaris, married Dr. Asa Cannaday, father of Dr. Albert A. Cannaday of
Roanoke, Va. She is still living (1921) at the age of eighty or
more.

II. Daniel Shelor (1750-1830), eldest son of Lawrence by
his second wife, was a captain in the Revolutionary War, having
enlisted in the County of Frederick, Maryland, on January 22,
1777, as a Lieutenant. He saw service for awhile in New Jersey
under the command of General Thomas Johnston and Colonel

James Johnston. While later serving in Maryland, he received orders from Major Bailey. His commissions were signed by the governor of Maryland. Daniel appeared to have been a man of means. After coming to Virginia he built the first iron furnace in the southwestern part of the state. He married Mary Wickham, sister of Nathaniel, and they had eight children:

A. Elizabeth Shelor married a Mr. Wade, and they had one child.

B. George Shelor married Ruth (1783-1875), daughter of John and Deborah (Cassell) Banks. John Banks (b. 1757) had been a resident of New Jersey before coming to Virginia and as a soldier from that state fought in the Revolutionary War. Major Thomas Banks (b. 1803), a lifelong resident of Floyd County, was a younger brother of Ruth. The children of George and Ruth (Banks) Shelor were: 1. Harriet m. George Kitterman; 2. Mary (1815-1891) m. Isaac Cannaday; 3. William B. (1820-1914) m. Elizabeth, daughter of "River John" Helms; and 4. Sarah J. (Nov. 9, 1825-June 22, 1923) m. William A. Cannaday (1819-1900), son of James.

William B. Shelor (Colonel of 54th regiment, CSA), and Elizabeth (Helms) Shelor had the following children: Emma m. John Coles; Eliza m. Captain William Francis; George W. m. Mary Becker; Henry C. m. Marcella Payne; Sarah m. Hughes Howery; Nannie m. Mont Thompson. (See page 277).

Sarah J., sister of Col. William B. Shelor, is still living (1921) at Salem, Virginia, at age 96. Their children were: Thomas m. Malinda Helms; Malinda m. Jacob Helms; John H. m. Minerva Williams; Samuel, died while a student at Roanoke College; Nannie, unmarried; Richard F. m. Emma Huff; Elizabeth (Betty), unmarried; Emma m. Ballard P. Shelor, Jr.; William, died as a young man; and Edward J. m. Cora Payne.

C. William Shelor married Annie, daughter of Major Thomas Goodson; they had six children who lived to be grown:

1. Rhoda m. Philip Epperly, and they had three children.

2. Sarah married Major Howard and they had one child: Sarah Amanda, who married Mat Helms.

3. Mary (Polly) married a Mr. Goodson, and they had

two children.

4. Thomas G., a preacher, married a Miss Pierce, and they had seven children, of whom one, Ellen, married Dr. C. M. Stigleman, a well-known physician of Floyd County. (He commanded the first company organized in Floyd County for service in the Civil War.) A son of Thomas G. Shelor was killed near Staunton, Va., in the same war.

5. George m. Elizabeth Bower, and they had one son, Rufus.

6. Elizabeth m. Captain Job Wells (his second wife), and they had six children: John T., a physician: Dr. George Milton, also a physician, still living (1921) at Portland, Oregon; Harvey; Rowena m. a Mr. Davidson, a minister; Mary Jane (b. 1844) m. Dr. Douthat, a professor at West Virginia University; and William, lives in the West.

D. Sarah Shelor married Thomas Scott, and they had several children.

E. Daniel Shelor, Jr., married Mary, daughter of Major Thomas Goodson of Turtle Rock, and they had four daughters and two sons:

1. Jane m. Colonel Joseph Howard, son of Peter.
2. Elizabeth m. Topelo O. Watkins.
3. Ruth m. a Mr. Vest.
4. Mary Ann married John Poage.
5. Thomas B. m. Mary, daughter of Isham Barnard; they had nine children:

   (a) Ballard P. m. Sarah, daughter of William Goodson.
   (b) James F. m. Louise, daughter of Edward Jefferson.
   (c) William Marion m. Nannie Luvenia, daughter of Edward Jefferson.
   (d) Sarah Ann m. Frank Hall.
   (e) Isham Barnard m. Mahala Wade.
   (f) Daniel M. died young.
   (g) Mary Jane m. William Robertson.
   (h) Thomas G. m. Levina Wade.
   (i) Elizabeth, died in infancy.

6. Floyd G. m. a Miss Carter.

Three of the sons were members of Stuart's Horse Artillery.

F. Jacob Shelor married Annie Tuggle, and they had eight children: Elizabeth, Randolph, Daniel, Sarah, George (died as a soldier of the Confederacy), Mary, William and Elvira.

G. John Shelor married a Miss Howell, and they had five children, two sons, both of whom were killed in the Civil War, and three daughters: Statiria, Roxena, and one name not recorded.

H. Mary (Polly) Shelor married Captain John Thompson, and they had four children; names of three daughters: Louisa, Mary and Vashti. The family lives in South Carolina.

III. Jacob Shelor married a Miss Ryland from eastern Virginia; and they had four children: Mary, Thomas R., Sarah and Joseph R. With the exception of Sarah, all removed to South Carolina, where their descendants now reside.

Short

William Short, the first of the family in Virginia, was born in England, about 1613, as shown by his deposition in the records of Charles City County, Virginia. He came to Virginia about the year 1649, "transported" by Robert Moseley, Esq. The records show that he "took over" from Robert Moseley, in 1657, 1,100 acres of land lying at the head of Upper Chipoaks Creek, between Surry and Charles City counties. This portion of Charles City County became Prince George County. The Shorts lived so near the border that their records appear in both counties.

The emigrant settler, William Short (I) was still alive, April 20, 1658, when he appeared in two law suits in Charles City County, and was probably dead before July 2, 1659, when his widow, Elizabeth Short, bought an Indian boy from King of the Wameoakes.

His son, William Short (II) made deed of gift to lands to his brother, Thomas Short, Aug. 22, 1668, and the same was acknowledged in Court, May 4, 1669; the same day that a similar deed was acknowledged to George Middleton, husband of Sarah

Short, a sister of both William and Thomas Short.

The records show that this eldest son of the emigrant, William Short (II), died in the year 1676, as his will was proved in Court, March 28, 1676. He was survived by his mother, his wife, Mary, and by two minor children: William Short (III), and Elizabeth.

William Short (III) was probably the man who, with his wife Elizabeth, made deed to Travis Morris in Prince George County (formerly Charles City County), Dec. 12, 1715.

The exact order of descent of the families of the William Shorts and the Thomas Shorts -- there being several of each name -- of Surry, Amelia and Chesterfield counties fails to appear from the Court records examined, but circumstantial evidence is very strong that they were all descended from William Short (I). This includes William Short who was Secretary of Legation to France with Jefferson, who was from Surry County, and the William Short who was a Vestryman in Bristol Parish in 1742.

William Short of Surry County, born Sept. 30, 1759, was educated at William and Mary College. He was Secretary of Legation to France in 1784, Charge d'affairs to France 1789, Minister Resident in 1794, and Minister to the Hague 1797 and to Spain in 1794. He married Elizabeth, daughter of Sir William Skipwith, Bart., and had children: 1. William; 2. Peyton; 3. Edmunds; 4. Elizabeth, m. Dr. Ridgely of Kentucky; 5. Jane, m. Charles Wilkins. Peyton Short was a member of Kentucky State Senate of Fayette County 1792-6. He became Minister Resident in 1794, and at the departure of former associates concluded the negotiations and signed the treaty of friendship, commerce and boundaries on October 27, 1795. He died in Philadelphia, Pa., December 5, 1849. Under caption "W-M Library Recipient of Interesting New Gifts," in *Alumni Gazette* of Friday, Jan. 31, 1936: "In an interesting collection of books recently purchased from the Short heirs, are several books that were owned by William Short, the distinguished ambassador to Spain and Holland, and Secretary to Thomas Jefferson. William Short was a student in the College from 1779-1780. These books have either the book label of William Short, or that of his brother Peyton Short. They are in excellent condition."

William Short of Chesterfield County made his will on Sept. 11, 1756, which follows: "Parish of Dale, County of Chesterfield. To my eldest son Young Short 5 pounds and no more. To grandson, Grief Short, 100 acres of land, but Thomas Short the father to have the said land during his life time. To son Samuel Short, same (100 acres), and lands also to son John Short (who married Olive Sassine), and wife Barbary Short to have one half personal estate, the other half to sons: Samuel and John. Son Young Short and George Lovel to be executors."

The above William Short was still living two years later -- April 7, 1758 -- when he made a deed of gift to his son Young Short of a tract of land of 76 acres, which was recorded the same day in Chesterfield County, Deed Book 3, page 252:

"George the Second by the grace of God of Great Brittain France and Ireland King Defender of the faith & ce. To all to whom these presents Shall Come Greeting Know Ye that I William Short of Chesterfield County for Divers good Causes and Considerations thereunto me Mooving Have given Granted and Confirmed and by these presents Doe give grant Alien enfeoff and Confirm Unto my Son Young Short of the County a foresaid and to his Heirs and Assighns for ever Seventy Acres of Land Situate Lying and being in the County aforesaid and Parish of King William Bounded as followeth (towit) Beginning at a Corner Black Oak and Gum, thence North fifty Six and one third Degrees West Thirty four Poles to a Corner Black Oak, thence South Sixty Degrees West One Hundred and Sixty one Poles to Pointers On Hills line thence on Hills line North Eleven Degrees East One Hundred and fifty two Poles to the place began at Including the Plantation whereon my Said Son now Liveth with all houses orchards Gardens fenses woods underwood waters and water Courses thereunto Belonging or in any wise appertaining with the reversion and reversions remainder and remainders to To have and To hold the aforesaid Land and Premises with their Appurtenances to the Only Proper Use and Behoof of him the Said Young Short his heirs and Assighns for ever in Witness where of I have hereunto Set my Hand and

Affixed my Seal this Seventh Day of April One thousand Seven Hundred and Fifty Eight In the presence of John Bransford (Signed) Wm. Short."

John Landrum
Nath Larys (unsure who)

Note: --On this farm Young Short and Marie Bilbo, his wife, went to live just after their marriage February 3, 1756, and on which place they were living when the above deed was executed. This is on James River, about twelve to eighteen miles from Richmond, and within the then limits of Manakin Town. Here the five children of Young Short were born: Archibald Short, c. 1758; Nancy, Elizabeth, Mary, Reuben -- January 10, 1769; and Young William Short. When his father made his will two years before (Sept. 11, 1756), it was evidently understood that his son Young Short was then living so hence the: "5 pounds and no more," given to Young Short in the will.

The children of William Short of Chesterfield are:

	(1. Young Short—	(Archibald, b. Dec. 1758, m. Levina.
	(wife, Marie Bilbo	(Nancy, m. Isaac Robertson.
Wm. Short made		(Elizabeth, b. Mar. 7, 1764.
deed of gift		(Mary, b. Sept. 14, 1766.
to Young Short		(Reuben, b. Jan. 10, 1769.
in 1758	(2. Samuel	(Young William Short, b. about
		(1771.
Wife of Wm.	wife, Elizabeth	(Pleasant, Fleming and "another yet
	LeSueur	to be born.")
Short, Barbara	(3. William Short (II) died 1763: See Will.	
	(4. John Short—dau. Judia m. John Shipwash.	
	(5. Thomas Short—son Grief Short.	

As stated before, his son William Short (II) had died two years before and his will is here quoted:

Will Book, 1, page 450: All property to be equally divided among his four brothers: Young Short, Thomas Short, Samuel Short and John Short. "Brother Young Short to be executor." Dated Aug. 22, 1763. The inventory was taken on Oct. 22, 1763. Teste: William Short, Thomas Vawter, Barbary Short--Evidently both his father and mother witnessed his will.

Samuel Short made his will June 19, 1780: Will Book 3, page 305 in Chesterfield County--His wife, Elizabeth (LeSueur), sons were Pleasant Short, Fleming Short, "and another yet to be born." Executors: Charles Clark and Martell LeSueur (Martell LeSueur was a Rev. Sol.), and William Barnet.

The five sons of William Short, Sr., of Chesterfield County were:

I. Young Short, m. Mary Bilbo, February 3, 1756.

II. Thomas Short, m. Ann Payne, Jan. 10, 1762—Judith, a daughter was born to them Feb. 5, 1765, bapt. May 19, 1765.

III. Samuel Short, m. Elizabeth LeSueur, Feb. 20, 1774. See his will.

IV. William Short, Jr., died in 1763—See his will above.

V. John Short, m. Olive Sassins, Sept. 18, 1766—William, a son born to them Feb. 29, 1768, bapt. May 15, 1768.

These dates were found recorded in "Douglas' Register," a record of marriages, births and deaths occurring in the churches in the County of Chesterfield, and in King William Parish and vicinity, including the Huguenot settlement of Manakin Town. Collected and compiled by Rev. Douglas.

Young Short, married Mary Bilbo (Marie Billiebo), Feb. 3, 1756. In the index to Ship List, Meale and Census, the Huguenot immigration to Manakintown, is Jacque Billiebo. On page 13, **Huguenot Emigration to Virginia** by R. A. Brock (a translation from the original French records), is found in 1714, Jacques Bilbaud (also given in this book Billiebo, Bilbo) with wife and one son. This doubtlessly was father of Jean Pierre Bilbo, for the birth of the first son of Jean Pierre namely, Jacque, is recorded in Brock's, page 84, June 30, 1730 as follows: "June 30th, 1730, was born Jacque Billiebo, a son of Jean Billiebo and Susane his wife." On page 92, the name is spelled Bilbo.

The following reference is from **Huguenot Emigration to America** by Charles W. Baird, D.D., Vol. II, P. 16: "Jean Bilbaud fled from Port des Barques in 1681 to England. Jacques Billebau (Bilboa, Bilbaud, Billiebo), one of the inhabitants of Manakintown, 1700-1723 was doubtlessly of this family." This Jean Bilbaud settled in the North, New Jersey or New York, most likely. In **Virginia Magazine of History and Biography**, Vol. II, P. 295, a reference states that Jacques Billebaud came from Saintoge, France, to Manakintown. In the same volume, P. 431, under "List of Tithable Persons" of the present year, 1711, in

King William Parish is Jacques Bilbaud; in the year 1730, **V.M.H.B.**, Vol. XII, P. 382, is listed Jean Pierro Bilbo, "Tithable in King William Parish."

From the foregoing argument: Jacques Bilbaud (Billiebo, Bilbo) with wife and one son emigrated to Manakintown, Va., they were father and mother of Jean Pierre Bilbo, evidently the name of the "one son." In 1722, this Jean Pierre Bilbo owned 162 acres of land in King William Parish; in 1723 he was listed as one of the tithables--though he was listed as one of the household of Pierre Dutoy, who gave in 5 tithables, one of whom was Bilbo (or Billiebo), the name was variously spelled. (I) Jacques Bilbaud (Billiebo, Bilbo) "with wife and one son." (II) Jean Pierre Bilbo (Anglicized) and Susane his wife.

The following record of Jean Pierre Bilbo and Susane his wife:-- On June 30, 1730, Jacque Billiebo, a son was born,--baptized (in the Episcopal Church) Aug. 16, 1730.

On June 23, 1733, Marie Billiebo, a daughter was born,-- baptized Dec. 23, 1733.

On November 13, 1739, Elizabeth, a daughter was born – and died Mar. 20, 1740.

On December 30, 1740, Elizabeth, a daughter was born-- (named for the one who had died?)

(III) Marie Billiebo (Bilbo), dau. of Jean Pierre Bilbo and Susane, his wife, was born June 23, 1733, baptized December 23, 1733, – and had for Godfather, Antoine Benin, and for Godmothers, Barbarie and Mariane Dutoy – perhaps, Susane was a daughter of the Dutoy family, with which Jean Pierre Bilbo had lived.

In 1731 Jean Pierre Bilbo was appointed Processioner for lands in King William Parish --and in the same year, he and his wife were listed as two tithables. They were so listed each year until about 1750. He was made Church Vestryman, and took the oath prescribed for the same on March 15, 1734. And on October 30, 1742, he took the oath of Church Warden, highest elective office within the gift of the people of the Parish. He was listed as owning two slaves.

Young Short, son of William and Barbara Short, married

Mary Bilbo in Manakin Town, Virginia, December 3, 1756, and their eldest son, Archibald was born, December, 1759. Archibald Short was a Revolutionary soldier. The next oldest was probably Nancy Short, who married Isaac Robertson. The third was Elizabeth Short, born March 7, 1764; then Mary Short, born Sept. 14, 1766; Reuben Short, born January 10, 1769, baptized March 4, 1769 in the Episcopal Church--and when leaving Chesterfield County for the present Floyd County in 1800-1804, he deeded one-half acre of land from his land received from his father, to the Baptist Church.. Deed Book, 17, page 266: 1806 Deed to Reuben Short's plantation of 430½ acres for 1000 pounds--½ acre next to the meeting house reserved, and deeded to the "Baptist Society" of Spring Creek Church, this is recorded in Deed Book 15, page 341. "October 1801 Deed of Gift Reuben Short to Baptist Society of Spring Creek Church, one-half acre for two dollars," (this charge of two dollars to bind the gift). The next year, Young Short made deeds of gift to his two youngest sons: Reuben Short, and Young William Short of 430½ acres to each. Young William Short was born about 1771, and was named for both his father and his grandfather. To recapitulate, the children of Young Short and Mary Bilbo, his wife, were:

    I.   Archibald, born Dec., 1758, wife Lavina. (He was a Rev. soldier).

    II.   Nancy, born about 1760, m. Isaac Robertson, Piedmont, Va.

    III.   Elizabeth, b. Mar. 7, 1764--See "Douglas' Register."

    IV.   Mary, born September 14, 1766.

    V.   Reuben, born January 10, 1769, bapt. March 4, 1769.

    VI.   Young William (Short), born about 1771.

Deed Book 16, page 237; 1803, May: Ann Short to John and Judith Shipwash--Judith was the daughter of Thomas Short and Ann (Payne), his wife--only daughter of Charles Payne. (Could this John Shipwash have been John Skipwith?--if so, then perhaps the same family as that of Elizabeth Skipwith, who married Col. William Short, and was the mother of William Short, the diplomat--**This paragraph properly belongs under heading of William Short**).

Deed Book 11, page 101: 1786, March: Deed of gift from

Young Short to Archibald Short. After the gift to Archibald and in the year 1795, Young Short owned 670 acres of land in Chesterfield County and eight slaves--one billiard table, and had ordinary license--and in the same year, Archibald Short had 200 acres of land, and owned two slaves. In 1796, Young Short made deeds of gift to his two youngest sons: Reuben Short, and Young William Short, to 430½--four hundred and thirty and one half acres--to each. This seems to be about the year of young Short's death, as there is no mention of him or of his estate after 1796.

Archibald Short was a Revolutionary Soldier. McAllister's **Virginia Militia in the Revolutionary War:** "Archibald Short, Powhatan, Co., Va., Aug. 15, 1832. Born in Chesterfield, Dec., 1758. Took oath in 1776. About 1777 enlisted as regular for three years under Captain Francis Smith, a recruiting officer of the First Regiment. After a few weeks procured a substitute. About June, 1780, substituted for Samuel Short of Chesterfield, under Archibald Walthall. Waited at Randolph's Mill till the militia from Caroline, Hanover and Henrico came up. Col. Faulkner led the regiment to Hillsboro, where it lay till the Virginia and North Carolina militia assembled. After General Gates arrived, the army proceeded to near Camden, where it was defeated, but rallied at Salisbury. Affiant was in hospital there about a month more. A third tour was to guard the ferries at Westham and Tuckahoe. A fourth tour of about five weeks was under Captain David Patterson. Was discharged before the battle of Guilford under same captain he served at seige of Yorktown, and then guarded prisoners under Captain Spencer, of Charlotte. Total services about two years."

Nancy Short, married Isaac Robertson in Chesterfield Co., Virginia, and later came to the Piedmont section of Virginia with her husband and children--one of whom was John Robertson, who settled on an adjoining farm to that of his uncle, Reuben Short. This was on the crest of the Blue Ridge Mountains, in what was then Franklin County, which became a part of Floyd County in 1873. The children of Isaac and Nancy Short were: Thomas L. Robertson, a Baptist minister of Floyd County, who married Perminta Graham; Frances, wife of John Barton; Nancy, wife of William Agee;----Greer, wife of Pleasant Greer;

Isaac Robertson, who married a Huff; Emmaline, wife of William Ingram; and Jesse Robertson, late of Rocky Mount, Franklin Co., Va., a well-known hotel proprietor, who married Ida Connelly of Franklin County, Va.

Reuben Short, fifth child of Young Short and Mary (Bilbo), his wife, was born in Chesterfield County, Virginia, January 10, 1769, baptized March 4, 1769, in the Episcopal Church of King William Parish in Chesterfield County. He married Lydia Clark in Chesterfield County--she was born July 20, 1767, the daughter of John Clark, and Susan Nix, his second wife. John Clark was the son of Allison, Sr., of Chesterfield, and John Clark and his brother Jesse were Revolutionary soldiers of the Line, and served under Colonel John Gibson in the Western Detachment in the vicinity of the present Pittsburgh, Pa., from January 1, 1780 to Dec. 6, 1781, see pages 281 and 282 of Saffell's **Records of the Revolutionary War.** Other Chesterfield Clarks serving in the Revolutionary War were his nephews: Allison Clark (III), Joseph and James Clark. About 1800, Reuben and Lydia Short with their family moved from Chesterfield County, Va., and settled within the present limits of Floyd County, Virginia--on the crest of the Blue Ridge Mountains on a farm which was then in Franklin County.

About the same year, other Chesterfield County families came to the present Floyd County and its vicinity. They were: John Clark, and Susan Nix, his second wife, and their family, one of whom was Henry Clark, who later married Deborah Banks in Floyd County. All of John Clark's four children (two by his first marriage), came with him to the present county of Floyd; Joshua Russell and family; Martell LeSueur and family; Field Jefferson to Franklin County, Va.; Isaac Robertson to the Piedmont section of Va.; and John Robertson and family to the crest of the Blue Ridge in the present Floyd County.

Reuben Short's lands — As stated before, Reuben Short and his younger brother, Young William Short, each received 430½ acres of land from their father in 1796. Reuben owned in addition to this land, three slaves, and upon his land were five houses, as shown by the land tax books of Chesterfield County. Before leaving Chesterfield County, he deeded one-half acre of land "next to the meeting house" to the "Baptist Society of

Spring Creek Church," and in 1806 he sold his 430 acres of land to Cornelius Buck for 1,000 pounds--deed recorded in Deed Book 17, page 266--at which time he entered a paper, showing that it would be very inconvenient for Lydia, his wife, to come to the County of Chesterfield to make out the papers, so she signed away her dower, properly attested, (they were in the present county of Floyd). In the year 1804, Reuben Short bought 353 acres of land in Franklin Co., Va., from Andrew Donald of Bedford County, for 220 pounds--See Franklin Deed Book 5, page 11. And on Feb. 22, 1806 Reuben Short of Patrick Co. made deed of trust to John Hall of the same county, conveying a tract of land, the "Bear Spring," being the same conveyed by Andrew Donald to the said Reuben Short. Deed of trust to run till Dec. 25, 1807. In 1808, Deed Book: March 21: Roland Salmons of Montgomery County made deed to Reuben Short of Franklin County to 180 acres of land on west side of Runnet Bag and Shooting Creeks for 42 pounds. 1810, Nov. 12th: John Hall of the County of Patrick made deed to Reuben Short of the County of Franklin for $100 to land in County of Franklin,-- line crossing a branch of Runnet Bag to cucumber tree in Sauners' line, etc. Reuben Short's home was in that portion of Franklin County, which was annexed to Floyd County in the year 1870.

Reuben Short, and his wife, Lydia Clark, were both born and baptized in the Episcopal Church in Chesterfield Co., Va., as shown by "Douglas' Register," but both later joined the Baptist Church, and Reuben was one of the local Baptist ministers. It is said he baptized his wife, Lydia, into the Baptist Church. One of his grandsons, Asa D., a son of Joseph Nix Short, was for many years Pastor of County Line Baptist Church, which was within two miles of the Reuben Short home in Floyd Co. Reuben Short died in 1852. He and his wife Lydia are buried on the farm, which was their home, and which was later the home of his grandson, Naaman J. Short. In the same family graveyard, are buried his son Joseph Nix Short (and his two wives: first, Mary (Polly) Thomas; and, secondly, Fannie Bryant), and Naaman J. Short and his wife. In 1839 Reuben Short and wife Lydia deeded their lands thus: "December 4, 1839: Reuben Short and Lydia his wife of Franklin County to Nathaniel B. Wickham of same county two tracts on waters of Runnet

Bag and Shooting Creeks including all the lands of said Reuben Short adjoining lands of Elisha Rakes and others"--recorded in Deed Book 16, page 290, in Franklin County, Va. This Nathaniel B. Wickham was his son-in-law.

The children of Reuben and Lydia Short were: I. Reuben Short, Jr., died young; II. Mary Short; III. John Young Short (b. 1796-d. 1877); IV. Lydia Short, married James Banks; V. Joseph Nix Short (b. 1803-d. 1876); and VI. Calvin R. Short, in the Mexican War of 1848.

II. Mary Short, daughter of Reuben and Lydia, married Nathaniel Wickham, one of the largest landowners of Floyd County. They were the parents of: (a) Mary A., married Joel Shanks; (b) Cornelius, educated under Professor Gannaway and died young; (c) Dallis, a Baptist minister; (d) Curtis; and (e) Olivia, married Francis Snead, and was his second wife. Nathaniel B. Wickham was a member of Zion Lutheran Church at Floyd.

IV. The tradition is that Lydia Short, daughter of Reuben and Lydia, married James Banks, a son of John and moved West about the time that Henry Clark and Deborah (Banks), his wife, went West.

III. John Young Short, son of Reuben and Lydia, was born in Chesterfield County, Va., in 1796, and came as a babe-in-arms with his parents about 1800 to Floyd County. He married Judith Thomas (b. 1803-d. 1902), daughter of Pleasant and Mary (Cannaday), daughter of James Cannaday and Elizabeth (Raikes), his wife, who lived to be 105 years old. James Cannaday was a Revolutionary soldier, serving under General Nathaniel Greene. John Young Short lived for many years in Patrick County. His farm and home was one mile east of Old Charity Meetinghouse. In 1846 he moved to the Flat Top Mountain in Mercer County, Virginia, now West Virginia. John Young purchased a farm of eleven hundred acres and lived there about one year. Then he sold his Flat Top farm and moved back to Patrick County. A copy from the Mercer Co. Clerk's Office follows:

1. By deed dated January 8, 1846, and recorded in Deed

Book No. 2, page 301, Edwin Lilly and Elizabeth Lilly, conveyed to John Y. Short eleven hundred acres of land on the waters of Mountain Creek and Glade Fork Creek, which empties into Mountain Creek. The consideration was $200.00 cash paid. This land is fully described by metes and bounds and runs from a point near where the Lilly Reunion grounds are (the Lilly Reunion grounds are on the Bluefield-Beckley highway on the top of Flat Top Mountain at the junction of Mercer and Raleigh counties), in an eastern direction probably for about four miles.

2. By deed dated January 1, 1848, and recorded in Deed Book No. 2, page 421, John Y. Shortt, Sr., and Juda Short, conveyed five hundred acres of this land to Jonathan Brammer for $800.00.

3. By deed dated January 1, 1848, and recorded in Deed Book No. 3, page 329, John Y. Shortt, Sr., and Juda Shortt conveyed five hundred acres of this land to Jonathan Brammer for $500.00. This deed was acknowledged in Patrick County, Virginia, before Jeremiah Burnett and Charles Thomas, two justices of the peace.

4. By deed dated November 2, 1852, and recorded in Book Book 3, page 482, John Y. Short and Juda Short conveyed the remaining 200 acres of this land to Augustus Ball. This deed was acknowledged in Patrick County, Virginia, before James Coliver and Elkanah B. Turner, two justices of the peace.

Therefore, the records show that he purchased eleven hundred acres for $200.00 and sold it off in three conveyances for the total sum of $1300.00, at least. The deed to Ball does not state what the consideration was except $100.00 and other valuable considerations. This land is probably owned by twenty different people at this time (1935). In some of the deeds his name was spelled **Short** and in others **Shortt**.

James Brammer and Jonathan Brammer are doubtlessly brothers and they came to Mercer County from either Patrick or Floyd County, about the time they purchased this land. They have a great number of descendants in Raleigh and Mercer counties.

After moving back to Patrick County in 1848, John Young

Shortt and his family lived for many years one mile east of Charity Meetinghouse on Smiths River. Then later they lived on Runnet Bag in Franklin County at what was later the James Hash farm. In Floyd they lived at what was known as the Snuffer place--later known as the "Jim Martin" farm. Then they bought and worked as their last home, the Col. Tom. Banks place, which was a part of the original John Banks home.

The eleven children of John Young Short and Judith (Thomas), his wife, were:

1. Reuben, Jr.; 2. Pleasant; 3. Charles--all of whom died in childhood;

4. Lydia, who married Joshua Cannaday--one of Patrick Bill's sons--and later moved with their large family to Gallipolis, Ohio.

5. Naaman J. (b. 1829-d. 1911), m. Nancy Lemon, dau. of Isaac,--see below for longer sketch of Naaman J. Short.

6. Susan, married, first, Jefferson Turner--children: John and Judith; and, secondly, Isaac Lemon (was his second wife)--child: Minerva, married Samuel Rakes.

7. Judith Annie, b. Feb. 17, 1834, d. Aug. 30, 1899--married Richard Johnson Wood, Feb. 5, 1852, and lived through the Civil War period in Patrick County, after which they lived in Floyd County, six miles east of Floyd Court House. Their nine children were: (a) Susan Emaline; and (b) Rachel Elvira--both of whom died in infancy; (c) Jefferson Pinkard, m. Belinda Brammer; (d) Daniel Hillsman, m., first, Ruth Corn, and secondly, Fannie Stovall; (e) George Bunyan, m. Elizabeth Brammer; (f) Greenville Darius, m., first, Melissa Graham, and, secondly, Lilly Barnard; (g) Amos DeRussia, m. Annie Chapman Johnston; (h) Sparrel Asa, m., first, Jesse Scales and, secondly, India Goodwyn; and (i) Doc. Robertson, m. Gertrude Howard. Richard Johnson Wood, father of this family, was born October 27, 1828, died December 20, 1917, and is buried with his wife in the New County Line Churchyard, six miles east of the county seat.

8. Martha, m., first, William Lemon--children: Isaac, Lucinda, Thomas and Sallie; and, secondly, Flemon Janney--children: Aaron, Hibernia, William and Malinda.

9. Elizabeth, m., first, Jordan Thomas--children: Alice and

others; and, secondly, James Greer--children: James Greer, Jr., and others.

10. John P. Short, m. Victoria, dau. of John Young. John P. Short was a member of Company A, 54th Virginia Infantry in the Confederate army, and was captured along with his cousin Asa D. Short, at Missionary Ridge, Nov. 24, 1863, and imprisoned at Rock Island, Ill., until the close of the War. He was a prominent citizen of Floyd County--long a justice of the peace, who resided four miles south of Floyd Court House. About 1885, he sold his home in Floyd County and moved with family to Parsons, Kansas, where he died in 1927 at the age of about 90 years. Their children were: Emmet, Palmer, Edward, John, Harry, Wilmer, Lilly, India and Frank--all of whom reside in or near Parsons, Kansas.

11. Lucinda, born November 1, 1841, died February 8, 1936-aged 94 years, 3 months and 7 days. She married, first, Joseph Young, son of George--children: Tula and Jefferson; and, secondly, Nathaniel Thomas, son of Peter--children: Clayborn, Kemper, Dee, and others. She is buried in Bluefield, by the side of her daughter Tula Peters, who died in 1934.

(5) Naaman J. Short, son of John Y. and Judith, married Nancy Lemon, daughter of Isaac by his first marriage. He was a prosperous farmer, who kept open house. Their children were: (a) Amanda, m. Madison Brammer; (b) John W., m. Mary Eliza Thomas (ch.: Minerva, George, Lydia, Posey, Leona, Daisy, Loula, Zerah, Forest and David); (c) Prince E., m. Annie Watkins (ch.: Hilda); (d) Zera H., m. Mary Robertson, dau. of Isaac (ch.: a son and daughter); (e) Jefferson D., m. Loula Huff, dau. of Peter (no children); (f) Everett T., m. India Hoback, dau. of Dr. A. J. Hoback (ch., Woody); (g) Callahill, m. (no children); (h) Thomas, never married; (i) Sylvanus, died in infancy; (j) Lydia, died in infancy.

V. Joseph Nix Short, son of Reuben and Lydia, was the first child born to them after they came to the Blue Ridge section. He was born in 1803, and died in 1876. He married, first, Polly (Mary) Thomas, daughter of Charles and Judith (Ripley) of Patrick County, and lived five miles east of Floyd. Their children were: (a) Lydia, wife of John Russell; (b) Emmeline, wife of William Davis--one son, John; (c) Asa D. Short, a well-known Baptist minister--see below; (d) Ira H. Short, m. Sarah Hatcher--one daughter, Birtie. Ira Short died in the Confederate army--was in Co- H, 54th Virginia Infantry; (e) Sarah J. McDaniel, wife of James. They lived in the west end of the county of Floyd--several children. James McDaniel died in the Confederate army. He was in Co. H. 54th Va. Infantry; (f) Elizabeth McDaniel, wife of Lucian--nine children, one of whom was Joseph McDaniel. Lucian McDaniel was a member of Co. H, 54th Va. Infantry; (g) Marion Monroe Short, died in the Civil War, in Co. D, 51st. Va. Infantry; (h) Deborah C. Smith, wife of Eli--children: Asa Smith and five other children. Ira Smith was a member of Co. I, 54th Va. Infantry; (i) Judith Hatcher, wife of Elkanah--no children. He was a soldier in the Confederate army; (j) Mahala Short--no record. (k) Lurinda Jones, wife of Robert--no children. Robert Jones was in the Confederate army.

(c) Asa D. Short, born April 17, 1842, died May 31, 1917. He married Sarah Graham, dau. of Alexander, and raised a large family, who were: Iowa, m. George Williams; Lucinda Mary, never married; Albett, aged 13, and George, aged 5 years, died of diphtheria; Amos; Lydia; Senora; Cleo; and Rena. Asa D. Short was a farmer and a Primitive Baptist Minister. He was Pastor of County Line Church and a member of other churches in the county of Floyd. In the Civil War, he was a member of Company A, 54th Virginia Infantry, under Captain Andrew Dickerson, and was captured along with his cousin, John U. Short at Missionary Ridge, Nov. 24, 1863, and imprisoned at Rock Island, Illinois, until the close of the War.

After the death of Polly, his first wife, Joseph Nix Short married, secondly, Fannie Bryant, a daughter of Ambrose, and sister of Joseph of the Blue Ridge section of Floyd and Patrick counties. She was also a sister of Nancy Bryant, who married Henry Wood and moved to Sullivan County, Indiana, in 1836. Joseph Nix and Fannie had no children.

Perhaps it is appropriate to state why Joseph N. Short's middle name was Nix. John Clark, Joseph N. Short's grandfather, married as his second wife, Susan Nix, daughter of Joseph Nix, and granddaughter of George Nix, Sr., of Spottsylvania County, and later of Orange County, Va. The children born to John Clark and his second wife Susan Nix, were: Lydia and Henry. Lydia Clark married Reuben Short; and Henry Clark married Deborah Banks, daughter of John Banks—both John Clark and John Banks were Revolutionary soldiers. The will of George Nix, Sr. is found in Chalkley's **Abstracts of Augusta County.**

Susan Nix, as John Clark's second wife, came with him from Chesterfield to the present county of Floyd about 1800, and she and her husband lived some three or four miles southeast of the courthouse, and are thought to be buried in the Howell Graveyard on the Old Floyd Patrick Pike some four miles south of Floyd Court House.

The Court records were searched by Mrs. Jesse S. Carter, now Mrs. John M. Bell of Chester, South Carolina; Civil War records from the Muster Rolls through courtesy of the Confederate Veterans; Mrs. Deborah C. Smith, widow of Eli Smith, and a daughter of Joseph Nix Short was a valuable contributor; as were many others of the Short family, who aided with documents, etc., all of which made this sketch possible.

[There has been very little editing of this sketch-ed.]

Henry Showalter

The Floyd County family of the Showalter name traces its origin to one of three brothers who immigrated to America in the year of 1770 and settled in Pennsylvania. Of these, Henry Showalter moved to Virginia and settled in the present county of Pulaski.

He had a son Daniel, born June 28, 1806, who married Sarah Griffith, and their son, Henry B. Showalter, was born July 29, 1830. He married Elizabeth Turpin of Pulaski County and moved to the Indian Valley section of Floyd County in the year 1860. He died in Floyd County, August 8, 1916, at the age of 86. Their children were nine daughters and one son:

1. Martha; 2. Salome; 3. Naomi; 4. Virginia; 5. Ruth; 6. Sarah; 7. Elizabeth; 8. Florence; 9. Minnie;

10. Isaac Daniel (July 4, 1862-Oct. 13, 1907) married Minnie Criner, daughter of William G.; their children were:

(a) Forest F. (b. June 1885) m. Braskey Kenley; their children: Roy (b. Jan. 4, 1909), Mable and Lena.

(b) Nathaniel Prior (b. 1892) married Callie Turpin.

(c) Daniel Bruce (b. 1894) married Canary Buckner.

(d) Giles Henry (b. 1902) married Clona Huff.

(e) Elizabeth married Vander Bishop.

(f) Dora married Harvey P. Wade.

The Simmons Family

Charles Simmons came from the eastern portion of Franklin County, Virginia. and about 1772 took up a large boundary of land five miles north of the present town of Floyd in the present Wills Ridge section. His first wife was a Miss Reed; they raised a family, two of whom, Ned and John, moved to the State of Ohio when that state was admitted to the Union early in the 19th century. [One account states that Thomas Simmons came with Charles to Floyd County, but this is not substantiated by existing records.]

Charles Simmons married, secondly, a Miss Weeks, and had three sons (names of daughters not given);

I. William Simmons - no further information.

II. Cara (Carey) Simmons (b. April 11, 1793), lived on West Fork six miles west of the present county seat where he operated a grist mill; he married Catherine Slusher (July 26, 1790-Dec. 11, 1880); they were the parents of nine children:

A. Charles L. Simmons (Oct. 12, 1818-June 6, 1886), married Lucy Bishop; their children:

1. Dr. Elkana (b. June 30, 1848), moved to Indiana.

2. Margaret C. (b. Oct. 25, 1849)

3. Mary A. (b. Dec. 10, 1852), second wife of Lanan Harman, son of Benjamin.

4. John (b. Dec. 30, 1855), married Ellen Spangler, moved to State of Washington.

5. Nancy E. (b. Sept. 1, 1858), married William Shelor, son of Thomas.

6. Burdine (b. Sept. 13, 1867), moved to Indiana, but came back to Floyd and married Judah, daughter of Jesse Pratt, went West again.

7. Luvina (b. June 6, 1864), married Greene Harris, son of Abraham.

8. Homer L. (b. Dec. 30, 1867), married Ellen Slusher.

B. Noah Simmons (b. July 9, 1827), married Eliza Phlegar, daughter of Joseph; their children:

1. Mary (b. Sept. 17, 1861), married William J. Boone, son of Benjamin; their children:

(a) Asa m. Lucy Hylton; their children: Treva m. Newton Weddle; Rena; Raymond; Oneta; Ruth and Mauyer.

(b) Stella; (c) Lillie; (d) Henrietta;

(e) Annie m. Sam H. Smith; their children: Willie and Pauline.

(f) Maggie married Peyton Graham; their children: Iva; Ibra; Mary; Banjoline and Eva.

(g) Elmer married Chloe Weddle; their children: Vada and W. J.

2. Monroe (b. June 1, 1865), m. Lydia Dickerson, daughter of Amos; their children: Harmon; Lillian m. Olie Shelor; Olivia; Percy; Howard; Verbena and Hugh.

3. Sarah (b. Aug. 13, 1867), married George Harvey Smith, son of George; they had one child, Earnest.

4. Calvin (b. May 26, 1869), married Mary Weddle, daughter of G. L.; their children: Troy and one daughter.

5. Joseph (b. Feb. 6, 1871), married Almena Sumpter, daughter of Joseph; their children were: Ray, Lane and Ava.

6. Henry (b. Aug. 10, 1875), married Maude Dillon, daughter of Henry B.; their children: Julian, Kate, Mallie and Allie.

7. Elmetta (b. June 16, 1877), married Rev. Leroy M. Weddle, son of Isaac.

C. Obediah Simmons (Oct. 15, 1830-Jan. 14, 1899), married Eliza Wade, daughter of Isaac; their daughter, Minnie, married Tap Howard, son of Joseph L., and lives in Floyd.

Obediah Simmons was a farmer and cattleman.

D. Barbara Simmons married Jesse Pratt; their children:

1. James W. Pratt, died in Civil War.

2. Louanna Pratt m. Levi Hylton.

3. Susanna Pratt m. Clay Burnett.

4. Bennett H. Pratt m. Mrs. Catherine Hylton Pratt, daughter of Henry Hylton.

5. George W. Pratt m. Emma Webb, daughter of Henry.

6. Stephen, died in infancy.

7. Nancy, died of diphtheria.

8. Cara, died of diphtheria.

9. Catherine, died of diphtheria.

E. Elizabeth Simmons (d. April 4, 1903), never married.

F. Louanna Simmons married Rev. John B. Weddle; their children, in part: Dow, Jabe and Ellen m. a Mr. Starr.

G. Mary Simmons married Joshua Weddle; their children: George m. Young; Thomas; Roley; Eliza m. Hylton; Belle; Arline m. Bowman and Malinda m. Harman.

H. Eva Simmons, died in infancy.

I. Catherine Simmons (b. July 27, 1836), married Dennis Hylton; their children:

1. David E. (b. June 26, 1859).

2. Cordelia A. m., first, Leroy Quesenberry, secondly, W. R. Kitterman.

3. Amanda A. m. Cook Weaver, son of George.

4. Burdine H. (b. June 18, 1867), m. Mattie, daughter of W. A. Ballinger.

5. Harvey W. (b. Oct. 12, 1869), m. Nora, daughter of Burdine Dickerson.

6. Laura E. (b. June 13, 1872), m. Carl Moses, son of John.

7. George W. (b. Dec. 25, 1874).

8. Cassie E. (b. Aug. 3, 1878), m. W. A. Smith, son of George.

III. Thomas W. Simmons (b. 1798), married Delilah Boothe (b. 1798); their children, in part:

A. Otey T. Simmons (b. 1818), married a Miss Agnew.

B. Mary Simmons (b. 1824), married William T. Lester;

they were the parents, among others, of Elder Posey G. Lester, who served in the U. S. Congress for two terms (1889-93), and is a widely-known minister of the Primitive Baptist Church; he is now pastor of a church in Roanoke.

C. Dr. William B. Simmons, a physician of Georgia.

D. Roley M. Simmons (b. 1826), married Malinda Nancy, daughter of Col. John W. Helms of Burks Fork. They lived at the old Charles Simmons homestead. Roley Simmons was educated under Professor William T. Gannaway at his school for young men at Jacksonville, after which he was for some years one of the schoolteachers of Floyd and Henry counties: among his pupils were Rear Admiral Robley D. Evans, Hon. Posey G. Lester, and others who attained honor and usefulness. He was Treasurer of Floyd County for the years 1887-91. Children of Roley and Nancy Simmons were:

1. Dr. John W. (b. 1859), who was for many years located at Floyd where he practiced medicine, and was Superintendent of Schools. He was the Republican nominee for Congress in the Fifth District against Judge E. W. Saunders. He moved to Martinsville, Va., in 1898, where he continues his practice of medicine. He married Elizabeth, daughter of Captain William H. Morgan; their children: Nancy Lee m. L. A. O'Brien of Winston-Salem, N. C.; Richard Morgan m. Margaret Sydnor of Mt. Airy, N. C.; Anna; Alice; and John W., Jr., m. Ruth Long of Charlottesville, Va. (See page 278).

2. Dr. Thomas W. married Willie Thomas of Southampton Co., Va., and located in Martinsville, Va., where he practiced medicine up to his death in 1898. He had three children.

3. George W., a large farmer and grazier who resides in Floyd County on part of the old Simmons farm, married Laura, daughter of Noah B. Moore; they had twin daughters: Annie Weston m. Joseph Proffit; and Olivia Moore m., first, Hugh Boyd, son of Captain J. M. Boyd, and, after his death, married Peter Archer Willis, son of George A. Willis.

4. Judge Tazewell M., a lawyer, lives in Huron, South Dakota; never married.

5. Hamilton W. (d. 1917), was Commonwealth's Attor-

ney of Floyd County for twelve years; never married.

6. Olivia married Charles B. Keesee, and lives in Martinsville.

7. Mattie married James D. Martin (deceased), of Leaksville, N. C., and lives in Martinsville.

In the Confederate army: Thomas H. Simmons, Fourth Sergeant, killed at Hatcher's Run, and Charles A. Simmons, killed at Frazier's Farm; they were members of Company A, 24th Virginia Infantry. In Company A, 54th Virginia Infantry were: Tazewell, Gideon, William, James A. (captured at Bentonville, N. C., and taken to Rock Island) ; and Daniel R. Simmons (captured July 20, 1864, near Atlanta and taken to Camp Douglas and paroled, June 16, 1865). In Company I, 54th Virginia Infantry were: Harvey D., Erasmus (fifer) and G. W. Simmons. Roley M. Simmons was in Stuart's Horse Artillery; Otey T. and Charles L. Simmons were members of Captain James B. Headen's Reserves.

In the World War was Hosea G. Simmons.

The Simpkins Family

Robert Simpkins and his brothers immigrated to America from England. They landed in the present state of New York where the brothers settled. Robert moved South and took up land by land warrant on the waters of Indian Creek in the present county of Floyd about the year 1770. The name of his wife is unknown. Their children were:

I. William Simpkins, whose wife is unknown, had the following children: Jackson, Back, Joseph, James and William, Jr.

II. Henry Simpkins (1800-1885) married Elizabeth Duncan and lived in the Indian Valley section. He is buried in the Sumpter Graveyard. Their children:

A. Crockett Simpkins (1828-1903) married Julia Ann, daughter of Marvel Trail of Franklin County; he is buried near Hiwassee, Pulaski County; their children: 1. John; 2. Lewis; 3. Legrand (b. 1851) m. Minerva Duncan, dau. of Benjamin and Nannie; their children: George Sidney, Susan, Benjamin, Ennis, Allie, Noah and Sarah; 4. Aaron; 5. Gabriel; 6. Marion;

7. Riley; 8. Sarah; 9. Polly; 10. Elizabeth; and 11. Margaret.

B. Floyd Simpkins married Sarah Sumpter; their children: Mary, Malinda and Harriet.

C. Richard Simpkins, married Polly Quesenberry; their children: Garland, George, Jackson, James, Lucy, Louise and Sallie.

III. Eli Simpkins, left the county when a young man.

IV. Thomas Simpkins, married Margaret Duncan; their children: Joshua, Gabriel, George, Peter, Nannie and Eliza.

V. Lawrence Simpkins, moved to Kentucky.

Richard L. Simpkins was a soldier in the Confederate army, a member of Company A, 24th Virginia Infantry, under Captain C. M. Stigleman. He was captured at Five Forks, taken to Point Lookout prison, and released in June 1865. Baxter Simpkins was a soldier in Company A, 54th Virginia Infantry, under Captain Andrew Dickerson.

Simpson

The Floyd County family is derived from the father of Allen Simpson, who emigrated to America in the year 1752-53, from Ireland, and settled in the state of New Jersey. Here Allen was born in the year 1757. He married Susanna Biles, who died May 22, 1827; Allen Simpson died March 19, 1820, both in the present county of Floyd. Their children were: William, James, Solomon, John and Catherine (Kitty).

A. William Simpson was born December [1793?], died September 28, 1879. He was an officer in the Mexican War. His home was near Simpsons in Floyd County, and at one time he owned practically all the land around Simpsons, including nearly all the land that is now called Locust Grove. At the time he [could this have been Allen, the father?] came to Floyd there was no cleared land, it was in the fall of the year, and no roads, only riding paths, or trails. "He thought he was at his journey's end and could get no further. They lived on peaches for three weeks, William, then but four years old, became so tired of peaches, it is said, he never ate another peach during his long life."

B. James Simpson was born in the present county of Floyd,

August 1799, and lived all his life in the county; he died in his eightieth year on March 24, 1879. Two of his children were Matilda E. and William A.

1. Matilda E. married William Walters, a Confederate soldier, who lost his life in the battle of Chancellorsville, Virginia, May 9, 1863. He was killed just behind William A. Simpson, his brother-in-law, who buried him the next day under a peach tree on the battlefield.

2. William A. Simpson was born Nov. 22, 1836, and lived in Floyd County at the old William Simpson home place, in his eighty-sixth year. He was a Confederate soldier, a member of Stuart's Light Horse Artillery, was with General Jackson's army (?), three days and three nights, going around General McClellan's army. They had very little to eat, and what little they did have they ate sitting on their horses. He was on the firing line until the very close of the war. The rations near the end of the war were one pint of cornmeal and one gill of molasses per day. He came out of the war without a wound and returned to Floyd County to recoup his waning fortunes, and has since lived in the county, a worthy and well-known citizen.

The Slusher Family

The Slushers, like many of the early German immigrants, lived for a time in Pennsylvania, and then moved south into Virginia with the tide of German migration between the years 1769 and 1800. Christopher Schlosser (Slusher) appears as attending St. Paul's Lutheran Church at Strasburg, Virginia, in 1794. Among those who subscribed and paid into the fund which was sent to Germany for the first pipe organ, Dec. 27, 1794, were: Christopher Schlosser, the Widow Gutekunst, Georg Phluger, Jacob Theiss.

Christopher Slusher came to present Floyd County and settled on West Fork of Little River. His family consisted of five sons and five daughters:

I. Peter Slusher had three sons and three daughters.

II. Solomon Slusher had three sons: William, Solomon, Jr.,

and Allen.

III. David Slusher had five daughters (names unknown) and four sons: Sparrel, Hamilton, George and Ananias.

A. Ananias Slusher had four sons:

1. Lafayette, a physician.

2. Floyd, a very successful farmer.

3. Monroe.

4. David married Margaret, oldest daughter of Peter Bowman; they raised a family of eleven children, one of whom is Dr. William C. Slusher of Bluefield, W. Va. David Slusher was Sheriff of Floyd County for 16 years.

IV. Jacob Slusher (Sept. 2, 1797-1871) married Tabitha Hylton; their six children:

A. John, whose children were, in part: Taylor, John, Jr.

B. Jeremiah, an elder of the Brethren Church, married Sally Weddle, daughter of Andrew, and granddaughter of Benjamin, the settler; their children:

1. France married Lizzie Harter; their children were: Adam m. Rachel Hylton; Edward m. Lura Barringer; Margaret m. Josiah Howell.

2. Bennett married Nannie Dickerson; their children were: Jacob, Arthur, Walter, Hiley, Julina and Lillie.

3. Millard married Sarah Jane Finn; their children: Francis, Samuel and Louannie.

4. Andrew, no record.

5. Darius married Susan Slusher; their children, Dr. Hamilton; Delilah; and Sarah.

6. Elizabeth married John Hylton.

7. Nancy married John Bennett Turman.

8. Rosabelle married William Weeks.

C. Marion Slusher married Lucy Turman; their children: Leroy, Tazewell, Thomas, Sarah Ellen, Adeline, Adaway, Lena and Dollie.

D. Oliver Perry Slusher married Mary J. Wood, daughter of John R. and Lucinda (DeHart) Wood; they lived northwest of the courthouse on West Fork where he was one of the progressive farmers of the section; their children:

1. Jacob, and 2. John, both of whom died in infancy.

3. Asa L., died at age 21.

4. Flournoy married Eliza Jenkins, daughter of William and Delilah (Smith) Jenkins, and now lives in Ohio; their children: Edgar m. Nellie Burke of Roanoke County; Earnest Wm.; Oliver m. Lucy Nixon; Carmel F.; and Meda Mae m. Guy Altizer.

5. George William married, first, Clementine D. Corn, daughter of Rev. Peter and Tina (Turner) Corn of Patrick County, and, secondly, Mrs. Della Howery. Children of the first marriage; S. Claude m. Ida Hylton; Peter Asa, died age 3; Romney L. m. Ada Harman; Mary T. m. Edgar Harman; Nola L. m. George M. Hylton; Roger O. m. Pearl Sutphin; Bessie R. m. Earle W. Sutphin; Martha E. m. Joseph G. Conduff; Effie V. m. H. Cline Sowers; George, Jr.; Lelia A.; Kate W.; Freeman M.; and Eva Doyle (Dotte).

6. Louisa married Abraham, son of Riley and Hannah (Wade) Hylton.

7. Angeline married Abraham Snead, son of Francis; their children: Abner m. Willie Agee; Arnton.

8. Rosie Roena married Homer Hylton, son of Riley and Hannah.

9. Ellen married Ephraim Hall, son of Burrell and Martha (Viar) Hall.

10. Lelia Kansas (d. 1902) married Callie Sowers, son of David and Mary (Ridinger) Sowers; they had two sons: Orris and Orland.

E. George Slusher married Leah Wood (twin to Rachel), daughter of John R. and Lucinda; they lived in Floyd County; their children: Eliza; Kittie m. Samuel Emerson; Sarah.

F. Mary Melissa Slusher (1838-1853) died at age 14.

V. Christopher Slusher, Jr.

VI. Tabithia Slusher.

VII. Cynthia Slusher.

VIII. Susan Slusher.

IX. Elizabeth Slusher.

X. Julianna Slusher.

The Smith Family

The Smith family is of German origin, the name being originally spelled **Schmidt**. William Smith bought 1000 acres of land in the county of Montgomery, now Floyd. His wife brought Easter lily bulbs over on the boat in her apron pocket and planted them at the original home place, now known as the Easter flower patch.

Casper Smith, son of William, married Catherine Schlosser (Slusher) in Germany where their first three children were born; John, Frederick and Henry, the latter born in 1793. The family immigrated to America while Henry was a babe in arms. They settled in Pennsylvania and here three more children were born: Christopher, Eva and Mary. About 1800, the family moved South, settling some three miles south of the present county seat of Floyd on the waters of Dodds Creek. Casper and Catherine were affiliated with Zion Lutheran Church, as shown by the church records: their daughter, Elizabeth, born February 1, 1805, baptized April 30, 1805, sponsors Christopher Slusher and wife. This record indicates that their daughter Elizabeth was born after their settlement in Virginia.

I. Henry Smith (1793-1851) married Catherine (Katie) Harman, eldest daughter of Jacob and Christina (Mock) Harman, and lived two miles south of the present county seat. Their eleven children:

A. Christina (1818-1903), never married.

B. Isaac (1819-1907) married Naomi Weaver, daughter of John; their children:

1. Rosabelle (b. 1843)

2. Noah (1854-1911) married D. C. Harman, daughter of Peter.

3. Flournoy (b. 1856) married Adeline Bowling, daughter of Henry: their children: Hubert Lee, Mattie, Maude, Naomi, Samuel, Amos, Abigail, Burks, Annie and Ashby.

4. Mahala married Washington Weeks; their children: Isaac and Letitia.

5. Abednego married Alice Weeks; their children: Dorah, Rowena, Elza, Mathew, Rosetta, Lillian and Clayton.

6.   Louanna (1867-1915) married Benjamin Harman; no children.

C.   Eli (1821-1905), twin brother to Eliza, married Dec. 23, 1858, Deborah Clark Shortt, daughter of Joseph, and lived six miles south of the courthouse; their five children:

1.   Asa S. (b. 1865).

2.   Victoria A. (b. 1871).

3.   Emma G. (1868-1899) married Henry J. Weddle; their children: Elbert, Hattie, Posey, Lida, Caleb, Carrie and Dewey.

4.   Malinda M. (b. 1874) married T. A. Weeks in 1898; their children: Elmer, Clara, Gladys, John, Hymen, Reva, Elsie, Lelia, Zora, Clarence and Howard.

5.   Minnie F. (b. 1879) married, first, Daniel B. Weddle in 1899; their children: Marie, Vernon, Raymond and Edward.   Minnie married, secondly, in 1913, E. C. Wickham of Iowa; their children: Pauline, Anna, Ella and Robert.   They live near Gage post office.

D.   Eliza (1821-1901) married Samuel Agnew, Jr.; their children: Isabella, Tazewell, Ellen, Susan, Henry, Emmazetta, John and Nannie.

E.   Maza (1823-1900) married John Wade; their children: Levi and Amanda.

F.   Flemon (1825-1905) married Mary J. Gill, daughter of John; their children: Sallie, Solomon, Cora, Henry and Naomi.

G.   Delilah (1827-1909) married William Jenkins, son of Jonathan; their children: Angeline, Virginia and Eliza.

H.   George (1830-1905) married Catherine Russell, daughter of Jeremiah; their children: James Bennett, John Floyd, George H., Charles P., Sarah A., Daniel F. and William A.

I.   John (1832-1912) married Elmira Morricle, daughter of Samuel; their children: Catherine, Annie and Samuel.

J.   Martha (1834-1918) married John Basham and lived ten miles north of the county seat; their children: Flemon, Sallie and Annie.

K.   Jacob (b. 1837) married Jane Nixon, daughter of Thomas, and lived, after 1888, in Indian Valley District, where he has been Supervisor of the county and a prominent farmer;

their children: Lizzie, Thomas, Alfred, Catherine, Mary, Laura and Arthur.

II. Christopher Smith, better known as "Stuffle," married Wilmouth Watkins, daughter of Ebenezer, and settled two miles south of the present county seat, where he operated a flouring mill. The old mill site is now the property of Giles W. Whitlow. Here Robert (Bob) Whitlow kept a tollgate on the Mabry Gap Turnpike in the days before the Civil War. Children of Stuffle Smith and wife were:

A. Sarah, married Mason Jenkins.

B. Julie Ann, first wife of John Earles.

C. Mary Jane, second wife of John Earles.

D. Christina, married George Whitlock.

E. Eliza E., married Hosea Correll.

F. Emmazetta, married George W. Weaver.

The Smiths from this family in the Confederate army: Jacob and John Smith were members of Company A, 24th Virginia Infantry; Jacob was wounded three times, both were captured at Five Forks and taken to Point Lookout prison. Henry L. Smith was Second Lieutenant in Company I, 54th Virginia Infantry, and in the same company were Eli, wounded at Resaca, Georgia, on May 15, 1864, and Fleming, wounded at Mt. Zion, June 25, 1864. Isaac Smith was in Captain J. B. Headen's Reserves. In Company B., 42nd Infantry, were: William R., William P., John A., John, Thomas and Jonathan L. Smith. Thomas and Jonathan L. were wounded and died in the service, time and place unknown. George Smith was a member of Company H, 51st Virginia, and was captured at Waynesboro, Va., and taken to Fort Delaware. Others who served were Bill Smith and B. F. Smith.

Luke Smith The Settler

In 1840, Luke Smith and Mary Naff, his wife, moved with their family from Franklin County and settled six miles east of the county seat. The Smith family had lived for years in Franklin County; Luke's brother, John A. Smith, was Sheriff of the county. Their father may have been Philemon

(Phil) Smith who married Nancy Abshire, daughter of Luke Abshire, in 1794. The eight children of Luke and Mary (Naff) Smith, were:

A. Josiah Smith, married Amanda Richards, daughter of Walter Richards; their children, in part:

1. John S. Smith, a Lutheran Minister, has been pastor of a church at Ephrata, Pennsylvania, for a third of a century.

2. James Smith.

3. Jefferson Smith, married India Harman, daughter of David, and lived for many years in the town of Floyd where he was a cattle dealer.

4. Josiah S. Smith, a physician of Radford, Virginia.

5. Kyle Smith, lives at the old homestead three miles east of the courthouse.

B. John Smith, no record.

C. Shelburne Smith.

D. Susan Smith, married Jacob Bower (1829-1881), their children: Josiah, Amanda, Abraham, Ellen, George, Rosa, Isaac, Marion.

E. Martha Smith.

F. Christina Smith.

G. Elizabeth Smith, married Daniel Bower, son of Christopher the settler; their children: Mary, Ann, Jane, Luke, Joseph, Eliza, Martin, Homer, Florence.

H. Hannah Smith, married James A. Hoback, a minister of the Church of the Brethren, and lived in the east end of the county.

In the Confederate army: Josiah and John Smith were members of Stuart's Horse Artillery in Pelham's Battery, and Shelburne Smith was a member of Company A, 54th Virginia Infantry under Captain Andrew Dickerson.

The Snuffer Family

The Snuffer family was one of the many Franklin County settlers who came over the Blue Ridge to find homes in Floyd County. The Snuffers lived on Pig River in Franklin County; two sons of this family were Isaac, who married Malinda Rakes, daughter of Samuel of Patrick County, and Peter, married Betsy Cannaday.

I. John Snuffer married Susan Huff, daughter of John, the settler, and they lived at Graysville, Floyd County. At the time, John and Susan lived on the Cannaday's Gap road at the Marion Agee place.

II. Elizabeth Snuffer married Isaac, son of John and Mary (Tony) Huff, and lived for some years on Otter Creek in Franklin County, later moving to Floyd in the Pine Creek section. They were the parents of Jacob, Isaac, Peter and John.

III. Peter Snuffer, brother of Elizabeth and John, lived at the late Jonathan Brammer place, some six miles east of the county seat. Susan, daughter of Peter, married Christopher Bower, Jr., and their children were: John, William and Tabitha.

The Snuffers were members of the Baptist Church.

Sowers

John Sowers, born in Floyd County, married Catherine Lester of Montgomery County, and raised the following children:

A. Hulen L. Sowers, married Margaret Yearout; their children:

1. James A. Sowers (b. Jan. 26, 1850) married Eliza A. LeSueur, daughter of James W., their children: Mary Alma m. Arthur Winchester; Ruby Lee m. Thurman Akers; Joseph A. m. Lucy Scott; Edwin F. m. Pearl Munsey.

2. Joseph A. J. Sowers, married Malinda Lampy.

3. John W. Sowers, married Caldonia Lampy; their children: Charles m. Pearl Epperly; Lee m. Ruby Howery; Maud m. Charles Howery; Houstin; Everett; Ernest; Jacob Shell.

4. Mary E. Sowers, married A. W. Lester.

5. Catherine Sowers, married Abraham Bower.

6. Amanda H. Sowers, married Harley Cumming; their children: Clayton; Lessley; Willie; Mary m. Howard Hylton; Ruth m. Rex Dangerfield; Eva m. Johnson.

B. Joseph D. Sowers, married Julia Ann Slusher.

C. Ellen Sowers, married David Winter.

D. Mary Sowers, married B. C. Wickham.

The Spangler Family

The Spanglers came from Pennsylvania, according to family tradition, and settled first in Franklin County, Virginia. Records there show that in 1786 Daniel Spangler, Sr., and Daniel Spangler, Jr., served on the grand jury. In 1787 the will of Daniel Spangler, bearing date November 1787, was exhibited by Mary Spangler, executrix. This Daniel Spangler was doubtless the husband of Mary Spangler, widow, who settled near the mouth of Pine Creek in present Floyd County. Her tombstone in Pine Creek Cemetery shows that she died in 1820, aged over 100 years.

In 1792, Daniel Spangler, II bought the mill on Pine Creek from William Logan, the same mill which William Logan bought from Joshua Terry in 1787. The mill has been in the Spangler family from that time: it was held by Daniel Spangler, II from him to his son Samuel, then to his son, Samuel, Jr., and from Samuel, Jr., to his son Walter H. Spangler, the present owner and of the fifth generation of Spanglers in Floyd County.

Daniel Spangler, II, died Feb. 4, 1823, at the age of seventy-six, and is buried in Pine Creek Cemetery. His wife Sarah died May 8, 1839, at the age of eighty-six. The first court held in Floyd County was "at the late residence of Daniel Spangler, deceased, on Monday, May 16th, 1831." This log house was not far from Spangler's Mill near the mouth of Pine Creek. Children of Daniel, II, and Sarah Spangler were:

I. John Spangler (b. April 8, 1783) settled at Meadows of Dan, name of wife unknown; their five children were: Richard, Fleming, Thomas, George Washington and Mary Ann.

II. Daniel Spangler, III, (b. Aug. 25, 1784), married Betsy Sowers, June 4, 1805, moved to Tennessee.

III. George Spangler (b. July 18, 1786), married Elizabeth Epperly, April 1, 1806, moved to Tennessee.

IV. Mary Spangler (b. Dec. 28, 1789), married George Sowers, Jr.

V. William Spangler (Sept. 18, 1792-1862), married Mary Irvin (1808-1880) and lived in Floyd County; they were the parents of eleven children. They are buried in Pine Creek Cemetery. Their children were: Harvey, Daniel, David, Tazewell,

John, Calvin, Nancy, Mary Ann, Lina, Elizabeth, and one son who died in infancy.

VI. Samuel Spangler (b. Jan. 2, 1795), married, first, Catherine Hylton. He served in the Mexican War; he died April 26, 1875, and is buried in the Spangler Cemetery. After the death of his first wife, Catherine, Samuel married, secondly, Phoebe Webster (d. July 5, 1876, buried in Spangler Cemetery) ; they had no issue. Samuel anod Catherine had eleven children:

A. Henry (1819-1902), married, first, Elizabeth Shelor, and lived in Floyd County; their eight children: Eden, William Ira, Catherine, Emily, Matilda, Mary Isabel, Nancy Jane, and Lydia. Henry married, secondly, Artie Lane; their children: Benjamin, Nora and Mattie.

B. Asa (1822-1901), married, first, Caroline Payton and settled in West Virginia; their children: Perry, Samuel, John, Roena, Isabel, Phoebe and Martha. Asa married, secondly, Rebecca Martin Kidd; no issue.

C. William (1824-1857), married Hannah Sowers (1828-1910) ; their children: Ananias; Abraham; Samuel (b. 1853) m. Mary O. Agee, their children: William L., James S. m. Martha Reed, W. B., Charles, Eliza, and Judith; William; Ellen; Annie; and Sallie.

D. Solomon married Mary Carroll and lived in Floyd County; their nine children: Samuel, Lafayett, Ellen, Malinda, Sallie, Elizabeth, Mellie, Susan, and Daniel.

E. Jacob married Ruth Graham and lived in West Virginia; their five children: Bartley, James, and daughters, names unknown.

F. Isaac Spangler married Henrietta Creasy and lived in Floyd County; their children: Catherine, Phoebe and Henrietta.

G. Samuel (1836-1901), married Adaline Sowers (1838-1909), and lived in Floyd County; their children: Charles, Walter, Glenn and Rosa.

H. Sarah Spangler.

I. Elizabeth Spangler.

J. Octavia Spangler.

K. Daughter, died in infancy.

VII. Jacob (b. June 2, 1799), settled in Missouri.

VIII. David (b. Sept. 16, 1801), married, first, Sarah

[Margaret] Sowers, lived in Floyd County: their children: John, Sarah, Mary, Nancy and Eliza. David married, secondly, Amelia Boothe; their children: Joseph, George, Christian, Daniel, Henderson, Isaac, James, David, Elmira, Adaline, and Margaret.

(See page 279 for Spangler's Mill).

Jacob Strickler The Settler

Abraham Strickler, of Zurich, Switzerland, came to America and settled in Pennsylvania, then moved to Virginia. Abraham brought with him a German Bible printed in Zurich in 1536, and this book is still cherished by his descendants. The name of his wife is not known; they had at least four sons and a daughter: Jacob, Joseph, Benjamin, John, Mary, and there may have been other children.

Jacob Strickler, eldest son of Abraham; his home, a combination dwelling and fort, was built on the thousand-acre estate which he inherited from his father, named Egypt. Jacob married, first, Nancy Kauffman and after her death he married Magdalene Moorman. Jacob Strickler died in 1784, leaving thirteen children, six of whom were by his first wife, Nancy.

Samuel Strickler, second child of Jacob and Nancy (Kauffman) Strickler, was born about 1765 and died in 1833. He lived opposite Horseshoe Bend on Smith's Creek, near New Market, Va. His old home is still standing. He married Mary Maggot (or Maggard); they had at least three children: Jacob, Abraham, Mary.

I. Jacob Strickler (1786-1867), eldest son of Samuel, is the ancestor of the Floyd County family. He married Mary Kagey (1797-1880), daughter of Henry Kagey of Smith's Creek, son of Henry Kagey of Pennsylvania. He moved from the Valley of Virginia to present Floyd County and settled on the Bent Mountain pike, eight miles northeast of the county seat. Their eight children:

A. Mary Ann Strickler (b. Oct. 11, 1818), married in

1844 Mathew Scott, son of John Scott of Floyd, and their children were: Samuel; James; Martha m. James M. Boyd and had one daughter, Etta m. Bittle Harless and lives in Christiansburg; Winfield; Alice m. James Stultz; Walter, unmarried; and Mary m. Birdine Bishop.

B. Samuel (b. Sept. 17, 1820), married Nancy Ann Helms, daughter of John and Sallie (Livcsay) Helms of Little River, and lived six miles east of the courthouse; their ten children:

1. Ann Eliza (b. 1845), m. Akin Epperly, no children.

2. Sarah Rosabelle (b. 1847), m. Thomas Keen DeWitt; they have two sons: Samuel Zachariah m. Maggie Florence Vest, and James Strickler m. Eunice E. Furrow.

3. John Ballard (b. 1849), m. Celeste Sowder, daughter of William and Mary Ann (Thrash) Sowder; their children: William T., Samuel A., Nancy M., Cammie, Herbert Helms, Eliza B., Kate and Clyde.

4. Millard Jacob (1850-1863), killed by "falling of a tree."

5. Mary Josephine (b. 1853) m. Robert Thurman, son of David; they had one child, Robert Melvin m. Lelia Cannaday, and moved to Anthony, Kansas.

6. Samuel Homer (b. 1855) married Feb. 27, 1878, Harriet Conner, daughter of Jonathan and Mahala; they lived for many years in Floyd and later moved to Iaeger, W. Va.; their children:

(a) Annie Eliza m. J. F. Simpson, son of Tazewell and Elizabeth Simpson; their children: Sherman, Violet, Almeda, Harman S., B. M., Sarah, Katherine, and Amos Lee.

(b) Warfield m. Letitia Richardson, daughter of John.

(c) Valentine Thrash m. Marjory Annie Carter (d. Oct. 23, 1919), daughter of Thompson and Virginia Carter; their children: Jack Carter, Harriet B., Ida Nell, Margie Ann.

(d) Wise m. Sadie Huff.

(e) Julia m. Robert Mullins; their children: Alvin, Juanita, Strickler, Samuel and Almeda.

(f) Mary m. John Parker; their children: Lucile, William, Edna and Virginia.

    (g)   Elizabeth m. Henry Christian, one child, Elbert.

    (h)   Belle m. Wesley Johnston and has one child, James.

    (i)   Elbert, unmarried.

    7.   Christian Flurnoy (b. 1858), m. Geraldine Whitenack, daughter of Jonathan, and lives in Floyd County; they have four children: Sallie A., Hyburnia, Lala, Alene.

    8.   Nancy Abia (1862-1864).

    9.   James William Warfield (1864-1865).

    10.   Lenora Davis (b. 1869), m. John T. Thurman, son of David and Ann (Livesay) Thurman, and moved to Anthony, Kansas; their children: Myrtle, David, Helms, Herthel and Forest.

    C.   Catherine (b. 1822), never married.

    D.   Elizabeth married William J. Williams; their children: Jacob, Julia, Mary, Ellen, Thomas and Samuel. The family moved to Texas about 1859.

    E.   Henry, died in infancy.

    F.   Sarah, married Eli M. Williams; their children: James, Callahill, Henry, Charles, Samuel and Mary. The family moved to Texas about 1890.

    G.   Barbara married, first, Alvin Whitlock; their children: John, William, Josephine and Sarah. Barbara married, secondly, John M. Graham.

    H.   Ruth married Andrew Cross and moved West; they have eight children, among them: Sarah, James, Samuel.

Sumpter

    Edmund Sumpter, Jr., states in the Draper Mss. that his great-grandfather came from England, settled near Richmond, Va.; that his grandfather's name was George but he does not remember any of George's brothers; that his grandfather married Elizabeth Gross, probably from Charlotte County, Virginia. He says, "My father's name was Edmund Sumpter and he married Elisabeth Kingery from Franklin County, Va. He had two brothers, Uncle Richard went to Ohio to his wife's relatives, he and my father married sisters; Uncle George married

Catherine Prillaman in Franklin County, Va., then moved to Indiana and later to Georgia. My father served in the War of 1812. My grandfather, George Sumpter, died in the County of Montgomery, but now Floyd County, he was accidentally killed by his son Richard cutting a dead sapling on him at a chopping at one of his neighbors while he (grandfather) was repairing a helve for an axe; he was a workman. I don't know how old he was."

George Sumpter signed his will Sept. 3, 1800, and from this he appears to have been a large landowner and a man of considerable business capacity. George Sumpter was born Feb. 5, 1713, near Richmond, Va., and married Elizabeth Gross (b. June 16, 1714). They were the parents of three daughters, whose names are not recalled, and three sons:

1. George Sumpter, Jr., married Catherine Prillaman and moved to Indiana.

II. Richard Sumpter married Kingery and moved to Ohio.

III. Edmund Sumpter (Feb. 25, 1770-April 10, 1856) was in the War of 1812; married Elisabeth Kingery (Dec. 22, 1770-Oct. 19, 1857), and lived at the old homestead at the junction of Dodd's Creek with the West Fork of Little River. Their children were:

A. John Sumpter (b. Feb. 10, 1796), moved to Indiana.

B. Jacob Sumpter (b. March 29, 1797).

C. Martha Sumpter (b. Sept. 3, 1798), married Sowder.

D. Sarah Sumpter (b. July 17, 1800).

E. Richard Sumpter (b. Dec. 19, 1801), lived at his father's old homestead, married Catherine Sowder; their children: 1. Asa (b. March 15, 1825); 2. Tymandra (b. May 8, 1826); 3. Letitia (b. Oct. 5, 1827); 4. Salathiel (b. Apr. 12, 1831); 5. Harvey (b. Jan. 20, 1834); 6. Elizabeth (b. Oct. 1835); 7. Emily (b. June 28, 1837); 8. Joseph (b. Aug. 25, 1839); 9. Matilda (b. June 21, 1841); 10. Martha (b. June 21, 1844).

F. Edmund Sumpter, Jr. (Dec. 13, 1803-Aug. 27, 1883) married Delilah Eskew (April 15, 1799-June 15, 1899), and settled in the Indian Valley Township in 1841; their children:

1. Elizabeth (b. April 18, 1832).

2. Malinda (b. March 13, 1833).

3. Octavia (b. July 14, 1834).

4. Sarah (b. July 20, 1836), married Riley Sutphin.

5. John (b. March 23, 1838).

6. Ruth (b. March 9, 1840).

7. Jacob (b. Feb. 18, 1844), married Mary Hambrick (Oct. 20, 1848-July 22, 1921), and lived in Indian Valley; their children:

(a) George (b. June 23, 1870).

(b) Annie Lawsa (b. Jan. 16, 1873).

(c) Monroe G. (b. Feb. 2, 1875), moved to Logan County, W. Va., and married Louemma Stafford, their children: Kyle, Archie W. (U. S. Army), Willie E. (enlisted in World War May 4, 1917, and saw active service in France), Wilmer A., Ruth, Walter, Ethel, Hazel and Luther.

(d) Forest (b. July 19, 1876).

(e) Mason D. (b. Oct. 20, 1881).

(f) Frank C. (b. July 7, 1887), m. Della Akers and lives on New River in Giles County, Va., their children: Delmas (b. May 23, 1907), Bonnie D. (b. April 10, 1910), Sam E. (Oct. 31, 1912), May (b. May 22, 1915), Wise M. (b. Jan. 14, 1919), Mary V. (b. Jan. 14, 1922).

8. Joseph (b. Feb. 18, 1844), twin to Jacob.

9. Araminta (b. Dec. 6, 1846), m. John W. Altizer.

10. Laban (b. Nov. 12, 1850).

G. Fannie Sumpter (b. March 2, 1806), m. Burnett.

In the Confederate army were: Joseph Sumpter, Third Corporal in Company A, 54th Virginia Infantry under Captain Andrew Dickerson, wounded at Missionary Ridge, June 26, 1863; Asa Sumpter was a private in the same company; Jacob Sumpter was a member of Company B, 54th Virginia Infantry under Captain Jackson Godbey; R. D. Sumpter was a member of Captain James B. Headen's Company of Reserves under Col. Robert L. Preston.

In the World War were: John S., Bernice A., and Martin L. Sumpter from Floyd County.

Sutphin

The Sutphins were natives of Belgium and spelled their name **Zutphen.** They immigrated to the British Isles and then to America, settling in New York and in eastern Virginia. In the early 1800s, Hendrick Sutphin came to present Floyd County with his large family and settled on Burks Fork Creek near the Floyd-Carroll line. His wife's name is not known; they had twelve children:

I.   John Sutphin, married Leola or Leah Hylton, daughter of Henry and Elizabeth, she was a sister of Austin Hylton.

II.   Leonard Sutphin married Susannah Hylton (b. abt. 1794), daughter of Henry and Elizabeth.

III.   William Sutphin, no record.

IV.   Daniel Sutphin, no record.

V.   Henry (Hollie) Sutphin married Polly Keith; their nine children:

A.   Riley Sutphin married Mary Houchins; they had the following children: Lafayette; Marion; Washington; Henrietta m. Lorton; Martha Ann m. Judge John L. Meredith, no children; Madilla m. Madison Martin.

B.   Booker Sutphin, never married.

C.   John Sutphin married Mary Dick, no children.

D.   Byrd Sutphin married Rebecca Keith; their children:

1.   Taylor m. Catherine Knowles; their children: Mollie, Nina, Lelia, Lafayette, Martin, Elbert, Paris and Malinda.

2.   George m. Diana Knowles.

3.   Nelson m. Weddle.

4.   Malinda m. Kelse Reynolds.

5.   Joshua, never married.

6.   Milton m. Widow Martin, no children.

E.   Rolen Sutphin married Sophia Sutphin, his cousin;

their children:

1. Callahill m. Samanthia Clay, no children.
2. Louisa, never married.
3. Susannah, never married.
4. Maisie, never married.
5. Nancy m. Matt Duncan and had two girls, Sophia Catherine and Lydia Frankie.
6. Peyton m. Lydia Howell and had twin girls: Almeda m. Dorsie Phillips, and Lizena m. Dura Keith.

F.   Henderson Sutphin married Mary Becklehamer; their children: Thomas m. Spangler; James, never married; John; Levi; Ida and Etta.

G.   Martha Sutphin, never married.

H.   Eli Sutphin married Sarah Ann Martin; their twelve children:

1.   William Ransom m. Roena Becklehamer; their children:

(a)   Laura m. Richard Lawrence.

(b)   Maybell m. Jack Nally.

(c)   Thomas m. Lillie Jones, their children: Lee, Hazel, Sarah Jane.

(d)   Benjamin, never married.

(e)   McKinley m. Vernia Lafferty, their children: William Reginald, Mildred, Edna.

(f)   Hobart m. Widow Carrie Mead Gullet, their three children: Virginia, Charles, Abby Daye.

(g)   Annie Ethel m. Grover Treadway, they had one daughter: Virginia.

(h)   Eli m. Venia Iddings, their children: Ward, Cecil, Laura Jane.

2.   James Abraham Lincoln m. Eliza Ann Hylton; their children:

(a)   Carl H. m. Lillian Susan Dickerson; one son, Carl H., Jr.

(b)   Pearl Clyde m. Roger Oliver Slusher, a farmer of Brush Fork; their five children: Neva Dell, Edith Pearl, Roger Oliver, Jr., Ruth Ann, and Jewel Clementine.

(c)   Earl W. (served two years in France in the World War) m. Bessie Ruth Slusher; their two girls: Helen Earl and

Ruth Merle.

(d) Kate Merle m. Fieldon Harman, an ex-soldier of the World War, no children.

(e) Russell Howard m. Woodie Grant Moore, no children.

(f) Ruby Lee m. Lawrence Miller Bowman, businessman of Boones Mill; one daughter: Colleen Miller.

(g) Ina Dura, a nurse in Richmond, Va.

(h) Hazel James.

(i) Lorraine Ann.

3. Mellon Larkin m. Bessie Rank in Illinois and has one son, Ethelbert, who is married and living at Mena, Arkansas.

4. Mary Ann m. Henry Keith; their children: Meekin m. McPeak of Girard, Illinois; Lura m. Blacker of Girard, Ill.; Jessie m. Willhite; Ray.

5. Jane m. Eric J. Israelson, no children.

6. Hulda m. Leslie L. Harris, their children: Dollie; Georgia m. Hyle; Herbert; Burnice; Dorothy; and Eileen.

7. David m. Ida Bell; they have one daughter, Naomi Irene.

8. Henry m. Ella Harris; their children: Erma, Hallie, Eddison, and two other children.

9. Hines m. Ella Rellerford, no children.

10. Hite m. Louanna Sutphin, their children: Martha, Louise, Marvin Lee and Howard Erick.

11. Martha Ellen, died in infancy.

12. Liona Agnes, died in infancy.

I. Elizabeth married Levi Keith who was killed in a mill, no children.

VI. Christopher Sutphin married Susannah Harman (b. Jan. 3, 1800, baptized April 6, 1800, Zion Lutheran Church, Strasburg, Va.), daughter of Jacob and Christina (Mock) Harman; Christopher had 130 acres on Greasy Creek in 1831; their seven children:

A. Jacob Sutphin m. Polly DeLong.

B. Elizabeth Sutphin m. Leonard Keith.

C. Christina Sutphin m. Daniel Keith.

D. Rachel Sutphin, never married.

    E. Hendrick Sutphin, Jr., m. Parthena McPeak.

    F. Mary Sutphin, died in infancy.

    G. Sophia Sutphin m. Rolen Sutphin, son of Hollie.

  VII. Thomas Sutphin, no record.

  VIII. Hannah Sutphin, married John Alderman, Sr., of Burks Fork, they had ten children.

  IX. Nancy Sutphin, no record.

  X. Alice Sutphin, no record.

  XI. Daniel Sutphin, no record.

  XII. Catherine Sutphin, no record.

In the Confederate army: William Sutphin, Company A, 24th Virginia Infantry under Captain C. M. Stigleman, died at Culpeper Court House: Hendrick Sutphin, Company G, 54th Virginia Infantry; Jacob and W. L. Sutphin were in Captain James B. Headen's Company of Reserves under Col. Robert L. Preston; Jacob Sutphin was in Captain Andrew J. Graham's Company in the same Reserves; W. S. Stuphin, Company G, 21st Virginia Cavalry under Captain A. O. Dobyns, transferred to the 24th Virginia Infantry. Those in Company D, 54th Virginia Infantry under Captain Henry Slusher were: Hendrick, Rolen, Henderson, John H., Harrison and Asa L. Sutphin who died while on furlough at home. Lafayette Sutphin, son of Taylor, was killed in battle.

In the World War were: Earl W. Sutphin, Samuel L. Sutphin (died in France), and Lonnie L. Sutphin from Floyd County.

The Swinney (Sweeney) Family

The Swinney family in Virginia is considered an early family, but not a large one.

Samuel Swinney (1828-1906) was a well-known constable in the Little River District for thirty or more years. He married Margaret Thomas (1837-1894), daughter of Charles Thomas of Patrick County, and lived on the River about two miles from Pizarro, where he was also engaged in farming. Nine of their children were: Elkanah, Lizzie, Delia, Mary Jane,

Samuel, Jr., Dock, Peter, Nannie and Leonard.

Edward Swinney, brother of Samuel, lived also on Little River, where he was a farmer.

The Thomas Family

The rather fragmentary family tradition is that Charles Thomas and Judith Patterson, his wife, came with their family from Appomattox County, Virginia, and settled in Patrick County on Smiths River, three miles east of old Charity Meetinghouse on a farm later owned by Turner F. Rakes, who married a descendant. This family is said to be of Welch descent, and Charles Thomas the settler was the son of the immigrant who first settled in Maryland. The nine children of Charles and Judith Thomas were:

I. Charles Thomas, Jr. (b. 1768) married Deborah Jordan and lived on Poplar Creek in Patrick County. He was a farmer and one of the early justices of the peace. Their six known children were:

A. Mary (Polly) married Joseph Nix Shortt, son of Reuben Shortt; their children, in part: 1. Elder Asa D. Shortt m. Sallie Graham, daughter of Alexander; 2. Sarah Short m. James McDaniel; 3. Betty m. Lucian McDaniel; 4. Emily m. William Davis; 5. Judith m. Elkany Hatcher; 6.Deborah m. Eli Smith; 7. Lydia m. John Russell; 8. Rennie m. Robert Jones.

B. Fleming Thomas married ———— Hill; their children, in part: 1. George m. Susan Thomas; 2. Tom Pete m. ———— Griffith, sister of Tyler Griffith; 3. Polly, never married, still living, nearly 90 years old; 4. 'Merica m. Marshall Wright.

C. Peter Thomas married Sally Akers, daughter of Nathaniel and sister of Captain Burwell Akers; they were the parents of 22 children, some of whom were: 1. Nathaniel m. Lucinda Young Shortt (her second husband); 2. Fleming m. Martha Rakes; 3. Jordan m. Betty Shortt, daughter of John Y. Shortt; 4. Emeline; 5. Lucretia m. Richard Nolen, son of "Rusty," and grandson of John Nolen the settler; 6. Elizabeth m. William Nolen, brother of Richard; 7. Sarah m. William F. Nolen; 8. Ruth m. Jackson Rakes, brother of Richard, Alex, Lum.

D. Nicholas Thomas, never married.

E. Judith Thomas married Charles Thomas, son of Pleasant; their children: Tug, Sarah, and others.

F. Nancy Thomas married Francis Turner, son of Adam; their children: 1. Charles m. Viola Hall; 2. Samuel F. m. Rachel Wood, daughter of John R.; 3. Jefferson m. Susan Shortt, daughter of John Y. Shortt; 4. Fleming m. Nancy Rakes, daughter of Samuel Rakes; 5. Anna m. Alexander Rakes, son of Samuel and Lucinda (Nolen) Rakes; and 6. Debra m. Richard R. Rakes, son of Samuel.

II. Pleasant Thomas (1770-1848) married Mary Cannaday (1770-1847), daughter of James; they lived four miles east of Charity on Smiths River in Patrick County; their eight children:

A. Charles Thomas married, first, a Cannaday, sister of Bailey Cannaday; their children: Bailey, Jackson, and others; Charles married, secondly, Judith Thomas, daughter of Charles; their children: Tug, Sarah and others.

B. Pleasant Thomas married the widow Fannie Kennett; their children: Amanda m. Louis Thomas, son of Joseph; Tazewell; Charles (called "Strut") m. Rakes; Sarah m. John Hall, son of Harden; and Elizabeth m. John Burnett, son of Jeremiah.

C. Richard Thomas married Elizabeth _____ and moved to Illinois; Dr. Thomas of this family was a prominent physician.

D. James Thomas married Cynthia, daughter of Joseph Thomas, and lived on Poplar Camp Creek in Patrick County near the Floyd County line; their children: 1. Pleasant m. Amanda, daughter of Wilson Nolen, and moved West; their children: Lemons, Samuel and others; 2. Richard m. Elizabeth, daughter of Wilson Nolen; their children: Mary Jane, Abram, Larkin, Minerva, Lillie, Cora Lee and Patterson; 3. Jerry; 4. Lewis; 5. William; 6. Adaline; and 7. Onie.

E. Judith (1803-1902) married John Young Shortt (1796-1897), son of Reuben and Lydia (Clark) Shortt; their children:

1. Reuben, 2. Pleasant, 3. Charles, 4. Annie, all died in childhood.

5. Polly m. John Brammer, son of Jesse; their children: James and others.

6. Lydia m. Joshua Cannaday, son of Billie and Pat-

tie; their children: Martha, Naaman, James, "Bub," Louisa and others; this family moved to Gallipolis, Ohio.

7. Naaman m. Nancy Lemon, daughter of Isaac and Sallie (Young) Lemon; their children: Amanda, John W., Prince E., Zerah H., Jefferson Davis, Everett Tyler, Callahill, Thomas, Sylvanus, Malinda.

8. Susan m., first, Jefferson Turner, son of Francis; their children: John F. and Judith; Susan married, secondly, Isaac Lemon; they had one daughter, Minerva.

9. Judith Anne (Annie) m. Richard J. Wood, son of John R. Wood; their children: Emmeline, Elvira, Jefferson P., Daniel Hillsman, George B., Greenville D., Amos D., Sparrel A. and Doc R.

10. Elizabeth (Betty) married, first, Jordan Thomas, son of Peter; their children: Martha, Judith, Sparrel, Alice and William; Betty married, secondly, Jehu Greer, son of James; their children: James, Izetta, and others.

11. Martha married, first, William Lemon, son of Isaac and Sallie (Young); their children: Lucinda G., Isaac, Thomas J., Sallie J.; Martha married, secondly, Flemon Janney, son of John and Elizabeth (Underwood); their children: Aaron, Hybernia, William and Malinda Susan.

12. Lucinda married, first, Joseph Young, son of George; their children: Tula and Jeffrey; she married, secondly, Nathaniel Thomas, son of Peter; their children: Ophelia, Dee, Emmett, Walter, Maude, Kemper, Thadius.

13. John P. married Victoria Young, daughter of John and Delphia (Turner); their children: Emmett, Wilmer, Lillie, Palmer, John, Elkany, and others.

F. Susan Thomas married Fleming Cannaday.

G. Elizabeth (Betty) Thomas married Tice.

H. Mary (Polly) Thomas married Naaman Harbour; their children: Zach, Chap and others.

III. Joseph Thomas (1772-1855) married Annie Turner; their children:

A. Judith Thomas, lived to be over 100 years old, outlived all her brothers and sisters, married James Agee, son of Joshua and his wife who was a Brammer; their children: Annie m.

Floyd Dickerson; Onie m. Sam Spangler; Cynthis m. a Rakes; Adaline, never married; William, never married; Mintie m. J. D. Wood, son of John G.

B. Rachel married Stephen H. Wood, son of John R.; their children:

1. Ann m. Chas. McAlexander; their children: Asa, Gee, Osburn G., Ella, Daniel, Callahill, Louannie, and Mary Etta.

2. Sparrel m. Ida Rakes, daughter of Richard; their children: Samuel, Lillie, Minnie, Abram, Conner, Elisha, Robert, Katherine and Venie.

3. Lewis m. Eck Hall, daughter of Harden Hall; their children: Stephen, John W. (called "Buck"), Sylvanus, Ella, Clemmie and Clara.

4. John I. m. "Puss" Hall, daughter of Harden; their children: Stephen, Sylvanus, John.

5. S. Green m. Judith Rakes, daughter of German Rakes; their children: Mary Ellen, Asa P., German H., Stephen M., Sparrel Abe, Amos R., Lenard D., Ada B., and Loula M.

6. Adaline m. Pinkard Robertson; their children: Thalus, Ophus, Posie, Oscar, and Bella.

7. Ellen m. Peter Thompson; their children: Bunyan, Tula and others.

C. Mary (Polly) Thomas married __ Thomas; names of children unknown.

D. Onie married ____ Thomas; family unknown.
   The families of both Polly and Onie are in Floyd County, Thomas Grove Meeting House.

E. Sallie Thomas, never married, lived to be 90 years old.

F. Lucinda Thomas married Charles N. Nolen, son of Alex; their children: William T., Mary Ann, Sarah, John A., Thomas S., George and Cinderella.

G. Cynthia married James Thomas, son of Pleasant; their children: Pled, Richard, Jerry, Lewis, William, Onie and Adaline.

H. Susan Thomas married George, son of Fleming Thomas; their children: Ira, Stephen, Crawford, "Tinny," Caroline, and one other.

I. Lewis married Amanda Thomas, daughter of Pleasant; their children: Frances Ann, Wm. Rufus, Malinda, John, Tilden, and Green.

IV. Richard Thomas married, first, Elizabeth Ferrell; their children: A. Charles moved to Missouri; B. Carroll married Rebecca DeHart; C. Alfred died in childhood; D. Lucy m. Washington Turner; E. Sally m. Jackson Johnson; F. Mary m. Boothe; G. Maxie m. Jerry Foley; H. Judith m. James Foley. Richard married, secondly, Martha Turner; their children:

I. Wellington m. Martha Hall.

J. Walter Henry (1829-1919) m. Judith Virginia Harbour and lived on Smiths River; their children:

1. Flora A. married S. Tyler Turner, son of Charles.

2. Mary Kansas married Thomas Anglin.

3. James W.

4. Martha (Mattie) married Ernest Lester.

5. Lina.

6. Nannie P. Anglin.

7. Richard F.

8. Dr. Charles Walter, a well-known physician of Floyd.

9. Abraham L.

10. Gillie married Nina Brammer, daughter of Tazewell.

K. Tyler L. Thomas (1830-1914) married Malinda Prillaman; their children:

1. Mary Eliza (Nov. 20, 1861) m. John W. Shortt, son of Naaman J.

2. Martha Ellen (b. Sept. 24, 1863) m. Turner F. Rakes, son of Alexander.

3. George Lee m. Martha Rakes, daughter of Alexander.

4. Victoria E. (Betty) (b. Feb. 2, 1868) m. Jefferson Turner, son of Samuel.

5. Susannah B., never married.

6. John Dilla (b. Jan. 29, 1873).

7. Daniel L. (Jan. 10, 1876) m. Lillie Nowlin.

8. Nannie B. (b. Jan. 28, 1879) m. Abram Houchins.

9. Thomas R. (b. Mar. 5, 1881) m. Minnie Nowlin, daugh-

ter of Charles.

    10. Henderson S. (b. Dec. 31, 1883) m. Martha Hall.

    L. Tazewell Thomas married Letitia Lackey.

    M. James Thomas, never married, died in the Confederate army.

    N. Andrew Jackson Thomas married Sally Terry.

    V. Mary Thomas married John Nowlin the settler, and was the mother and grandmother of all the Nowlins of the name in the Blue Ridge section of Franklin, Patrick and Floyd counties.

    VI. Cornelius Thomas married Elizabeth Slaughter April 7, 1806.

    VII. John Thomas, no record.

    VIII. Nicholas Thomas, died in childhood.

    IX. Susan Thomas married Jourdan.

Thomas Grove Meeting House, named for this family, is on the Floyd-Patrick County line, seven miles south of the town of Floyd, on the crest of the Blue Ridge Mountains.

In the Confederate army: In Company A, 54th Virginia Infantry under Captain Andrew Dickerson were James J. Thomas, died, time and place unknown; Fleming Thomas, died at Christiansburg; and Charles Thomas, wounded at Resaca, Georgia, May 16, 1864. Bailey Thomas was a member of Company B, 42nd Virginia Infantry under Captain Henry Lane. H. H. Thomas was a member of Company D, 54th Infantry. In Company H, 54th Virginia Infantry under Sparrel H. Griffith were: Jordan, A. J. and Charles Thomas. Woodley Thomas was a member of Third Arkansas. In Company I, 54th Infantry were Joseph and John Thomas, the latter was mortally wounded at Resaca, Georgia, May 15, 1864. First Lieut, John Thomas and Third Lieut. E. P. Thomas were members of Col. Robert L. Preston's Reserves.

Swanton Thomas enlisted in the World War from Floyd County.

Thrash

Among the early settlers of the Head of the River section of what is now Floyd County is the Thrash family. John Thrash, the settler, born in 1781, married Lydia Cole (sister to Byrd Cole), daughter of John Cole, a Revolutionary soldier, who was also one of the first settlers of this east-end section of the county. Thrash settled near a small mountain, which has since borne the name "Thrash's Mountain." He was on the county line, as shown by the **Acts of Assembly,** 1831, which reads: "Beginning at the widow Litterell's; thence a straight line to John Thrasher's (Thrash's), thence a straight line to John Cooper's old place."

John and Lydia Thrash were the parents of two sons: John, Jr., who, in his early life moved to Missouri; and Valentine (b. 1806), married Harriet, daughter of Joseph Gray the settler, and lived at the old Thrash homestead, near "Thrash's Mountain." Valentine was one of the early justices of the peace when the Locust Grove District was first formed; he was a member of the Legislature of Virginia during the Civil War and was of much service to the families of soldiers in Floyd County. He built a fine brick house and dispensed old-time Southern hospitality. He lived to the great age of 97 years, dying in 1903. Their children were:

1. Mary Ann, married William Sowder and lived all of her life in the Copper Hill section; their six children: Celestia m. John Ballard Strickler; Augustus Thrash m. Eliza Hancock, their children: Clifton, John, Maude, Eugene, Mamie, Kate, Sam and Eliza; Jacob Rush m. Mary West, daughter of John; Wheeler m. Octavia West, daughter of John; Valentine M. m. Susan, daughter of Floyd W. Edwards, their children: Mary, Harriet and Valentine; and Nora m. Morgan Hancock, their children: Grace, Clyde and Harry.

William Sowder was a soldier in the Confederate army.

2. Mahala, daughter of Valentine and Harriet, married Jonathan Conner, son of William, and lived at the Head of the River. Their children were: Valentine T. Conner m. Nancy

Akers, daughter of William; Priscilla Conner m. Pleasant Manning, son of Karyl; Shelton Lee Conner m. Sally Hall, daughter of John; Harriet E. m. Samuel Homer Strickler and moved to West Virginia after residing many years in Floyd; Lucy m. Mark King, son of Joseph; and Robert Lee Conner m. Abbie Yeatts, daughter of Anthony.

Thurman

David S. Thurman of Franklin County, Virginia, son of David Thurman, also of Franklin County, came to Floyd County about 1840, and settled two miles east of the village of Turtle Rock, now Pizarro. He married Ann A. Livesay, daughter of Peter, and lived at the old Peter Livesay homestead the balance of his life. They had the following children:

1. Dr. J. Wilton Thurman married, first, Attaway Lancaster, daughter of Robert and Octavia (Underwood) Lancaster, and has lived all of his life at the old Peter Livesay place; their only daughter: Lena Attaway, married John Edgar Wood, son of Jefferson Pinkard and Sarah M. (Brammer) Wood. After the death of his wife, J. Wilton married, secondly, a Miss Shanks, daughter of Joel Shanks, and they had one daughter. Dr. J. Wilton Thurman, a graduate of the University of Virginia and the Jefferson Medical College of Philadelphia, has an extensive practice in the east end of the county.

2. Robert Thurman married Josephine, daughter of Samuel Strickler; they had only one son, Robert Melvin, who married Lelia Cannaday, and moved to Anthony, Kansas.

3. John Thurman married Nora D., daughter of Samuel Strickler; and moved to Anthony, Kansas; they have a family of four sons: David, Helms, Herthel and Forest.

4. Emma Thurman married A. Lincoln Vest, son of Jacob and Jane (Shockey) Vest, and lives on the old Floyd-Franklin Pike, four miles east of the county seat. They are the parents of: Allen m. Gertrude Wood; A. Harry m. a Miss Bailey. Allen and Harry Vest are in the hardware business at Matoaka, West Virginia.

The Tice Family

Jacob Tice, a German from Pennsylvania, and member of the Lutheran Church, settled in Floyd County. Three of his children were Nicholas, Christina and Manassah Tice.

Christina Tice married John Weaver, the settler, and lived on the Weaver farm two miles west of the present county seat. Nicholas and Elizabeth, his wife, lived about one and a half miles northwest of the county seat. In 1831, Nicholas Tice and family moved to the State of Illinois, settling in Menard County near the City of Petersburg, at a place later known as Tice Station. Nicholas and Elizabeth had eight children, three of whom were John, Wilson and Amanda Bryan of Oklahoma. John Tice (b. Feb. 22, 1823, Floyd Co.) became a very useful and distinguished man in Menard County. He was judge of the county court, assessor, surveyor and treasurer of the county, besides many other positions of trust and honor, including sheriff of the county. He died Nov. 24, 1904, at the age of 81 years.

Manassah Tice (b. Jan. 24, 1796) married Cynthia, daughter of Benjamin Dodd, the settler, and lived in what is now the town of Floyd. When the county seat was being formed, he donated land for public use, including land for a school, on which the Brick Academy now stands. The deed was so worded that should this property cease to be used for school purposes, it should then revert to the Tice estate. Manassah and Cynthia Tice had eleven children:

1. Susannah Tice married Claybourne Dodd, son of William; they had three daughters: Lelia, Laura and Florence.

2. Caleb Tice married Emeline, daughter of Isaac Lemon; he lived in the town of Floyd where he was a well-known citizen long after the close of the Civil War; their five children: Nettie May m. George T. Spangler, their children: Maudie, Ward and Irvin; Benjamin m. Florence Howell and had two sons, Benjamin, Jr., and Howell; Minnie married Mortimer T. Phelps and lives at Bloom, Kansas, where she has been postmistress for many years; Ward married Elizabeth Calhoun and their children were: Elizabeth, Ward, Jr., Alton and Harold; Fleming married Lottie O'Chester, their children: Esther, Edna, Edith,

Mary, and Everett.

3. John William Tice married Alma Brame and had one daughter, Lula, who married Rufus Altizer and had two sons, Dr. Ray Tice of Norfolk, and Harold of Bluefield.

4. Elizabeth Tice married Levi Atkins and had one daughter, Alice; after the death of her husband, Elizabeth married J. M. Stigleman.

5. Benjamin Tice was killed at the Battle of Chancellorsville in the Civil War.

6. Fleming Tice died of smallpox while a soldier in the Civil War.

7. Abner Tice, twin of Fleming, never married, died 1921 in Soldier's Home, Richmond, Va.

8. Joseph Tice, no record.

9. Jacob Tice, no record.

10. Abraham Tice, no record.

11. Daughter, died in infancy.

Kaliff (Laban?) Tice, whose relationship to Jacob Tice is not known, lived in the east end of the county. His children were:

1. Andrew Jackson Tice married Mary Snuffer.

2. Daniel W. Tice married Martha Snuffer, sister of Mary.

3. Martha Tice, married James Light.

4. William Edward Tice (1841-1920) married Henrietta Kefauver, daughter of George Kefauver; their children: John Jackson m. Clara Jones, lives in Bluefield, W.Va.; Loura m. Irvin Clinginpeel; Annie, unmarried; Oscar m. Irene Webster; Fannie m. George Jamison; Flora m. Edward Kern DeHart; Isaac Eldridge married and lives in Detroit; and George m. Clora Conner.

The Turner Family

According to family tradition, about 1735 three brothers, Shadrach, Meshach and Abednego Turner emigrated from England to America and settled in Lunenburg County in Piedmont Virginia. They were Baptist in religion and had a religious background as evidenced by their names. Abednego settled in the section that is now Bedford County; Shadrach, in present Patrick County and later removed to the State of Georgia; while Meshach settled in the west end of present Franklin County on Town Creek.

When Shadrach Turner left Patrick County and settled in Georgia, tradition says that at least one of his sons remained in Patrick County, or that one of his descendants returned to Patrick County and is the ancestor of Shaws, Shadrach and Wilson Turner. Elder Charles L. Ross, a descendant of both Meshach and Abednego Turner, states: "I cannot give the connecting link of Francis Turner but feel reasonably sure that he was a descendant of Shadrach Turner."

James Turner and Mary, his wife, emigrated from Ireland with their eldest child, Francis, and settled near Elamsville in Patrick County about 1790. Their children were: Francis, Adam, Richard, Nancy, Elizabeth, Sallie, Mary.

A. Francis Turner (1789-1880) married Nancy Thomas, daughter of Charles and Deborah of Patrick County, and settled near his father's homestead. They had seven sons and five daughters:

1. Charles Turner (1817-1857) married Violet Hall, daughter of Thomas of Patrick County, and settled in Floyd County on the top of the Blue Ridge, seven miles southeast of the present town of Floyd; their children:

(a) S. Tyler Turner, farmer and member of the Virginia State Senate, married Flora Thomas, daughter of Walter of Patrick County, and lived near the Cannaday Gap in the Blue Ridge Mountains; their children: Emma K. m. George W. Hale; Stanton m. Ella Trail; Cameron m. Dora A. Wood; Ollie m. Robert Fralin; Laura m. Harvey Trail; Arizona (Zonie) m. Arthur Peters; Benjamin H. m. Lura Bowling; and Morton m. Minnie Thomas.

(b) Caroline Turner married Francis Snead; their children: Texas m. Callahill Lester; Minerva; Florida; Sarah U.; Martha V.; Tekorah; Green; Thomas; and Abraham.

(c) Adaline Turner married Peter Cannaday, son of Isaac, Supervisor of Little River District; their children: Amos

L. Cannaday, who resides in the west end of the county on Little River and who has been a member of the Legislature of Virginia; and Sarah E. m. Stanton Brammer, their children: Amos and Ezra.

(d) Onie Turner married, first, Ira Hatcher; their children: Peter and Senorah; Onie married, secondly, David Hall.

(e) Serrepta Turner married Alexander Nowlin and lived near the Charles Turner homestead; their children: Addie, Loula, Maudie; Dollie; Cabble; Sylvatus; and Floyd.

(f) Abigail Turner married Joseph Sowers; their children: May; Ellen; Kate; Frazier; Archie and Harley.

(g) Victoria Turner married Ira Thomas; their children: Louaddie; Florida; Susie; Sarah; Toka; Amos; Joel and Hosie.

(h) Amanda Turner married William Houchins; their children: Birtie; Emma; Abraham; Cabble; Walter and John.

2. John Turner, who was deaf and dumb, lived near the Floyd-Patrick line; he married, first, Nancy Thomas, daughter of Charles of Patrick County; their children: Green, Delilah Ann, Annie, all died in childhood; John married, secondly, Martha Thompson; their children: Elizabeth m. Flem Ingram; George m. Minerva Nolen; Jefferson m. Ruth Robertson; Nannie m. _____ Turner; and Fannie m. Samuel Nolen.

3. Peter Turner married Pernina Brammer, daughter of William of Floyd County, and lived on the Franklin Turnpike near Turtle Rock, six miles east of the town of Floyd; their only son, William, m., first, Eliza Smith and, secondly, Fannie Hoback.

4. Nicholas Turner died when a small child.

5. Samuel F. Turner married Rachel Wood, (her dates are given in Wood family) daughter of John R. of Floyd County, and lived nine miles east of the town of Floyd where he was a farmer and stock raiser; their children:

(a) John m. Jathina Barnard; their children: Samuel Peter; James Matterson; Hattie E.; Annie L.; John T.; Minnie O. and Fannie D. (twins); Effie; Rachel E.; and Henry Washington.

(b) Arminda m. Daniel Webb; their children: John
F.; Turner A.; Jefferson J.; and Mary Etta.

(c) Mary Elizabeth m. John Conner Barnard; their
children: Lillie; Rachel; Howard; Samuel E.; Lura A.; Adeline
S.; Maud A.; Myrtle A.; John T.; and an infant unnamed.

(d) Jefferson m. Victoria Elizabeth Thomas; their
children: Samuel Tyler; Ollie; Claude S.; and Annie B.

(e) Annie m. John T. Beckner; their children: Maud
E.; Cash D.; Minnie Ora; and Elliott T.

(f) Ardella E. m., first, James Howery; their children: Anabel L.; Evelyn Cleo; and Marie Althea; Ardella m.,
secondly, George W. Slusher.

6. Fleming Turner married Nancy Rakes, daughter of
Samuel; their children: Elizabeth m. William Smith; Mary m.
Ernest Lester; Thomas, never married.

7. Rebecca married Abraham Snead; their children:
Mahala m. Thomas Profitt; Elizabeth m. Samuel Nolen; Leatha
m. William Edwards; John; Jefferson; Thomas m. Martha Nolen; Daniel m. Nancy Jane Cannaday; and Fleming m. Edwards.

8. Judith Turner married William Hatcher; their children: Sarah m., first, Ira Shortt and, secondly, Cat Ingram; Ira
m. Onie Turner; James m. Laura Underwood; and Charles.

9. Deborah Turner married Richard Rakes, son of Sam-
uel of Patrick County; their children: (a) Israel m. Loula Lee;
(b) Charles m. Ella Ross; (c) Judith m. Charles Nolen; (d)
Magruder (Gooda) m. Ophelia Thomas; (e) Ida Bell m. Sparrel
Wood; (f) William m. Lillie Nolen; (g) Adaline m. Robert
Lee; and (h) Samuel m. Cinderilla Nolen.

10. Elizabeth Turner married William Conner, son of
Daniel, a noted Primitive Baptist preacher; their children: Lon
and Nannie.

11. Jefferson Turner married Susan Shortt, daughter of
John Y., of Floyd County, and settled on a farm near the Haycock Mountain at the head of Shooting Creek Gap; he died during the Civil War of disease due to exposure while a soldier; they

were the parents of:

(a)   John F. Turner, lived near the old homestead for many years, now of Woolwine, Va., m. Adaline Nowlin, daughter of Charles; their children: George and Abram.

(b)   Judith m. Alexander Nowlin, son of Charles of Patrick County; their chlidren: Edward, George, Posie, Lillie, Susan and Lon.

12.   Annie Turner married Alexander Rakes of Patrick County; their children:

(a)   Turner F. Rakes m. Martha Ellen Thomas, their children: Minnie, Minerva, Thomas Lee, Daniel G., Amos W., Callie, Buron L., Gladys;   (b) Elizabeth m. William Turner; (c) Onie m. William Ingram; (d) Martha m. George Lee Thomas;   (e) George m. Robertson;   (f) Richard m. Minnie Wood; (g) Samuel m. Minerva Lemons; (h) Abraham m. Alma Harris; (i) Jefferson;   (j) Della m. Smith;   (k) Cassell.

Of this large family of Turner men, five were in the Civil War: Charles, Peter, Jefferson, Samuel F., and Fleming.

B.   Adam Turner, wife unknown; children were: Martha; Judith; Nancy and James.

C.   Richard Turner married, first, Celia George; their children: Martha, John, James, Charles and Nancy; Richard married, secondly, Lucinda Boyd; their children: Sarah, Rebecca, Judith, Adaline, Isaac, William, and Fleming.

D.   Nancy Turner.

E.   Elizabeth Turner.

F.   Sallie Turner.

G.   Mary Turner.

II.   Meshach Turner of Franklin County, had two (known) sons: Josiah and William.

A.   Josiah Turner, born about 1748 in Franklin County, lived one-half mile north of Henry Station on Town Creek. He married a German girl. They had three (known) sons:

1.   Constantine Turner married _____ Lavinder of Henry County; one son was Elder Joseph Turner of Floyd County.

2.   Thomas Turner; a grandson was Timothy Prillaman.

3.   William Turner married Elizabeth Philpott, daughter

of Neddy Philpott; Clark Turner was a son; U. G. Turner was a grandson on his maternal side.

B. William Turner (b. abt. 1750), son of Meshach, married about 1774, Jane Hunter, daughter of John Hunter; John Hunter owned and lived at the Meshach Turner place, and so did William Turner. William and Jane had thirteen children:

1. George Turner, born in 1775 (he was teased and told he was born a slave of George III), and died in 1850, justice of the peace for thirty years, married Millie Stone of Franklin County; their children:

(a) Stephen, who owned and lived in the "Cap" Turner house near Henry Station, Franklin County, married Ruth Prillaman of Franklin County.

(b) Obediah.

(c) George m. ____ Menefee, of Franklin County.

(d) Captain James O. Turner married, first, a sister of Col. W. T. James, and, secondly, ____ Philpott, and, thirdly, Jennie Woods.

(e) several daughters.

2. Elder John Turner (1777-1873), a Baptist preacher of Patrick County, married ____ Burnett of Patrick County; their (known) children:

(a) Stephen m. Ruth Turner, represented Patrick County for several years in the Virginia House of Delegates, he had several daughters and was the grandfather of Elder A. B. Philpott.

(b) Colonel Elkanah was a member of the State Senate from Patrick County, never married.

(c) Delphia m. John Young of Floyd County.

(d) Crawford was the father of Rufus and Murry Turner, who were popular men of Patrick County, alternately holding the office of Sheriff of the county for many years.

(e) several daughters.

3. William Turner, moved to Tennessee.

4. James Turner, moved to Tennessee.

5. Josiah Turner married Pricy Philpott of Henry County; he lived to be 84 years old; he was justice of the peace for

many years; their children: (a) Meshach m. ____ Deshazo of Henry County; (b) Robert m. ____ McGuffin of Franklin County; (c) James m. Sallie Cahill of Henry County; (d) Joseph m. ____ Ingram of Franklin County; (e) John m. Sallie Turner, daughter of Stephen and Ruth; (f) William; and several daughters.

6. Adelphia Turner married Shaws Turner, lived to be 94 years old.

7. Obediah Turner, died at the age of 4 years.

8. Sallie Turner married Christian Snidow.

9. Jane Turner married Berty Stone, lived to be 90 years old.

10. Andrew Turner married Frances Holland of Franklin County, he lived to be 84; their children: (a) William m. ____ McGhee of Franklin County; (b) John; (c) Abner m. ____ Wade of Franklin County; (d) C. M. m. ____ Menefee of Franklin County; (e) Andrew m. Eliza Cannaday of Franklin County; and several daughters.

11. Meshach Turner, Jr., married Nancy Martin, daughter of William B. and Sallie Martin of Henry County; he lived to be 79; their children: (a) Andrew, now (1918) in his 92nd year, m. Martha Prillaman, daughter of George and Dicy Prillaman and granddaughter of Daniel Ross.

(b) William B. Turner m. Frances Goode, daughter of George and Sallie Goode of Franklin County.

(c) John D. Turner m. Mary W. Jamerson, daughter of Wiley and Frances Jamerson of Franklin County.

(d) Lucinda Turner m. Robert V. Ross, son of Sutherland and Docia (Turner); they were the parents of Elder Charles Lee Ross, a well-known preacher of the Primitive Baptist Church, now living on Town Creek in Franklin County; two of his sons, William E. Ross, an attorney, and Virgel E. Ross, Commonwealth's Attorney of Mercer County, live in Bluefield, West Virginia. (Elder C. L. Ross is the source of much of the information on the Turner family and has assisted the compiler with this sketch.)

(e) Seven other daughters.

12. Elder Elkanah Turner (1801-1888) married, first, __

Hurd, and, secondly, Elizabeth Wingfield, daughter of Col. Wingfield of Franklin County. He was a Primitive Baptist preacher for 40 years; a member of the House of Delegates from Henry County, a justice of the peace for a number of years, and Supervisor for several terms. His children:

    (a) Dr. Jesse Turner m., first, _____ Barrow of Henry County, second wife unknown.

    (b) Elder Taylor Turner m., first, daughter of Lewis Jamison, secondly, Hattie Cook of Pittsylvania County.

    (c) James m. _____ Davis of Henry County.

    (d) George m. _____ Jenkins.

    (e) Clay.

    (f) Elkanah m. Bettie Shumate.

    (g) Several daughters.

    13. Elizabeth Turner m. Ned Philpott; she was the grandmother of Elder A. B. Philpott.

    III. Abednego Turner located in Bedford County where there is yet a large number of his descendants. He had a son, Richard, who was great-grandfather of Elder Charles L. Ross on his father's side.

The Vest Family

Moses Vest came from Germany and settled in Maryland at a date unknown, and had one son named John, who came to Campbell County, Va., and settled. Then in 1795, he came to High Peak, Floyd County, Va., and brought with him six children: Berry, Charles, John, Joseph, Elizabeth and Fanny.

Little Berry Vest was born Nov. 28, 1774, died Nov. 14, 1868, age 94 years, 11 months and 14 days. He was married twice. His first wife was a Moor, and his second wife was a Miss Sarah James. To the first union were born six children— four sons and two daughters—John, Rolen, Chas., Samuel, Jane and Nancy.

John married Mary Smith and to this union were born four children—three boys and one girl—Samuel, James, Willis and Rosy. Rosy is the only one living.

Samuel was married three times. His first wife was Pollie

Vest, a daughter of uncle Charles, and to this union were born six children—two boys and four girls—John, Cable, Molly, Maltidy, Gilly and Lillie.

Rolen Vest married Deliah Vest, his cousin, a daughter of John Vest, Sr., and to this union were born four children—Joseph, Mary Jane, Susan and Vina. His second wife was Edith Hawkins and to this union were born four children: Arthur, Calla, Edith and Georgiana.

Joseph married Laura Caster and to this union were born three girls—Cora, Alice and Audra. Cora married a Love, Alice married a Rutrough, Audra died unmarried.

Mary Jane married a Null and to this union were born two girls—Sadie and Nerva. Sadie married a Johnston, Nerva a Boobults.

Susan married a Newman and Vina married a Rogers. All the last children married and had families.

Charles married an Iddings and to this union were born four children: Abbie, Pollie, Sallie and Lydia. Abbie married a Cole and had one son, Valentine; Pollie married her cousin, Samuel Vest; Sallie married Jonathan Whitenack and had eight children; Lydia married James Whitenack and had three children.

Samuel L. Vest was born June 8, 1813, died Sept. 22, 1890, age 77 years, three months and 14 days, just three months after the death of his wife. He was married to Sarah Iddings, Sept. 24, 1833, and to this union were born 13 children: Henry L., Berry, Charles, John, James, William, Abbie, Martha, Mary, Samuel, Sarah, Isaac and Hannah.

Henry L. Vest was born June 18, 1834, and died in the Confederate army, October 22, 1862. He was married to Becky Hall, Dec. 19, 1854, and to this union were born three children— Charley Will, Sarilda and Letcher.

Charlie Will married Octavia Iddings March 9, 1876, and to this union were born nine children—Letcher, Janey, Jiner, Samuel, Cella, Linda, Albert, Ada and May. Letcher married a King, Janey married a Conner, Jiner married a Carr, Samuel married a Lawrence, Cella married a Conner, Linda married a Compton and Albert married a McNeil; Ada and May are single.

Sarilda married Burl Eanes and to this union were born ten

children: Ida, Etta, Cephas, Charles, Carl, Don, Lola, Wilmer, Gracie and Glenn.

Letcher died in infancy.

Berry Vest, Jr., was born April 15, 1836, and was married to Harriett Swebster, Nov. 11, 1858, and to this union were born three children: David, Lorena and John Henry.

David married Addie Conner and to this union were born three children—Cleo, Gertrude and Grace. Cleo married Effie Sink, Gertrude married a Shank and Gracy a Whitenack.

Lorena married G. L. Lawrence but had no children.

John Henry married Lettie Light and to this union were born four children: Edgar, Letcher, Flossie and Essie. Edgar married Ethel Vest, Flossie married Eldridge Wright, Essie is single, Letcher died in infancy. Losing his first wife, he then married Pollie Tice and to this union were born six children; Wade, Louis, Susie, Ralph, Audra and Alene.

Charles Vest was born April 1, 1838, died March 2, 1878, age 39 years, 11 months and 13 days. He was married to Marget Hoback, Sept., 26, 1865, and to this union were born five children: Jacob died in youth; James married Rettie Lawrence and to this union were born two children—Clara and Carl; William married Tibitha Rierson and to this union were born 10 children —Annie, Ellen, Morris, Robert, Thomas, Elizabeth, Soy, Chyle and Ruby; Sarah married P. M. King and has two children, Wallace and Unis; Maggie married Z. K. DeWitt and to this union were born nine children: Charlie, Mosby, Ralph, Murl, Kate, Daisy, Roscoe, Fanny and Louis.

John Vest was born February 23, 1840, and was married to Juanna Hall, Sept. 12, 1868, and to this union were born 8 children: Ellen, Norah, Ida, May, Jessie, Joseph, Almeda and Andy. Ellen married A. P. Vest and to this union were born 12 children: Luella, Ethel, Pearl, Annie, Hugh, Brethard, Maggie, Clifford, Teddy, Roscoe, Giles and Beatrice. Norah married J. W. Conner and had one child, that died in infancy. May married Elbert Vest and had 5 boys. Jessie married Etta Vest and has 5 children. Joe married Jennie Wright and has one child. Almeda married Louis Conner and has two children. Andy married Minnie Perdue and has one child. Ida is still unwed.

James Vest was born Oct. 30, 1842, died Oct. 4, 1882, age 39 years, 11 months and 26 days. He was married to Maranda Conner in 1866 and to this union were born two children: Melvina and Alzora. Melvina married John Akers and had several children and Alzora married a Bradberry.

William Vest, Sr., was born Nov. 5, 1844, married Elizabeth Conner, and to this union were born ten children: Samuel, James, Charles, Robert, Cuzzy, Maranda, Liza and Mobey. Samuel married Helen Whitenack and to this union were born 6 children: Lacy, Lula, Verney, Jasper, Havey and Sam Barnard. James married Stella Whitenack and to this union were born three children: Mamie, Harley and Reba. Charles married Lidy Anne Conner and has five boys: Howard, Okley, Berkley, Elmer and Woodrow. Robert married Lucy Mucy and has several children. Cuzzy married a Kingrea and had one child. Liza married a Whitlock and has several children. Maranda married Dock Vest and has seven children. Mobey married a Stump.

Abbie Vest was born May 12, 1846, married James M. Furrow and to this union were born 2 girls—Sarah and Malisy. Sarah has never married. Malisy married John Keaton and had 13 children.

Martha Vest was born April 9, 1848; and married James McDaniel and to this union were born 12 children: Osker, Jackson, Sarah, Jane, Mary John, Thomas, Horace, Charles, Addie, Samuel, Emmett, Laura and Walter.

Mary E. Vest was born March 23, 1850, and married J. A. Conner, Jan. 3, 1867, and to this union were born 6 children: James, Melvina, Patry, Dora, Nathern and Alfred.

Samuel Vest was born April 11, 1852, and married Deliah Moran, Nov. 21, 1871, and to this union were born 8 children: Monroe, Charles, Emma, Nora, William, Lila, Betty and Sadie. Monroe married Lena Belcher. Charles married Sallie Kennett and has 7 girls—Nellie, Edith, Laurnel, Evelyn, Louis, Mirium and Claudine. Emma married a Shilling and has three girls. Nora married a Kennett and he has several children. Betty married a Shilling and has several children. William married a Hall and has three children. Lila married a Thomas and has two children. Sadie is at home.

Sarah A. Vest was born April 27, 1854. She married Valentine Conner, Jan. 8, 1873, and to this union were born 4 children: Rosy, Daniel, Millard and Maltidy.

Isaac H. Vest was born June 13, 1856, and was married to Sarah Vest, Dec. 31, 1876, and to this union were born 10 children: Abbie, Josie, Charles, Peter, Laura, George, James, Banks and two who died in infancy. Abbie was married to N. A. Conner, May 5, 1908, and to this union were born six children: Ugen, Virginia, Ethel, Willie, Beatrice and Mildred. Josie married John H. Eanes March 12, 1905, and to this union were born two children—John Henry, who died in infancy, and Walter Scott. Charles married Neva Bailey, April 17, 1909, and to this union were born two children—Byron and Inez. Peter married Docia Hale Aug. 2, 1905, and to this union were born four children: Olive, Ellet, Ora and Georgeanna. James married Luella Vest, Jan. 17, 1915, and to this union were born two children—Ward and Lottie. George died, Feb. 20, 1905, at the age of 17. Laura and Banks are still at home.

Hanah F. Vest was born April 20, 1858, and to this union were born five children: William, Julie, Minnie, Lee and Robert.

Little Berry Vest had by his last wife, ten children: Isaac, Abraham, Jacob, William, Peter, Washington, Elizabeth, Mary, Rachael and Frankey.

Isaac Vest, Sr., was born April 28, 1827, died Sept. 1905. He married Nancy Wilson and to this union were born four children: Elizabeth, Louise, Mahaly and Sallie. Elizabeth married a Link, Mahaly married Whitenack, Sallie married an Austin and Louisa is still unwed.

Abraham Vest married Lidy Wilson and to this union were born two boys—Floyd and Isaac. Floyd married an Angle and had several children: Isaac married a Conner and had four children.

Jacob Vest married Jane Shockey and to this union were born seven children: James, Lincoln, Pierce, Charles, Henry, Dock and Mary. James married Mary Brooks and had several children; Lincoln married Emma Thurman and has two boys—Allen and Harry; Pierce married Ellen Vest and had 12 children;

Charles married a Poff and has several children; Henry married a Walters and has two girls; Dock married Maranda Vest and has several children; Mary married a Hall and had two children.

William Vest married Jane Walters and has several children.

Peter R. Vest was born May 6, 1834, and was married to Charlotte Shockey and to this union were born nine children: Cally Hill, William, George, Louis, Noah, Byre, Sarah, Nancy and Fanny.

Cally Hill married Rosy Poff, and had 8 children: Alma, Lula, Nellie, Chester, Lemuel, Ras, Frank and Clye. Alma married a Walters, Lula married a Light, Chester a Trump, Lemuel a Kingery, the rest of the children are unmarried.

William married Mary Boone and to this union were born five children: Walter E., Will C., Robert C., Alice and Essie. Walter married Sadie Blankinship and has one son, Walter, Jr.; Will married Sallie Whitenack and died in March, 1916; Robert married Lucy Whitenack; Alice is at home; Essie died in infancy.

George married Lilly Angle and to this union were born five children: Shirley, Brainard, Lorenza, Noah and Eddy. Louis married Odell Craghead and to this union were born three children. Maude married Posy Sisson and Robert and Clarence are at home; Noah and Byre died unmarried. Sarah married Isaac Vest and had ten children, Nancy married Luther McNiel and had three children; Carrie married a Poff, Will and Everette are at home. Fanny married an Austin and had two girls— Mary and Burnace.

Washington Vest married Beckie Likens and had 10 children. William, Ira, George, Nancy, Sarah, Lucy, Isabelle, John, Elbert and Etta.

Elizabeth Vest married a Kennett and had two children.

Polly Vest married a Richard and had nine children: Steve, John, Nancy, Elizabeth, Sarah, Octavia, Berry, Jim and Lincoln all married and have families.

Rachael Vest married a Beckleheimer and had two children—

Charles and Elizabeth.

This completes all I know of the Vest family.

We have several letters we want connected with this.

Since the above writing, Rev. Peter R. Vest died April 22, 1917, at the age of 82 years.

Gotten up and Written by,
Laura L. Vest

John Wade The Settler

John Wade, the Floyd County settler, was a member of the Wade family of Franklin County, Virginia, where many of the name still reside. He came with his family in the early days and settled nine miles west of the present county seat. On Feb. 2, 1792, he married Hannah Jones, daughter of Henry Jones. Their children, in part:

I. Henry Wade (b. 1799) married Elizabeth Cox (b. 1802), daughter of Ambrose, and lived on Burks Fork. Two of their sons were: 1. Jacob; and 2. John (1825-1864), married Ruth Cox, daughter of Luke, and lived on Burks Fork; their children were: John W. (b. Oct. 17, 1864), Eli and Mary E. John Wade lost his life while a soldier in the Confederate army.

II. Nathan Wade.

III. John Wade, Jr., twice married, his second wife was Amazy Smith.

IV. Owen Wade (May 21, 1809-1884) married Aug. 16, 1832, Lavina Phlegar (Oct. 17, 1813-1890), daughter of Abraham, and lived on Burks Fork where he was one of the prominent men of the county. He was one of the early justices of the peace and was for a time Presiding Justice. Owen and Lavina Wade had 12 children:

A. William Burwell (1833-1918) married Eliza Jane Summers, daughter of William W. and Cynthia, and moved to Missouri.

B. Abraham (1834-1921) married Mary Allen, daughter of Ethan and Ann Rachel (Musgrove) Allen, and lived in Missouri. Their only child was Anna Lavinia m. James Warren

Brown; their children were James Wade and Robert Allen.

C. Eli (1837-1922) married Elizabeth F. Albin, and lived in Missouri; their children were: Robert, and Laura m. Lewis,

D. Amanda Margaret (b. 1839) married Henry M. Goody-koontz; their children: Winton, Louella, Webster, Edward, Flora and Ida H.

E. Hannah (b. 1840) married J. B. Albright; they were the parents of ten children: David, Charles, Amanda, Nina, Lil-lie, Emmet, Henry, Lucy, Marks and Ella.

F. Julia Ann (1843-1917) married William L. Bird; their children: Eli, died young; and Ann m. Rev. Sollie Hylton.

G. Sarah (1844-1899) married Cornelius Clayton Weeks, son of Mathew; their children: Stella F., Esper R. and Kyle M.

H. Rev. Peyton John (Aug. 26, 1847-1925) married 1876, Susannah P. Hylton (d. 1920); he was a well-known minister of the Lutheran Church and lived many years in Floyd County, moved to Fredrick, Maryland; their children: Edward W., a druggist of Richmond, Virginia; Rev. William Arthur (b. Nov. 4, 1879), a minister of the Lutheran Church of Baltimore, Mary-land, married Ursula Cotta, daughter of Rev. Asa Richard Cotta; and Lena E., of Frederick, Md.

I. Eliza Attaway (b. 1849) married Lorenzo Dow Weddle, son of John B. and grandson of Andrew, and lived in the west end of the county; they had one son, William Weddle m. Dollie DeHart; their son Dewey m. Nancy Thurman.

J. Joseph (1851-1892) married Ann Fisher and lived near Willis, Virginia; their two sons were: Charles B. and William O. Wade.

K. Mary (1853-1918) married first, Isaac Taylor, lived near Willis, Va., and had one daughter, Clara Taylor; Mary Wade married, secondly, Monroe Slusher, no children.

L. David B. (1856-1862) died while a boy at the age of six.

V. Isaac Wade.

VI. Annie Wade married Cox.

VII. Mary (Polly) Wade married Samuel Weddle.

VIII. Nancy Wade.

Eli Wade was Fourth Sergeant in Company D, 54th Virgin-ia Infantry under Captain Henry Slusher. F. B. and H. S. Wade were in Company G, 21st Virginia Cavalry under Captain Armp O. Dobyns. John C. Wade was a member of Stuart's Horse Artillery. Peyton J. and John C. Wade were members of Captain James B. Headen's Company of Reserves under Col. Robert L. Preston.

Martin L., Guy Mosby, Kyle J., Hiley J., Harvey W., Wyatt W., and Henry C. Wade were soldiers in the World War.

James W. Walton The Settler

The Floyd County family of Waltons traces its origin to one of three brothers who emigrated to America from England in 1773 and settled in the Colony of Georgia. Three years later, George Walton (1740-Feb. 2, 1804), the ancestor of the Floyd County family, was a member of the Continental Congress, or Continental Committee, which issued the Declaration of Independence. George Walton was one of the signers of this famous document. There are two brass cannon in the Navy Yard at Norfolk, Virginia, which he helped to take from the English while he was serving in the Continental Army of the Revolution.

James Walton, son of George, moved from Georgia to Virginia and settled in the county of Halifax. He served in the War of 1812. He lived to the great age of 104 years, and in the latter part of his life moved to Pittsylvania County.

James W. Walton, son of James and Sally (Goodman) Walton, and grandson of George, was born and reared in Pittsylvania County. He married Louise M. Walton, a cousin, and their children were: W. H., S. L., and J. N. He lived to the great age of 94 years, and in 1845 moved to Floyd County and settled on a farm two miles from Salem Baptist Church. His son, James W. Walton, Jr., resides at the old homesite. He was born in 1848 and married Mary J. Conner; their children: 1. D. W. Walton; 2. Martha W. Rierson; 3. Laura R. Conner; 4. Elvira G. Wilson; 5. K. K. Walton; and 6. Nora F. Wilson.

The Waltons of Floyd County were members of the Primitive Baptist Church.

James W. Walton, Jr., and Jesse L. Walton were members of Company I, 54th Virginia Infantry under Captain Burwell

Akers; Cephas L. Walton was in Company B, 42nd Infantry under Captain Henry Lane in the Confederate army.

The Weaver Family

John Weaver, the settler, came to the present county of Floyd from Surry County, North Carolina, and settled two miles west of the present town of Floyd. His homesite was in the original forest, which he cleared; it is to this day known as the "Weaver farm." John Weaver is spoken of as having been a "wealthy man, and a slave owner." He was listed as one of the largest taxpayers when the county was organized in 1831. His first marriage was to Christina Tice, daughter of Jacob. Their family of children were:

1. Daniel (b. July 20, 1813) married, first, Elizabeth Dodd on Dec. 20, 1840; their children were: Sarah (b. Oct. 18, 1841); Margaret J. (b. Jan. 20, 1844); James T. (b. Dec. 7, 1845); John, Jr. (b. April 13, 1848); Jesse M. (b. Nov. 1850); Nancy Jane (b. Sept. 10, 1853); Daniel B. (b. Feb. 11, 1856); and Isaac E. (b. Apr. 4, 1858). Daniel married, secondly, Mintora DeHart on Nov. 23, 1870; their children: Walter G. (b. Nov. 2, 1871); and Emma T. (b. Sept. 17, 1874).

2. Isaac was a soldier in the Mexican War, 1848; some of his children were: Martha, Julia and Joseph.

3. Solomon married Sabrina Dodd (b. 1810), daughter of Benjamin; their family of children were three sons and four daughters, one of whom was George W. Weaver (1836-May 17, 1920) who married Emmazetta (d. June 9, 1920), youngest daughter of Christopher Smith.

4. Sally (Sarah) (d. 1865 at age 46), married John T. Gill; their children: Harvey W.; Mary J.; Ann M.; Emeline; and Albert W.

5. Naomi married Isaac Smith (Sept. 8, 1819-Feb. 25, 1907), oldest son of Henry; their children: Rosabella, Noah, Flournoy, Mahala, Abednego and Louanna.

John Weaver's second wife was Polly Boone, of Franklin County; and their children were: Joseph; Martha m. Steve Borden and had a daughter Martha Ellen, moved to Indiana; and others.

Benjamin Weddle

The Floyd County family of Weddles is descended from Johan Michael Waidele (Weddle) who came to Philadelphia on the ship **Francis & Elizabeth,** which docked Sept. 21, 1742. The family came from Germany on the left bank of the Rhine. They settled in Lancaster County, Pa., where they lived for some years. Benjamin Weddle, son of Elijah, and grandson of Michael, married Annie Maria Eiler in Lancaster County, and moved south to "Horseshoe Bend" on New River, just east of the present city of Radford. While there he was enlisted in the militia of Augusta County, Virginia, fighting the Indians. He was captain of a company of militia under General Andrew Lewis at the Battle of Point Pleasant, fought in 1774. He held the front line of battle until General Lewis gained the rear, when the Indians under the celebrated Chief Cornstalk were completely routed. The tradition is that a price was placed on the head of Captain Weddle, who removed his family from the "Horseshoe Bend" to Bent Mountain in the east end of the present county of Floyd. He lived there for a short while, then settled permanently on the West Fork of Little River, about seven miles west of the courthouse, where Daniel Spangler now (1926) lives. The old log house erected by Benjamin Weddle, though added to and changed to some extent, is yet standing. Benjamin Weddle bought 1568 acres of land, Feb. 27, 1790; family records indicate that the land warrants were signed by Patrick Henry, Governor of Virginia. The land joined the lands of Elijah Hylton, and here these two settlers lived and their children intermarried. Benjamin Weddle died and was buried on Bent Mountain in the year 1807. Benjamin and Anna Maria Weddle had ten children:

I. David Weddle (May 1, 1774-Oct. 22, 1859) married, first, Margaret Morricle; their children:

A. Mary married Thomas Helms; their children: Benjamin m. Nancy Booth; Jacob m. Adaline Helms; George m. Caroline Keith; John m. Levina McAlexander; Peter m., first, Diana Booth, and, secondly, Ruth Hylton; Adam m. Dorothy Knowles; Abarilla m. Naaman Knowles; Mary Ann m. Thomas Alderman; Margaret m. Alan Slusher; Joseph m. Melissa Ann

Earles; and Elizabeth m. Floyd Keith.

B.   Elizabeth married Henry Duncan, son of Blanch.

C.   Andrew.

D.   John married Jane Weeks; their children: Andrew m., first, Barbara Weddle, secondly, Eliza Lemon, and, thirdly, Mrs. Sarah Davis Havens; his children: John D., Milton, Allan, Chapman, Walker, Armelda, Archelaus, and Beverly; Elijah m. Mary J., daughter of A. F. Stigleman; Margaret m. Robert Weddle, their children: William m. Harter, Malvina m. Utt, Laura, Emma; Allan m. Amanda E. Gill; Finetta m. George W. Weeks; and David m. Letitia Stigleman, daughter of A. F. Stigleman, their children: Fultz, Daris, Clyde, Dollie, and Grace.

E.   Valentine.

F.   Benjamin.

G.   William.

H.   David, Jr., married Mary Manning; their children: Harriet m. Jasper Dillon; Simon Peery went West; Elizabeth and m. Emma Earles, daughter of John, their children: Linda A. m. m. Emma Earles, daughter of John, their children: Linda A. m. I. L. Epperly, Mary M. m. R. A. DeHart, John D. m. Elizabeth Wall, Simon C. m. Minnie Kirk, Julia E. m. K. Leslie Dove, William McKinley; and Sevilla Adelina m. Benjamin F. Hancock.

I.   Joel.

David Weddle, Sr., married, secondly, Catherine Stigleman, daughter of Philip and Margaret (Weaver) Stigleman; their children:

J.   Alexander was a man of considerable prominence in the county, was a teacher in the public schools for a number of years and a justice of the peace for several terms of office. He married, first, Susan, daughter of Samuel Weddle; their children: James P. m. Louisa Cannaday; Elizabeth m. James Marshall of Carroll; Letitia m. Enoch Hylton; B. Franklin, m., first Sarah E. Slusher and, secondly, Laura Maberry; Ann M. m. Roley Weddle; Louisa F. m. Leroy Slusher; John S. m. Callie Spangler; Harry A. went West and married Etta Stigleman; Lavina and Amanda who died in infancy. Alex Weddle married, secondly, Keturah Mitchell.

K.   Ira married, first, Nancy Thompson, daughter of

Elisha; their children: Emezetta m. D. A. Ratliff and lives in Los Angeles, California; Nancy C., died in infancy; Perida Thompson, died in childhood. Ira married, secondly, Susan Lancaster; their children: Florentine, Margaret, Oscar, Eliza, Simon P., and Homer. The family moved to Indiana. Oscar, Eliza and Homer are still living.

L. Simon P. Weddle married, first, Sarah Thompson, daughter of Elisha; their children: Joel, Isabelle and Catherine. The family moved to Hendricks County, Indiana, where Joel married Amanda Mahan, Isabelle m. Tazewell Gill, and Catherine married Henry Hunt. Simon P. married, secondly, Mrs. Angeline Bishop Harter, daughter of Asa Bishop of Floyd County; their children: Benjamin, Charles E., Asa E. and Elizabeth, all of whom married and are living in Indiana. Simon P. Weddle was still living in the year 1922, at Brownsburg, Indiana, at the age of 91 years.

M. Margaret J. Weddle married William Baliff who died during the Civil War, leaving the following children: David m. Adaline Slusher; William m. Mrs. Charity Poiner; the family moved to Indiana.

N. Nancy C. Weddle married James J. Thompson, son of Claibourne, their children: Nancy C.; Samuel E. m. Carrie E. Howard of Bloomingdale, Tenn.; A. Claibourn, never married; Margaret E. m. G. B. Harman, son of Christopher, prominent farmer and chairman of the Board of Supervisors of Floyd Co.; and John A. m. Melissa A. Phlegar, daughter of Isaac.

II. John Weddle, whose descendants live in Carroll County, Virginia.

III. Marton Weddle married Patty, daughter of Elijah Hylton.

IV. Jonas Weddle (1774-1843).

V. Sarah Weddle married Jacob Harter.

VI. Catherine Weddle (1784-1863) married (1804) Archelaus Hylton, son of Elijah.

VII. Elizabeth Weddle married Jesse Hylton.

VIII. Barbara Weddle, never married.

IX. Margaret Weddle married Robert Huff.

X. Andrew Weddle (Aug. 13, 1787-Aug. 3, 1847)

named for General Andrew Lewis, married Elizabeth Boone (Sept. 3, 1791-Nov. 9, 1850), daughter of Jacob Boone; their children:,

1. Samuel Weddle (Sept. 26, 1812-1893) married, first, Mary Wade; their children: Caleb m. Cyrena, daughter of Jacob Harman; Joshua m. Sallie Woods; Sarah m. Elijah, son of Cyrus Keith; Owen m. Elizabeth, daughter of John Lee; Malachi, Eli, Allie, Louana and Noah, all of whom died in childhood, some from diphtheria. Samuel married, secondly, Mrs. Mary Bowman Hylton, daughter of Christopher Bowman; their children: Elizabeth m. John Keith; Martha m. Elijah Dickerson; Joseph m. Flora, daughter of J. W. Hylton; Susannah, Lydia, Samuel, all of whom died in childhood.

2. Mary Weddle (b. March 8, 1815) married Benjamin, son of George Phlegar.

3. Benjamin Weddle (b. March 12, 1817) married Nancy, daughter of Henry Link; their children: Elizabeth m. Christ. Spangler, son of David; Mary, never married; Asa, killed in the Civil War; Adaline; Emmeline m. Christopher Cox; Sue m. Joseph Weller; and Elijah m. Sarah Dick.

4. Levi Weddle (Aug. 22, 1819-June 23, 1892) married Catherine, daughter of Adam Harter; their children: Eld. Harvey m. Margaret Harman, daughter of John; Eld. Joel m. Martha Hylton, daughter of George; Samuel m. Catherine Harman; J. Calvin m. Christina Harman, daughter of John; Eld. Andrew J. m. Annie Harman, daughter of John; Francis M. m., first, Julia Keith and, secondly, Sallie Bryant; Elkanah A. m. Emezetta Cannaday, daughter of Stephen; Elizabeth m. Austin Hylton; Margaret m. James Slaughter; and Martha Ellen m. Owen Harman, son of George.

5. Sara Weddle married Jeremiah Slusher.

6. Elder John Weddle (d. March 12, 1871) married Louanna Simmons, daughter of Cara; their children: Lorenzo Dow m. Eliza A. Wade, daughter of Owen, they had one son John William m. Dolly DeHart, and their son was Dewey C.; Darius William m. Anna Studebaker; Callahill Minnis m. Studebaker, daughter of Isaac, Darius and C. M. moved to Ohio; Lafayette

G. m. Martha Dodd; Jabez m. Nancy Harter; Ellen C. m. Steward Starr.

7. Elder Joseph Weddle (Mar. 30, 1826-April 3, 1862), married Susannah, daughter of Christopher Bowman; their children: Mary M. (b. 1850) m. Daniel Spangler, son of Abraham; Hannah m. Eli Marshall; Elizabeth (b. 1854) m. Winfield McDaniel; Sarah m. John Flora, son of Abraham; Christina (1860-1872); and Josephine m. Josiah Flora, son of Abraham.

8. Isaac Weddle (Aug. 6, 1828-Apr. 29, 1900), married, first, Catherine Sutphin; their children: Joseph S. (b. 1856) m. Lydia E. Howell, daughter of William; Cornelia J. (b. 1861) m. William E. Marshall of Carroll County; J. Abner (b. 1863) m. Cora E., daughter of T. P. Brammer of Patrick County; Nancy E. (1865-1887); Abraham (1867-1889); Elder Leroy M. (b. 1871) m. Elmetta Simmons, daughter of Noah; and John A. (b. 1872) m., first, Eliza Hill and, secondly, Mary Dickerson, he moved to Missouri. Isaac Weddle married, secondly, Violet Harman, daughter of Benjamin; both of their children died in infancy.

9. Joshua Weddle (Oct. 4, 1830-June 23, 1914), married, first, Mary Simmons, daughter of Cara; their children: Elder George W. m. Elizabeth Young; Elder Roley M. m., first, Anne Weddle, daughter of Alexander, and secondly, Eliza Frost, he moved to the State of Kansas; Orlena m. Daniel Bowman of Franklin County; Eliza m. M. M. Hylton, son of Riley; Malinda m. Samuel M. Harman, son of George; Laura I. went to Kansas and married there; Thomas P. m. Ella Harman, daughter of George; and Mollie m. Decator E. Phillips of Tennessee. Malinda, Thomas and Mollie are now living somewhere in the West.

10. Eliza Weddle (b. May 7, 1833) m. John Spangler, son of David.

Benjamin Weddle was in the habit of making a trip each year in a six-horse wagon to Lynchburg, Virginia, bringing back salt, sugar and such supplies that were needed in those days. On the return of such a trip in the year 1807, he was taken sick on the top of Bent Mountain and died, and was buried there.

His granddaughter, Mrs. Daniel Spangler, who lives in his old home, has a much prized possession, a large pewter dish or platter, fifteen or sixteen inches in diameter, which was in the wagonload of goods at the time of his death.

Elijah Weeks The Settler

Elijah Weeks, the settler, lived in Loudoun County, Virginia, where he married a Miss Thompson and moved to Bedford County, Virginia. He lived there for a number of years and raised a large family of children. He moved from Bedford with his family of eleven children and settled in the west end of the present county of Floyd. Most of his children moved to Western states when they grew to maturity. His children were: 1. Alderson; 2. Elijah, Jr.; 3. Thompson; 4. John; 5. Lewis; 6. Alfred; 7. Chapman; 8. Mathew; 9. Finneta; 10. Jane; and 11. Elizabeth.

7. Chapman Weeks was a local Methodist minister, whose sons were: Elbert, Andrew and Ephraim.

8. Mathew Weeks married a Miss Maberry and lived in the west end of Floyd County where he raised a large family of children who were well-known citizens; they were:

(a) Cornelius C. married Sarah Wade, daughter of Owen, and had three children: Esper R., Stella F., and Kyle M. Kyle M. Weeks is a well-known lawyer of Floyd, who was State Senator.

(b) Quinqua Darius is a well-known minister of the Primitive Baptist Church in Floyd County. He married Elizabeth Hylton and their children are: Landon D., Edward G., Obediah, Locky and Cullen.

(c) Mathew A. married Virginia Page.

(d) Elijah G. married Catherine Smith.

(e) Semiramis.

(f) Rosetta.

(g) Emmarillia.

(h) Laura.

Those in the Confederate army in the Civil War were: P. A., and John were in Company D, 54th Virginia Infantry under

Captain Henry Slusher; Charles C. was in Company A, 24th Virginia Infantry under Captain C. M. Stigleman; Lewis U., General, Louis S., and James R. were with Captain Andrew Dickerson in Company A, 54th Virginia Infantry; Washington and Archibald (Archibald died in the service, time and place unknown), Augustus (died in the service, time and place unknown), F. M. Weeks and Elijah Weeks were with Captain Henry Slusher in Company D, 54th Virginia Infantry. John and W. H. Weeks were with Captain W. H. Price in Company H, 51st Virginia Infantry; and William and George Weeks were members of Col. Robert L. Preston's Reserves.

In the World War were: Joseph L., Herbert G., and Kyle M. Weeks from Floyd County.

Wells

Richard Wells (Apr. 30, 1754-Aug. 28, 1832) and wife Jane (1754-1836?) came from near Zanesville, Ohio, and settled in the present county of Floyd near the covered bridge on Little River. Here he laid warrants on over one thousand acres of land. He had no children and soon his nephew, Job Sidwell Wells, came to make his home with him, and eventually fell heir to all of Richard's possessions in Floyd County.

Job Sidwell Wells was born April 6, 1798, died Nov. 2, 1860. He married, first, Sarah, daughter of Peter and Sarah (Strickland) Howard. They had two children: Major H., who died in 1836 at the age of 12 years, and Richard (b. 1826). Job married, secondly, Elizabeth (1811-1891), daughter of William and Mary (Goodson) Shelor. They were the parents of eight children:

1. Rowena Wells (1835-1913) married Rev. Marshall Anthony Davidson; they had five sons and one daughter.

2. Dr. George Milton Wells (b. 1837) married in 1864, Lucinda P. Goodwin, daughter of James Goodwin of Catawba County. He was educated at Hale's Ford Academy, Jacksonville Academy and Roanoke College, and spent the first twenty-five years of his life in his native county of Floyd. He enlisted in Company A, 54th Virginia Infantry under Captain C. M.

Stigleman, was later assigned to the Commissary of the Twenty-fourth Virginia Regiment, Pickett's Division, and in this capacity served throughout the war and was on the ground at Appomattox when the surrender came. He graduated from the Medical College of Virginia in 1866 and then practiced medicine for two years at Floyd Court House in partnership with Dr. C. M. Stigleman, after which he removed to Portland, Oregon, where he was for many years a busy practitioner and a successful businessman. He was Professor of Diseases of Children in the University of Oregon for thirty years. He traveled extensively and was a man of wide experience. They were the parents of four children: (a) Dr. James Hunter Wells, a Medical Missionary of the Presbyterian Church in Korea for 25 years; (b) Dr. John M. Wells, a physician of Chelsea, Mass.; (c) Frank M. Wells, an attorney-at-law of New York City; and (d) William Bittle Wells, of Portland, Oregon.

3. Emily Jean Wells (1839-1863).

4. Harvey Deskins Wells (b. 1842) married Jennie Lewis.

5. Mary Jane Wells (b. 1844) married Dr. Robert William Douthat, son of David Greiner and Mary Ann Straton Adams Douthat of Christiansburg, Virginia, on January 16, 1865. Dr. Douthat was professor of Greek and Latin at the University of West Virginia. Their children: Claudius David; Leland, died in infancy; Rudenz S. (Clerk of the County Court of Cabell County, Huntington, W. Va.); Luther Lee and Robert Marvin; Lucie Emma; Mary Elizabeth; Dana Glen; and Genevieve Lane.

6. Dr. John Thomas Wells (1846-1882) married Alice, daughter of Jackson Godbey, and was a noted surgeon of Portland, Oregon.

7. William Butler Wells married Addie Douthat, moved to Los Angeles, Cal.

8. Tazewell Headen Wells, died in infancy.

In the Confederate army: George Milton and Harvey Deskins Wells were members of Company A, 24th Virginia Infantry. In Company G, 21st Virginia Cavalry, were John T. Wells, promoted to Corporal; Harvey D. Wells, captured Nov. 12, 1864, and imprisoned at Point Lookout; W. B., Richard H., and Burwell Wells.

Whiteneck (Whitenack)

Benjamin Whiteneck was the immigrant ancestor of the Floyd County family, whose son William Whiteneck settled in the east end of the present county of Floyd in 1827. William married Bidsey Lambert; their family of nine children were:

I. Benjamin, moved West.

II. Anderson married and moved West.

III. Jonathan, m. first, Sallie vest; their children: Leander; Oscar W.; Geraldine D. m. Christian Strickler; Mabie; Helen; Birtie; Maude; Stella and Gay. He married, secondly, Mahala Vest, no children.

IV. James m. Lydia Vest, their children: Eliza, Charles M. and Arthur R.

IV. Thompson m. Mary Sisson; their children: Delaware, Enoch, Albert, Richard, Rilda, Rena, Flora, Lucy, Sally and Shannie.

VI. Martha m. Henry Iddings; their children: James, Lafayette, Charles, Octavia, Sally, Elenor, Lucy and Alice.

VII. William, Jr., m., first, Sarah J. Clower; their children: Robert, James, Wilburn, Rosa, Laura, Callie and Florence. He married, secondly, Sarah Vest; their children: Jasper, Barnard, Elvy and Dorma.

VIII. Joseph went to Indiana where he was a schoolteacher.

IX. Clementine m. William Clower, no record.

In the Confederate army: James R. Whiteneck was a member of Co. B, 42nd Virginia Infantry under Captain Henry Lane, wounded May 2, 1863, at Chancellorsville, Va., and had a fragment of shell taken from his side weighing 12 ounces. In the same company was William H. Whiteneck, wounded at Kernstown, May 23, 1862. J. A. Whiteneck was a member of Co. I, 54th Va. Infantry under Captain Burwell Akers. Henry T. Whiteneck was in the World War.

Whitlock

The Whitlock family is of Irish descent and lived in Halifax County, Virginia, before moving to Patrick County. Henry Wilburn Whitlock was a farmer in Halifax County; after his death, the widow and children came to Patrick County about 1815 and settled near the old James Cannaday mill in the northern part of the county. The family of children were, in part: Henry; Zebedee; Riley; Richard; and Thomas.

I. Henry Whitlock (b. 1805) married Elizabeth, daughter of Jonathan and Polly (Shelor) Graham, the settler, and made his home in the county of Floyd on Little River, some eight miles northeast of the present county seat. He was a well-known citizen whose family of children were:

1. Jonathan married Elizabeth Gardner; their seven children: Leroy C.; Ferdinand; Phillip; Waitman; Mary Susan; John, Jr.; and Matilda E.

2. Alvin married Barbara, daughter of Jacob and Mary (Kagey) Strickler; their children were: John; William; Josephine; and Sarah.

3. Isaac (b. 1833) married May 4, 1865, Elizabeth (b. July 26, 1839), daughter of Calvin and Nancy (Kenzie) Wickham; their children: (a) Virginia.A. (May 24, 1866-Aug. 1919) m. J. W. West, their children: Henry, Addie, Maud, Kate, Virginia, Fletcher, Norris, Henry and others; (b) Nancy M. (b. Mar. 2, 1868) m. Will Williams, their children: Oscar, Nancy, Elsie, Mattie, Eugenie, and Mary and Joseph (twins); (c) Noah B. (b. July 4, 1870); (d) Joseph (b. Dec. 22, 1872); (e) Daniel T. (b. July 6, 1875); (f) Mazura (died in infancy); (g) Annabelle (b. Nov. 27, 1880); and (h) Hannah (b. 1878).

4. Mahlon (b. 1835), a well-known stonecutter and farmer, lives two miles southeast of the courthouse on the Cannaday's Gap Road; he married Matilda Sumpter; their children were: Wilburn, Shelburn, Mahlon, Joseph, Elizabeth and Lillian.

5. Elinus Whitlock (1837-1916) married Octavia Spangler, daughter of Samuel, and lived ten miles east of the courthouse; their children: Lincoln, Isaac, Laura, Rosa, Maggie,

Grant, Elijah, Augustus, Dove and Catherine.

6. Hyatt Whitlock married Sarah Spangler, daughter of Samuel, and lived five miles northeast of the courthouse; their children: Samuel, Henry, Elinus, Malinda and George.

7. George Whitlock married Charlotte, daughter of Moses Blackwell, and lived near Stonewall schoolhouse in the east end of the county; their children: William, Mintie, Christian, Otho, Mary, Joseph and Eugenia.

8. Mary Whitlock married Augustus Beamer, and lived in Roanoke, Virginia.

II. Zebedee Whitlock married Celia (b. 1806), daughter of Jonathan Graham, and lived in Floyd County; they were the parents of Asa Whitlock who married Elizabeth Sumpter; their children were: Dennis, Albert, Ataway, Laura, Olivia and Inez.

III. Riley Whitlock married Anna Cockram, daughter of Edward Cockram, Jr.; they had one son, Harden m. Alla Boyd, daughter of Samuel.

In the Confederate army: Alfred Whitlock, Co. A, 54th Virginia Infantry under Captain Andrew Dickerson, was captured and taken prisoner to Fort Douglas, where he died. In Company B, 54th Virginia Infantry under Captain Jackson Godbey, were: Isaac, Elinus, Joseph H. and George Whitlock, the latter wounded, time and place unknown. George Whitlock served in Company I, 54th Virginia Infantry, under Captain Burwell Akers.

The Wickham Family

The Wickham family is of English origin. Nathaniel and Calvin Wickham are descendants of the first settler who settled on the Roanoke River.

I. Nathaniel Wickham married Mary B. (Polly) Shortt, daughter of Reuben and Lydia (Clark) Shortt, and they lived on Little River in Floyd County. He was one of the early carpenters. He built a very fine house for Major Thomas Banks which is still standing—over one hundred years old. The children of Nathaniel were:

1. Corneliuus, educated at the Gannaway School, died

at age 24 of tuberculosis, unmarried; a short sketch about him appeared in the **Mountain Boomer** in 1891 and also a sample of his poetry.

2. Reuben, also died young.

3. Dallis was a well-known Primitive Baptist minister, married Emmazetta O'Bryant and lived on Little River. He had one daughter, Loula.

4. Curtis married Frances Agee, daughter of William; their four children were: Elliott, Mollie, Daisy and Elmettie.

5. Mary A. married Joel Shanks, and lived on Little River. They were the parents of twelve children: Jefferson, Wade, Richard, Olivia, Nannie, Dora, Agatha, Bulah, Maud, Eugenia, Frances and Glynn.

6. Olivia married Francis F. Snead (she was his second wife); their children: James, Essie and David.

II. Calvin Wickham, brother of Nathaniel, married Nancy Kenzie (b. Jan. 3, 1811) on August 30, 1838. He lived on Little River; their children:

1. Samuel K. (b. 1841) married Mary Jane Deweese.

2. Elizabeth (b. 1839) married Isaac Whitlock.

3. Benjamin (b. 1842) married Polly Sowers; their children: Homer, Jane, John Kyle, George (b. Aug. 23, 1884), Lillie and Ocie.

4. Hannah (b. 1842, Benjamin and Hannah were twins) married a Mr. Carroll.

5. Mary Frances (b. 1846) married John Weaver.

6. Noah (b. 1848) married Alice Riner.

7. Christian A. (b. 1850) married Lina Cole.

8. Nancy Isabelle (b. 1852) married Pleasant Cole and lives in Cambria, Montgomery County, Virginia.

The Phillip Williams Family

In 1804, Phillip Williams (1773-Apr. 7, 1834) married Jane Poag (1779-1851), a descendant of the family of President James Polk, and moved to the present county of Floyd. They settled on Pine Creek, about four miles east of the present county seat (Naaman and Wilton Brammer now own and reside on this place). Their children were:

I. Joseph Williams (Sept. 1813-1875) married Susan Huff (1825-1902), daughter of Isaac (1794-1872) and Elizabeth (Winfrey) Huff (1800-1872), annd settled one mile northeast of his father's home on a part of the Phillip Williams land. He was a good farmer; their eight children:

A. Isaac Phillip (1847-1914) married Bertie Robertson, daughter of Elder Thomas L. Robertson of the Primitive Baptist Church. They lived on the Floyd-Franklin Pike, four or five miles east of the Court House. Their children were: Lula, Lila, Tom and others.

B. John Franklin Williams (1850-1888) married Martha Moore, daughter of Noah B. Moore of Floyd County. Their children: Joseph, Jerome, Jesse, Isaac, Frank, William, Maude, Peter and John.

C. Jacob Og. Williams (1856-1916) married Clementine Moore, daughter of Noah B. Moore; their children: Susan (d. in infancy), Peter, Luther, and others.

D. James Peter Williams married Rena J. Shortt, daughter of Elder Asa D. Shortt of the Primitive Baptist Church. They live at the old Joseph Williams homestead where he is engaged in farming.

E. George Bright Williams (1866-1920) married Iowa E., daughter of Elder Asa D. Shortt, and lived three miles east of the town of Floyd.

F. Elizabeth Jane Williams married Edward Howery.

G. Mary Williams (1853-1905) married, first, Elbert Young and, secondly, Daily Akers.

H. Tula Williams married Samuel Thomas.

II. Col. John Williams (Sept. 1, 1817-Dec. 4, 1880) married Amanda Lemon (Jan. 15, 1828-Feb. 21, 1906), daughter of Isaac and Sallie (Young) Lemon. They lived at the old Phillip Williams homestead where he built a substantial stone residence and erected a sawmill on Pine Creek, which ran very near the home. Col. John Williams was one of Floyd County's best-known citizens. They had but one child, Minerva Jane, who married John H. Cannaday, son of William A., and they were the parents of Dr. Dexter Cannaday, a prominent young physician, and Ada, Samuel and Fannie.

III. James R. Williams married Mary, daughter of Jacob Bower of Floyd County; their daughters: Sarah Jane ("Duck") m. Johnson Agnew; Emma m. William Burnett; Drucilla m. Cape Jones; Ellie m. Dalton; and Celia m. Phillips; their sons (?): George, James, Fred and Charles.

IV. Elizabeth Williams (b. Aug. 14, 1801) married Sparrel Janney of Floyd County; their children: James Monroe, died young; William Powell; and Philip.

V. Sarah Williams (b. Oct. 15, 1815) married Thomas Lancaster (1811-1884), known as Dr. Tom Lancaster, who practiced medicine as an herb or "Thompsonian doctor," as did his father (Dr. Lewis Lancaster) before him. They lived on Pine Creek on the Floyd-Cannaday Gap Road, just east of New Haven Baptist Church. Their children: Andrew m. Teressa Haynes; Phillip m. Mary Sue Corbin; Garland; Zack, never married; Mary m. James W. Walton; Sarah m. Landon Stone; Nannie m. Jonathan Lee; Eliza m. Rice Young; and Lucinda, never married.

VI. Isabel Williams married William Guthrie; their children, in part: Philip married Burnett, sister to Abe Burnett; James m. Conduff, sister to J. H. Conduff; Joseph, never married; Annie; Jane.

In the Confederate army: Jarret Williams was First Sergeant under Captain Henry Lane in Company B, 42nd Virginia Infantry. Eli M. Williams served under Captain Jackson Godbey in Company B, 54th Virginia Infantry. John Wliliams and James R. Williams were members of Stuart's Horse Artillery. R. B. Williams served under Captain W. H. Price in Company H, 51st Virginia Infantry. Isaac P. Williams was a member of Captain Bill Smith's Company, Company F, 14th Virginia Cavalry.

The William Williams Family

William and Mary Williams were the parents of another Williams family, unrelated to the Phillip Williams family, two of whose sons were Powhatan and Hector.

I. Powhatan Williams (1813-1893) married Elizabeth (Betsy) Dickerson, daughter of Moses, and lived on Pine Creek, just north of the Floyd-Franklin Pike. Their children:

A. Demaris married Isaac Epperly, son of Jacob; their children were: Charles T., Thomas E., Kent, Frank, Lizzie and Lula.

B. Minerva married Captain Darius (Druss) W. Sowers; they were the parents of Professor Trigg D. Sowers, one of Floyd's prominent teachers; William Aaron, editor and proprietor of *Floyd Press;* Walter R., and Rev. Robert R., a prominent minister of the Lutheran Church.

C. Thomas married Anna Saunders; their children: John, Blanche and George.

D. David married Lina Spangler, daughter of William; their children: Aaron T., Thomas W. and Alma.

E. George married Sarah Epperly, daughter of Eli W.; their children: Zora; Arthur; Lena; Walter; Eula; Samuel; Elsie; Luther; Jewett; Roy.

F. William T. married Albina Young, daughter of John, and lived in Floyd Court House; their children: Byron T., Bunyan; Hattie; Gay; Bessie; Harry; and Annie.

G. Henry married Florence Young, daughter of John, sister to Albina, and moved to Missouri; their children: Una, Frank, Lala, Helen.

II. Hector Williams married Susan Morricle and lived in Floyd County. Their children: Darius Edgar; Emeline; Asbury; Jennie; Alice (Allie); Nannie; Albert (Tom); Charlie; Nettie.

In the Confederate army: Darius E. Williams was a member of Company A, 54th Virginia Infantry, who went out at the beginning of the war under Captain C. M. Stigleman; he was killed in battle at Plymouth, North Carolina, date unknown. In Company A, 54th Virginia Infantry under Captain Andrew Dickerson, were David Williams, wounded at Bentonville, March

19, 1865; George M. D. and Mathew Williams. In Captain J. B. Headen's Company of Col. Robert L. Preston's Reserves were: John, Hector and William T. Williams; and in the same under Captain Andrew J. Graham was Asbury B. Williams, First Lieutenant.

The Williamson Family

The Williamson family is from Franklin County, Virginia. About 1830, George Williamson, who married a Miss Wood of Franklin County, moved his family from that county and settled on West Fork, some four miles west of the Court House. His neighbors were the Goodykoontzes, the Wades, the Harmans, the Slushers and the Simmonses. Their children were, in part: Thomas W., Sarah, Wyatt and Mary. Sarah Williamson married George Goodykoontz (1812-1888), son of George and Miriam (Beaver), and moved to Missouri. Wyatt and Mary Williamson did likewise.

Thomas W. Williamson married Nancy, daughter of Dr. John and Dicey (Cox) Bishop, and lived for some years in Indian Valley. He opened the first general store in that section, hauling his "goods" with four- and six-horse teams over the mountains from Lynchburg, Virginia. He later moved to Jacksonville (Floyd) where he was a popular tavernkeeper before and during the Civil War. His tavern, or hotel, was on the south side of Main Street, directly across from the Court House. Mr. Ferguson was the previous operator, and Flemmon Howery followed Thomas Williamson. Bryant Hylton was a contemporary with Mr. Williamson in the tavern business.

Mary Williamson (b. 1836), daughter of Thomas and Nancy, married George W. Goodykoontz, son of David and Ruth (Harter), and moved to Radford, Virginia, where she is still living at the age of 86. George and Mary Goodykoontz were the parents of: Nancy, William, Alfred, John T., Ida, Charles H., Lena and Harry. Charles H. and Harry are well-known druggists of Bluefield, West Virginia.

George W. Goodykoontz and his brother William were

soldiers in the Confederate army, both of whom were severely wounded in action.

The Willis Family

The Willis family is of English extraction and [according to tradition] the first of the name came from Normandy with William the Conqueror.

Bennett Willis was corporal, then sergeant, of Captain Magagno's Company of Infantry of the Line, 5th Virginia Militia regiment, in the War of 1812. He enlisted September 16, 1813, and died in camp January 18, 1814, and was buried in Norfolk. He was survived by his wife, Catherine, and the following children: John, Hugh, David, Jonathan, Polly, Elizabeth, Rachel.

Jonathan Willis (1807-1889), fourth son of Bennett and Catherine, came from Franklin County in 1833 and settled on Burks Fork, four miles south of the present village of Willis. He married Arabella, daughter of Abraham Phlegar and they raised a family of ten sons and four daughters: Margaret (1835-1921); David (April 13, 1836-1925); Hamilton (b. 1837); Bennet (b. 1839); Lavinia (1841-1916); Thomas (b. 1842), Samuel B. (1843); Simon Peter (1845-1916); James (b. 1848); Mary and Martha, twins (b. 1849); John (b. 1850); George (b. 1853); and William Henry (b. 1856).

Of their ten sons, six served in the Confederate army. Bennet, a sergeant in Company D, 54th Virginia Volunteers, died in camp of diphtheria. Samuel was desperately wounded in battle, captured and died on a prison ship; he is buried in a Federal cemetery in South Carolina. David was First Lieutenant in Company D, 54th Virginia Volunteers, and was severely wounded in Georgia on the retreat before Sherman. Thomas was also wounded. Jonathan Willis, the father, belonged to the Home Guard.

Margaret married George Williamson and went West. Her children live at Sundance, Wyoming.

David married Ellen Phlegar in 1866, daughter of Benjamin, and has lived since 1865 at the old Abraham Phlegar homestead in the town of Floyd. Their children: Azula Rhoda m. H. P. Hinman; Margaret (Maggie) M., never married; Mary Ella, never married; Arabella Lillie m. Harvey R. Bishop; and Anna Lee m. M. F. Brumbaugh.

Hamilton emigrated to Missouri after the Civil War.

Thomas lives in Texas; among his children are: Margaret, Olive Virginia, Wade.

Peter was one of the public-spirited and progressive men of the county. He lived at Willis, Virginia. He married, first, Lydia Hylton, and, secondly, Emma Riner; their children (second marriage): Bessie P., Martha, Bennett Riner.

Martha married Jonas Harman; her children: Arabella m. Sowers; Dora m. Weeks; Thomas m. McMartin; Jennie m. Belton; and Lavinia m. Potter.

Lavinia was Jonas Harman's second wife (after the death of Martha); her daughter is Della m. Dickerson.

The Rev. James Willis, now retired, lives in Washington, D. C. He married Ione Miller; their children: Thomas Capel; Houston; Russell (daughter) m. Frank Grimes; Bennett; and Sidney. Houston and Thomas are lawyers. Houston and Sidney were both in action in the World War, both officers.

John lives at Willis, never married.

George married Anna Lavinia Brumbaugh in 1883; their children: Eula Meade m. Jesse S. Carter; Julius Dreher, physician, m. Mary Butler Evans, lives in Roanoke; Peter Archer m. Olivia Simmons Boyd; George Armand Jr., m. Fannie Copenhaver; and Lena m. William McDonald. George A. Willis, Sr., was a citizen of Floyd County for 65 years, but now lives at Rocks, Maryland. He was Superintendent of Schools of Floyd County for eleven years. His son, Peter Archer, was 2nd Lieutenant in the World War, and was in France one year. Julius D. was a medical officer.

William Henry lives at Willis, Virginia. He married, first, Laura Isabel Guthrie and had a son, Edward Bennett; he married, secondly, Elizabeth Fisher, and had a son, Walter Neal; he married, thirdly, Sarah Catherine Eller.

Peter Wilson The Settler

Peter Wilson emigrated from England to America and settled in the east end of the present county of Floyd in 1783. His wife's name is unknown. Their five children were:

I. Randolph (Feb. 17, 1812-Dec. 23, 1861) married Anna Gray, daughter of Joseph, the settler, and lived in Floyd County all of his life. Four of their children were: A. Joseph H. married Eliza J. Gray; B. Noah married Lizena Bell Poff; C. Giles R. married Aleann Walters; and D. Anna Rhoda, died in infancy from diphtheria.

II. Elijah (b. 1814)married a Miss Light; their children, in part: A. Jonas; B. Taylor; and C. Calla Arr.

III. James married a Miss Smith and moved to West Virginia many years ago. Their children were: Tazewell, Charles, John and others.

IV. Rhoda married James Howard Gray, son of Joseph, the settler; their children: James M., Joseph M., Osborne W., Rhoda and Juliet.

V. Livey married Crockett Muncy.

Those of the name from Floyd County serving in the Confederate army were: Cary D. and Joseph Wilson in Company B, 42nd Virginia Infantry, under Captain Henry Lane; Joseph Wilson was wounded, captured and taken to prison at Elmira, New York, where he died in prison. Valentine, Peter R., Jonas, James, John T. and Laban Wilson were members of Company I, 54th Virginia Infantry, under Captain Burwell Akers. David Wilson was a member of Col. Robert L. Preston's Reserves.

Walter H. and Noah D. Wilson were soldiers in the World War.

Paulus Winter The Settler

The Floyd County family is of German descent and the tradition in the family follows: "Paulus Winter was born in Germany about the year 1757, and, being very anxious to get to America, came across the Atlantic as a stowaway (an indentured servant) and was sold (or indentured) to defray the cost of his transportation across the ocean. He was a skilled mechanic, having served fourteen years apprenticeship in Germany, seven years as a stonemason and seven as a journeyman. He was purchased by, or indentured to, a man who wanted a house built and in its construction badly needed a stonemason."

Paulus Winter later built a dam across the James River, some distance above the present site of Lynchburg, Virginia, which stood for many years. He married Sally Little, a young woman of Irish descent and lived for many years in Botetourt County, Virginia. Later, about 1825, he removed to Terry's Creek in the eastern part of the present county of Floyd. His home was six or seven miles northeast of the county seat, where he purchased 600 acres of land at 25c per acre. It is said he brought the first "big plough" or turning plough, and the first wagon to the county. He died at his home on Terry's Creek in 1839 at the age of 82. Of Paulus Winter's family of children, two settled in Floyd County. They were: I. David, and II. George.

I. David Winter was born in 1825, and married Mary Blackwell, daughter of Moses, the settler. They lived near Stonewall schoolhouse in the east end of the county. Their two children were: 1. Paulus, Jr., who moved West, and 2. Lizzie Dickerson, wife of George W., who lived on Brush Creek in Montgomery County.

II. George Winter was born in 1828, died in 1888, and married, first Elizabeth Slusher, (1837-1881), daughter of David, and, secondly, Martha J. Howery. The first set of children of George and Elizabeth were: 1. Emily B. (b. 1864) m. David Moore, son of Noah B.; 2. Albert Grant (b. 1867) m. Annie L. Gibson and lives on Pine Creek where he owns a very fine farm known as the "Peter Huff farm." They are the parents of four daughters and two sons: Stella Georgia, Nancy Blanche, Mary Alice, John Simmons, Annie Grant and Herman Daniel. There was one daughter of the second marriage: Willie E. m. Purse Williams of Roanoke City.

In the Confederate army, Daniel and John P. Winter were members of Company A, 54th Virginia Infantry, under Captain Andrew Dickerson.

**Stephen H. Wood (1822-1890),
Son of John Richard Wood**

The Wood Family

(I) Stephen Wood was born between 1700 and 1720, and died after 1781, the date of his will. Joseph Johnson of Lunenburg County, Virginia, deeded a tract of land in Lunenburg County, in 1756, to his son-in-law, Stephen Wood. Stephen Wood left a will in Lunenburg County, Virginia, dated 1781, proved in 1782: wife, Ann; children mentioned: John, Sally (m. Jordan), David, Patsy, Johnson (m. Fannie Thompson), George and Henry. Perhaps his oldest son was Stephen who had already received his part of his father's estate. If this were correct, it would account for both Stephen's Line and John's Line of the Wood Family. Members of both lines were known to be closely akin.

STEPHEN'S LINE

(II)   Stephen Wood, b. in Lunenburg about 1740, m. June 4, 1765, Ann Smith, daughter of Samuel. Their marriage was recorded in Halifax County, Virginia. They had seven children:

1. Samuel Wood, lived near New London, Va., was killed by a wagon.

2. Thomas Wood m. Sally Pasley, marriage recorded in Franklin, as follows: "Thomas Wood & Sally Pasley, dau of Robert, Dec. 17, 1802, surety Henry Dillon, minister John Saunders," had two children, one of whom was Gilly Wood, m. Daniel Angle: "Daniel Angle and Gilda Wood, Apr. 26, 1828, surety Thomas Wood, minister Moses Greer." Their son Stephen married Nancy Cabaniss: "Stephen Woods, Jr. (Wood) & Nancy Cabaniss, May 1, 1837, surety Cassimer Cabaniss, minister Theo. F. Webb."

3. Stephen Wood (III)—see below.

4. Nancy Wood (b. 1770) m. Alexander Ferguson, Jr., Dec. 1, 1788, surety Stephen Wood, minister Thomas Douglas, marriage recorded in Franklin. They had five children: (a) Thomas; his daughter Mary m. Lyons, a tobacco dealer of Lynchburg, Va.; (b) Mary m. Anthony Simmons, they had four children, of whom Sparrel Simmons of Salem, Virginia, had a daughter Eliza m. Dr. Joseph A. Gale, Chief Surgeon of the Norfolk and Western Railway; Emma Simmons m. Dr. Koiner, and after her death Dr. Koiner m. Lizzie Simmons; after his death Lizzie m. McClung of Salem; Lem. Simmons, brother of Sparrel, m. Julianna Wood; Serepta Simmons m. Joseph

Meador.

5. Susan Wood m. Moses Greer and lived at Gogginsville: "Moses Greer and Susannah Wood, Feb. 4, 1794, minister Randolph Hall." Moses Greer was a Baptist preacher and long represented Patrick County in the Legislature. Their children were: Samuel, went to Missouri; Moses m. Juliana Simmons and moved to Illinois; William lived and died in Franklin County; Mary m. Daniel Noble, Sept. 9, 1823, had three sons, went to California. Moses Greer had two children whose names are not known.

6. Betsy Wood m. Burnet Law: "Burnet Law & Betsy Wood, 1789, minister Thomas Douglas." They had two sons, one of whom was Thomas, lived in Pittsylvania County, Va.

7. Fannie Wood m. William Chambers: "William Chambers & Franky Wood, April 24, 1809, surety John Smith, Minister John Ashworth." They had six sons, lived on Blackwater in Franklin Co., Va., sons were: Washington, Smithen, and Cephas, went to Kentucky when young; Silas, John and William, lived in Franklin Co., Va.

(III) Stephen Wood, son of Stephen Wood and Ann (Smith), settled on Blackwater in northeastern part of Franklin Co., Va., where he died Aug. 1, 1850. He is buried on the old home place, three miles from Hardy Station on the Virginian Railroad. He married Lydia Holland: "Stephen Woods (Wood) & Lydia Holland, Feb. 2, 1812, minister John Ashworth," the record is in Franklin County. He was High Sheriff of Franklin County, Va., and was an Ironside Baptist preacher. Their children were:

1. Thomas m. Fannie Harvey; they had six children, of whom: Lucy m. McGuire Davis; Sarah m. John Holland and had nine or ten children: Samuel m. Jamie Howell of Pittsylvania Co.; Jack m. Josephine Poindexter of Pittsylvania Co., and

had six children; Louisa m. John Smith of Sandy Level, Pittsylvania Co., Va.

2. Susan m. Paul Thrasher: "Paul Thrasher & Susannah Wood, January 18, 1841, surety Samuel G. Wood, minister Benjamin Meador," and lived near Vinton, Va.; their children: James, killed in battle at Gettysburg; Mary m. Smith; Nannie m. Short; Stephen; and John.

3. Samuel Gilbert (b. Nov. 18, 1818) d. at Bonsacks, Roanoke Co., Va., July 16, 1896; m. Amanda Gish, Dec. 25, 1844. He was a captain in the Confederate army. Their children: Stephen Thomas, Lynchburg, Va.; Mittie m. N. J. Vinyard; Mary (b. Feb. 19, 1851) m. John Williams; David Gish (b. Sept. 19, 1853); William Garrison (b. Feb. 11, 1856) at Bonsacks, Va., m. Anna Powell Thrasher of Arch Mills, Va., they had seven children, one of whom is William Wilson, Bluefield, W. Va.; Samuel B. (b. July 31, 1858); Calvin (b. April 1, 1860); Emma (b. 1864) m. Pace; and James E. (b. 1870).

4. Nancy, died aged 24 years, never married.

5. Stephen S., lived to be 80 years old; m., first Eliza Vinyard and, secondly, Elizabeth Jones. He lived on Blackwater in Franklin County. Richard Johnson Wood, of the John Wood line, knew this old man and knew of their close kinship; they talked it over together.

6. Fanny, lived to be 77 years old, m. Crocket Bandy and lived at Ballyhack, Va., no heirs.

7. Calvin, died young, no heirs.

8. Julina (b. 1831) m., first, Lem. Simmons.

9. Mary Josephine (b. 1837) m. Tazewell Meador, two sons: John, and Wood.

10. Martha Ann (b. Jan. 19, 1839) m., first, Jonathan McGuire, one son: Wood McGuire; she m.,

secondly, Jack Kasey, three children: Thomas, Louery and Maggie. She was living in Vinton in 1925.

11. William m. Fanny Pace, and died in California.

12. Elizabeth (b. abt 1835) m. Henry Pollard. The marriage recorded in Franklin: "Henry C. Pollard & Elizabeth L. Wood, January 17, 1852, minister Theo. F. Webb." They had nine children.

(End STEPHEN'S LINE)

JOHN'S LINE

(II) John Wood, son of Stephen Wood and Ann Johnson, his wife, mentioned in Stephen Wood's will as one of his heirs, was born about 1745, and was living May 18, 1816, when he witnessed the will of Edward Cockram, Sr., in Franklin County, Va. At this time he was living at the top of Woods Gap on the line of Patrick and Montgomery counties (now Floyd), his son, Richard, had married the daughter of Edward Cockram, Sr. John Wood, in 1782, the year his father's will was probated, secured Land Office Treasury Warrant for 50 acres of land, the same that now includes Woods Gap. This was located and surveyed at the top of the Blue Ridge in 18__; the line adjoining James McCutchen's line and the line of Charles Thomas, marked "C.T." John was twice married; one of his wives was named Nellie. He had two (known) sons: Richard, of Woods Gap, and Henry, who went West, probably to Missouri. Franklin County Marriage Records show that he was the father of two daughters: Ellender, who married Henry W. Boyd: "Henry W. Boyd & Ellender Wood, June 28, 1806, surety John Wood, minister Benjamin Sweeney," and Elizabeth, who married Francis Hill: "Francis Hill and Elizabeth Woods (Wood), surety John Woods (Wood), minister Thomas Douglas, February 24, 1796."

(III) Richard (Dickey) Wood was born in 1769 and died at the top of Woods Gap in Patrick County, Virginia, in 1859, aged 90 years. He married, first, Rachel Cockram, daughter of Edward Cockram, Sr.; secondly, Fannie Brammer, no children; thirdly, Betsey DeHart, four children; fourthly, Lucy Via, six children.

Richard (Dickey) and Rachel Wood had eight children:

1. Henry (1798-1883) m. Nancy Bryant, and in 1836 moved to Sullivan County, Indiana; they had eight children: Matilda m. Johnson; Louisa m. McCarty; Sarah m. Joseph; Lucinda m. Wolverton; Nancy m. Alsop; Ambrose m. Sarah Ditch; German m. Amanda Ward; Henry, Jr., (b. 1824).

2. John Richard (b. 1799) m., first, Lucinda DeHart (see below).

3. Annie (b. 1807) m. David Cockram, son of Isham, Sr., and lived to be over 100 years old; they had eleven children:

(a) Alexander m. a daughter of Jerry Wood; children: Larkin, Gale, Jeff.

(b) Richard m. a daughter of Jerry Wood; children: Malinda, Jackson.

(c) Isham m. Elizabeth Salmons; children: Rufus, Joney, Robert, Buren, Alice.

(d) Jackson m. Martha Salmons; no children.

(e) Harvey m. Milly Jane DeHart, daughter of Wilson; children: James D. (the Primitive Baptist preacher); Asa; Amos; Joe; Green; Matthew; Rebecca Ann; Lilly; and Allie.

(f) David m. Ellen Cannaday, first, and, secondly, Iowa Griffith; no children.

(g) Peter m. Mahalie Cannaday, daughter of Constant; children: John William; David; German; Leah; and Annie.

(h) German m. Mary Wood, daughter of Jerry; no children.

(i) Leah m. John Ashworth; children: Green; Sarah; Lelia; Tazewell.

(j) Nancy m. Jonathan Salmons; children: John M.; Waller C.; Sarah; and Martha Ann.

(k) Sarah m. Mark Salmons; children: Rena, and

others.

4. Alexander m. Bethina Brammer, and later moved to Raleigh County, West Va., and is buried in Old Baptist Churchyard near "Lilly Reunion Grounds" on Flat Top; he was a militia captain and drillmaster in Patrick County before the Civil War; they had eight children: (a) Crawford m. Vineca Howell, no children; (b) Richard A. m. Lucinda Wood; children: William A., James, Nancy, John; (c) Wesley, name of wife unknown, children: Daniel, Joe, Poncy J., Belle, Eliza, Whittie, one other; (d) Sallie m., first, John Brammer and, secondly, Rankin Keaton; (e) Keziah m. Newton Sweeney; children: Jeff, Jack, William and Belle; (f) Jane m. Absalom Birchfield; (g) Louise m. Alex Goode; and (h) Joel, moved to Wisconsin.

5. Jeremiah (1801-1891) m. Polly DeHart, daughter of Wilson, and lived all of his life in Patrick County; they had thirteen children:

(a) Annie m. Richard Cockram.

(b) Isaac m. Akers; children: William, George, James, Henry, and perhaps others.

(c) Lucinda m. R. A. Wood, son of Alex and grandson of Dickey; children: William A., James, Nancy, John, and others.

(d) Charity m. Harden Hylton.

(e) Gabriel m. Luella Akers; children: Hayden m. Amanda Harvey, and had two children, Lunda and Hayden.

(f) Sallie m. Alex Cockram.

(g) Jerry moved to Ohio, no record.

(h) John, killed in the battle of Gettysburg.

(i) Mary m. German Cockram.

(j) Stephen m. (name of wife unknown).

(k) Nancy m. John Harris.

(l) Mahala m. Crawford (?) Hall; children: J. H.

V. T., Mrs. C. D. Moye, Mrs. J. R. Lilly, Mrs. Lewis Lilly, Mrs. Cora Neely, Mrs. Guy Moye.

(m)   Judith.

6.   Peter (1808-1897) m., first, Nancy Moran, and moved with his family to Raleigh County, West Va.; they had six children:

(a)   Mary Ann m. Davis Hylton; children: Nancy Ann, Elizabeth, Janie, Lucinda, Jacob, Peter and James.

(b)   James Nelson m. Nancy Sweeney; children: William M., Martin G., Alex, German, George J., Elder Stephen L., Vincent, John, Henry Newton, Nancy Ann, Janie, Arminta and Emma.

(c)   Martha Elizabeth m. Lewis Meador; children: Tyler, Alex, Granville, Frank, Nancy, Mary Jane, and Rosa.

(d)   John Lee, died young.

(e)   William Marion, died young.

(f)   David Anderson, died young.
      Peter married, secondly, Rhoda Jane Thompson; one child:

(g)   Lewis A.

7.   German m. Nancy Wright, and moved with his family to Mercer County, West Va.; they had seven children:

(a)   Alex m. ___ Massie; children: Belle, Janie, Daniel, and others.

(b)   James Wesley m. Jane Hylton; moved to Oregon, no record.

(c)   Octavia m. Green Ferguson; children: John, Ira, Hayden, and others.

(d)   Arminda m. Jacob Walker; children: Henry, German, Zina, Ned, Hayden, and Belle.

(e)   Sallie m. Calvin Walker; two children: Myrtle and Leona.

(f)   Martha m. Council Walker, no further record.

(g)   Mary, died young.

8.   Edward m. Mary (Polly) Moran, daughter of Nelson,

and lived in Patrick Co., Va.; their children: Alex; Tom; Elder Elijah, a Primitive Baptist preacher; Eli; German; and John.

(IV)   John Richard Wood (1799-1886), second son of Richard (Dickey) and Rachel, was buried on the old home place at the foot of Woods Gap.   He married Lucinda DeHart, daughter of James and Ellen (Dennis), his wife, and granddaughter of Aaron DeHart.   Ellen Dennis was from Franklin County and lived to be 104 years old.   After the death of Lucinda in 1853, John Richard married, in his old age, Nancy Hubbard, no children.

The children of John Richard and Lucinda (DeHart) Wood were:

1.   Annie m. Elder John Hubbard, later they moved to Summers County, West Va., where John Hubbard was a Primitive Baptist preacher; they had two sons and four daughters: Lucinda and Joseph are recalled.

2.   Stephen H. (1822-1890) m. Rachel Thomas, daughter of Joseph and granddaughter of Charles Thomas the settler, of Patrick County; (See page 259, their nine children:

(a)   Ann m. Charles McAlexander, justice of the peace of Franklin County; their children: Ausbern G. m. __ Ingram, he was State Senator from Franklin and Floyd counties; George m. Judith Nolen; Asa m. Elizabeth Ann Nolen; Callahill, never married; Daniel m. __ Snead; Ella m. Lewis Nolen; Mary Etta m. Samuel Bowling; Lou Annie m. Tyler Thomas, and, secondly, Zach Helms.

(b)   Sparrel m. Ida Rakes, daughter of Richard, and lives at the foot of Woods Gap in Patrick County on the old Jeremiah Burnett homestead; their children:

(1)   Samuel, unmarried.

(2)   Lillie m. William Christman and lives in North

Carolina; children: Vesta, Vada, Clifford, Ocie, and Mae.

(3) Minnie m. Richard Rakes, son of Alexander, and lives at Rocky Mount, Va.; children: Eura, Glen, Chester, and Richard.

(4) Abram m. Ruth Rakes, daughter of Millard; children: Ralph, Orvil, Pauline, Maury, and others.

(5) Conner m. Clementine Martin, daughter of Preston; children: Bernice and Herbert.

(6) Elisha m. Bertie Rakes, daughter of Millard; children: Auburn, Buford and Elsie.

(7) Robert m. Myrtle Turner, daughter of Alvie J. and Nancy; no children.

(8) Nannie Susannah (Kate) m., first, Hosea Thomas, son of Ira; children: Alpha; m., secondly, Robert Eads of Siloam, N.C.

(9) Venie m. Claude Turner, son of Alvie J.; children: Albert and Ralph.

(c) John I. m. "Puss" Hall, daughter of Bland, of Patrick County; children: Stephen m. __ Hall; Sylvan m. Venie Hall, daughter of Henry H. and Ruth (Turner), one child, Murray; John m. Della Hall, daughter of John and Sarah (Thomas).

(d) Lewis m. Exonie (Eck) Hall, daughter of Hardin; children: Stephen m. Linda Thomas, children, Arthur, Ruth; John W., not married; Sylvanus m. Lillie Nolen, one child, Flossie; Clementine m. Amos Thomas, son of Ira and Victoria (Turner), no children; Ella m. Frank Howell; Clara m. George Robertson, son of Abe, one child, Norine.

(e) Stephen Green m. Judith Rakes, daughter of German; they have nine children:

(1) Mary Ellen m. Rev. James D. Cockram, Primitive Baptist preacher; their children: J. Bernard; J.D., Jr.; John (Teddy); Virginia C.; Geneva

Marie; Mary Joy.

(2) Asa P., merchant of Kimball, West Va.; unmarried.

(3) German H. m. Lillie Brammer, daughter of Jesse; children: Virginia Dare, Woodrow, Sunshine.

(4) Stephen M., unmarried.

(5) Sparrel Abram, in business in Bluefield, West Va., unmarried.

(6) Amos R. m. Blanche Robertson, daughter of James B. and Judith Jane; child: Ernest Goodson.

(7) Lenard D., unmarried.

(8) Ada B. m. D. N. Scales.

(9) Lula M., unmarried.

(f) Adaline m. Pinkard Robertson, son of David and Nancy; children: Thalus m. — Williams of Spray, N.C.; Ophus; Posey; Oscar; Della; and Eulalia m. Brammer.

(g) Ellen m. Peter Thompson, son of Jennings, they live in Franklin County; children: Bunyan; Eula; Bertha; Olliver; Mae; and Kermit.

(h) Bunyan m. Lucy Dixon; their children: James Lundy m. Lena Turner; Ellis m. Bertha Nolen.

(i) Joseph.

3. Mary m. Perry Slusher, son of Jacob, and lived in Floyd County; they had ten children.

4. Delilah m. Richard Hatcher, son of James, and lived in Floyd County; they had several children, some of whom were: Charles m. Alice Thomas; Letha; William; and Rosa Belle.

5. Richard Johnson (see below)

6. Leah (b. Aug. 25, 1834), twin of Rachel; m. George Slusher, son of Jacob and brother of Perry. She lived to be 92 years old. They had three daughters.

7. Rachel (Aug. 25, 1834-1935), twin of Leah; she lived to be 101 years old; m. Samuel F. Turner, son of Francis; their children: John m. Jathina Barnard; Melinda m. Daniel Webb; Mary Eliza-

beth m. Conner Barnard; Jefferson m. Victoria
Elizabeth Thomas; Annie m. John Bechner; and
Della m. James Howery.

(V) Richard Johnson Wood (Oct. 27, 1828-Dec.
20, 1917) married, February 5, 1852, Judith Anne Shortt (February 17,
1834-August 30, 1899), daughter of John Young Shortt and
Judith (Thomas), his wife. Richard Johnson was militia captain in Patrick County before the Civil War. He volunteered
as a private in Company D, 51st Regiment of Virginia Militia,
under Captain D. Lee Ross. He attended the local schools, which
were inadequate and poor; yet he had as a teacher for a short
time, Nathaniel Henry, son of the distinguished Virginian, Patrick Henry. Their nine children were:

1. Susan Emeline (Feb. 24, 1853-June 17, 1858).

2. Rachel Elvira (May 30, 1855-July 3, 1858).

3. Jefferson Pinkard (b. November 4, 1858) m. Sarah
   Belinda Brammer, daughter' of Jonathan and
   Juliana (Burnett), and lives in Floyd County
   where he has been a farmer and justice of the
   peace for forty years. Belinda Wood died March
   1, 1931; their children: (a) Stanton H.; (b)
   Dora; (c) John E.; (d) Benjamin Frederick;
   (e) Gertrude; and (f) Ethel. Jefferson Pinkard died Dec. 10, 1955.

4. Daniel Hillsman (b. November 3, 1860) married,
   first, April 14, 1881, Ruth Malinda Corn, daughter of Rev. Peter and Clementine (Turner), of
   Franklin County, and lived for some years in
   Floyd County. They later moved to Patrick
   where he is a farmer living near Woolwine, Va.
   He has represented Patrick in the Virginia Legislature; and has been School Commissioner.
   Their children:

(a) Susan Ardella (b. Mar. 14, 1882) m., Sept. 8, 1907,
    W. L. Harger.

(b) George Cleveland (b. Nov. 21, 1884) m., Oct. 15,
    1907, Kate Handy; their children: G. C. Wood,

Jr., Richard, Billie (dec'd), Laurence Hale.

(c) Kate (b. Oct. 8, 1887) m., Sept. 10, 1911, Daniel C. Spencer; their children: Ruth Emma; Daniel C., Jr.; and Bruce.

(d) May (b. May 31, 1889).

After Ruth's death, November 26, 1892, Daniel Hillsman married, secondly, August 31, 1893, Fannie J. Stovall (b. Sept. 13, 1864-d. 1936) daughter of Joseph M. and Permelia (Corn). Daniel Hillsman died Jan. 22, 1954.

5. George Bunyan (May 13, 1863-June 12, 1930), m. Elizabeth Brammer of Floyd County; they had one son, William Jefferson, now deceased. Elizabeth died July, 1930.

6. Greenville Darius (b. November 9, 1866) m., first Melissa Graham (d. 1892), daughter of Andrew and Senorah (Turner), no heirs; m., secondly, Lilly Barnard, daughter of Conner and Mary Elizabeth (Turner); their children: (a) Dr. R. Hugh Wood, a physician of Atlanta; (b) Susan Lee; (c) Elizabeth; (d) Greenville; and (e) John. Greenville Wood is a merchant and farmer of Floyd County. He died in 1943.

7. Amos DeRussia [the complier] (b. May 16, 1869); he is a physician, residing in Bluefield, West Virginia. He married Annie Chapman Johnston (d. 1947) in Portland, Oregon, daughter of Judge David E. Johnston. Their children: Sara Pearis (d. four years old); John David (d. in infancy); and Richard Johnston, who is with the Appalachian Electric Power Co., Pulaski, Virginia. Dr. Amos Wood died in 1942.

8. Sparrel Asa (b. October 30, 1873) m., first, Jessie Scales (d. 1906) of Martinsville, Va.; one daughter, Evelyn Martin, died in infancy. Sparrel m., secondly, India Goodwyn, daughter of Judge Goodwyn of Nottaway, Va.; one daughter, Judith, graduate of George Washington

272

University, and teacher in the public schools of Washington, D. C. Sparrel Asa is now retired from a long career of teaching in the public schools of Virginia. Sparrel died in 1959.

9. Doc Robertson (b. February 1, 1877) m. Gertrude Christian Howard, daughter of Peter L. and Belle, of Floyd, Va. They have one son, Dexter Robley, a banker of Pulaski, Virginia, and two daughters, Virginia Howard and Catherine Ball. D. Robertson is a National Bank Examiner, residing at Pulaski, Va. Gertrude died 1939, D. Robertson died in 1952.

[Dates of deaths in recent years have been added—Ed.]

Mrs. Amos D. Wood (nee Annie Johnston) in the backyard of her father's home in Bluefield, WVA

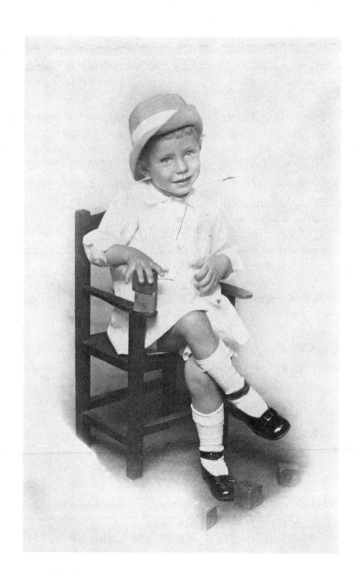

Richard J. Wood, the Author's Son
About Four Years Old

Young

Captain Peter Young and his wife, Mary, lived in the west end of Franklin County; they had six sons and two daughters. Two of his sons moved to Floyd County and were among the early prominent settlers:

I. William Young and Jane, his wife, originally settled in the Turtle Rock section of the new county; he was a member of the first Court of Justices when the county was organized. Later they moved to Alabama, and there is no further record of the family.

II. Joshua Young and Nancy (Walker), his wife, came across the Blue Ridge to live on a farm five miles east of the courthouse. This place was later the home of his son, George, and later the home of Ferdinand Huff. At present it is the home and property of Robert Huff. On this farm are buried Joshua and Nancy Young, their son George, the Wickhams and many of their neighbors. The children of Joshua and Nancy Young as remembered were:

1. George (b. 1817) married Nancy Jane, daughter of Samuel Agnew, the settler, and lived and died at the old Joshua Young homestead; their children:

(a) Burwell married America, daughter of Isaac and Sally Lemon; their children: Norman, George, Lizzie, Nerva and Nora.

(b) Joseph married Lucinda, daughter of John Y. Shortt; they had two children: Jefferson and Tula.

Burwell and Joseph Young were members of Company H, 54th Virginia Infantry, under Captain Sparrel H. Griffith in the Confederate army, and were killed in the battle at Resaca, Georgia, May 15, 1864.

(c) William married Berta Phlegar; their children: Bertie and Minoris.

(d) Elbert married Mary Williams; their children: Charlie, Elbert, Lena, Rosa, Tula and Eugenia.

(e) Peter married Malinda Bower; their children: James, Lemuel, Frazier, Nannie, Mallie and Abner.

(f) Thomas married Clementine Epperly; their children: Sam, Jasper, Joseph, Clay, Ella, Mattie, Flora and Willa.

(g) Susan married Walker Jones; their children: Preston, Thomas, Iford, George, Virginia, Martha, Elena, Nettie and Leah.

(h) Leah married Thomas Hall; their children: Irvin and Adaway.

(i) Eliza married William P. Lawrence, son of Thomas; their children: Dove, Hope, Florence, Pearl, Pattie, Byrd and Willie.

(j) Adaline married Henry Lawrence, son of Thomas; their children: Taylor, Thomas, Derusia, Ollie, Dora and Lillie.

2. John Young (b. 1819) married in 1840 Delphia, daughter of Elder John Turner, widely known Baptist preacher of Patrick County, and lived for some years at the John Banks home place, and later on the headwaters of Pine Creek. He was an expert carpenter and cabinetmaker. Their children were:

(a) Victoria (b. 1843) married John T. Shortt (b. 1841), son of John Y. Shortt, and moved to Parsons, Kansas; their nine children: Emmert, Palmer, John, Harry, Edd, Wilmer, Lillie, India and Frank.

(b) Nancy married Jefferson Vaughan; their children: Zora and Alice.

(c) Albina married William T. Williams; their children; Byron, Bunyan, Hattie, Gay, Bessie, Harry, Annie.

(d) Florence married Henry Williams; their children: Lala, Helen, Una, Frank.

(e) Rice married Eliza Lancaster, daughter of Thomas; their children: Trumbull, Rosco and Gertrude.

(f) Elkana, never married.

(g) Laura married James Sowers; their children: Nana, Harry, Mabel, Helen.

(h) Leota married Theodore Elmey (?); their children: Elizabeth and Ward.

(i) Asa married Laura Phlegar.

(j) Nora married John Sowers; two children: Beula and Ward.

3. Elizabeth Young married Pleasant, son of William and Patsy Cannaday; their children: Isaac, Mitchell, Sally and

Ellen.

4. Sally Young (1811-1862) married Isaac Lemon (his first wife).

5. Mary Young married, first, Anderson Jones; their children: Walker, Landron, Callahill, Charity, Orpha, Rosa and Luemma. Mary married, secondly, Stephen Hill; their children: Elizabeth, Nancy, Octavia and Swinfield (?).

6. David Young married Sally Fisher; they lived for a while in Floyd County and later moved West.

7. William.

8. Jennie.

Colonel William B. Shelor
(1820-1914)

John W. Simmons
(1859-1938)

Spangler's Mill established late 1700's

Mrs. Elizabeth Shelor Wells in her dressy coif.
(1811-1891)

CHAPTER II

FLOYD COUNTY

To appreciate any person or place, one must know their history. To know Floyd County is to love it. To the natives, particularly, nature has done more for Floyd County than any other county in the state.

Along this Blue Ridge, Highland and Foothill section one will find apples, cherries, peaches and berries on the open hillsides. Nature has spread this tableland with a lavish hand.

Floyd County is one of the most elevated counties in the state-- a natural watershed area. Part of the water reaches the Gulf of Mexico and part reaches the Atlantic Ocean. The county is unique in the fact that not a drop of water flows into the county from any other county.

Facts About Floyd County

Floyd was formed in 1831 from Montgomery and was named in honor of John Floyd, Governor of Virginia from 1830 to 1834.

Population: 13,115 (1922).

Area: 238,578 acres.

2,432 feet above sea level.

The Buffalo, highest point in the county.

Floyd County is a grain and grazing section of Southwest Virginia. The value of livestock and poultry was $1,501,683 in 1920.

The healthy atmosphere of Floyd County has led a goodly number of her senior citizens past the century line.

Plateau Region

Floyd County occupies a plateau region in Southwest Virginia between the Blue Ridge and the Alleghany Mountains; in area it contains 238,578 acres. It is shaped in the form of an elongated triangle with its base joining Carroll County and the apex in the northeast at the junction of Franklin, Roanoke and Floyd. Its surface is broken and uneven, containing many small mountains and ridges, with numerous small valleys between. It is watered and drained by Little River and its tributaries, "'The first River in New Brittaine which runneth West, a River of long extent," the most eastern source of the New River. A unique feature is that no water flows into the county from without, but all of its water arises within its borders and flows out of the county.

THE BLUE RIDGE MOUNTAINS, the mountain range forming the great watershed dividing the eastern waters from the western, here form the county line for some thirty or thirty-five miles from the Patrick-Carroll junction in the southwest to the Roanoke-Franklin junction in the northeast. A number of passes or gaps are found in this portion of the mountain forming the boundary, some of which are: Tuggle's Gap, Wood's Gap, Cannaday's Gap, Shooting Creek, Runnet Bag Creek and Daniel's Run.

THE BUFFALO KNOB, situated in the southwestern part of the county, a spur of the Blue Ridge Mountains, is the highest knob in the county and can be seen for miles around. Rising almost abruptly from the surrounding country to a height of sixteen hundred feet (some 4000 feet above sea level), it forms an impressive mountain scene. The mountain stands in the shape of the buffalo which once grazed near its slopes, the head and shoulders turned to the north or northwest, formed of huge, bare, blue rocks piled one upon another in a rugged bold manner. Holes in these hard, gray-blue rocks have been given names: the Raven's Nest, Kettles, and the Rattlesnake Den. It is said that in the old days there were many rattlesnakes in and around The Buffalo and in early spring it was an annual sporting event for adventurous young men to take their stand with shotguns and kill the sluggish serpents as they crawled out into the sunshine. One spring more than a hundred snakes were killed in a day. As late as in the 1880's a wolf was killed on top of The Buffalo. Bailey Sutphin discovered a wolf track in the light snow and gathered a band of men around the mountain while others beat the bushes for the wolf. William Sowers of Burks Fork was near a large boulder on top of the knob when the wolf came up from the eastern side "out of the ivies," whereupon Sowers killed him. Rev. and Mrs. John K. Harris were in the habit of taking their entire school to The Buffalo in the spring of the year and spending a day and a night on the knob. They made the trip of some twenty miles in covered wagons, with plenty to eat and blankets for the night. The object of the outing was to take in the extensive view and to watch the sun rise from the top of the knob.

STORKER'S (STOCKER'S) KNOB is situated in the center of the county near and overlooking the town of Floyd. It is a knob of some elevation which affords an excellent view of the surrounding country. The tradition is that it took its name from a man by the name of Stocker who deserted from Tarleton's army in the time of the Revolutionary War and settled on this knob. Here he lived a lonely life and, like all deserters and shirkers, he left an unsavory memory. He kept hounds and was fond of hunting. It is said he was a rude musician and often amused the early settlers with his fiddle. The carousing and noises heard late at night from the knob filled some of the early German settlers with a superstitious awe.

WILLS RIDGE lies some five miles north of the courthouse, extending from the West Fork of Little River in a southwestern direction for some twelve or thirteen miles. It is a ridge or mountain of considerable elevation above the surrounding country; much of it is still well timbered. In the early days it was the home of the bear, the panther, the deer, the wildcat, the wild turkey and an abundance of smaller game, making this a desirable hunting ground. The ridge took its name from a man by the name of Wills from Franklin County, Virginia, who built a hunting lodge here and was in the habit of coming once or twice a year and spending a month or so in hunting and fishing.

ALUM RIDGE, so named from the large deposits of alum

found in the hills, extends from Little River some ten miles west into the Indian Valley section. Along the north side of this ridge and along Little River in this section of its course, were the early homes of the Lesters, the Akerses, the Showalters, the Petermans, the Altizers and others. Between Alum Ridge and Wills Ridge and along the banks of Beaver Creek were the homes of the Simmonses, the Boothes, the Coopers, the Ellers, the Reeds, the Dulaneys and the Akerses.

INDIAN RIDGE dies in the west central portion of the county, extending from West Fork of Little River in a western direction to the Carroll County line, some six or eight miles in length. It separates the Greasy Creek and Burks Fork valleys, is of moderate elevation, and has many fine, fertile farms on its slopes. It derived its name from the many Indian relics, broken stone pots and other cooking utensils, spears and arrowheads, found along its slopes.

LAUREL RIDGE, of low elevation above the surrounding country, is the county line between Montgomery and Floyd for a distance of about nine miles. Laurel Creek runs along the south side of this ridge, and Brush Creek is on the north side over in Montgomery County, though the latter does rise in Floyd County and flows around the east end of Laurel Ridge. The Coles, the Huffs and others lived along Laurel Ridge, while the Wimmers settled on the headwaters of Brush Creek. The LeSueurs lived on Camp Creek, farther to the south.

LITTLE RIVER is formed by three main branches or "forks": East Fork of Little River (Little River proper), West Fork, and South Fork (Dodd's Creek). The East Fork of Little River rises in the extreme east end of the county near the crest of the Blue Ridge and is joined along its course by many small creeks and streams; Boothe's Creek, Pipestem Branch and Payne's Creek join the East Fork to form the head of Little River proper. Some of the larger creeks which it receives along its course are: Beaverdam Creek, Pine Creek, Camp Creek, Terry's Creek and Laurel Creek. Along Little River are some very fine farms on which were the homes of the Boothes, the Howards, the Wellses, the Watkinses, the Moores, the Shelors, the Wickhams, the Stricklers, the Helmses, the Whitlocks, the Winterses, the Bowmans, the Spanglers; around the "head of the river" lived the Conners, the Kelleys, the Vests, the Poffs, the Cannadays, the Grays, and others of the early settlers.

WEST FORK of Little River has its source in several heads in the Blue Ridge Mountains which at this portion form the Patrick County line. It flows north and northeast through the central portion of the county and is joined in its course by Howell's Creek, Rush Fork, Spurlock's Creek and other streams, and, two miles north of the county seat, by the South Fork of Little River, or Dodd's Creek. After this it turns north and flows for six or eight miles to its junction with the East Fork or Little River proper. Solomon Harman and his wife Elizabeth Slusher, settled on West Fork seven miles west of the town of Floyd and here they built one of the first mills of Floyd County. A few miles upstream was the old Cary Simmons mill, later run by his son, Obediah Simmons. Among others to settle along this watercourse were the Hyltons, the Weddles, the Slushers, the Wades, the Goodykoontzes, the Williamsons; and lower down on the stream, the Dickersons, the Simmonses, the Lesters, the Boothes, the Reeds, the Sumpters and others.

SOUTH FORK, or Dodd's Creek, rises in the Haycock Mountain near the head of Pine Creek, southeast of the county seat, and flows in a large curve around and to the west of the town of Floyd and joins the West Fork two miles north of the courthouse. It took its name from the settler, Benjamin Dodd, who came here from Franklin County and settled one mile west of present Floyd. On this stream Christopher Smith, a German from Pennsylvania, built one of the first flour mills in Floyd County; the old mill house is now owned by G. W. Whitlow. Howard's Mill (Epperly's Mill), a landmark, which has been burnt down and rebuilt two or three times, is on this stream some three miles southwest of the town of Floyd, and Scott's fine rolling mill is two miles north at the mouth of the creek. Others to settle along this watercourse were the Gilhams, the Agnews and the Slushers.

BURK'S FORK, a tributary of Reed Island Creek, rises along the Blue Ridge in the southwestern portion of the county. It is a stream of some fifteen miles in length and along its banks are some of the finest farms to be found in the county. Here were the homes of the Willises, the Wades, the Hyltons, the Helmses, the Vaughans, O'Neals, Barringers, Bolts and others. This stream was named for James Burke, the pioneer, who came to this section after he was driven out of "Burke's Garden" in the year 1755.

GREASY CREEK heads east of the town of Willis and runs west to empty into Reed Island Creek, a stream of twelve or fifteen miles in length and of considerable size at its mouth. It is said Greasy Creek took its name from the hunter, James Burke, who killed so many bears on its banks and threw so much greasy bear meat in the stream that the early settlers called it "Greasy Creek." Along the banks of this stream was "The Quarters," the farm owned in the early days of the county by the Saunders family of Franklin County. They kept cattle here and a number of slaves, hence the name of "The Quarters." The Slushers, the Burnetts, the Phillipses and the Hollandsworths lived along this stream.

INDIAN CREEK rises near the town of Willis and runs north for some twelve miles and, with its tributary streams, drains the Indian Valley section. If flows into Little River at the east end of Mack's Mountain at the junction of Floyd, Montgomery and Pulaski counties. The Indian Creek section was a favorite hunting ground of the Indians, from which fact it took its name. A tribe of Canawhay (Kanawha) Indians had a camping ground used for hunting in this area; they regularly passed this way over a trail going from their settlement on New River, said to be near present Radford, to points in North Carolina. The trout fishing in this stream in the early days was very good and hunters from many miles distant would come to this section to hunt and fish. A man by the name of Ashby was so fond of fishing and hunting in this section that he spent a whole winter and spring here on one of its branches which he named after himself, "Ashby's Branch." Ambrose Cox lived on Little Indian Creek. This valley was the home of the Bishops, the Coxes, the Akerses, the Hambricks, the Mitchells, the Halls, the Duncans, the Teels and the Reeds, who were well-known early settlers of

Floyd County.

BEAVER CREEK, a small but very beautiful stream, flows through a valley between Wills Ridge and Alum Ridge and empties into Little River. On this stream Bonsack's Carding Machine was located and was operated for many years prior to and during the Civil War. Bonsack lived near the present city of Roanoke. George Eller came from Roanoke County to take charge of the machine about 1868, and he ran it for many years, later purchasing it. They also made linseed oil and for some time it was known as the Oil Mill.

PINE CREEK rises in the Haycock Mountain near the Shooting Creek gap and flows north for some ten miles to empty into Little River near the old home of the widow Mary Spangler and Spangler's Mill. The first court of Floyd County was held near the mouth of this stream. Along this creek were the early homes of the Epperlys, the Williamses, the Guthries, the Huffs, the Lancasters, the Smiths, the Sowerses, and others.

PAYNE'S CREEK is a small stream, some three or four miles in length, which has its source in the Blue Ridge Mountains in the extreme southeastern part of the county and flows north to empty into the East Fork of Little River on the old Daniel Howery farm. This creek took its name from Lewis Payne, the settler, who came from Warrenton, Virginia, and settled on this stream in 1825. Later and higher up on this creek was built the Payne's Creek Primitive Baptist Church. Others to make their homes along this creek were the Howerys, the Kelleys, the Ogles, the Murphys and the Radfords.

TERRY'S CREEK, which flows into Little River just below Pine Creek, was named for a family of Tory sympathizers who settled here, one of whom was Jonathan Terry, the builder and first owner of Spangler's Mill. This was in the time of the Revolutionary War when this territory was part of Montgomery County and the Tories formed a large element in the county. The Easom plantation, which was visited by Captain Wade and his company of rangers in the year 1758, was on this creek, as was the early Winter home.

BRUSH CREEK rises in Floyd County in the northeastern

section, and flows west, north of Laurel Ridge. Laurel Ridge divides the Brush Creek valley from the Laurel Creek valley, which is entirely in Floyd County. Laurel Creek falls into Little River at Sowers, several miles above the mouth of Brush Creek. Huffville is on the headwaters of Brush Creek. The Wimmers, Huffs, Whitenacks, Scotts and others lived in this part of the county.

DODDS CREEK rises principally in the Haycock Mountain near the head of Pine Creek, and runs in a large curve around (just west) of the Town of Floyd. It was named for Benjamin Dodd, the settler, whose farm was one mile west of Floyd. Many beautiful farms are on this creek and two fine mills: Howard's mill (now Epperly's mill) nearly two miles southwest of the courthouse, one of the old mills of the county which has been burned down and rebuilt two or three times, and Scott's rolling mill, situated near the junction of this creek with West Fork, some two miles north of the courthouse.

REED ISLAND CREEK, a tributary of New River arises or flows through the very extreme southwest corner of the county and enters Carroll County, and further north again re-enters Floyd County and flows for some miles, when it again passes over into Carroll County and flows northwest to empty into New River.

MACK'S MOUNTAIN lies in the extreme western part of Floyd County and forms a part of the boundary line for some ten miles between Floyd and Pulaski counties, continuing in a southwestern direction forming the dividing line between Carroll and Pulaski counties. The mountain is noted for its high peaks, fine timber, rattlesnakes, copperheads and huckleberries.

MINERALS OF FLOYD COUNTY

Nickel & Cobalt

The property owned by the Virginia Nickel Corporation is located in the extreme northern part of Floyd County along the boundaries of Montgomery and Roanoke counties. The openings thus far made are wholly in Floyd County. The principal ones being directly on Lick Fork, within a few hundred feet of its confluence with Flat Run southeast headwaters of the South Fork of the Roanoke River.

The Lick Fork openings are further located in a direct line from Shawsville, the nearest railway station.

(Watson, **Mineral Resources of Va., p. 580-1.**)

Copper

The Toncray copper mine is located about eight miles southeast of Floyd Courthouse. It was last operated by the New York & Virginia Copper Company.

The property has been developed by several tunnels and shafts.

(Watson, **Mineral Resources of Va. p. 517.**)

Iron

Gossan was mined in the southwestern part of the county on the West Fork of Little River at the Toncray mine for the Shelor & West Fork furnaces.

The county is without a railway, and there have been no modern iron ore operations.

(Watson, **Mineral Resources of Va. p. 475.**)

Soapstone

Curry mentions a thin seam of soapstone running through Floyd County within two miles of the courthouse.

(Watson, **Mineral Resources of Va. p. 293.**)

Acts of Assembly

Floyd County

An Act appointing Commissioners to select a site for the seat of justice for the County of Floyd.

Passed January 5th, 1832; Henry Edmundson, of the County of Montgomery; Samuel McCamant, of the County of Grayson; Matthew Sandefer, of the County of Patrick; George W. Wilson, of the County of Botetourt; and Moses Greer, of the County of Franklin, appointed Commissioners, to meet at the house of Daniel Spangler, deceased, in the County of Floyd, to select a place for the County seat of Floyd County.

A report shall be made to the County Court of Floyd County, designating the place fixed upon for holding courts and erecting public buildings.

(Acts. 1831-2. P. 261.)

An Act providing that whenever there shall be an election held in the County of Floyd, in which all the lawful voters of of the County are required to vote, there shall be at the same time a separate poll opened for such elections at the house now the residence of James Litterell, situated in the eastern part of said County, on the waters of Little River.

Passed January 8th, 1833.

(Acts. 1832-33. P. 32.)

An Act providing for the incorporation of "The Mawbrey's Gap Turnpike Company," and appointing Commissioners for receiving subscriptions to an amount not exceeding thirty thousand dollars, in shares, of twenty-five dollars each, to constitute a joint capital stock for constructing a turnpike road from some point on the Danville and Fincastle turnpike road in the County of Pittsylvania by Henry Courthouse, through Patrick County, crossing the mountains at Mawbrey's Gap, thence passing along the main cross street of Jacksonville at Floyd courthouse, to Christiansburg in Montgomery County.

Passed March 7, 1848.

(Acts. 1847-48. P. 198.)

The Old Toll Road from Floyd to Christiansburg

The Toll Road from Floyd to Christiansburg was completed during the late 1850's, but during the War it went down considerably. It was revived after the close of the Civil War and toll gates were erected; one of these was at the residence of Topelo Watkins, one mile north of the Little River Bridge. Another toll gate was erected at Union Mills in Montgomery County, four miles south of Christiansburg. Over this road has traversed most of the merchandise sold and bought in the county in all of its years of progress, except, of course, in the last few decades, when the Bent Mountain hard-surfaced road has come into general use. Years ago the merchants and farmers made wagon trips with four- and six-horse teams to the City of Lynchburg, Virginia, then the Southern market for Southwest Virginia.

First Land Warrants and Surveys
In What Is Now Floyd Co.

1774—Uriah Akers 333 acres on Little River & Blackburn Akers (48 and 150 ac. 1775 & 1782).

1774—George Hairston on South Fork Little River in all 3096 acres--this up to 1782. He was very wealthy, and had many slaves and was a tobacco grower, iron manufacturer--and his iron had a great reputation for its toughness. He was a Revolutionary Soldier from Henry County. His home was at "Hoardsville" on Smiths River, just a short distance below the present town of Bassett, Va., and where his old brick home still stands. It is said one at this early date could walk 17 miles on Hairston's lands leading west of Martinsville.

1774—John Bishop, on South Fork of Little River: 71 and 144 acres up to 1782.

1774—Abraham Goad, 106 and 316 acres on North side of Burks Fork--up to 1782.

1774—Isreal Willis, 284 acres on Little River.

1774 to 1786—William, John & David Spurlock 975 acres on Pine

Creek.

1774-1782—Richard Reynolds 887 acres on Pine Creek & Old Field Creek.

1774-1787—Thomas Goodson, Sr. & Sons 2989 acres on Pine Creek & Little River. Thomas Goodson was a Revolutionary Soldier.

1782-1787—The Dickersons on Little River to 2197 acres--They were Griffith Dickerson, Sr. & Jr.; Moses and Obediah Dickerson. Probably the Dickersons were from Franklin County--there is a place in Franklin County still known as Dickersons.

1782-1785—Daniel Conner laid land warrants on 665 acres on Meadow Run.

1782-1785—John and Christian Cooper laid warrants on 915 acres in the vicinity of Brush Fork--and later in 1831, when Floyd County line was run, it ran over his lands.

1783—Jacob Graham, 400 acres on Pine Creek.

1783—Samuel Eason, 841 acres on Terry's Creek and Brush Fork.

1783-1787—Mathew & Thomas Scott 691 acres on Beaver Dam Creek. Mathew Scott was Rev. Sol--See bounty warrants, war. 4, p. 351.

1782-1785—Robert McElhany 1572 acres on Brush Creek.

1783-1787—Humphrey Smith 830 acres on Brush Creek & Laurel Creek. Humphrey Smith & Byrd Smith were large land traders for years. Byrd Smith was a Revolutionary Soldier:--See Aud. Acct. XVIII, page 682.

1782—John Wood land office treasury warrant no. 382 for 50 acres. Sep. 24, 1782. Lands adjoining James McCutchin and Charles Thomas on South Fork Little River near Haycock Mountain. His lands were near the large 3096 acres taken up by Revolutionary Soldier, George "Rusty" Hairston of Henry County.

1787-1788—Francis Turner to land office treasury warrant 237 acres on West Fork and Burks Fork.

1790—Roland Salmonds 420 acres Top of mountain including headwaters of Pine and Shooting Creeks.

1783—David Nowland 204 acres on East Side of Little River.

1787—Zachariah Stanley 997 acres on Beaver Dam Creek.

1775—Reuben Keith 384 acres on Greasy Creek.

1782-1789—Samuel, Peter and George Reed 346 acres on Beaver Creek.

1782—Mathew Cox 293 acres on Forks of Beaver Creek.

1786—Peter Saunders, 417 acres on Little Creek---The descendants of this Peter Saunders later had a large body of land on West Fork, and kept many slaves there and grazed cattle, and called their place "The Quarters." These Saunderses were from Franklin County. Peter Saunders, Capt. Henry Militia in Rev.

1774-1783—Hercules Ogle 870 acres Head of Little River, and East End of the present Floyd County.

1782—Joseph Cole 97 acres Headwaters of Beaver Dam Creek. Rev. Soldier.

1783—Thomas, John and Joseph Huff 400 acres on West Fork of Little River.

1784-1787—Daniel and Jacob Shelor 975 acres on Pine Creek, Little River and Oldfield Creek. This Daniel Shelor was Captain Daniel Shelor, a Revolutionary Soldier--drew a pension for services as such 1835: Pension Records page 154.

1784—John Short 298 acres on Pine Creek.

1785—Richard Wells 284 acres on Terry's Creek and Little River. Richard Wells was a Revolutionary Soldier and received a "Bounty Warrant" for his services--Daniel Wells was member Montgomery Militia in the Revolutionary War.

1783—Moses Greer, Laid Land Office Treasury Warrant to lands on Burks Fork;--This Moses Greer, Capt. in Revolutionary War, rec'd. pension for services 1835: Pension Records page 136. Moses Greer, married Susan Wood, daughter of Stephen Wood and Ann Smith—marriage certificate recorded in Halifax Co. Was member Virginia House of Delegates from Franklin County 1793/4; 1798/99; 1799/1800; 1800/1801; 1801/1802; 1802/1803;

1803/1804; 1806/1807.

1782—George Quesenberry 165 acres on Greasy Creek.

1782—Tobias Phillips, 190 acres on Greasy Creek. The Phillipses settled first just across in Grayson County, but many of the family lived in Floyd County.

1783—David Ross 270 acres on Greasy Creek.

1782-1787—Isreal and Jacob Lorton 545 acres on branches of Little River. These Lortons intermarried with the Howards.

1783—Thomas Indicut (perhaps Endicot) 200 acres on Little River.

1783—John Dunkin 185 acres on Laurel Creek of Little River.

1782-1785—Jacob and Abraham Picklesimor 574 acres on Brush Fork.

1782—William Lawson lands on Sugar Run, branch of Little River.

1783—Edmund Vancel 200 acres on Little River.

1774—Steele and William Lafferty 811 acres on Indian Creek and in 1783, 400 acres more--making 1211 acres.

1807—Nathaniel Burwell obtained a Land Grant for 109 acres,-- "Plantation whereon said Burwell lives." This Nathaniel Burwell in 1809 married Lucy Carter of Shirley, a sister of General Robert Edward Lee's mother. This Nathaniel Burwell was Captain and Aid to General Howe in 1779--was Captain of Company 2, of Col. Charles Harrison's Virginia and Maryland Regiment of Artillery. His name is among a list of officers, for whose Revolutionary services Virginia Military Land Warrants were issued, prior to December 31, 1784:---Saffell's **Records of the Revolutionary War.** Spring Camp, the home of the Burwell's is a part of an original tract (nineteen thousand and more acres, in Floyd County, Patrick and Carroll) granted by the State of Virginia to General Henry (Light Horse Harry) Lee for services rendered by him to the Colonies during the American Revoultion. The section southwest of the Buffalo Knob, being a part of this tract, was known as "The Orders."

MEN IN FLOYD, AS SHOWN BY RECORDS OF "BOUGHT & SOLD"

1799—John Turman
Samuel Ferguson
on Little River.

1799—Andrew McHenry
Thomas Goodson on
Panther Knob of
Little River

1799—Moses Brown
Jacob Sowder
(This Jacob Sowder
was Rev. Sol. Aud.
Acct. 1779-1800, page
173.)
Daniel Shelor
George Epperly
Christian Epperly
Joseph Huff
Daniel Spangler
George Sowers
Joseph Moore
James Light
Abijah Boothe
Adam Pate
Jeremiah Pate
George Taylor
Alex Smythe
Agt. Loyal Co.
Thomas Lee
Henry Bishop
John Lester, Jr.
Conelius Reed
Thomas Lee to
Joel Walker
William Griffith
Robert Johnson

David Porter 1799
Jacob Robins to
William Ferguson
John Spangler
Isaac Jackson 1799
Peter Kingrey
Christian Harter, 1800
Conrad Harter
John Zilling (Shilling) 1800
Hercules Ogle
John George
Ruth Huff, to
Thomas Lee
John Chace
Jacob Pate

1796—John Wickham to Joseph Wickham
Joseph Moore, John Wood

1798—Andrew Lewis, Elijah McClanahan
Isaac Renfro, Robert King
Philip Hogan, Byrd Smith

WEST FORK
1799—Joel Walker
Dan Parkerson
Charles Turman
George Micksell
William Logan
Thomas Crutcher
Henry Jones

1800—William Turman
John Hook--the
eccentric, but
very wealthy
Tory Scotchman

1797—Henry Jones
William Spurlock
Byrd Smith

Guy Smith

INDIAN VALLEY

1800—Samuel Vancele
Ambrose Cox

BURKS FORK

1799—William Clifton
Thomas Warden

BRUSH CREEK

1799—Samuel Hilton
Allen Unthank
1800—Jesse Wilson
Absolom Stewart

SOUTH FORK

1799—Ben Howell
Jere Buchanan
Jos. Rentfro
John Kitterman
Thomas P. Jordan
Peter Saunders

PINE CREEK

1799—Sam Landon
Peter Hornbarger
Humphrey Smith
Jacob Sowder
Silas Terry
Wm. Goodson

1800—John Wickham
Robert Johnson
Philip Williams
Humphrey Smith
Jasper Terry

GREASY CREEK

1799—John Ward
Ed. Chote
Jno. England

Jno. Smith

WEST FORK

John Banks, Rev. Sol. 1835 Pen. Book 2, page 139

1795—Court Records show, that on Dec. 25, 1795 William Banks, son of the settler, sold to Byrd Smith 400 acres of land, lying on West Fork of Little River for 350 pounds--He, William Banks moved to Grayson (now Carroll) County, where he was a prominent citizen.

BURKS FORK

1787—John Cock to Andrew Cock

SOUTH FORK LITTLE RIVER

1792—George Hairston to Robert Jones

1791—Elias Harbour to James Bartlett

1794—Isaac Jones

1794—Daniel Howell

1794—John Thurman to Jesse Jones

1796—John Kitterman, Thomas Gordon, John Hook.

1794—Benjamin Howell, Amos Combs, Jeremiah Buchanan.

SOME FRANKLIN COUNTY LAND GRANTS, TO FLOYD COUNTY CITIZENS--LATER TO BE FLOYD COUNTY RESIDENTS

1804—Richard Wood, June 12, 1804 116 acres on Shooting Creek:--from Land Book No. 53, page 129.

1804—Nathan Cockram, July 3, 1804 (does not give number of acres) from Land Book 53, page 244.

1806—Henry Pedigo, June 18, 1806 150 acres on Runnet Bag Creek, from Land Book 55, page 527.

1803—Henry Pedigo, April 28, 1803 168 acres on both sides Shooting Creek, from Land Book No. 51, page 272.

1796—William Cannaday, Jr. July 18, 1796, 128 acres on a branch of Runnet Bag Creek,--Land Book No. 34, page 446.

From Henry County Records

1787 Edward Cockerham, July 30, 1787 165 acres on South
Branch of Stewarts Creek adjoining Jacob Caton, from
Land Book No. 1, page 609.

OTHER FLOYD COUNTY GRANTS

1785—John Lester obtained a Land Grant to 100 acres on Little
River September 10, 1785,–Land Office Records.
1782—Charles Simmons obtained two Land Grants for 300 acres,
and 350 acres, both lying on Beaver Creek.

1804—Reuben Short, L220, for 353 acres on Headwaters of Runnet Bag Deed Book 5, page 11-This in that portion of
Floyd County that was cut off from Franklin County and
joined to Floyd in 1870.

Political Organization of Floyd County

The location of the county seat was the work of a com-
mission appointed by Governor John Floyd as provided in the
Act of the General Assembly creating the county. This com-
mission was composed of one member from each of the ad-
joining counties: Hamilton Wade from Montgomery County,
Archibald Stuart from Patrick County, Edward Johnson from
Botetourt County, William Jones from Franklin County, John
Cock from Grayson County.

The county courthouse and jail situate on lands donated
by Abraham Phlegar and wife to the county for the said purpose, as expressed in the deed conveying the same:

"This Indenture made this 16th day of July 1832, Between
Abraham Phlegar and Margaret his wife of the one part and
George Shelor, Jacob Helms, George Godbey, Joseph Howard,
Peter Guerrant, John Lester, Benjamin Howell, William Young,
William Hancock, John Wilson, Lewis Payne, and Bryant Hylton,
Justices of the Peace of Floyd County, of the other part:
Witnesseth that for and in consideration of the location of the
county seat of said county being located on and adjoining the

lands of said Phlegar he doth hereby give grant and convey to the Justices of the peace as aforesaid for the use and benefit of said county of Floyd one acre of land lying on the Ridge adjoining the land of Manassah Tice and John Kitterman part of which Aker of land is included in lott No. 1 purchased by Harvey Deskins and the other part together with a small parcel taken from the lands of the said Manassah Tice, forming the Public square as located by the commissioners appointed by the legislature of Virginia in 1832 to erect Publick Buildings on, for said county, also doth hereby convey all that part of lott No. 3, Back of the jail purchased by James Bolt which is taken from the lands of said Phlegar's land, also all the land of said Phlegar which is included in lott No. 1 purchased by Joshua B. Wickham which is agreeable to a bond executed to said commissioners as aforesaid and also an arrangement made this day with said Phlegar by commissioners for and in behalf of said county and the said Abraham Phlegar and Margaret Phlegar his wife doth hereby forever warrant and defend a good and lawful right and title to the above recited parcel and parcels of land free from the claim or claims of them the said Abraham Phlegar and Margaret Phlegar his wife and their heirs as well also as all and every other person or persons whatsoever as witness whereof we have hereunto set our hands and seals this day and year above written.

Abraham Phlegar   (SEAL)
(SEAL)

List of Largest Landowners in Floyd County As They Appear in the Land Tax Book for 1831

Samuel Agnew	Isaac Boothe
Nicholas Alley	Daniel Boothe
William Aldridge	William Bishop
Archibald Atkins	Henry Banks
George Boothe	Benjamin Bostwick
Abner Boothe	Charles Bolt
Abijah Boothe	Christopher Bower
Joseph Boothe	James Bartlett

John Carter
Ambrose Cox
Carter Cox
Matthew Cox
Thomas Craig
George Craig
Andrew Conner
William Conner
John Cooper
Bolen Childers [Childress]
Christopher Clark
Henry Calloway
Blanch Duncan
John Duncan, Jr.
Benjamin Dodd
Charles Diven
Marchus Evans
Jacob Epperly
William Ferguson
David Fishburn
Major Howard
John Hook*
George Hylton
Archelaus Hylton
Samuel Huff
Henry Huff
Solomon Harman
Jacob Helms
Thomas Helms
John Ingles
James Keath
John Kitterman
John Kersey
John Lester
James Light
Henry Link

George Layman
William Morrical
Edwin Matthews
Jacob Nester
Catherine Nester
Lewis Payne
George Peterman
Abraham Pflieger
George Pflieger
John Poff
Henry Poff
William Phillips
Randolph Phillips
George Reed
Joseph Reed
Thomas Riffey
Jacob Snuffer
Thomas Simmons
Charles Simmons
Edmund Sumpter
William Simpson
William Shelor
Elijah Turman
William Terry
Samuel Thompson
Manassa Tice
Joseph Underwood
Allan Unthank
Elias Vancel
Richard Wells
David Weddle
Andrew Weddle
Ebenezer Watkins
Nathaniel Wickham
John Weaver

*John Hook laid land warrants on nearly 10,000 acres of land in present Floyd County, on the waters of Burks Fork Creek, during the years 1783-1794. (From records of Montgomery County office)

LIST OF LAND TAX, 1831, made by JOSEPH HOWARD, COMMISSIONER OF REVENUE

NAME	RESIDENCE	NO. ACRES		DESCRIPTION OF LOCATION
Nicholas Alley's Rept.	Unknown	941	acres	In Little River District
Thos. Alley's Rept.	Montgomery	100	acres	West Fork Lit. Riv.
Blackbourn Akers	Floyd	67	acres	Waters Lit. Riv.
Wm. Aldridge's Repts.	Floyd	280	acres	Waters Lit. Riv.
Leonard Aldridge	Floyd	160	acres	Head waters Lit. Riv.
Ezekiel Aldridge's Repts.	Floyd	300	acres	Head waters Lit. Riv. & S. F. Roanoke
Thomas Aldridge	Unknown	200	acres	Waters Burke Fork
Archibald Atkins', Rept.	Floyd	233½	acres	Lit. Riv. **Wm. Bishop**
Emery Altizer	Floyd	80	**acres**	Waters **Beaver Cr.**
George Boothe	Floyd	120	acres	Beaver Cr.
Abner Boothe	Floyd	137	acres	Beaver Dam Cr.
Abijah Boothe	Floyd	805	acres	J. Graham L. (joining)
George Boothe, Jr.	Floyd	320	acres	Lit. River
Stephen Boothe's Repts.	Floyd	100	acres	West Fork Lit. Riv.
Joseph Boothe	Unknown	200	acres	A. Wiley
Austin Boothe	Missouri	30	acres	West F. Lit. Riv.
Isaac Boothe, Sr.	Floyd	667	acres	On & near Lit. Riv.
Daniel Boothe	Floyd	205	acres	Mouth Beaver Cr.
Isaac Boothe, Jr.	Montgomery	100	acres	Beaver Cr. of Lit. Riv.
Riley Boothe	Floyd	179	acres	West F. Lit. Riv.
Same & Austin Boothe	Floyd	130	acres	Waters Lit. Riv.
George Boothe	Floyd	350	acres	Head wat. Beaver Cr. & Reed
George J. Boothe	Floyd	140	acres	Buck Shoals & Litt. Riv.
Same & Henry Trip	Floyd	125	acres	Little River
Henry Bishop, Sr.	Floyd	80	acres	Little River
Henry Bishop, Jr.	Floyd	80	acres	Little River
Henry Bishop, Jr.	Floyd	150	acres	Waters Indian Cr.
Wm. Bishop	Floyd	50	acres	Laurel & Camp Creeks

NAME	RESIDENCE	NO. ACRES		DESCRIPTION OF LOCATION
John Bishop	Floyd	50	acres	Laurel & Camp Creeks
John Becket, Sr.	Floyd	183	acres	Beaver Dam Cr.
James Barnett's Repts.	Montgomery	186	acres	Head Beaver Dam Cr.
John Banks	Patrick	167	acres	Adj. Thomas Goodson, Lit. Riv.
Wm. Banks	Patrick	139	acres	Thomas Goodson
Henry Banks	Richmond	1,000	acres	Jones Ridge Pig Run fork
Henry Banks	Richmond	1,000	acres	Ford Glade Cr.
Henry Banks	Richmond	500	acres	West side Laurel Ridge Cr.
Henry Banks	Richmond	500	acres	Head Glade Br.
Henry Banks	Richmond	350	acres	Glade Cr. Wat. Lit. Riv.
Wm. Brooks	Franklin	66	acres	Wat. Lit. Riv.
John Bowman	Franklin	270	acres	Wat. Lit. Riv.
Thomas Boyd	Unknown	100	acres	Wat. Lit. Riv.
Chas. Bowman's Repts.	Floyd	100	acres	West F. Lit. Riv.
James Bowman	Unknown	690	acres	S. F. Roanoke, Flint nob.
Benj. Bostwick's Repts.	New York	40,000	acres	Wat. Lit. Riv. (valued @ 121/2c per A)
Wm. Brown	Unknown	44	acres	Penning Cr.
Chas. Bott (Bolt?), Sr.	Floyd	300	acres	Burks Fork & Reed Island
Charles Bolt, Jr.	Floyd	100	acres	Burks Fork & Reed Island
Christ. Bower's Repts.	Floyd	156	acres	Cronk & Hawbert line
John Bishop	Floyd	36	acres	Wat. Lit. Riv.
Ambrose Bryant	Floyd	130	acres	Wat. S. Fork Lit. Riv.
Wm. Bartlett-Thomas Bartlett's				interest in land of Gardner Bartlett, dec'd.
John Beckett, Jr.	Floyd	16	acres	Lit. River
Gardner Bartlett's Repts.	Floyd	314	acres	Smith A. Lewis
Same & Thomas Littrell	Floyd	83	acres	Adj. 151 tract
John Carter	Floyd	373	acres	S. Fork Lit. River

NAME	RESIDENCE	NO. ACRES	DESCRIPTION OF LOCATION
Bailey Carter	Floyd	110 acres	S. F. Lit. Riv.
Amos Combs	Unknown	165 acres	S. F. Lit. Riv.
Ambrose Cox, Sr.	Floyd	596 acres	Indian Cr.
Braxton Cox	Floyd	105 acres	Indian Cr.
Luke Cox	Floyd	230 acres	Home place & Adj. Home place
John Cox' Rept.	Unknown	241½ acres	Lit. Riv.
Carter Cox	Floyd	363 acres	Indian & Greasy Cr.
Mathew Cox	Floyd	100 acres	Beaver D. Cr.
Ambrose Cox, Jr.	Floyd	200 acres	Indian Cr.
Robt. Craig	Montgomery	56 acres	Lit. Riv. D. Connors
Thomas B. Craig	Montgomery	135 acres	Wat. Bea. Dam. Cr.
George Craig	Montgomery	290 acres	Beaver Dam, Piney Cr. & Lit. Riv.
Joseph Coal, Sr.	Carolina	197 acres	Elliott's Cr., House Place Lit. Riv. Brush Cr.
John & Sam'l Coal	Unknown	50 acres	Burks Fork
Andrew Connor	Floyd	340 acres	Wat. Roanoke B. Connor
Andrew Connor	Floyd	245 acres	Meadow Run Wat. Lit. Riv.
Wm. Connor	Floyd	190 acres	Adj. Connor
Wm. Connor	Floyd	150 acres	N. Alley
Wm. Connor	Floyd	50 acres	Muster Ground Branch
John Cooper's Rept.	Floyd	462 acres	W. Brush Cr. & S. F. Roanoke
James Craig	Floyd	221½ acres	Brush Cr. & Laurel Cr.
Boulden Childress	Floyd	377 acres	Flat Run Wat. Lit. Riv. & S. F. Roanoke
Frederick Crusenberry	Floyd	250 acres	Greasy Cr.
Edward Choat	Floyd	80 acres	Greasy Cr. H. Holaday
John Chapman	Montgomery	194 acres	Lit. Riv.
Henley Chapman	Giles	89 acres	Lit. Riv.

NAME	RESIDENCE	NO. ACRES		DESCRIPTION OF LOCATION
Christopher Clark's Rept.				
Henry Calloway	Unknown	1,200	acres	Burks F., Howel's Cr. Shelor's Iron Works
	Franklin	1,145	acres	Pine Cr. Adj. Thos Goodson & Lit. Riv.
Henry Cronk	Floyd	260	acres	Wat. Lit. Riv.
Wm. Cronk	Floyd	95	acres	S. W. Side
Nathan Cockram	Floyd	420	acres	Head Pine Cr. & Shoot. Cr.
William Clifton	Floyd	104	acres	Lit. Riv.
Robert Clifton	Montgomery	100	acres	Lit. Riv.
M. W., Jno. & Lemuel Clay	Floyd	820	acres	Greasy Cr. Adj. Kent's
Otey Divers	Franklin	204	acres	W. Lit. Riv.
John Duncan	Floyd	150	acres	Indian Cr.
Blanch Duncan, Sr.	Floyd	253	acres	Indian Cr., Pine Swamp, Alum Ridge
Blanch Duncan, Jr.	Floyd	172	acres	Lit. Riv.
Henry Duncan	Floyd	450	acres	Indian Cr.
Benjamin Dodd	Floyd	786	acres	Sou. Fork Lit. Riv. Col. Helms & John Boon's
Wm. Dulaney	Floyd	96	acres	Beaver Cr.
Richard Dulaney	Floyd	100	acres	Lost Bent Creek
Mary Dewese	Floyd	140	acres	Head W. S. F. Roanoke
Hannah Dewese	Floyd	135	acres	Lit. Riv.
Moses Dickerson, Sr.	Floyd	300	acres	W. F. Lit. Riv.
Leonard Dickerson, Sr.	Floyd	150	acres	Indian Ridge
Robert Dowthat	Richmond	600	acres	Greasy Cr.
Charles Diven	Floyd	214	acres	Lit. River
John Dennis	Franklin	237	acres	Brush Cr. S. Huff
Jacob Epperly	Floyd	250	acres	Lit. Riv. P. Winters'
Christian Epperly	Floyd	444	acres	Old Field Cr.

NAME	RESIDENCE	NO. ACRES		DESCRIPTION OF LOCATION
Jacob Epperly, Jr.	Floyd	80	acres	C. Creek, R. Wells
John Epperly & Jno. Helms	Floyd	72	acres	Between C. Creek & Scraggs Branch
Soloman Epperly's Rept.	Floyd	60	acres	Terry's Br.
Samuel Agnew	Floyd	285	acres	S. F. Lit. Riv.
Marinus Evans	Floyd	200	acres	Wa. Lit. Riv. & Roanoke
Jacob Epperly & son	Indiana	169½	acres	Pine Cr.
Sophia Furguson	Franklin	306	acres	Wat. Greasy Cr.
Charles Furguson	Franklin	206	acres	Wat. Greasy Cr.
Standerfer Furguson	Franklin	180	acres	W. F. Lit. Riv.
Edwin Furguson	Franklin	377	acres	S. F. Lit. Riv.
Wm. Furguson's Rept.	Franklin	815	acres	Lit. Riv. J. Weddle
David Fishburn	Franklin	130	acres	Huckleberry Cr.
Henry Fowler	Franklin	185	acres	Wa. Lt. Riv. D. Run
Daniel Field	Floyd	160	acres	Pine Creek—P. Williams
John Floyd	Montgomery	200	acres	Beaver D. Lit. Riv.
Same & Sires Robertson	Montgomery	185	acres	Adj. Miss Scott's
Thomas Goodson, Sr.	Floyd	634	acres	Lit. Riv.
John Goodson, Sr.	Floyd	12	acres	W. F. Lit. Riv.
Thomas Goodson, Jr.	Tennessee	200	acres	Adj. James Underwood
Thomas Goodson, Jr.	Floyd	422½	acres	Pine Cr. J. Grayham
Robt. Goodson	Floyd	360	acres	Lit. Riv. J. West
Wm. Goodson	Floyd	605	acres	W. F. Lit. Riv.
				Wa. Lit. Riv. J. C. West & Pine Cr. Lit. R.
Elizabeth Goodson	Floyd	150	acres	S. F. Lit. Riv.
Abram Goard	Floyd	60	acres	Greasy Cr.
George Godby	Floyd	360	acres	Indian Cr. & N. side Lit. Riv.

NAME	RESIDENCE	NO. ACRES		DESCRIPTION OF LOCATION
Jack & Crockett Godbey	Floyd	495	acres	Indian Cr. & W. side Lit. Riv.—J. Howbert
James Goard	Floyd	140	acres	Greasy Cr.
Jonathan Grayham's Rept.	Floyd	205	acres	Pine Cr. F. Goodson & Wm. Hungate
Same & Jacob Grayham, Sr.	Floyd	483	acres	Pine Cr.
Jacob Grayham, Jr.	Floyd	190	acres	Wa. Lit. Riv. & West F. Lit. Riv.
Lawrence Grayham	Floyd	80	acres	Adj. J. Grayham
Robt. Grayham	Floyd	340	acres	Alum Ridge—G. Reed
George Goodekoontz' Rept.	Floyd	970½	acres	West F. Lit. Riv. & Store Place
Daniel Goodykoontz	Grayson	10	acres	W. F. Lit. Riv.
Jacob Goodekoontz	Floyd	140	acres	W. F. Lit. Riv.
Wm. Gilham	Floyd	290	acres	S. F. Lit. Riv.
Ezekiel Gilham	Floyd	100	acres	Wa. Lit. Riv.
Thomas Gearheart	Franklin	237	acres	Pine Cr.—Shelor
Wm. Gray	Floyd	225	acres	Pine Cr.—J. Moor's
Edward Gray	Floyd	100	acres	Lit. Riv.
Joseph Gray	Floyd	361	acres	Lit. Riv.
Joseph Galligo's Rept.	Richmond	10,000	acres	W. F. Lit. Riv.
Jacob Gearst, Jr.	Botetourt	150	acres	Wa. S. F. Lit. Riv.
James Gardner	Floyd	293	acres	Alum Ridge & Wa. Lit. Riv.
Robt. Gardner	Montgomery	50	acres	S. F. Lit. Riv.
Peter Guerrant, Sr.	Franklin	1,098½	acres	Lit. Riv. Roanoke & Head Wa. Lit. Riv.
Peter Guerrant, Jr.	Floyd	50	acres	Wa. S. F. Roanoke
Thomas B. Greer	Franklin	120	acres	W. F. Lit. River
Peter Guerrant & H. Iddings		360	acres	B. Dam Cr. Licking Br.
John Grayham	Floyd	25	acres	W. Indian Cr.
Alexander Gardner	Floyd	100	acres	Alum Ridge—J. Lester

NAME	RESIDENCE	NO. ACRES		DESCRIPTION OF LOCATION
John Gardner	Montgomery	50	acres	Adj. Ben Howel
David Howel, Sr.	Floyd	194	acres	House Place, Mill Place S. F. L.
David Howel, Miller	Floyd	375	acres	Riv.
David N. Howel	Floyd	140	acres	S. F. Lit. R.
Benjamin Howel	Floyd	110	acres	S. F. Lit. Riv.
Mary Howel	Floyd	194	acres	S. F. Lit. Riv.
Thomas Howel	Floyd	100	acres	W. F. Lit. Riv.
Mark Howel	Floyd	190	acres	S. F. Lit. Riv.—South Side—
				Jones
Daniel Howel, Sr.	Floyd	190	acres	Adj. Jno. Carter
Jno. Howel & Son	Floyd	117	acres	S. F. Lit. Riv.
Alexander & Anderson Howard		460	acres	S. Side Alum Ridge (They live
				in Wythe)
Joseph Howard	Floyd	250	acres	Wa. Lit. Riv.
Major Howard	Floyd	585	acres	Wa. Lit. Riv. & Beaver Dam
Ira Howard	Floyd	138	acres	Lit. Riv.—R. Wells
John Hook's Rept.	Bedford	3,406	acres	Unknown & Wa. Lit. Riv.—
				Thos. Goodson
John Hughett	Floyd	300	acres	N. drains of Greasy Cr.—Jas
				Goard
Wm. Hughett	Floyd	150	acres	Home Place
Daniel Howel, Jr.	Floyd	20	acres	Burks Fork
George Hylton	Floyd	1,419	acres	Wa. W. F. Lit. Riv. Burks F.
				Black Ridge
Archelaus Hylton	Floyd	2,711	acres	W. F. Lit. Riv. & Burks Fork—
				J. Hook's
Henry Hylton's Rept.	Floyd	48	acres	W. F. Lit. Riv.

NAME	RESIDENCE	NO. ACRES		DESCRIPTION OF LOCATION
Jesse Hylton	Floyd	131	acres	S. Fork—Thompson & Howel's Cr.
Elijah Hylton's Rept.	Floyd	185	acres	Greasy Cr.
John Hylton	Floyd	130	acres	W. Fork. G. Hylton's
Samuel Hylton	Floyd	275	acres	Big Reed Island
Burwell Hylton	Floyd	304	acres	West Fork
Hylton Children	Floyd	34	acres	Adj. J. Hylton
Soloman Hylton	Floyd	66	acres	N. side Burks Fork
Austin Hylton	Floyd	130	acres	N. side Burks Fork
Henry Hylton	Floyd	114	acres	N. side Burks Fork
Gordan Hylton	Floyd	183	acres	Wa. W. Fork
Samuel Huff B.C. Rept.	Floyd	400	acres	Brush Cr.
James Huff	Floyd	340	acres	Big Ridge—J. King—Hy Huff
Samuel Huff	Floyd	30	acres	West Fork—M. Lesures
J. & P. Huff	Unknown	185	acres	W. F. Lit. River
Joseph Huff	Unknown	217	acres	Burks Fork & Greasy Cr.
Henry Huff	Floyd	234	acres	Home Place
John Huff	Franklin	195	acres	Adj. Ogle's Old Place
Wm. Hungate	Floyd	194	acres	Lit. Riv.
Jacob Harman's Rept.	Floyd	250	acres	Weddle (Creek)
Soloman Harman	Floyd	713½	acres	West Fork
Wm. Hancock	Floyd	8	acres	West F.
Francis Harter	Unknown	80	acres	Mill Cr.
Christian Harter, Sr.	Floyd	150	acres	Lit. Riv.
Christian Harter, Jr.	Floyd	109	acres	S. F. Lit. Riv.
Henry Harter	Floyd	217	acres	S. F. Lit. Riv.
Adam Harter	Floyd	83	acres	On Mill Cr.
Abner Hunt	Unknown	75	acres	Burks Fork
Asa Hunt	Unknown	200	acres	S. Side Fork

NAME	RESIDENCE	NO. ACRES	DESCRIPTION OF LOCATION
George Hornbarger	Floyd	170 acres	Lit. Riv. J. King
Michael Howry	Floyd	250 acres	Pine Cr. Meeting House
Jacob Helms	Floyd	2,3981/2 acres	W. F., S. F. Black Ridge, etc.
Same & J. W. Helms	Floyd	290 acres	West Fork
Thomas Helms	Franklin	1,3231/2 acres	S. F. Lit. River, J. Terry, J. Ogles
Same & John Hy. Samuel	Franklin	1581/2 acres	Old field or J. Ogle
James Helms	Floyd	302 acres	Lit. Riv.
Thomas Helms, Jr.	Floyd	303 acres	Lit. Riv.
Samuel Harsten	Franklin	237 acres	Pine Cr.
Levi Holladay	Floyd	73 acres	Waters Beaver Cr.
Robt. Holladay	New York	6,000 acres	Terry's Cr. B. D.
Michael Howbert	Floyd	150 acres	Bowers & Epperly
John Houts	Botetourt	280 acres	Shelor & Goodson
Jacob Hoback	Floyd	111 acres	Lit. Riv.
Samuel Harris	Floyd	100 acres	Waters Lau. Cr.
Joseph Harris	Floyd	130 acres	L. River
Henry Idings	Floyd	526 acres	E. F. Lit. Riv. S. F. Roanoke
William Idings	Floyd	100 acres	L. br. Water L. Riv.
Henry Jones, Sr.	Floyd	293 acres	Wa. Lit. Riv.
Jonathan Jones	Unknown	215 acres	S. F. Lit. Riv.
Isaac Jackson	Unknown	80 acres	Waters Lit. Riv.
John Journall	Unknown	100 acres	Wa. Lit. Riv.
John Ingles, Sr.	Montgomery	3,585 acres	Greasy Cr. and its headwaters
Same, Smith & Isham	Montgomery	1,540 acres	Mira Fork of Greasy Cr.
Susan Kinger	Montgomery	116 acres	Little River
John King P. M.	Floyd	356 acres	Roanoke J. Paden, P. Huff
Anthony King	Floyd	200 acres	Lit. Riv. J. King
Joseph King	Montgomery	1,658 acres	Lit. Riv.

NAME	RESIDENCE	NO. ACRES	DESCRIPTION OF LOCATION
Peter & Soloman Kennett	Montgomery	103 acres	Flat run Wa. S. F. Roanoke
John & Joseph Kent	Wythe	1,035 acres	Big Meadow G. Creek
James Keath, Jr.	Floyd	190 acres	Greasy Cr.
James Keath, Sr.	Floyd	75 acres	Head waters G. Cr.
John Kitterman	Floyd	477½ acres	South F. Lit. Riv.
George Kitterman	Floyd	200 acres	Pine Cr. Adj. Howery
Isaac Kersey	Floyd	60 acres	S. F. Lit. Riv.
John Kersey	Floyd	100 acres	Brush Cr.
John Lester	Floyd	732 acres	West F. Lit. Riv. Brush Cr. Adj. Winters
Abner Lester	Floyd	500 acres	Middle Ridge & B. Run
Wm. Lester	Floyd	153½ acres	Lit. Riv. and Adj. Simmons
James Lester	Floyd	340 acres	Laurel Cr. Wa. Lit. Riv.
James Light	Floyd	158 acres	Wa. Lit. Riv. & Roanoke
Henry Light's Rept.	Floyd	158½ acres	Old field Creek J. Ogles
John Long	Floyd	200 acres	P. Guarrant L. Riv.
James Likins	Floyd	132 acres	Wat. S. F. Roanoke Flat run
Daniel Lammon	Unknown	320 acres	So. F. Lit. Riv. & Terry's Cr.
Moseby Lesure's Rept.	Floyd	390 acres	W. F. L. Riv. & Greasy Cr.
William Link	Unknown	143 acres	L. River. J. Howard's
Henry Link	Floyd	200 acres	Beaver Dam Cr.
Stephen Law	Unknown	160 acres	Pine—D. Fields
James Littrell	Floyd	119 acres	Wat. Lit. Riv.
George Layman	Floyd	160 acres	Laurel fork of B. Fork
James Loving			(J. Loyd's interest in lands of P. Huntsman, dec'd)
William Morrical	Floyd	262½ acres	Lit. Riv. & W. F. Lit. Riv. surveys
Jacob Morrical, Jr.	Floyd	182 acres	Spurlock Creek

NAME	RESIDENCE	NO.	ACRES	DESCRIPTION OF LOCATION
Thos. McHenry's Rept.	Alabama	150	acres	W. F. Lit. Riv.
Thomas McGeorge	Unknown	50	acres	Alum Ridge
Joseph Michaux	Unknown	1,635	acres	Burke Fork Adj. Hook's Land
George McCutcheon	Unknown	200	acres	South Fork J. McCutcheon
Alexander McAlexander	Floyd	200	acres	Wat. Lit. Riv.
Theodosia Masse	Unknown	350	acres	Burks Fork A. Hunt
Jesse Milicar and Mrs. Smith		16	acres	Adj. Fowler's lands
Patrick Martin	Unknown	160	acres	Adj. Hook's land
Mary Maddox	Floyd	400	acres	Greasy Creek
Edwin Mathews	Floyd	390	acres	Head West Fork
Thomas McClanahan	Floyd	83	acres	Same contained in . . .?
Jacob Nester's Rept.	Floyd	100	acres	Indian Cr. A. Cox
Catherine Nester	Floyd	240	acres	N. E. Indian Creek
Daniel Nester	Floyd	50	acres	Greasy Creek
Jonathan Otey	Floyd	284	acres	Lit. Riv. Adj. Rutrough Adj. Thos. Banks
Lewis Payne	Floyd	560	acres	Wat. Lit. Riv.
Michael Peterman	Montgomery	200	acres	Wat. Lit. Riv. J. Gardner
George A. Peterman	Floyd	214	acres	West side Camp Cr.
Same & J. Epperly	Floyd	149	acres	West side Camp Cr.
Abraham Pflieger	Floyd	633	acres	Adj. J. Kitterman
Michael Pflieger	Floyd	67	acres	S. F. Lit. Riv.
George Pflieger	Floyd	421	acres	Pine Cr. L. Riv.—Home Place & W. F. Lit. Riv.
Isaac Pflieger	Floyd	260	acres	Pine Cr. W. F. Lit. Riv.
Joseph Pflieger	Floyd	376	acres	Black Ridge, Big Branch Goodekoontz & B. Fork
John Poff	Floyd	80	acres	Adj. Home place
Henry Poff	Floyd	66	acres	Wat. Lit. Riv.

NAME	RESIDENCE	NO. ACRES	DESCRIPTION OF LOCATION
Anthony Poff	Floyd	97 acres	Mill Place & Home place
Charles Poff	Floyd	200 acres	Waters Lit. Riv.
Peter Poff, Jr.	Floyd	112 acres	Wat. Lit. Riv.
Samuel Poff	Floyd	192 acres	Part home place
Michael Poff	Floyd	116 acres	Wat. Lit. Riv.
Obedience Pratt	Floyd	100 acres	Wat. B. Fork
Joshua Pratt	Floyd	130 acres	Wat. B. Fork
John Pratt	Floyd	100 acres	Wat. B. Fork
John Parkerson	Unknown	486 acres	On Pine Cr.
James Parker	Unknown	232 acres	Beaver Dam Cr.
William Phillips, Sr.	Floyd	130 acres	Greasy Cr. J. Goad
William Phillips, Jr.	Floyd	100 acres	Greasy Cr. J. Goad
Randolph Phillips	Floyd	110 acres	Thomas Smith
Tobias Phillips	Floyd	110 acres	Thomas Smith
Jehu Phillips	Floyd	200 acres	Thomas Smith
Stephen Phillips	Floyd	150 acres	Wat. W. F. Lit. Riv.
David Patison's Rept.	Unknown	4,275 acres	Burks F. (Valued at 9¢ per acre)
David Paterson's Rept.	Unknown	75 acres	Burks Fork
Steven Peters	Unknown	150 acres	On Burks Fork
Jacob Prillaman	Franklin	280 acres	Laurel Cr. Wa. Lit. Riv.
Amariah Phares', Rept.	Floyd	75 acres	Wat. Lit. Riv.
Showers Price	Franklin	238 acres	Wat. Lit. Riv.
Peggy H. Price	Montgomery	130 acres	Lau. Cr.
Joseph Price	Franklin	200 acres	Adj. M. Scott's old place
Henry Poff	Floyd	220 acres	E. F. Lit. Riv.
Michael Plaister	Floyd	100 acres	L. Riv.
Burk Priddy & P. Barber	Floyd	100 acres	Adj. Jno. Thomas et al
Henry Platt	Floyd	225 acres	Becket's old place
Jacob Prubecker	Unknown	80 acres	Old Field Cr.

NAME	RESIDENCE	NO. ACRES	DESCRIPTION OF LOCATION
Elisha Rakes	Franklin	183 acres	On Rush Fork
Robert Radford	Franklin	200 acres	Adj. Thomas Goodson
William Richard	Floyd	73 acres	Little R.—D. Spangler
George Reed W. son	Floyd	145 acres	Beaver Cr.
Michael Reed	Floyd	190 acres	Wat. L. River
Humphrey Reed. A. son	Floyd	150 acres	Beaver Cr.
Humphrey Reed P. son	Floyd	214 acres	Indian Cr.
Humphrey Reed's Rept.	Floyd	43 acres	Beaver Cr.
George Reed P. son	Floyd	240 acres	Indian Cr. adj. P. Reed
Griffith Reed	Floyd	820 acres	Wat. Beaver Cr. & Lit. Riv.
George Reed A. son	Floyd	150 acres	Adj. A. Reed, Sr.
Andrew Reed A. son	Floyd	150 acres	Beaver Creek
Spancer(?) Reed	Floyd	280 acres	Indian Cr.
Humphrey E. Reed	Floyd	86 acres	Land of Humphrey Reed, dec'd
Andrew E. Reed	Floyd	130 acres	Part of same
Peter E. Reed	Floyd	197½ acres	East side Lit. River & Beaver Cr.
Humphrey Reed	Floyd	130 acres	Indian Cr.
Wil. & Silas Ratliff	Unknown	180 acres	Cedar Run
George Ridinger	Unknown	69 acres	Chestnut Camp
Israel Ronalds	Unknown	284 acres	Wa. Terry's branch
John Ronalds	Floyd	196½ acres	W. L. Riv.
Robert Ross' Rept.	Unknown	100 acres	Not known
Charles B. Ronalds	Floyd	340 acres	Wa. Lit. River & Meadow run
Thomas Riffey	Floyd	100 acres	L. River adj. H. Cronk
Jacob Snuffer's Rept.	Floyd	232 acres	Home place adj. Zilling's place
John Snuffer	Floyd	255 acres	Adj. J. Snuffer Wa. L. Riv.
David Slusher	Floyd	959 acres	Huckleberry Cr. E. Snuffer & Burks F.

NAME	RESIDENCE	NO. ACRES	DESCRIPTION OF LOCATION
Christopher Slusher, Sr.	Floyd	1,605 acres	W. F. L. Riv. Huckleberry Cr. Peaks Cr.
Peter Slusher	Floyd	250 acres	Wa. Greasy Cr.
Mathew Scott's Repts.	Floyd	342 acres	Beaver Dam Cr.
John Scott	Floyd	290 acres	Beaver Dam Cr.
Charles Simmons	Floyd	924 acres	Camp Cr. & Little Riv.
Same & Thos Hill	Floyd	1,510 acres	Alum Ridge
John Simmons' Repts.	Floyd	420 acres	Alum Ridge
Cary Simmons	Floyd	170 acres	Beaver Creek
William Simmons	Floyd	155 acres	Beaver Creek
Henry Sowers, Sr.	Floyd	146 acres	Wa. Lit. Riv.
John Sowers H. son	Floyd	88 acres	Wa. Lit. Riv.
George Sowers, Sr.	Floyd	220 acres	House place
Jacob Sowers	Floyd	159 acres	Wa. Old Field Cr.
John Sowers	Unknown	140 acres	Adj. Mathew Scott
Wm. Sowers J. son	Floyd	100 acres	Indian Cr.
John Sowers G. son	Floyd	94 acres	Wa. Lit. Riv.—Hungate's
John Sowers J. son	Floyd	160 acres	Obediance Br. Indian Cr.
George Sowers, Jr.	Floyd	94 acres	Wa. Little Riv.
Peter Smith	Floyd	311 acres	Adj. Thos. Littrell's
Col. John Smith	Montgomery	820 acres	Head of Indian Cr.
Humphrey Smith	Floyd	708 acres	House place—Idings & West F. Lit. Riv.
Thomas H. Smith	Unknown	720 acres	Not Known
Casper Smith's Repts.	Floyd	250 acres	S. Side Lit. Riv.
Jabez H. Smith	Floyd	180 acres	Adj. B. Childress. S. F. Roanoke
Henry A. Smith	Floyd	200 acres	Adj. H. Harter
Jacob Smith, Jr.	Floyd	50 acres	S. F. Lit. Riv.

NAME	RESIDENCE	NO. ACRES	DESCRIPTION OF LOCATION
John W. Smith's Repts.	Floyd	85 acres	Head wa. Lit. Riv. Also Beaver Dam Br.
Daniel Spangler's Rept.	Floyd	100 acres	Pine Cr.
D. W. & Samuel Spangler	Floyd	345 acres	Pine Cr.
Daniel Spangler	Floyd	50 acres	Pine Cr.
David Spangler	Floyd	80 acres	Christie's Cr. Lit. Riv.
George Sumpter	Floyd	175 acres	W. F. Lit. Riv.
Edmund Sumpter	Floyd	342 acres	House place. E. Watkins & W. F. Lit. Riv.
Martin Stegall	Floyd	275 acres	Greasy Cr. Adj. A. H. Isom's
Wm. Shelor	Floyd	796 acres	Little River—Old Field Cr.
Same & heirs	Floyd	619½ acres	Adj. House place
George Shelor	Floyd	377 acres	Lit. Riv. S. L. R. C. Epperly
James Simpson	Floyd	436 acres	Adj. T. Helms
Wm. & Catherine Simpson	Floyd	490 acres	House place, Wa. Pig run
Hezekiah Sumner's Repts.	Floyd	325 acres	Hill's Mill. W. F. L. River
Owen Sumner	Floyd	100 acres	W. F. Lit. River
Peter Saunders	Franklin	230 acres	Wa. Lit. River
Anthony Sowder	Franklin	140 acres	Wa. Lit. Riv.
Anthony Sowder	Franklin		Dr. Hickman's interest in 4 tracts of J. Snuffer dec'd
David Sowder	Floyd	100 acres	Lit. Riv. A. King
Jacob Sowder's Repts.	Floyd	238 acres	Lit. River
George Shively	Unknown	182 acres	Not known
George Shilling	Floyd	28 acres	Head wa. S. F. Roanoke
Jacob Shilling's Repts.	Floyd	182 acres	P. Smith
Joseph Sullenbarger	Unknown	75 acres	Laurel Cr.
John Spence's Repts.	Floyd	215 acres	Indian Cr. G. Reed
Christopher Sutphin	Floyd	130 acres	Wa. G. Cr.

NAME	RESIDENCE	NO.	ACRES	DESCRIPTION OF LOCATION
Wm. Slaughter	Floyd	290	acres	Burks Fork
Joseph Shoe	Floyd	100	acres	L. River
Stephen Slusher	Floyd	100	acres	Head wa. G. Cr.
Joseph N. Short	Floyd	165	acres	Flag Br.
Jacob Songer	Wythe	148	acres	Wa. Lit. River
Mankin Teal	Franklin	625	acres	West F. Lit. Riv. Black Ridge
Charles Turman	Floyd	415	acres	West F. Lit. Riv.
Elijah Turman	Grayson	813	acres	West F. Lit. Riv. & Beaver Cr.
George Turman	Floyd	190	acres	West F. Lit. Riv.
Norbourn Thomas	Unknown	1,030	acres	Burks Fork Reed Island
John Thomas	Floyd	176	acres	S. Fork Lit. Riv.
William Terry's Repts.	Floyd	1,177	acres	Brush Cr. Humphrey Smith
Gasper Terry's Repts.	Floyd	34	acres	Wat. Lit. Riv. W. Shelor
Jonathan Terry	Floyd	200	acres	West F. Lit. Riv. Mid. Cr.
Silas Terry's Repts.	Floyd	524	acres	Adj. Hartman
James Trail	Floyd	333	acres	Lit. Riv. J. Huff
James Thompson	Floyd	192	acres	S. Fork Lit. Riv.
James Thompson, Jr.	Floyd	20	acres	Both sides Lit. Riv.
Samuel Thompson	Floyd	169	acres	Lit. Riv. Broad Shoals
Adam Thompson	Floyd	118	acres	Hy. Rakes
Nathaniel Thompson	Floyd	400	acres	Head wa. Burks Fork
William Thompson	Floyd	169	acres	Mill Cr.
Jacob Tice	Floyd	1,170	acres	Wa. Ind. Cr. & So. Fork. Lit. Riv.
Nicholas Tice	Floyd	227	acres	So. Fork Lit. Riv.
Manassa Tice	Floyd	228	acres	So. Fork Lit. Riv.
Henry Trip	Floyd	80	acres	Lit. Riv. G. Hornbarger
Polly Townsley	Floyd	50	acres	Piney Cr. G. Craig
Thomas Templeton	Ohio	78	acres	W. Lit. Riv. W. Scott

NAME	RESIDENCE	NO. ACRES	DESCRIPTION OF LOCATION
Wm. Thompson	Floyd	75 acres	a part of 172 acres
Thomas Townsey	Unknown	176 acres	Gardner's old machine
Joseph Underwood	Floyd	75 acres	Adj. Thomas Goodson
Allen Unthank	Unknown	172 acres	Wa. Burks Fork
Elias Vancel	Unknown	173 acres	Lit. Riv. Laurel Creek
Richard Wells	Floyd	1,268 acres	Wa. Lit. Riv. Home place
John Wells	Floyd	100 acres	Lit. Riv. Adj. R. Wells
John Wilson	Floyd	360 acres	West Fork Lit. Riv.
Peter Wilson	Floyd	60 acres	Adj. J. Smith
Samuel K. Wilson	Floyd	50 acres	Camp Cr.
Andrew Wilson	Floyd	1,000 acres	S. F. Roanoke
George Wright	Unknown	112 acres	Ja. Harman's
Jacob Weddle	Floyd	264 acres	Adj. D. Weddle
Martin Weddle	Scott	160 acres	Burks Fork & W. F. Lit. Riv.
Isaac Vest's Repts.	Floyd	640 acres	Lit. Riv. D. Shelor
David Weddle	Floyd	458½ acres	W. F. Lit. Riv.
Andrew Weddle	Floyd	690 acres	Adj. Jacob Goodekoontz Home place
Jonas Weddle	Floyd	563½ acres	Adj. D. Weddle & Reed Island
John West's Repts.	Floyd	600 acres	L. River
Thomas West	Unknown	100 acres	Wa. S. F. Lit. Riv.
John Western & J. C. Price	Unknown	1,144 acres	Wa. S. F. Lit. Riv. Helms
Samuel Wilks	Unknown	175 acres	Not known
Henry Winfrey	Chesterfield	850 acres	Wa. Lit. Riv.
Jacob Wimmer	Floyd	526 acres	Wa. Lit. Riv.
Paulus Winther	Floyd	1,044 acres	E. Fork Lit. Riv. R. Wells Terry Cr.
Philip Williams	Floyd	650 acres	Adj. Ja. Callaway & Pine Cr.
Orin Williams	Richmond	10 acres	Wa. Lit. Riv.

NAME	RESIDENCE	NO. ACRES		DESCRIPTION OF LOCATION
George Walters, Sr.	Montgomery	500	acres	Beaver Dam Cr.
William Walters	Floyd	292	acres	Adj. Wm. Simpson
Alexander Wiley's Repts.	Floyd	320	acres	Head wa. Lit. Riv. East Fork
John Wigington	Unknown	7271½	acres	Wa. Lit. Riv. Ja. Lester
James Ward	Unknown	224	acres	Burks Fork
Ebenezer Watkins	Floyd	1,285	acres	S. F. Lit. Riv. Home place, Pine Cr.
Nathaniel Wickham	Floyd	248	acres	S. F. Lit. Riv. Adj. Epperly
Joshua Wickham		440	acres	Wa. Lit. Riv. M. H.
John Wade	Floyd	851	acres	West Fork. H. Jones
William Wade's Rept.	Floyd	145	acres	S. F. Lit. Riv.
Anderson Wade	Floyd	100	acres	S. F. Lit. Riv.
John F. Wade	Franklin	235	acres	Little River
John Weaver	Floyd	554	acres	Lit. River
George Weaver	Floyd	144	acres	Beaver Cr.
Daniel Webster	Floyd	153	acres	Wa. Lit. River
Henry Wood	Floyd	127	acres	S. F. Lit. River
Samuel Weddle	Floyd	240	acres	Wa. Lit. Riv.
Henry Walker	Franklin	133	acres	W. F. Lit. Riv.
Martin S. Wilson	Floyd	100	acres	Greasy Creek
Joseph Weeks	Bedford	170	acres	S. Fork Lit. Riv.
Wm. Wilson	Bedford	234	acres	Home place
Joshua Young	Floyd	428	acres	Waters Lit. Riv.—Greasy Cr.
Thomas Young	Floyd	365	acres	Hy Harter
William Young	Floyd	175	acres	Pine Cr.
John Zentmeyer	Floyd	441	acres	S. Fork Lit. Riv. Old Field Cr.

I, William Goodson Clerk of the County of Floyd do hereby certify that I have carefully and deliberately examined the foregoing land Book that I have compared it with the land book of the Preceding year with the records in my office where necessary and with the law and that I find the same to be correct, given under my hand this 10th day of June, 1831.

William Goodson, Ck.

Note.

The valuation of the lands ranged from fifteen cents per acre to thirteen dollars and fifty two cents and a half in the case of George Goodekoontz's store place and seventeen dollars in the case of Jacob Helms' 132 A. tract on S. F. Little River, but these are extreme cases—the average was probably about two dollars per acre. Of course these figures do not closely approximate actual values, so this note is of little real value.

ITEMS FROM THE FIRST ORDER BOOK
OF FLOYD COUNTY

March Court, 1831.—The following attorneys who were licensed to practice were: Robert Craig, Archibald Stuart, Edmond Johnston, James C. Tate, Norborne M. Taliaferro, Robert T. Woods, John D. Cheatham, Samuel McCammant and Robert McClannahan, Gentlemen, who have been duly licensed to practice the law in the Courts of this Commonwealth, on their motion have leave to practice in this Court and thereupon they took the several oaths prescribed by law.

Ordered that Joseph Howard be appointed Commissioner of the Revenue for the County for the ensuing year.

Ordered that Job Wells, George Shelor and Mannassa Tice be appointed Commissioners, any two of whom may act, for the purpose of making all necessary arrangements with William Spangler for the Court to be held at his place and that they make report thereof to this Court.

Ordered that the Court be held at this place until the necessary buildings shall be constructed at the place designated by the Commissioners appointed by law for that purpose.

Ordered that William Shelor and Nathaniel Wickham be recommended to the Governor as fit and proper persons one of which to be commissioned as Coroner of this County for the ensuing year.

Ordered that William Gilham, Robert Goodson and George Shelor be recommended to the Governor as fit and proper persons to be commissioned as Sheriff of this County for the ensuing year.

The Court proceeded to lay off the County into districts, and to appoint Constables therein and doth order that the County be laid off into two districts, and that all that part of the County comprising the first battalion shall be called the first district, and that all that part of the County comprising the second Battalion shall be called the second district.

For the first district ordered that Thomas H. Steger, Ira Howard and Thomas Shelor be appointed Constables therein, and that Benjamin Howell, John W. Helms and Thomas S. Gardner be appointed Constables in the second district.

They took the several oaths as prescribed by law and gave bonds and security.

Commissioners were appointed to act with those of Montgomery County to run the county line: Peter Guerrant, Job Wells and Andrew Wilson.

April Term of Court, 1831—Present: Robert Goodson, George Shelor, Joseph Howard, John Lester and William Young, Gentlemen.

John Chapman and William Masterson, Gentlemen, were

licensed to practice law, took the several oaths.

Benjamin Howell commissioned by the Governor a Justice of the Peace appeared and took the several oaths as prescribed by law.

Ordered that John Howell, Jr., be appointed a Constable in the room of Benjamin Howell, who has been commissioned a Justice of the Peace.

William Shelor, who was commissioned as Coroner of the County appeared and took the several oaths as prescribed by law.

William Gilham was commissioned as Sheriff by the Governor, appeared and took the several oaths and gave bond. John W. Helms, appointed deputy sheriff.

William Ballard Preston was appointed by unanimous vote to the Court Commonwealth's Attorney in and for the County of Floyd, whereupon he qualified and took the several oaths, as prescribed by law.

Major Howard was appointed deputy sheriff under William Gilham, appeared and took the several oaths.

James Litterell was licensed to keep an useful and orderly house of Private Entertainment, a license is granted him to keep an House of Private Entertainment, at his house in this County until the next May term (one year) of the Court of County of Floyd. A fee of two dollars was paid.

THE FIRST ORDINARY

William Spangler granted license for an Ordinary House of Entertainment licensed until the May term of 1832, paid the fee of $18.00.

Sarah Howard was granted license to keep a House of

Private Entertainment, paid the fee of two dollars.

The First Grand Jury: Mastin Stegall foreman, John Goodson, Christian Epperley, John Sowers, Abner Boothe, Jesse Milkein, Henry Cronk, Jacob Graham, William Banks, Michael Howbare, Manassah Tice, George Ridinger, John Reynolds, David N. Howell, William Morricle, David Fields, William Simmons, Joseph Phlegar, John Carter, Sr., Nathan Cockram, Abner Phlegar and John Zentmeyer were drawn a Grand Jury of inquest for the body of this County and after having received their charge, withdrew to consult of their presentments— Present, Robert Goodson, Gent.

William Goodson was elected by the Court of Justices to be Clerk of the Court defeating the only other candidate, William Wade.

Moses G. Carper by the approbation of the Court is permitted to act as Dept. Clerk.

June Term of Court, 1831—The Constables in the first and second districts: Thomas H. Stegar, Ira Howard, Thomas Shelor, Hiram Bolt, John Howell, Ezekiel Gilham and Thomas S. Gardner entered into bond and security conditioned as the law directs, and took the oath of fidelity, the oath of office, the oath against dueling and also the oath to support the constitution of the United States.

Henry Iddings was granted license to keep an orderly House of Private Entertainment, and paid the fee of $2.00 for one year.

Martin Stegall was granted license to keep an orderly House of Private Entertainment.

June term of the Court, 1831.—Present, Robert Goodson, Gent.

The Court proceeded to make the County Levy in the

following manner:

Dr. the County of Floyd for scantling furnished
for the house to hold Court in 1.75

To Leonard Aldridge for Wolf Scalp 5.00

To William Quessenberry for Do. 5.00

To Elijah Dickerson, Jr. for three young Do. 7.50

To John Reynolds for one old Wolf Scalp 5.00

To Cover for two young Do. 1.00

To John Bolt, Jr. for benefit of John W. Helms
for six young Wolf Scalps at 15 .... 15.00

To James Helms for 2 young Red Fox scalps
@ 3/ 1.00

To Leonard Hall for one old Wolf Scalp 5.00

To Jonathan Terry for 2 young Red Fox scalps 1.00

To William Sowers, Surveyor of the Road for
1 days work .... .25

To Blanch Duncan Do. 4 days work 1.00

To John Carter Do. 2 Do. .... .50

To Bryant Hylton Do 10 Ditto 2.50

To John Wilson Ditto 3 Ditto .... .75

To Marcus Evans for a Red Fox Scalp 1.00

To Nathan Cox surveyor of Road 2 days .... .50

To Job Wells and Manassah Tice for work on
the house to hold Court in 3.00

To John Lester Surveyor of Road 3 days .... .75

To William B. Preston money for the
Commonwealth 75.00

To William Goodson Clerk for Ex officio
services 50.00

To William Gilham Sheriff for Ditto 45.00

To William Goodson Clerk for minute book 10.00
_____

$239.50

By 893 tithables @ 1.00 each $893.00
Deduct amount of ours 239.50
_____

Balance due County $653.50

June Term Court.—Joseph Gray licensed to keep House of Private Entertainment $1.68 for the remainder of the year, to May term, 1832.

Road from James Keith's to Indian Creek Road, Commissioners: Archelaus Hylton, Charles Bolt, Jr. and Bryant Hylton.

Road from Mouth of Indian Creek to the Fork of the Road at Ambrose Cox's field and that John Lester, Luke Cox and George Godbey, Esq., be appointed to allot the tithables within his precinct do put and keep the same in repair according to law.

No. 2. Ordered that Tobias Phillips be appointed Surveyor of road from the forks at Ambrose Cox's Field to the Grayson line.

No. 3. Ordered that Jacob Slusher be appointed Surveyor of the road from Howell's Road to the Branch of Emery Altizer's and that David Goodykoontz, Stephen Slusher and George Boothe do allot the tithables within the said precinct to him and that he put and keep the same in repair according to law.

No. 4. Ordered that William Lester be appointed Surveyor of Road from ?

No. 5. Ordered that Thomas Howell be appointed Surveyor of the Road from the Patrick Road at John Carter's to the Dug Spur Road at or near Soloman Harman's Mill and that he with the tithables allotted him by Adam Harter, Benjamin Howell and David Weddle, Sr., do put and keep the same in repair according to law.

No. 6. Ordered that John Long be appointed Surveyor of the Road from the Franklin line by Guerrant's and Simpson's to the Branch at Henry Iddings' and that he with the tithables allotted him by Jacob Hoback, Charles R. Reynolds and William

Simpson, do put and keep the same in repair according to law.

No. 7. Ordered that Byrd Cole be appointed Surveyor of the Road from the Branch at Henry Iddings to the Montgomery County line and that he with the tithables allotted to him by Charles R. Reynolds, Jacob Hoback and William Simpson do put and keep the same in repair according to law.

No. 8. Ordered that William A. Conner be appointed Surveyor of the Road from the head of Daniels Run to Simpsons and that Jacob Hoback, Charles R. Reynolds and William Simpson do allot the tithables in said precinct, who together with said Surveyor do put and keep the same in repair according to law.

Slaves Owned in Floyd County at Time of Formation 1831

(Only those over 12 years of age are listed)

Owner	Slaves Owned	Owner	Slaves Owned
Samuel Agnew	1	John Helms	1
Charles Bolt, Sr.	3	George Hylton	7
Isaac Boothe	1	Gordon Hylton	2
Abijah Boothe	1	Solomon Harman	2
Wm. Banks	2	Daniel Howel, Sr.	1
Thomas Banks	1	Wm. Hancock	4
Ambrose Cox, Sr.	4	John Kitterman	2
Benjamin Dodd	3	James Litrell	2
Peter Guerrant	6	James Light, Sr.	3
Thomas Goodson, Jr.	1	Henry Latham	2
Robert Goodson	1	Wm. Obrian	1
Archelaus Hylton, Sr.	2	Shoas Price	3
Sarah Howard	1	Tobias Phillips	1
Major Howard	3	Wm. Phillips, Sr.	2
Joseph Howard	3	Abram Phleger	1
Henry Huff	1	Charles B. Reynolds	5
James Huff	1	John W. Smith's Reps.	1
Jacob Helms	12	Mastin Stegall	4
John W. Helms	1	Christopher Sutphin	
Thomas Helms	3	& son	1
James Helms	1	Continued	

John Snuffer	1	Freeman Waynright	1
Lucretia Scott	1	John Weaver	1
Samuel Saunders	6	Easter West	1
George Shelor	2	Philip Williams	1
Wm. Shelor	4	Richard Wells	5
Jabez H. Smith	1	Job Wells	1
Peter Saunders	5	Paulus Winther	1
Thomas H. Steger	3	John Wade	1
Charles Turman	3	Eli Williams	1
Wm. Terry's Reps.	1	Thomas Young	1
Joseph Underwood, Sr.	1		

Register of the General Assembly Of Virginia
Floyd County

Jacob Helms, 1831/32, 1832/33, 1833/34

Thomas H. Steger, 1834/35, 1835/36

Harvey Deskins, 1836/37, 1838 (Jan.), 1839 (Jan.)

John Howell, 1839/40

Harvey Deskins, 1840/41, 1841/42, 1842/43

John W. Helms, 1844/45

Harvey Deskins, 1845/46

Samuel A. J. Evans, 1846/47

Joseph L. Howard, 1847/48, 1848/49

Peter Guerrant, 1849/50

Harvey Deskins, 1850/51

Tazewell Headen, 1852 (Jan.)

John Howell, 1853/54

Pleasant Howell, 1855/56

Preston Howery, 1857/58

Isaac Goodykoontz, 1859/60, 1861 (Jan.)

Harvey Deskins, Convention 1861

Valentine Thrash, 1861/62, 1862 (April) 1862 (Sept.), 1863 (Jan.)

Isaac Goodykoontz, 1863/64, 1864/65

N. B. Moore, 1865/66, 1866/67

George Young, 1869/70, 1870/71

John B. Payne, 1871/72, 1872/73

Joseph L. Howard, 1874 (Jan.), 1874/75, 1875/76, 1876/77

Amos Dickerson, 1877/78, 1879/80, 1881/82

Burdine Bishop, 1883/84, 1884 (Aug.)
Austin Hylton, 1885/86, 1887 (March)
S. H. McNeil, 1887/88
Zebrem Keith, 1889/90
V. M. Sowder, 1891/92
S. T. Turner, 1893/94, 1895/96, 1897/98 (Floyd & Franklin)
A. L. Cannaday, 1899/1900, 1901/02 (Floyd & Franklin)
Nathan Phillips, Convention 1901/02
G. H. Thomson, 1904
D. L. Eller, 1906, 1908
J. A. L. Sutphin, 1910, 1912
B. B. Franklin, 1914
W. E. Phillips, 1916
Peter Dickerson, 1918

CHAPTER III

Baptist Church in Floyd County

The early history of the Missionary Baptist Church in Floyd County is largely the history of the services of Rev. Daniel G. Taylor and his son, Rev. John Lee Taylor in this territory. Their labors in this field were in the infancy of its organization. A few Baptists had come into the county, mostly from Bedford County and had organized themselves into a church, but had no pastor or place of worship.

In September of 1847, Rev. Daniel G. Taylor made his first visit to Floyd County from his home near Mayo Church in Patrick County. He says:

"I found a few Baptists who had come from Bedford County. They had been organized into a church at Jacksonville; but they had no house of worship, no pastor and no regular preaching. I preached at the residence of Brother Lancaster. The people seemed eager to hear the truth. The harvest is plenteous in this community."

At this period the field was mostly filled with Anti-Mission Baptists. "At that time there was not on the entire field a house of worship belonging to our denomination. The Anti-Mission Baptists had houses in the territory. My preaching had to be done under trees and arbours, in school houses and private residences, wherever I could get the people together." He says that at this time, in the county of Patrick: "I found but one Missionary Baptist, though there may have been a few others." This was Elder John Turner.

In November, 1854, Rev. Daniel G. Taylor again visited Floyd County and preached for the Jacksonville Church at the residence of Mrs. Lancaster. The services were continued four days. In the following January he returned and preached for several days. For two years he continued his visits to Floyd at such times as he could be spared from services in other parts of his missionary field. In 1857 a meeting of unusual interest was held and the name of the church was changed from Jacksonville to New Haven. And too, it seemed that the town had not been a very desirable point for the meeting of this small church, and at this time New Haven Church was located some four miles southeast of the town. Several years later, under the ministry of Rev. John Lee Taylor a new church building was erected at Jacksonville, but was not much more successful than the old church. After the close of the Civil War, in 1870, Rev. Daniel G. Taylor again received a call from the New Haven Church and continued to serve it for a period of about two years.

In 1875 Rev. John Lee Taylor and Rev. Mr. Haymore conducted a two-weeks' revival meeting at New Haven Church, receiving seventy-five members into the church. After this Rev. John Lee Taylor located at Floyd Court House, Jacksonville, as a State Missionary, confined to the County of Floyd. Here he labored for many years. The Jacksonville Baptist Church was organized in the courthouse of Floyd County with thirty-three members, on the 13th day of April, 1876, with Rev. John Lee Taylor as pastor.

Rev. John Lee Taylor served the people of Floyd as pastor and State Missionary for a period of seven years, doing much to build up the church in the county. From **Daniel G. Taylor, A Country Preacher,** and **John Lee Taylor, Minister and Missionary.**

Rev. John F. Lancaster (1826), son of Thomas, Sr., married Annie Taylor, daughter of Rev. Daniel G. Taylor.

Rev. Davis G. Lancaster, son of Nathaniel, married Katherine Henley, and was long the pastor of New Haven Church.

Brethren Church

William Smith was the first minister we have any account of to preach in Floyd County. He came to this country from England and settled at the head of Daniels Run, now in Floyd

County. He was baptized and ordained by Elder Jacob Miller of Franklin County. He was called to the ministry by the church. The Lord blessed his humble efforts; souls were gathered into the fold; and about the year 1800 the first Brethren Church was organized in the territory which is now included mostly in Floyd County.

Elder Austin Hylton was one of the pioneer preachers, being called to the ministry in 1829. About 1850 he moved to East Tennessee. Other pioneer preachers were Chrisley Bowman, Jacob Weddle, Archie Thompson, Joshua Thompson, Andrew Weddle, H. P. Hylton, Andrew Reed, John Weddle, Joseph Weddle, William Reed, Isaac Reed, J. B. Hylton, Cornelius Reed and J. H. Slusher.

There being no church houses, services were held over the territory in dwelling houses, barns and groves. In 1857 the Brick Church was built seven miles west of Floyd Court House, being the first Brethren Church in the county. It was built by H. P. Hylton and Joseph Weddle at a cost of $1300; $800 was paid by members and friends and $500 by the builders. In 1896 the Brick Church was replaced by a frame building and the name changed to Topeco. The following preachers have served here: Elders Harvey Weddle, P. N. Hylton, Joel Weddle, C. D. Hylton, Ananias Harman, Jacob Hylton, A. N. Hylton, L. M. Weddle, G. W. Hylton, W. L. Jennings and S. Benton Alderman. All have died or moved away except A. N. Hylton, L. M. Weddle and S. Benton Alderman. Membership: 150.

In 1860, Pleasant Valley congregation north of Wills Ridge was cut off from Brick Church. This congregation has been cared for by the following ministers: Isaac Reed, Humphrey Duncan, Griffy Reed, Noah Reed, Henry Reed, Wyatt Reed. All these men are dead and the church is in the care of the following Brethren: S. P. Reed, Michael Reed, Dr. R. T. Akers, Isaac Reed, Jr., H. L. Reed, and Willie Dulaney. Membership: 130.

Red Oak Grove Church was organized about 1870. It was cut off from Pleasant Valley, and is located seven miles east of Floyd Court House on Little River. W. H. Naff, M. I. Dickerson, S. G. Spangler, J. F. Keith, Charles Williams. W. F. Vest and William Yearout have served as ministers; all are dead or moved away except W. F. Vest and William Yearout. Membership: 100.

Burks Fork congregation was organized in 1892, and was cut off from the old Brick Church, with A. J. Weddle, Joel Weddle, S. E. Hylton, Joseph Hylton and Austin Hylton. All these are still in the congregation except Joseph Hylton who has been dead for about five years. This church is located on the headwaters of Burks Fork Creek on the south side of Floyd County, six miles from Topeco. Membership: 100

Beaver Creek congregation was cut off from Pleasant Valley congregation about 1890. Ministers who have served there are: Noah Boothe, Jessee Boothe, Richard Reed, Samuel Mannon, J. F. Mannon, A. E. Sumner and Enoch Reed. All these are still in the congregation except Noah Boothe who has been dead about ten years. This congregation is on the north side of Wills Ridge about eight miles northwest of Floyd Court House. Membership: 100.

White Rock congregation was organized about 1895 and was also cut off from Pleasant Valley congregation. It is in the north side of Floyd County at Carthage, Virginia. It has been cared for by the following ministers: G. W. Akers and Wallace Akers. Wallace Akers is the only minister as G. W. Akers moved out of the congregation. Elder S. P. Reed is elder in charge. Membership: 75.

Pleasant Hill congregation was organized about 1898. This congregation was also cut off from Topeco and built one mile west of Willis, Virginia, on the Floyd-Carroll Pike. It has been served by the following ministers: Owen Barnhart, S. P. Hylton, M. F. Woods, Charlie Hylton, Zion Michell, J. B. Sowers. All these have moved away except J. B. Sowers who is assisted by A. N. Hylton. Membership: 100.

Laurel Branch congregation was the last one organized in the county, it being cut off from Topeco congregation in 1917. It is located on the south side of Wills Ridge, five miles northwest of Floyd Court House. Ananias Harman and G. W. Hylton were the ministers at the time of organization. Ananias Harman has died and Luther Bowman has been called to the ministry.

Topeco has two other houses in congregation, namely Fairview and Rock Hill, both south of Floyd C. H. near the Patrick line and about four miles apart.

By Elder Abram N. Hylton
Floyd, Va.

Methodism In Floyd County

About the beginning of the nineteenth century, two Methodist itinerants, Revs. Thomas and Samuel Kennerly, preached at Christiansburg. They were said to be the first Methodist preachers in Montgomery County (which at the time embraced all of present-day Floyd County). Then the great heralder of Methodism, Lorenzo Dow, preached to the enlisted soldiers in the War of 1812 at Christiansburg, sitting on his horse. Tradition holds that he also preached at Major Goodson's near Turtle Rock.

Methodist itinerants, according to tradition, visited at the home of Humphrey Smith in the eastern part of Floyd County. He always kept and fed the preachers and their horses. Once he was asked by a Mr. Poff how he could afford to feed the preachers' horses, and he replied for every bushel of grain he fed them, two bushels came in their place. The main preaching place was in the home of Bolen Childress, who, with his entire family, became devoted Methodists.

Around the year 1820, the first church was built near the little village of Simpsons, better known as Locust Grove. The first church was called "Iddings Chapel," because the land was donated by the aging Henry Iddings, Sr.

The first church in the western part of the county was a log structure near Willis, and it was built by William Thompson, better known as "Uncle Billy." Later, Bethel Church was located in that section.

For a number of years the Methodists used the

Presbyterian Church in the town of Floyd, later preaching was held in the old courthouse and also in the present one. Sunday school was held in the old male academy over the years. In 1860 the Methodist Church that now stands on East Main Street was begun, but with impending war, the structure was used to store hay for the Confederate army and was not completed until 1871. At this time, Rev. Dickey was the presiding elder and Rev. Phillips was the pastor.

Long before the Civil War, camp meetings were held. The first one was held on land belonging to George Goodykoontz; the second and third camp meetings were held on the farm of Samuel Kennerly. These were in the neighborhood of Falling Branch Church; the fourth and fifth camp meetings were held near Zion Lutheran Church; the sixth near the camp of the second and third, and the seventh and eighth near Locust Grove.

The history of Methodism in Floyd County would be incomplete without the names of Bolen Childress, Humphrey Smith, George, Isaac, David and Alfred Goodykoontz, Samuel Dobyns, whose mother (familiarly known as "Aunt Betsey") would pray in public and end by shouting; Frank Hogan, a class leader, Andrew Stephens, a choir leader, the Stimpson and LeSueur families, the Stuarts, Weeks, William M. Morgan, superintendent of the Sunday School for forty years, Dudley Peterman, steward for twenty-eight years, and many others.

Among the local preachers of the olden days were: William Thompson, George Godbey, Richard Buckingham, David Howell(?), Charles Bartlett, William Foster, Henry Bishop. Of a later date, there were: Abram Hogan (whose acute memory enabled him to tell children many stories told to him by his father and grandfather about the early settlement of this country), Charles Stuart, Christopher Keith, David Conner, Ethelbert Weeks, and many others.

The early preachers were: Zane Bland, Rev. Jamison, John Aken, Henry Bland, Alfred Goodykoontz, _____ Reed, _____ Hildebrand, _____ Wolfe, _____ Stransberry, J. W. Boteler, J. N. Davis, J. J. Engle, John Cecil, Elias Skelton, Ambrose B. Cox, Adam Q. Flaherty, A. Poe Boude, J. H. Lemon. Revs. Bean and Butt were the pastors during the Civil War.

Rev. Lenz stood on a stool while in the pulpit because he was just three feet in height. He and his faithful wife went south to help in the yellow fever epidemic and both fell victims. Rev. Quinn and Rev. Strickler were the last pastors while the charge belonged to the Baltimore Conference. Rev. Barnes was the first when it became a part of the Holston Conference.

Names of the other pastors are here recorded—Revs. Davidson, Rucker, Phillips, W. W. Hicks, L. W. Thompson, G. W. Sommers, B. W. S. Fielder, W. S. Bourne, William M. Dyer, R. S. Umbarger, C. W. Kelley, Walter Spence, J. E. Swecker, C. L. Stadley, J. B. Frazier, W. A. Goodpasture, G. M. Johnston, I. N. Munsey, J. W. Repass, H. E. Cole, H. S. Johnston, D. F. Wyrick, E. H. Bogle, C. A. Melton, J. W. Christian, W. R. Carbaugh, W. A. Warner, A. H. Gentry, Fred Gordan, J. D. Wright, H. L. Henshaw, J. A. L. Perkins, and perhaps others.

Among the presiding elders were Revs. Samuel Register, Dickey, George Miles, McTier, Long, J. Tyler Frazier, E. H. Cassidy, D. F. Hurley, and J. B. Ward.

Robley D. Evans, in **A Sailor's Log**, refers to early church services in Floyd thus:

Churches and schools were few and widely distributed. In place of the former we had the "circuit rider," who came and made himself at home almost as a member of the family, until his duties were performed, when he passed on to some other farmhouse, and so in turn visited the whole section. In the summer time camp meetings were organized, and then the horsemen and horsewomen gathered from all the surrounding mountains and enjoyed themselves in a very sensible way. Most of them prayed and sang until they were tired, and then withdrew to their tents and ate and drank the good things that had been prepared for them. Wheeled vehicles were not in use to any general extent for pleasure purposes, as the few roads we had were mere trails fit only for horses. Sometimes the camp would be made near a smooth stretch of road, and after the ministers and the shouters had done their work the young men would have their innings and speed their favourite horses; certainly there could not have been found a more healthful recreation or a happier way of passing a week during the heat of the summer. (Page 4)

Presbyterians In Floyd

The Jacksonville Presbyterian Church was organized March 20, 1853, by the Rev. B. V. Lacy of Salem, Virginia, with the following members: from Christiansburg Presbyterian Church - Mrs. George Shelor, Miss Mary Banks, Mrs. Paulus Winter, Mrs. Harriet Kitterman, Dr. and Mrs. Samuel A. J. Evans, Mrs. Jackson Godbey, Mrs. Henry J. Jones, Mrs. Lewis F. Woltz, William Lindsay and Dr. John D. Stuart; from the church of South Plains, Albemarle County - Mrs. James M. Wilson; from the church of Milton, North Carolina - Judge John Merritt. Mrs. Wade and Mrs. James Gill were received on examination. Dr. Samuel A. J. Evans, Dr. John Stuart and Judge John Merritt were elected ruling elders. Dr. Evans served as ruling elder up to the time of his death in the year 1856. J. M. Wilson served until he and Mrs. Wilson moved to Rodgersville, Tenn., in the fall of 1859.

The minutes indicate that the church had no regular pastor until Rev. G. T. Lyle took charge on May 4, 1866. He was a Licentiate of the Montgomery Presbytery. He ended his pastorate on Oct. 13, 1867.

Dr. John Stuart was dismissed by letter, May 4, 1866, when he moved to Wytheville, Virginia. Henry Dillon was elected an elder prior to Sept. 29, 1867.

Walter Pendleton was elected an elder on Nov. 19, 1867, and served until Dec. 20, 1878, when he moved to Hillsville, Virginia.

On June 30, 1872, Rev. John K. Harris took charge of the church, which he served as pastor until Aug. 20, 1882, when he moved West with his family.

Rev. W. R. Coppedge was in charge of the church as pastor from Jan. 14, 1883, until the fall of the year 1887.

Rev. P. C. Clark was in charge of the church during the year of 1888.

Rev. John K. Harris returned on Sept. 1, 1889, and held the pastorate until the time of his death, March 22, 1910.

During the first pastorate of Mr. Harris, a church was built at Turtle Rock (Pizarro) and some of the Jacksonville Church members transferred their membership there, and this congregation was active until shortly before Mr. Harris' death in 1910. Some members moved away, others died over the years and, as the church building was in bad condition, it was decided that the remaining members move their membership back to the parent church.

After the death of Mr. Harris the church was without a pastor for several months, when Rev. J. Kenton Parker was called and held the pastorate for a short time until he was called to the mission field.

For some time the church was under the management of the Home Missions, when Rev. R. Gamble See took charge of the field in and around the Jacksonville Church. During his pastorate a new church was built in place of the Turtle Rock church known as Harvestwood, named for three of the influential families in the neighborhood of the church: Harvey, Vest and Wood. At this place there is a good congregation.

Another preaching point with a good congregation is the Harris-Cannaday School, a mission school run by the Presbytery as The Harrison Mountain Schools, which takes in Shooting Creek School and other preaching points.

Dillon's Chapel is another preaching point with a good congregation. This chapel was named for Henry Dillon who faithfully served the church as ruling elder for many years.

THE PRIMITIVE BAPTISTS

In 1832 there was a general division among the Baptists in this country, those who espoused the doctrine of universal atonement and special application, which was introduced among the Baptists by Andrew Fuller in Kettering, England, in 1792, which was a modern doctrine as applied to Baptists, and became known as "New School," or Modern Baptists, and those who held to the ancient doctrine of special atonement and special application, according to the election of grace, became known as "Old School," or Primitive Baptists, hence the name

PRIMITIVE BAPTISTS.

The Baptists came to this part of the country from the Ebenezer Association of the Valley of Virginia, and constituted their first church on New River, near the mouth of Reed Island, in 1774, and called it "New River." From this body sprang the churches now comprising the "New River Association."

The doctrine held by these people prevailed through faith in the hearts of many of the earliest settlers of this part of the country.

In those days when the sturdy woodsman with his stalwart sons led the way for the wife and daughters, and defended them against the savage foe, these people were wont to assemble in some shady nook and worship the God of their fathers. Their manner of worship was much in harmony with the altar upon which they offered their devotions. They had no meeting houses, commonly called churches, in that day. When the weather permitted they met in the woods, as they do in this day, where they had cleared away the brush and erected a crude slab for a book board, and there upon the ungarnished foot-stool of their Creator and gracious Redeemer, they sang, and prayed, and preached, and praised, and thus planted seeds which have not ceased to bring forth fruit, and to keep in holiness unto the Lord these Bethels where He has so often commanded blessings of life, and peace, and joy in the Holy Ghost. The manner of worship in those days was characterized by a style held as sacred which added much to the solemnity of the services. The unaffected honesty, candor and simplicity of these people in their doctrine, faith and belief, together with their plainness of speech maintained for them in its simplest form the confidence of the people, which confidence they enjoy until now.

These associations never became so affected by the doctrine now held by the New School Baptists, as to produce division, and but very few have ever turned aside after that way, therefore the congregations have not suffered from this cause as they have in other sections of the country.

This church never having regarded an educated ministry as an essential requirement to the administration of the gospel of truth according to the scriptures, have always received their ministers as called of God from among the brethren, and so qualified of Him as to make their ministry such as He designed, and therefore such as the people require to supply their need. So, therefore, the Primitive Baptists have no schools of human learning in which to educate men to preach, however they have among them as a church at large, men as thoroughly educated, who are ordained elders, as the schools of our country produce.

They do not believe in men being sent of men to go and preach, and yet in their ministry there are those who travel as much as fifteen thousand miles during a single year and preach as they go. The churches in Floyd are not behind in this respect. The churches as a rule, believe that those who preach the gospel should live of the gospel—that is should live with, and of the things of which the brethren are blessed of the Lord, and yet their ministers are not inclined to evade the divine injunction that man shall eat bread in the sweat of his face.

The New River Association was constituted in 1794, and in 1857 was divided into two associations for convenience sake —the 10 churches west, retaining the old name, "New River" and the 10 churches east adopting the name, "Smith's River."

There are fourteen organized churches in the County of Floyd, as follows: Salem, Pine Creek, West Fork, County Line, Paynes Creek, Pine Forest, and Thomas Grove which belong to the Smith's River Association; and Indian Creek, White Oak Grove, Laurel Creek, Little Flock, Conners Grove, Greasy Creek, Floyd, and Mountain View which belong to the New River Association.

Salem

Salem, at first called Little River, is the oldest Baptist Church in the county, having been constituted in 1784. Elder William Howard was the first pastor of this church, who was one of the pioneer ministers in this part of the country. This church has been favored with a ministry represented by men of strong character and ability both as men and as ministers, as follows: Elders William Howard, Peter Howard, Michael Howery, George W. Kelley, John C. Hall and Asa D. Shortt with Elder H. V. Cole serving at this time. This has been for many years the strongest in number of members, and is today, numbering about sixty. The good influence of this church is instanced by the number and character of its membership, and the large and almost solid community which gives attendance at her meetings. Situated at the junction of the Blue Ridge and the Alleghany Mountains, their lofty peaks have served for about one hundred and seventy years as the altar at which this church has offered herself, and tendered her prayers and devotions unto the mighty God of Israel as the rock of her salvation. Her meetings are the second Sunday and Saturday before in each month, at which time without sound of bell, sackbut or psalter but as by the voice of their sleeping fathers, the rising sun, the bright new day and the whisperings of divine persuasion, the gray-haired grand sires, the mothers in Israel, the fathers and mothers, the little children, together with the young men and maidens may be seen on these days, wending their way toward this sanctuary of their fathers, until tens, and hundreds, and many times, thousands have assembled to wait upon the Lord and worship at his footstool.

Pine Creek

In 1796, the people gathered together and cleared away the brush and erected a crude stand for the worship of God, and agreed to sit together to hear of Him out of his word, and called the place "Pine Creek." An arm of Salem Church was extended to Pine Creek, and in 1797 a church was organized there with Elder William Howard as their first pastor, followed by Elders Peter Howard, Michael Howery, Thomas L. Roberson, Wilson H. Dodd, Amos Dickerson, H. V. Cole, with J. M. Dickerson, the present pastor. During the earlier history of this church, the Howards, Goodsons, Moores, Simmonses, Lesters and many other leading families, mingled their prayers and praises before the altar of their God at this old tabernacle, whose sleeping dust, and the savor of whose lives and characters render sacred still her hills and her devotions. For many years, Pine Creek was one of the most noted places in the county for the character of her faith and devotions, and the large assemblage of the people. One of the largest country cemeteries is at this church. In those days, the church set apart certain days for fasting and prayer. Their faith in the utility of prayer was such that it is said they would assemble for special prayer, for rain for instance, and that on at least one such occasion they were rewarded with rain and a good personal wetting before they reached their respective homes. The present membership of this church is forty-one. Peter Howard, Michael Howery, Thomas L. Roberson and Jacob F. Spangler were ordained elders in this church.

West Fork

The church at West Fork was constituted in 1803 with Robert Jones as pastor. For one hundred and twenty-two years this church has maintained its organized visibility and the doctrine as first espoused without interruption, and with but few exceptions its order has been desirable. Many of the most influential citizens in the community have come into her communion during these years and sat together with the humblest of the poor in heavenly places, and together worshipped the God of Jeshurun. She has been ably and soundly served as pastor by Elders Robert Jones and his son, Jessee Jones, Nathaniel Thompson, Green L. Tuggle, Wilson H. Dodd, with Q. D. Weeks and J. M. Dickerson, in present service. The present membership of this church is sixty-four. She has numbered among her members Elders Jessee Jones, Nathaniel Thompson, Wilson H. Dodd, Q. D. Weeks and Elijah Nester.

Indian Creek

The church called Indian Creek was constituted in 1844 with Elder Owen Sumner as pastor, who was succeeded by Elder

Thomas Dickens, Q. D. Weeks, and Asa Harris—Elder John M. Phillips, the present pastor. Elder Isaac L. Rigney, deceased, was a member of this church, and Elder Asa Harris was a member of her body. The wholesome influence of this church has been of great benefit to the community—many of whose citizens have from time to time found favor with the Lord and entered into the service of God with her. The present membership of this church is one hundred and sixteen.

White Oak Grove

White Oak Grove Church was constituted in 1847 with Elder Owen Sumner as pastor, who was succeeded in 1875 by Elder Amos Dickerson—the present pastors are Elders P. G. Lester and L. A. Cummings. During the seventy-eight years that this church has had a visibility, six of her members, at her request, have been ordained elders, to wit: Jacob Corell, John C. Hall, Jessee Sumner, Amos Dickerson, P. G. Lester and William L. Simmons. Elder Owen Sumner was a constituent member of this church, making seven elders who have during her history been numbered among her membership. This church has maintained an organization strong in doctrine and order, and in the number and character of her membership. An influence for good has been the heritage of the community in which this church is planted because of her steadfastness in the faith, the sublimity of her devotions and the order of her house. Her present membership numbers seventy-five.

Laurel Creek

The church at Laurel Creek was constituted in 1855 with Elder Owen Sumner as pastor. Elder Jacob Corell served this church as pastor for many years, succeeded by Elder Amos Dickerson, and Elder H. V. Cole, who is a member of her body, and present pastor. Elder William L. Simmons also served this church as assistant to Elder Corell. The doctrine, discipline and order of this church have been sound and effective, causing her influence to flow out and her usefulness to appear. Under the able ministry of Elders Amos Dickerson and H. V. Cole, her membership for years has been large in numbers and of good strength of character. The present membership numbers eighty-three.

County Line

The church called County Line was constituted in 1869 with Elder Amos Dickerson as pastor, who after a number of years was succeeded by Elder Asa D. Shortt, whose membership is also there, and he by Elders P. G. Lester, H. V. Cole and J. G. L. Hash. This church has proven the wisdom displayed in its location. The effect on the community at large has been for good. The seeds of sound doctrine and discipline faithfully sown by her pastors have produced orderly, wholesome fruit. The number of her membership is thirty-seven.

Little Flock

Little Flock Church was constituted in 1871 with Elder Amos Dickerson as pastor. For several years Elder R. M. Mabry who is a member of this church has served as pastor. Elder F. C. Reynolds was also a member of this church, as was also Elders Charles W. Vaughn and Amos D. Vaughn—present minister. Perhaps nowhere in this country has the saying that "The desert shall blossom as the rose" been more certainly fulfilled than in the community where this church is planted. Her influence grows and strengthens with the increasing years of her pilgrimage. Her membership is fifty-seven.

Paynes Creek

Paynes Creek Church was constituted in 1877 with Elder Wiley A. Via as pastor, succeeded by Elder Asa D. Shortt, with Elder J. H. Cummings, present pastor. Elder J. T. Turner is a member of this church. The effect of the good character of this church has proven a blessing to the section of the country in which it is situated. The present membership numbers forty-one.

Conners Grove

The church called Conners Grove was organized in 1886 with Elder R. M. Mabry as pastor. The late Elder Daniel T. Conner was a member of this church. His father, James Conner, was licensed to preach in this church. Elders Q. D. Weeks and J. M. Dickerson are the present pastors. This church numbers one hundred and five members.

Greasy Creek

The church called Greasy Creek was constituted in 1898 with Elder Q. D. Weeks as pastor, who thus serves it today. The church now called New Hope in Carroll County, when constituted in 1789 was called Greasy Creek. This new organization under the able ministration of Elder Weeks has been blessed with the strength and character of a good lively membership which makes it at once a blessing to the community in which it is situated. The membership numbers fifty.

Pine Forest

Pine Forest Church was constituted in 1898 with Elder David Sumner as pastor. Its meetings are well attended and its influence is wholesome. Its membership is twenty.

Floyd

The church at Floyd was constituted about 1900 with Elder P. G. Lester as pastor. Elder J. M. Dickerson is its present pastor and its services are well attended. Its membership numbers thirty-two.

Thomas Grove

Thomas Grove Church was constituted about 1900 with Elder P. G. Lester pastor; Elder J. D. Cockram—whose membership is with this church, with Elijah Nester are present pastors. This church is well situated to be of a wholesome influence in the community, and has a membership of about forty.

Mountain View

Mountain View Church was constituted of an arm from Laurel Creek Church with Elder S. L. Moran as pastor—who is also a constituent member. The situation of this church is such as to be of a wholesome influence to the community at large. Its membership is about twenty.

Resident Elders

Elders now resident in the County of Floyd and serving churches are: Elders Q. D. Weeks, H. V. Cole, J. T. Turner, J. H. Cummings, J. D. Cockram, R. M. Mabry, A. D. Vaughn, J. M. Dickerson, Elijah Nester, David Sumner and S. L. Moran.

The elders named as first pastors of the different churches are almost without exception the ones under whose ministry the churches were built up to their respective organization as churches qualified to do business for themselves. As a rule these churches acquire their individual organizations by an arm being extended from some organized church, by which the church agreed to hold conference or church meetings statedly at the new place designated, until a sufficient number had been received, it may have been but three, but generally more, and the indications were favorable for greater growth, whereupon the church called for a Presbytery of Elders, two or three, who met at the place of meeting of the arm, and upon examination finding the members orthodox in faith, constituted them into a church for the general transaction of church business. The first business for the new church is to select one or two of its members to be deacons, who are set before the presbytery which ordains them to that office. The church next calls one of her members to the office of clerk, and then calls a pastor to go in and out before them.

Primitive Baptist Ministers

These are first given liberty to speak in the bounds of the church where his membership is. Upon evidence of a gift to teach, he is licensed to make appointments wherever a door may be opened, and upon further evidence of aptness to teach and of general fitness of character he is ordained by a Presbytery of Elders, two or three, to the full functions of the Gospel ministry, and is called an elder, who according to his gift may fill the place of either of the gifts set forth in the Scriptures without the acquirement of a higher office, therefore they have none higher than elder. They do not use or recognize the title of "Reverend" as applied to men, believing it only applies to Him whose name is Holy and who only inhabiteth eternity, to whom it is applied but once in all the Scriptures.

Of some of the elders who have served the above churches or lived in the County of Floyd, I would briefly speak.

William Howard

This father in Israel was among the first to enter this part of the country, having been a constituent member of Salem, the oldest church in the county. When our public highways were mere Indian trails, and neighbors lived far apart, and those of like faith with him were few, this faithful man of God served with untiring energy in the cause of his gracious Master, planting at distant points, organizations which stand today to his memory, proving the genuineness of his call to the work and his labors of love in the Lord.

Peter Howard

Elder Peter Howard, son of Elder William Howard, succeeded his father in the service of churches, and long and faithfully did the work assigned to him, leaving the good savor of his name, which though he be dead yet speaketh peace by Jesus Christ, whom he preached.

Jessee Jones

Of this mighty man of valor, I have the following from an elderly gentleman who from his earliest recollection knew Elder Jones. "Of all the men I ever knew, Elder Jessee Jones, of the Primitive Baptist Church, was the most benign, gentle and humane in his Christian chcaracter. His voice was peculiarly soft and seemed to appeal to you in his distinctly clear and persuasive words. His soft beaming eyes were full of tenderness and drew you to him with the kindliest of feelings. He was in speech slow, deliberate and exact in the choice of his words and convincingly in earnest in all he said. However much anyone may have differed with him the doctrine he preached, no one ever doubted the honesty, sterling integrity and positive convictions of his Christ-like character." He died in 1859 at the advanced age of 93 years, and had been in the ministry seventy-three years.

Nathaniel Thompson

Elder Nathaniel Thompson served his day and generation in that fervency and zeal which characterizes one as a true servant of God. His manner in the ministry was earnest and effective, convincing his hearers of the high estimation in which he held the work assigned him.

Michael Howery

Elder Howery served in the ministry about fifty years. He was a man of clean sterling character, and so was his ministry. He wielded the sword of the Lord and of Gideon, unsheathed and without a shield except that of the faith which he preached. He was valiant for the truth and was honest, conscientious and true. He died in 1873.

Owen Sumner

Elder Sumner served churches about forty years. He was a man of strong convictions, and was among the ablest preachers of his day. He was a man of deep thought and was profound and logical in his conclusions. Several churches were built up under his ministry and among them was a number of able ministers, as special seals to the efficiency and divine character of his call and work in the vineyard of his Lord. He died in 1875.

George W. Kelley

Elder Kelley was a man naturally of strong mother-wit, and spirituality, of a sound and ready mind. He was earnest and zealous in the work to which he had been called, and proved himself to be well gifted in the ministration of the word of truth, a workman not ashamed of his calling. His ministry was fruitful to a good old age, at the end of which he died as he had lived.

Jacob Corell

Elder Corell was a man sound in the faith and of great zeal for the cause of his Master. Being of full German stock, his earnest manner of setting forth the truth was much in evidence of his nationality. His gift consisted largely in showing the character and doctrine of Christ to be according to prophecy and that he was therefore the true Messiah. He served churches for many years and was faithful to his calling, at the end of which he died in the peace and fellowship of his brethren and his gracious Redeemer.

John C. Hall

Elder John C. Hall, considered in all the lines of character which fell to him, and the able and efficient manner in which he handled the goods of his Lord entrusted to him, might well be said to have been one of, if not the ablest and most profound expounder of the Scriptures of divine truth in all the scope or bounds of his labors. Both as a man and a minister of the Gospel, he proved himself to have been a workman not to be ashamed. He fully enjoyed the unbounded confidence of the people as being a man whose words and actions truly indicated the purposes of his heart and mind. He was honest, sober, earnest and conscientious in his convictions of truth and in presenting them to the consideration of the people. His life was a continuous sermon and those with whom he came in contact were his auditors. To believe what he preached was not necessary to enable men who admire the nobility of real manhood, to note and appreciate the wholesome influence of his character as a man and as a minister. He called forth the best emotions of nature and encouraged the sublimest devotions to the God of all grace.

For more than forty years he preached the Gospel, and served churches as pastor, and for thirty years, he was the efficient clerk of the New River Association. In his death as it had been in his life, the saving triumphs of reigning grace were most assuredly and sweetly demonstrated.

Isaac L. Rigney

Elder Rigney was able in prayer, and exercised a gift in speaking before the people, that was well appreciated. His usefulness was brief, he having died in the midst of life.

Jessee Sumner

Elder Jessee Sumner, son of Elder Owen Sumner, lived but a few years after his ordination and died in the prime of life. His gift was useful.

Wilson H. Dodd

Elder Dodd's gift consisted largely in reviewing the scenes of the Old Scriptures and the dealings of God with ancient Israel and the triumphs by faith of the Patriarchs and Prophets. He served his day and generation in faithfulness. He lived and died in the confidence and fellowship of his brethren, and upon his ashes rests the benediction of peace.

Elder Asa Harris

Elder Asa Harris was a specially gifted man and served efficiently in the strength of the gospel of salvation by grace. He was held in high esteem by the brethren generally, and was an humble faithful pastor of churches.

Thomas L. Robertson

Elder Thomas L. Robertson was a fatherly well-beloved man —plain and simple in his everyday life and conservative in his ministry and his doctrine. He maintained a long and useful ministry in the service of his Master.

Elder Amos Dickerson

Elder Amos Dickerson was an able minister of the New Testament. He was a good pastor and minister in the service of his gracious Master. He served in the gospel of peace and was a keeper and feeder of sheep. He was a man of a strong clean character, and was sound in the doctrine, discipline and order of the church. He kept the faith and finished his course, and having fought a good fight, when the time of his departure was at hand he was ready to be offered.

Elder Asa D. Shortt

Elder Asa D. Shortt was a man of sterling qualities of character and citizenship. As a minister he was faithful in the service of churches. He was sound in the faith and conservative in the doctrine and commanded the confidence and respect of the general public to whom his life bequeathed the savor of a good name.

Elder Daniel T. Conner

Elder Conner was a man of great suffering and together with it was remarkably cheerful. His gift was pleasing and his manner was cheering and encouraging. His faithfulness was equal to his opportunities and his death was in the faith.

Elder William L. Simmons

Elder Simmons was ordained in Floyd and for a number of years preached and served churches here. He went to Missouri and after some years removed to West Virginia where he served churches with a peaceful end and died in the confidence and esteem of his brethren.

The ministers now resident in the county or having the care of churches pastors, or active in the ministry are— Elders R. M. Mabry, Q. D. Weeks, David Sumner, J. T. Turner, H. V. Cole, P. G. Lester, J. D. Cockram, J. H. Cummings, J. M. Dickerson and E. Nester.

Twenty-seven ordained elders have held their membership in churches situated in this county, sixteen of whom have fallen asleep and been laid unto their fathers, and eleven remain and are in active service.

The churches in this County of the Primitive Baptist order aggregate about eight hundred members. As a rule there is a larger percent of those who have an experience of grace holding with the Primitive Baptists, who are not members of the visible church, than any other denomination perhaps in the county.

Their membership is composed entirely of adults baptized into their fellowship. They resort to nothing but the preaching of the word and sound and wholesome exhortation to induce those of like faith to become members. Therefore, the actual membership does not indicate the strength that would be, were all of like experience members.

Because of the lack of necessary data, some points are omitted that might have been given, but such as I have is respectfully submitted.

From a manuscript by P. G. LESTER

Salem Church

Salem Church, known as the Head of the River Church, is an old established church. Here the Primitive Baptists are the strongest of any place in Floyd County. The first one to preach here was Isaac Jones, but no one can be found that can tell whether he remained here or how long. The next to preach here were Hiram and William Howard, brothers who came from England to America. They were both Primitive Baptist preachers and ably served the church. The next was Michal Howery, then George W. Kelly, then Elder John C. Hall. Mr. Hall was an able minister of the Gospel and most earnestly contended for the faith [ones delivered unto the Saints]. Under his care the church soon became very prosperous. At the present Elder H. V. Cole and Samuel Moran have the care of the church. A man by the name of John Ray who lived near the top of the Blue Ridge three miles south of Salem Church was said to be the first one to be buried at the Salem Cemetery. It has always been told that his grave was fenced with heavy new rails to prevent the wolves from digging into the grave. As Mr. Ray was a pioneer settler and the country being (mss. torn) . . . . one morning Mr. Ray on leaving his house discovered an Indian with a gun behind a pile of wood. Mr. Ray got his gun, and concealed himself behind his log cabin; when the Indian put his head out to look, the ball from Ray's rifle caught him in the mouth.

A very old family now living near Salem Church are the Waltons. George Walton and two brothers came from England to America in the year 1773. When the Revolutionary War broke out, George Walton was one of the signers of the Declaration of Independence. His son, James W. Walton died near here some 10 years ago at the age of 92; his son, James W. Walton, Jr., is now living in two miles of Salem Church, aged 75 years, is hale and hearty and owns three farms and is one of Floyd's best citizens.

Thomas Helms was another pioneer of this county and it was often said of him that he began life as a poor man, that at daylight of a morning he would take a piece of cornbread and fat meat, his axe, maul and wedge, and leave his cabin and stay until dark. He became a very wealthy man.

Another very prominent family who came to America was Joseph Gray, who came from England. He married Miss Mary Howard. Miss Howard was of English and French descent. They lived in one mile of Salem Church. They raised a family of fourteen children. Their youngest daughter, Rh . . . (mss. torn).

She died at the age of eighty-eight years, six months and 18 days, April 7, 1913. They had a family of four children. Their youngest, a daughter, Mrs. W. B. Gray lives in three miles of Salem Church. All of the Gray family, except four, went West.

Mrs. Sowder's sister, Harriet, married Valentine Thrash (1810-1906?), son of John Thrash, and he lived to be ninety-six years old. He died about sixteen years ago. His grandson, Valentine Thrash Conner owned the fine home until two years ago. It now belongs to Posey L. Angle. This fine farm is situated at the foot of Thrashes Mountain. The large brick dwelling is surrounded by a thick cluster of young pines left there by Mr. Thrash. He was a large, well proportioned man and very popular. He was Justice of the Peace many years and represented Floyd County in the Legislature of Virginia very satisfactory to his many friends. He owned several slaves and lived to this ripe age enjoying good health surrounded by his friends and grandchildren. (His high forehead seemed to be converted into iron.) Truly he was a remarkable man.

John B. Payne, son of Lewis Payne (you have mentioned in your letter), lived and died at the old home place on Payne's Creek. Mr. Payne was a man of considerable intelligence. He was very popular and was elected to the Virginia Legislature by an overwhelming majority though his opponent was a popular man. His family have all left Floyd County. His daughter Marcella married Henry Shelor, a son of William B. Shelor. Mr. Shelor also was a true type of the old Virginia gentleman, who died several years ago on Bent Mountain at the age of 87 years. His son Henry and wife now live in Roanoke City.

(Floyd County is fast coming to the front. The thick wooded portion is being cut away and many fine meadows now abound where a few years ago the wild turkey roamed plentiful. Deer that was found here, as well as wolves have faded away before the march of civilization. Good roads are being built and the people have almost forgotten the pioneers who felled the forest and paved the way for progress and civilization. Away back sixty-five years ago, which I well remember, the

people looked forward to time of husking corn when the entire neighborhood would gather at the neighbor's house and husk out the corn, and at night an old time dance would be in progress. The house would be cleared of all obstructing furniture and a log fire about 6 or 8 feet wide was blazing brightly. The tea-kettle would sing as the ginger stew was being prepared. A jug of good old apple brandy would be brought in; two boys with fiddle and banjo, then any one who enjoyed a good old time had full swing till morning light chased away the night. On some large farms at one of these husking bees where the good old darkey lived, all the colored people of the neighborhood would husk out the corn and with plenty apple brandy to make them merry, the white people would enjoy their singing such songs as Old Swaney River or the Jaybird Setting on a Hickory Lim (sic). Sometimes they would sing Old Massa's in the Cold, Cold Ground, really this very pathetic. So the people of today who live in luxury and refinement never enjoyed a more happy life than these primitive people who settled our county and left to their posterity all that we today enjoy.)
Dear Dr. Wood

I am mailing you some information as best I could. (I will have Mr. Weddle to fill up the blanks you sent me relating to the Conner & Poff families.) I am seventy-two years old and remember much I have written. As I am so crippled I can't get around much.

Sincerely your friend,
Noah Wilson

Salem Church
Head of the River Cemetery

(Recorded by pupils of Check High School in 1922 under the direction of William M. Weddle, Principal. Over 100 graves without tombstones.)

William M. Aldridge / born Oct. 8, 1826 / died July 16, 1914

Lucy Ann / wife of Wm. M. Aldridge / born March 6, 1831 / died Aug. 3, 1889

Elizabeth J. Byrd / wife of W. B. Reed / born May 7, 1839

/ died Oct. 27, 1919

Sarah Purdy / wife of Keaton / born Dec. 31, 1835 / died 1909

James M. Connor / born Sept. 16, 1874 / died March 2, 1917

Nathan Connor Sr. / was born Oct. 13, 1813 / departed this life April 11, 1880 / Age 67 yrs 5 mo 26 da

Levicy Connor / born 1812 / died April 26, 1909 / Aged 97 yrs

Mary Alice Walton / born Nov. 18, 1892 / died Oct. 7, 1900

James W. Poff / born Sept. 7, 1872 / died September 1874

Byrd Smith / born July 15, 1809 / died Feb. 22, 1896

Lydia Smith / wife of Byrd Smith / born Mar. 23, 1814 / died Oct. 12, 1884

Lydia Smith / born Oct. 12, 1884 / died Dec. 31, 1910

Jonathan I. Smith / son of Bird and Lydia Smith / who left this life / Sept. 20, 1862 / age 19 yrs 3 da

Henry Poff / born Feb. 13, 1792 / died April 26, 1854

Sarah / wife of Henry Poff / born March 25, 1794 / died Oct. 11, 1854

William H. Aldridge / born May 15, 1840 / died Sept. 23, 1902

John Sowder / born 1856 / died 1915

Lula Carr / born 1854 /died 1916

Velva Ellen Manning / born June 20, 1896 / died May 12, 1914

Martha E. Connor / wife of Daniel O. Connor / born 1828 / died 1888

E. Burton Hundley / born March 11, 1894 / died Dec. 1917 [killed in airplane in World War]

John Light / died 1884 / age 76 yrs 1 mo

Mary Light / died 1884 / age 76 yrs

Wife of M. Clingenpeel / born July 1859 / died Oct. 1889

Albert West / born 1852 / died 1865

Sarah West / born April 12, 1802 / died May 13, 1876

Sarah J. / wife of S. J. Conner / born 1853 / died 1896

W. A. Reed / born 1809 / died 1890

Charles Vest / born May 8, 1811 / died May 10, 1881

Elizabeth Ann Custer / born Feb. 20, 1837 / died Aug. 19, 1913

John King / born March 29, 1840 / died July 19, 1908

Mary / wife of J. H. Austin / born July 5, 1860 / died May 1, 1901

Lillie Miles / born 1863 / died 1877

Sarah Iddings / born Sept. 26, 1802 / died Dec. 23, 1881

Lillie V. Vest / born Nov. 28, 1774 / died Nov. 14, 1868

Katherine M. Reed / born April 11, 1811 / died Feb. 22, 1886

Emeline / wife of John King / born Dec. 9, 1846 / died 1897

Wife of J. H. Poff / born 1842 / died 1902

Wm. P. Connor / born 1821 / died 1906

Matthew Scott / died 1818

J. O. Connor / born 1814 / died 1910

Claudine Cecil Cannaday / born 1894 / died 1908

Albert Connor / born 1831 / died 1913

Thos Paul / son of G. B. and Naomi Nolan / born 1917 / died 1918

Julia Muncy / born 1836 / died March 21, 1896

Wm. H. Poff / born June 5, 1825 / died Jan. 12, 1908

May J. Poff / wife of W. H. Poff / born 1834 / died 1904

Alfred F. Poff / born 1873 / died 1906

Amanda Peradine Holt / born 1842 / died 1897

Mary M. / wife of J. T. West / born 1827 / died 1862

Aaron Connor / born 1811 / died 1887

Calesta Hale / born Nov. 19, 1878 / died Sept. 1881

Nancy / wife of H. W. Carr / born May 2, 1818 / died June 27, 1872

Henry W. Carr / born Jan. 19, 1809 / died Feb. 20, 1876

Mary Carr / born 1807 / died 1851

John T. West / born May 10, 1825 / died Sept. 27, 1909

Lydia / second wife of J. T. West / born 1834 / died 1884

Harry Lemons Aldridge / born July 24, 1882 / died Dec. 10, 1882

Dr. Asa Cannaday / born April 20, 1836 / died March 1908

James M. Connor / born Sept. 16, 1874 / died March 2, 1907

Naomi Ingram / wife of Josiah Poff / born 1888 / died 1918

Elizabeth / wife of W. F. West / born Nov. 1847 / died Sept. 16,

1887

Sarah B. / wife of W. T. Simpson / born 1845 / died 1888

Connie Connor / born 1887 / died 1898

Jonathan Connor / born 1831 / died 1914

Wife of Jonathan Connor / born 1830 / died 1907

Maggie Shockey / born 1852 / died 1916

Sarah Aldridge / born Jan. 25, 1848 / died 1918

John T. Poff / born Oct. 10, 1907 / died May 26, 1909

F. J. V. Poff / born March 10, 1865 / died Feb. 8, 1919

Elson Connor / born Nov. 12, 1849 / died July 21, 1916

Samuel Connor / born Sept. 1835 / died Feb. 7, 1889

Eliza / wife of J. P. Poff / born 1847 / died 1906

Isaac D. Wilson / born 1850 / died 1897

Flem H. Poff / born April 28, 1842 / died Sept. 15, 1904

Elmira J. Connor / born Aug. 2, 1838 / died Oct. 21, 1910

Nancy Furrow / born April 2, 1855 / died April 25, 1921

Lillie A. Aldridge / born Aug. 2, 1837 / died June 13, 1911

Charles O'Connor / born Jan. 11, 1862 / died Jan. 30, 1912

Daniel O'Connor / born 1813 / died 1897

Joseph H. Poff / born 1880 / died 1909

Elizabeth Charlotte / wife of Wm. Furrow / born 1850 / died 1917

Zora Furrow / born 1719 / died 1851 [error]

Jess J. Furrow / born 1884 / died 1886

Hannah Hale / born July 28, 1842 / died March 20, 1914

Flemmon Poff /   born June 7, 1816 / died Feb. 22, 1892

Mary / wife of W. O. Carr / died May 9, 1859

Nancy Ann Agnes Holt / born July 15, 1837 / died Nov. 5, 1909

W. T. Simpson / born 1838 / died 1898

Daughter of Mary Dina Poff / born Sept. 4, 1877 / died Dec. 29, 1889

Sallie A. Custer / born 1893 / died 1915

Lucinda / wife of J. O. Connor / born 1822 / died 1915

Carlyle / son of Zillah Manning / born 1873 / died 1889

Della Manning / born 1890 / died 1898
Sarah Light / born 1868 / died |no date]
Robt. Rierson / born 1828 / died 1830
Peter King / born 1794 / died 1804
Elizabeth / wife of Michael Sowder / born [illegible] / died 1803
James Furrow / born 1847 / died 1918

Jacksonville Academy

The Jacksonville Academy, known in after years as "The Old Brick Academy," was incorporated February 28, 1846. Three years later, the incorporators petitioned the Legislature for authority to change the name of the institution. The following act was passed March 15, 1849:

> "An Act providing for the change of the name of the Jacksonville Academy, incorporated February 28th, 1846, to that of "The Floyd Institute," and the Trustees authorized to hold property to the value of fifty thousand dollars." (Acts 1848-49, p. 172)

Soon after the incorporation of the Jacksonville Academy, the services of Professor William T. Gannaway of Wythe County, Virginia, were secured. Professor Gannaway was a recent graduate of Emory and Henry College, a man of fine literary and personal attainments. Under his leadership the school soon became a noted institution for learning, perhaps surpassing the adjoining counties in the facilities for learning. Soon many of the best young men from the neighboring counties came and entered Jacksonville Academy.

Among them were: J. E. B. Stuart, who became the famous cavalry General of the Confederate army, and his brother John, who in after years was Dr. John Stuart of Floyd and Wytheville; the Taliaferros of Franklin County; the Penns of Henry County; the Stapleses and Vias of Patrick County; the Tompkinses of Bedford County; and many others, as well as most of the prominent young men of Floyd County.

Dr. George Milton Wells writes of this school: "At the

time I entered Jacksonville Academy it was patronized by a large class of young men from Floyd and adjacent counties. The principal was a college-bred man, of fine personal and literary accomplishments, who introduced better methods and more advanced training than had been previously enjoyed; hence, young men trained in that school were stimulated to their best endeavors and became successful professional and business men."

Dr. C. M. Stigleman wrote: "What Floyd County owes to William T. Gannaway—than whom none ever within her borders gave a greater impulse to education—who can estimate the work of this man?"

Professor Gannaway found the climate too severe for his health and he gave up his useful work in Floyd and removed to the famous Bingham School in North Carolina, which was later Trinity College. Here he held a professorship for over thirty-five years, ranking among the ablest educators of his time. His sister, Miss Kate Gannaway, married Thomas M. Dobyns and was the mother of six children, one of whom was Samuel G. Dobyns of Patrick County.

In 1913, the Old Brick Academy was torn down to make way for the present high school building. The workmen found in the southwest corner a large black bottle, one of the old-time bottles about quart size. In this bottle was a part of a well preserved New York newspaper, on one side of which was printed the Declaration of Independence, and the facsimile signatures of all the signers thereto. Another paper in the bottle bore the names of the trustees and all contributors toward the erection of the Jacksonville Academy. This paper was dated April 1847, the date of laying of the cornerstone with Masonic rites. The preamble, which was very much faded, was signed by Thomas McCabe, followed by the following trustees and contributors:

Harvey Deskins, David Kitterman, Tazewell Headen, Samuel Dobyns, Major Howard, Manasseh Tice, Asa L. Howard, Samuel A. Evans, J. N. Zentmeyer, Alvin Graham, Fleming W. Lester, James B. Headen, Ira

Howard and Jackson Godbey.

On the back of this paper was written the following: "The Undertakers of this building are Henry Dillon, F. W. Lester, J. Gill, who do the work themselves."

All the above named men were very prominent in their time; their descendants have lived in the county up to the present.

Oxford Academy

In the year 1872, Rev. John K. Harris came to Floyd Court House and took charge of the pastorate of Jacksonville Presbyterian Church. He soon established, with the aid of Mrs. Harris, a school for young men and young women, known as Oxford Academy, which took rank with the best preparatory academies in the state and attracted students from many adjoining counties. This school was run continuously by Rev. and Mrs. Harris from its beginning until 1882, when the Harris family moved West. In the succeeding year, 1883, Rev. W. R. Coppedge assumed the pastorate of Jacksonville Presbyterian Church and carried on 'the work of the school which the Harrises had so ably started. The school had a prosperous four years until Rev. Coppedge moved from the county.

In the fall of 1889, Rev. and Mrs. Harris and their family returned to Floyd County and again took up the work and re-opened Oxford Academy which continued to be a noted place of education up to the time of the death of Rev. Harris in the year 1910. Many of the business and professional young men and women of this part of Virginia owe the chief part of their education to Oxford Academy and the lofty inspiration provided by Rev. and Mrs. Harris and Rev. Coppedge.

The Mountain Normal

This school was started at Willis, Virginia, and buildings erected by Professor John Wrightsman of Botetourt. It was a cooperative venture, those most interested being Dunkards.

It was opened about 1882, flourished for a few sessions, then failed. Later the property came into the hands of Professor J. H. Rutrough, who conducted there a summer "normal" which had many years of success. He often had as many as one hundred teachers and would-be teachers in his school, and taught them all himself!

CHAPTER IV

Now and Then

Leaving the old cottage home, revered—
With its wagons, play-mills and toys,
To take a longer journey,—tramp;
For we are now no longer boys.

Over hills and through many dales
Our deviating course will run;
Along many branches and creeks
On a man-hunt for yester's son.

A'down Runnet Bag, over Ridge of Blue,
Renfro Ridge and on to Poplar Camp,
Turkey Cock Creek and Raccoon Branch;
A wondrous, a very wondrous tramp.

Edward Cockram, venerable old—Rachel's dad:
Leah, Sarah Proffitt, Natty, Edd.
Nearby we stopped, a little visit had
With yester John, our great grandsire (dead).

Who was his father, his mother where?
Stephen Wood, John, Jesse, Ben?
Where did he live early in life,
And who was his first wife then?

Richard Wood for forty odd years,
Lived at the top of "Woods Gap."
The road was built through his lands,
And his was the name of the gap.

He was four times married,
Never had but one wife at a spell.
Was strongly opposed to polygamy,
But tried out monogamy well.

His numerous clan of Scottish descent,
Fills Patrick and Floyd with its faces;
In Raleigh, McDowell and Mercer counties
And very many other places.

Stephen Wood was Preacher and High Sheriff.
He would ma'rry, confess and jail,
   Sell you out for county taxes,
And then arrest, and bless the sale.

In Franklin County he married Lydia Holland,
And at home was a very good liver.
   He had a family of twelve children,
And he lived on Blackwater river.

We wended our way to old Wiggins Creek,
Under Rock Castle's hoary crest,
   And to Old Charity Meeting House,
Upon Old Patrick Billy's quest.

Billy had twenty four children,—a wife,
Oh, how did he ever feed them?
   I do not know how he could,
But now is now and then was then.

Question this not, thou doubting Thomas,
Here lived Charles Thomas, senior and son,
   Pleasant, Mary and Joseph too,
And Peter with twenty-two: daughter, son.

Both Peter Thomas and Billy Cannaday,
Knew their multiplications by rote,,
   They wrought in the fields early and late,
But with never a discordant note.

Ah well, then was then and now is now,
And ever apart will stay,
   Till time has run, till time has run,
And we at the judgment-day.

You ask me "this" and you ask me "that,"
I can only tell you "now,"
   For then was then and then was then,
But that only now is now.

Our longer trek leads us through,
Lunenburg, Chesterfield,—Powhatan,
   Born to Mary Bilbo and Young Short wed:
Archibald, Reuben Short, Lizzie, Nann.

Here Jacques Bilbaud, or Bilbo James,
Seventeen hundred or near that year,
Fled from France with wife and one son,
With the French Huguenots landed here.

They builded the village of Manakintowne,
On the banks of the lordly James,
Here lived the Bilbos, Jean Pierre Susane,
Until their little Mary came.

She married Young Short, William's son,
Was mother of Reuben, Lizzie, Nann,
And grandmother to all the Reuben tribe,
Her life was ended where it began.

Reuben won Lydia from John Clark,—Allison clan,
A patriot soldier's daughter,
And here they lived and prospered a while;
Then to the mountains he brought her.

About this time in Amherst County,
With a very good start,
But with only nine in family,
Lived Aaron DeHart.

The trail will run to back and back,
To the olden days of then and then,
To Surry County lower down,
To then and then and very early men.

Captain William Cockerham, Burgesser,
In Surry on Chioakes Creeke's water,
On land descended from Mr. William Spencer,
His wife was Mr. Spencer's daughter.

On Chipoakes Creeke and Hog Island Marsh,
By "Labor in Vaine" house it lay,
On Tap Pit Swamp Channel of Beauford's Creeke,
Eleven hundred acres, I say.

A goodly dowry, and right well he lived.
In Lownes Creeke Parish, he was "At Home."
Commissioner of Surry for many years,
Or a Gentleman Justice, of tone.

William Short, the first in Virginia,
Had a wife,—Elizabeth by name.
  Their children: William, Thomas and Sarah.
Their home was near by "Labor in Vaine."

King of the Wameoakes sold Elizabeth,
An Indian boy from his nation;
  But the House of Burgesses objected.
She had no right, no confirmation.

William Short, sixteen hundred-thirteen,
In England he was born and bred.
  Was "transported" by Robert Moseley, Esq.,
Into this Colony, "one head."

On Upper Chipoakes Creeke, in Surry,
For a certain consideration,
  He "took over" eleven hundred acres,—
This early olden Short plantation.

The trail has run through then and then,
You have carefully noted how,
  We travel those olden days no more,
But return to now and now.

[Assumed written by the compiler—Ed.]

Biography of the Seven Sons

R. J. Wood reared seven sons ------
A rural, rustic set.
Tho' he's passed to his reward,---
The Seven yet.

First is J. P. Wood, the Squire,
With will and brain enough
A "six foot" stalwart G. O. P.
A "Diamond in the Rough."
A member of Billy Sunday's Church
Judge of the "Country Court"
He owns a beautiful Floyd farm
And makes a fine support.

Second, D. H., the "Lesser" Squire
Mixed up with the county schools

"Hard-shell" scrapping Democrat
And chief among the fools.
Was once a Patrick delegate.
Some said: "Will he find the way?"
Yet he caught enough of the routine
To vote and draw his pay.
He now is called a "Rotten Duck"
Helps grind Republican axes
And thru some "Democratic Trick"
He's now assessing taxes.

Third, is George, his mother's love
A sunny, laughing clown,
Has rented out his river farm,
And selling goods in town.
He's joined nobody's contentious church,
But God must love his life.
He makes a friend of everybody,
And loves and pets his wife.
His politics smacks of Roosevelt,
But has not killed the bear
And he's 'nough like Ted himself.
To treat you good and square.

Fourth, G. D. . . country gentleman
Stout built and almost fat;
Director in the local bank,
Presbyterian and Democrat.
He has a dandy home and farm,
And wife most people like;
Imposing storehouse and barn
All on the Franklin Pike.
He catches all that is opportune,
Lets . . no good chances slip:
Makes business count for all its worth
And always guards his lip.

Fifth, is Dr. A. D. Wood,
Dispenser of drugs and pills

Who told women how they felt,
With all their aches and ills.
He squeezed their wrist, felt their pulse
And had to see their tongues,
And trust his head on either side
To listen to their lungs.
He's specialist now, does office work
Reads history for research
Belongs to the Democrats; I think
And the Presbyterian church.

Sixth, Prof. S. A. Wood,
From William and Mary College
And wonderful that one small head
Can carry all that knowledge.
Courteous, accomplished, immaculate
And ladies' diplomat,
Might dress a gate post out in silk
And he would lift his hat
Don't know his latest church and creed
Nor political affiliation
He lives in Washington City now;
The capitol of his nation.

And last not least is D. R. Wood,
The baby -- Seventh Son.
I'll chronicle something of his life
And then this work is done.
He wanted to work for Uncle Sam
And straighten the federal banks
Said: "Now D. H. land that job
And accept my many thanks."
I did not know his politics
Don't guess I ever will,
But blew him as a Democrat
And fed him thru the mill.
And now he has that post of honor
But forgets the brother "Runt"
The only one of The Seven Sons

That helped him pull that stunt.
This is not all 'bout, The Seven Sons
Nor is this all quite true.
But characteristics of each one:
I'm handing out to you.

---Second Son.

—From *Stuart Enterprise*

Poems by Charles Carter Lee
of "Spring Camp," Floyd County, Virginia
ROSABEL (A Song, Air "Lucy Long")

When Rosa was a baby,
    They asked that I would tell
A name for the little lady,
    And I called her Rosabel.
Take your time, Miss Rosa,
    Rosa, Rosabel;
Take your time, Miss Rosa,
    And learn your lesson well.

Now Rosa's like her namesake,
    That in the garden grows,
And when she blooms to more shape,
    Oh, how she'll plague the beaus.
But take your time, Miss Rosa,
    Rosa, Rosabel,
Take your time, Miss Rosa,
    And watch the fellows well.

For soon they'll come a courting,
    And wondrous things they'll tell
Of how their hearts are doting
    On pretty Rosabel.
But take your time, Miss Rosa,
    Rosa, Rosabel;
Take your time, Miss Rosa,
    No matter what they tell.

They'll say that you are losing
   The morning of your life,
And that you should be choosing
   To be somebody's wife.
But take your time, Miss Rosa,
   Rosa, Rosabel;
Take your time Miss Rosa,
   No matter what they tell.

And O, they will be sighing,
   To prove their passion true,
And vow that they are dying,
   But just to live with you.
So take your time, Miss Rosa,
   Rosa, Rosabel;
Take your time, Miss Rosa,
   No matter what they tell.

But while the Rose is blooming,
   Nobody minds the thorn;
Yet don't be too presuming,
   For soon the rose is gone
Don't over stay, Miss Rosa,
   Your time, Miss Rosabel;
To waste your Roses, Rosa,
   Is not to manage well.

But while your cheek is blooming,
   And many you command,
On some one be bestowing,
   At once your heart and hand.
For that's the way, Miss Rosa,
   Rosa, Rosabel;
That's the way, Miss Rosa,
   To wear your roses well.

LITERATURE AND RHYME

O, Sally! 'tis my chief delight
To gaze upon your eyes brite;
My luv fer you, by gosh, cirpasses
The luv I feal fer rum and 'Lasses.

THE SUICIDE

When William sent a letter to declare
That he was wedded to a fairer fair,
    Poor Lady shrieked, 'To life! — to
        all, adieu!

And in the indignation of despair,
She tore the letter and her raven hair,
    She beat her bosom and the post-
        boy too,

Then to an open window flew,
And madly flung herself into a chair.

Reminiscences About The Town

In 1856, Darius Howard had a general merchandise store on West Main Street in the brick building that is now occupied by W. P. Lawrence as a dwelling.

Ira Howard had a store on the corner of Main & Locust Streets where Hotel Brame now stands.

Harvey Deskins had a business on Main Street adjoining the house that once was occupied by Robley Evans and in which Mr. Deskins lived.

Thomas Moseley's business was on Main Street where the residence of Dr. W. G. Conduff now stands.

Samuel Dobyns' business was situated just across the alley from Moseley's on Main Street. The alley used to be called the Simmons' Alley.

Jackson Carter had a business about where the post office is now located.

There was another store on the southeast corner of Main and Locust Streets, but the name of the owner is forgotten.

Hylton's Tavern was kept by Bryant Hylton until after the surrender (Civil War), and was located on the southwest corner of Main and Locust Streets where the People's Bank of Floyd County now stands.

Another business was located where the Floyd Drug Store is now, and in 1860 it was run by a Mr. Ferguson. During the war it was kept by Flemmon Howery, later by Thomas Williamson (when it burned), but was rebuilt and burned again.

In olden times, court days were on Thursdays instead of Tuesdays as in later years, and they were attended by large crowds of people. Usually, there would be three or four fights in the afternoon. Every tavern had a barroom connected with it and liquor was easily gotten.

The Female Academy was a frame building with an immense fireplace. The Academy was situated north of Parsonage Street near the present residences of J. H. Sumpter and E. S. Salmons. Among the first teachers were: Miss Lizzie Ligon of Lynchburg, who later became the wife of Jackson Kirby of Floyd; Miss Delia Huff of Lynchburg; Miss Emma Poston and Mrs. Rogers. During the war, a Lutheran minister, Rev. William Wier (1863-7, pastor and teacher), and a very learned man, taught at the Academy. He would hold the final examinations in the Presbyterian Church during the day and the commencement exercises at night—each pupil bringing a tallow candle for lighting the church as there were no lamps during those days.

After the surrender and until the male and female academies were combined, school was taught by Miss Maria Smith of Salem, Mass. This lady was born in sight of George Peabody's home and used to tell her pupils about his little red house.

The Male Academy was a brick building located where the present high school building now stands. Among the early teachers were: Mr. Gannaway, Rev. Boude, Mr. Rogers (whose wife taught at the Female Academy), Rev. Abram Hogan, Rev. B. W. S. Bishop (during the war and afterwards became a noted pastor of the Methodist Church), Rev. Shirey, Dr. Hoback, and Rev. Obenchain.

Among the physicians before the war were: Dr. John Stuart, a brother of Gen. J. E. B. Stuart; Dr. Woltz; Dr. Hines,

372

Dr. Samuel Evans; and Dr. Stigleman.

Simon Rader and Peyton Richardson conducted tailor shops until the beginning of the war, and during the war a Mr. Simpson had a tailor shop.

Nathaniel Henry, a son of Patrick Henry, died in Floyd and is buried in the old cemetery in town.

"Odds and Ends"
Collected by Mrs. Anna Willis Brumbaugh

The first cooking stove brought to Floyd County was purchased by Dr. Samuel A. J. Evans, father of "Fighting Bob," about the year, 1847, and Abraham Phlegar bought the second one the following year.

The editor of *The Floyd Reporter,* of many years ago John (?) Sower, was a lineal descendant of Christopher Sauer. The second Bible printed in America was printed in the German language in 1743 by this same Christopher Sauer, at Germantown, Pennsylvania. The type for which was brought from Germany.

The first Lutheran Church in what is now Floyd County was erected on the grounds now owned by Zion Evangelical Lutheran Church. It was built by German families. The records were kept in the German language from 1796 to 1830. Zion Lutheran Church, 1838, was dedicated by Rev. Jacob Scherer and Rev. Samuel Sayford. This building was replaced by a new church sometime during 189__. Reverends Daniel J. Hauer, Richard Walter, and John C. Repass were among its pastors.

In the old German church book are found the names of many of the early settlers of the community, such as: George Pflieger, Benjamin Phlegar, Isaac Phlegar, Eli Phlegar, Michael Phlegar, Abraham Phlegar, Jacob Eberly (Epperly), David Kitterman, William Kronk, Jacob Sowers, Henry Sowers, John Zentmeyer, Jacob Bower and Moses Blackwell. Many of the members at the present time (1922) are descendants of these early church fathers.

Olive Hill Lutheran Church, though now falling to decay, was a hallowed place to many of the earlier settlers of the Burks Fork neighborhood, about four miles south of the village of Willis. This church was built about the year, 1868, mainly by Jonathan Willis and Owen Wade. James Willis, son of Jonathan, has been a Lutheran minister for at least 45 years. Owen Wade's son, Peyton J. Wade, and also Rev. P. J. Wade, son of William, are preachers in the Lutheran Church.

The Evans residence was the old brick residence later lived in by Pleasant Howell, and later still by Dr. William Pendleton. Though perhaps the Evans family resided a part of the time in a framed dwelling just west of the present Floyd County Bank building.

Jackson Godbey lived in the Judge Waller Howard residence. Andrew Stephens lived on east Main Street, next to the Methodist Church. Henry Jones lived on east Main Street, and later in the same property lived Henry Dillon for awhile, and then he moved to west Main Street into the property later owned by Jackson Kirby.

Fleming Lester was long a resident of Floyd in its early days.

A man by the name of Daniel Zentmire lived on West Main Street and had a tanyard. He later moved his tanyard one mile east of Floyd. He was associated with Abner McCabe.

Burwell Akers lived in the residence portion of the Jett Hotel, on the corner just across from the present Floyd County Bank building (was a large slave trader).

Samuel Dobyns lived in the property later the residence of Dr. John W. Simmons.

Abram Phlegar (who married Margaret Goodykoontz) lived in the property now the residence of David Willis. Ira Howard lived in a part of his store building, it serving as residence and store. This property was later the Col. Joseph Howard residence and store. Darius Howard resided in the property now owned by Mr. William P. Lawrence. Harvey Deskins resided on the north side of Main Street about where Brack Scott had his hotel. Harvey Deskins had a general store about where the Central Hotel (kept by Howard Spencer), later stood.

Alvin Graham lived in the residence later owned and resided in by Mrs. Mary Scott-Bishop.

David Kitterman lived below where Judge Waller Howard later had his dwelling in the S&W Scott's wagon lot. He owned about half of the land on which the town of Floyd is now situated, and all land toward Captain Luke Tompkins' residence. His brother also was a large landowner and lived nearby.

The Female Academy was north of Parsonage Street, near the Zack Dobyns residence. It was a framed building with an immense fireplace.

The Male Academy was where the present high school on North Locust Street stands. It was a brick building and among its early teachers were Wm. Gannaway, Rev. Boud, Mr. Rogers, (Rev. William Wire (1863-1867), during the war), taught in the Female Academy. Mrs. Rogers taught in the Female Academy while her husband taught in the Male Academy, Rev. Abraham Hogan, and during the war, Rev. Benj. W. S. Bishop (who later became a noted divine in the Methodist Church), Rev. Shirey, and later Dr. Andrew J. Hoback, Rev. Obenchain were among the teachers of the Male Academy.

Pupils of the Male Academy under Mr. Gannaway: Samuel Scott, Dr. Callihill M. Stigleman, Col. Joseph Howard, Giles Cannaday, John Tredwell Cannaday, Erasmus Graham, Swanson (of Pitt), Cornelius W. Wickham, Abraham Hogan, Dr. Andrew J. Hoback, Elijah D. Via (Patrick), John Staples of Patrick.

Miss Kate Smith and Miss Mariah came to Floyd just after the close of the war, being employed first by Samuel Dobyns to teach his family, and after that they stayed on and taught until they were old, living and dying there (they were middle-aged when they first came there from Salem, Mass).

EARLY CUSTOMS

Early customs among the Brethren German settlers of the county: We can all recall the very neat, but small plain bonnets worn by the younger women and girls of these families. Their dresses were neat and plain, as laces and ruffles were not permissible. The men wore no buttons on the back of their frock coats nor pocket straps. Suspenders were thought a superfluity and therefore condemned. An amusing incident was related to the author by the granddaughter of one of these pioneer families. A young man was called before the governing body of the church and questioned as to why he had violated the prescribed rules by wearing suspenders to his trousers.

The blushing young man had to answer in the presence of the whole church the cause. He stated that he being very slim had no hips and that it was necessary for him to wear suspenders to keep his trousers from falling down. This funny incident was in after years related by the boy's sweetheart to her daughter, who is now an honored lady of eighty years of age.

These people were not given to going to law over their business affairs, but should some difficulty arise it was taken before the church friends, brethren, and otherwise disinterested parties acted as advisors and a compromise usually effected. The matter was discussed in the church, prayed over and a friendly solution attained.

These frontier people lived their religion as they saw it much more than is usually the custom in later times. A saying amongst the author's grandparents was "not to let the sun go down on your anger," but should you have a difficulty with your neighbor or friend, this must be settled and friendship resumed before the close of the day. Anger was thought to grow with the brooding, hence an early settlement the better.

THE WEDDING

Manners and customs of the early Brethren German settlers: The marriages would often take place at early candlelight, and the ceremony would take place at the home of the bride; a girl-friend standing by the bride holding a lighted candle and one of the groom's young men friends standing to his right holding another lighted candle, for by this means only were the houses lighted, and at a wedding or other public gathering it of course took more candles. Then after this to the large table loaded to capacity with the best of everything good to eat, as only those good old homefolk of the long ago knew how to prepare. Turkey, venison, roast pork, chicken and dumplings, sweet potatoes, string-beans or "snaps," as they were called, apple dumplings, then the pastries: the old well-known "pound cake," and cakes of every description, pies of all the fruits to be had: apple pie, peach pie, cherry pie; must just have a little of this and you are urged to try this pie, or that cake, with a number of kinds of preserves, the delicious taste of which lingers. After this sumptious meal is over and the things cleared away, it would not be long before the young men began to rid the room of its furniture and other things which might be in their way and two or three young men would come in with their fiddles and banjos and an old-time dance was soon in full swing, in which all of the young folks for miles around would participate. Or on other occasions, simple games would be played with simple good old-time hearty participation; in which all had the time of their lives. If this took place in the winter or cooler times of the year the large six or eight foot fireplace was filled with a good sized log fire whose crackle and glow added to the happy cheer of the company. Truly these were times to long be remembered, and these primitive, frontier people enjoyed life perhaps as much or even more than the high strung, American neurotic of today. This was a country and a parentage of whom to justly be proud.

THE FUNERAL

Mark Twain said that if you wanted to know a people you must attend their funerals, but as Kippling says "this is another story, but well worth reading." Returning to the subject of the funeral, especially amongst these early German people who formed such a large part of our pioneer people of Floyd. A funeral sermon would be preached lasting from an hour to an hour and a half, following which the procession of sorrowing relatives and friends would start for the burying grounds or grave. The procession would be headed by the men who could sing, marching four abreast singing hymns from the home of the deceased all the way to the cemetery, which usually was no great distance. A favorite hymn they would sing on these occasions was: "I am going home to die no more," etc., which when rendered by those strong male voices, and almost all of them could sing, made those sad occasions long to be remembered, and causing the on-looker to ponder well the ultimate fate of man. Truly these were affecting scenes and brought forth many tears; people in those times were not above shedding tears for the departing loved ones, holding it no disgrace, as is the tendency in these later times, when one must as per force of custom "hold himself in" until you could not tell that he had even a cause of sorrow. Even the criminal has taken it up (we Americans are monkeys of imitators), and would for shame show the least of nervousness, going to the gallows with the firm and steady tread, apparently unconscious of the awful tragedy being enacted, holding himself in so to speak.

Superstitions

Star light, star bright,
First star I've seen tonight.
I wish I may, I wish I might,
Have the wish I wish tonight.

The above wish was thought to come true, if upon seeing the first star of an evening come out in the sky, you said or repeated the above wish in verse, as stated above.

If one counted the first nine stars to come out on nine consecutive nights and made the same wish each night, the wish would come true.

A child was told when having a milk tooth extracted that if the tongue was not put into the vacant space till the new tooth grew it would be a gold tooth.

A sleeping person could be induced to answer truthfully any question by putting his hands into cold water.

The person who took the last biscuit or piece of bread on the plate or platter would never marry.

———

If a person dropped a morsel of food it was to be supposed that someone grudged it.

———

Fish and milk eaten at the same meal were unwholesome.

———

The wishbone of a fowl, when broken by two persons, would indicate which would marry first—the shorter end going to the fortunate one.

———

Dew collected before sunrise on a May morning removed freckles.

———

Rainwater taken from a hollow stump would remove freckles.

———

Snow which fell in the month of March, melted and bottled, became a remedy for sore eyes and chilblains.

———

It is lucky to go fishing on Easter Monday.

———

When one sneezed his companion always said "Scat." (Quite a change from the European "God bless you.")

———

The dead are always buried facing Jerusalem.

———

The tree toad and the rain crow (yellow-billed cuckoo) sang only before and during rainy weather.

———

Playing with toads or frogs would cause warts to grow upon the hands.

———

If you killed a toad the cows gave bloody milk.

If you saw the new moon "clear" you would have a carefree month. If you saw it through the boughs of trees, clouds, or other obstructions you would have a "month of trouble."

When a bird flew into a house you might expect death or some dire calamity to be visited upon the household.

For a rabbit to cross your path was bad luck unless it went back again to the side from which it came.

Young girls were told the story of a man in search of a wife, who rode abroad begging at every household the scrapings from the bread tray to feed his horse. Each maiden tried to please the handsome youth by having a great many "leavings" from her bread making, for his stead, but none succeeded in winning his favor until he found a young woman who answered shortly and crustily that she never had any scraps left over, and that, as far as she was concerned, his horse might go unfed. Realizing that he had found one who would make a thrifty wife, he proceeded to his wooing. The moral is obvious.

To wear a new dress before the basting threads were pulled out was a sign the dress had not been paid for.

If the hem of your frock was accidentally tucked up it was a sign someone was thinking of you. If you turned it down at once before speaking, making a wish at the same time, the wish would come true. In case another girl turned down the tuck she would alienate the affection of your lover.

In all the old churches the women sat on one side of the church, the men on the other.

In a rectangular church in the olden days, a few pews were always arranged in the corners, on each side of the pulpit, to face the sides of the pulpit. These were called "Amen corners," and were usually occupied by the deacons, elders, and other "pillars" of the church.

If you made the picture of your enemy and buried it under the "drip" of the house, you would escape the witchcraft from which you were suffering.

A woman brought in an apronful of apples from the orchard, but found upon reaching the house that they had been changed by witchcraft to chips of wood.

Another girl said she saw two angels dressed in gold in the sky the night she was converted.

A "dumb supper" was a sort of dare to the powers controlling the future, and only a very brave person would undertake such a project. The hour must be midnight and the meal must be prepared in silence and solitude, every step being taken backward. When the supper was placed upon the table and two covers laid the look into outer darkness was opened and the wait began. If a marriage was to be expected the future husband walked into take his place at the board, if single life lay ahead a black cat came in, but if death was near at hand a coffin appeared. Chilling thoughts! It was permissible for two girls to try their fortunes together by laying covers for two couples.

It was unlucky to carry a hoe through any part of a dwelling; to walk under a ladder; to spill salt (in this case sometimes the ill luck might be averted by burning the spilled salt); to see the new moon over your left shoulder; to come into a room through one door and go out through another; to take up ashes after sunset; to own a crowing hen; to break a looking glass; to kill a cat.

A whistling girl and a crowing hen never come to a good end.

A whistling woman and a jumping sheep are the best pieces of property a man can keep.

———

Red hair indicated a hot temper.

———

You should plant your potatoes in the dark of the moon, and your beans and corn in the full moon.

———

The number thirteen was always unlucky, and it was not good form to seat thirteen at the table lest some guest be made uncomfortable.

———

A clear sunset indicated fair weather to follow.

———

Lightning in the north indicated rain within twenty-four hours.

———

Rain falling in sunshine was a sign of rain the following day.

———

The length and severity of a coming winter might be foretold by an expert by observing the breastbone of a goose or the "melt" of a pig.

———

Birds and insects might build their nests very low if the summer season was to be dry; but if there was to be much rain, with the watercourses overflowing their banks; all nests would be placed high.

———

Comets were always a sign of war.

———

A shooting star meant a death.

———

A "deathtick" in a wall in the dark hours of the night was fearsome to listen to.

———

Some folks thought the cry of an owl in the night was an omen of ill luck.

———

A certain sound from an open wood fire was called "treading snow" and was thought to mean a snowstorm.

———

If the cook burned her baking her husband or lover was said to be in a "bad humor."

———

A rooster crowing near a door foretold guests for dinner.

———

There were always stories of ghosts and graveyards and haunted houses; of chains rattling on the stairs in lonely country places; of groans in the night, and beds on trapdoors in murder-inns of long ago.

———

And in 1926, C. F. Counts of Carterton, Russell County, is the owner of a "madstone" that has attracted much attention for many years and many people who have been bitten by dogs or snakes have gone to Carterton to have their wounds "treated" by Mr. Counts' madstone.

Personal Reminiscences

In 1922, and in his late seventies, W. Edward Howery wrote some of his recollections of his early boyhood days:

"Our old farm was called the Old Ogle Place. The tradition is that the Ogles lived there during the Revolutionary War. There is a cliff of shelving rocks in a secluded place on the farm that is known as Ogle's Den. It is said that Ogle was a deserter during that war and that he hid under those shelving rocks, consequently the name, Ogle's Den. There was a cold spring nearby. Often when a child I visited this place and peered around under those shelving rocks. To my childish mind it was a place of awe. I was told by an old settler that the Ogle family was related to the old Scott family and that they were natural mechanics. For some reason that I don't know, the old farm was without an occupant for many years and what little that was cleared was partly overgrown. There were many wild crabapple trees, the fragrance from which in the spring when they were in full bloom was most delightful. Then there were wild plums and fox grapes. What times we children used to have, hunting and eating them! Long before my father moved there it was a great place for deer; hunters came from Franklin County to hunt there. Three streams entered the river on the farm: Payne's Creek, Booth's Branch and the Pipestem; Payne's Creek named because it flowed through the old Payne farm, Booth's Branch because it flowed through the old Booth farm, Pipestem Branch because on its banks grew shrubs that were hollow and suitable for pipestems. The river and those three streams were all full of brook trout in those days and it was fine sport fishing for those speckled beauties.

"When engineers were surveying different routes to find the most available route by which the then Virginia & Tennessee Railroad could get up the mountain, one route surveyed came through Franklin County and up Daniel's Run and through the old Divers farm and down the Pipestem Branch through our old farm.

"I remember when I was a boy we got mail once a week. My father made at least one trip to Lynchburg every fall with a four-horse team. He took down buckwheat flour, for which he got $3 per hundred pounds, and onions my mother raised in the garden for which he got $1 per bushel, and butter and some other produce. He brought back sugar, salt, molasses, bale cotton, coffee and such other necessaries as couldn't be made at home.

"My grandfather was subject to nightmares and he believed firmly that it was a witch riding him. He said he could see it sitting on his breast, it looked like a black cat, and he would try to knock it off but couldn't.

"In the spring of 1865, the last and the only raid made through our county (that I know of) by a brigade of Yankee Cavalry, stopped on our farm and fed their horses and burned fence rails and prepared their dinner. We had some wheat in the barn in the sheaf which they took and fed to their horses. I was in the army at the time and there was no one there but my aged grandfather and grandmother and one older sister and four younger children. They had got news of the Yankees coming and told our Negro man to take our horses out in the woods and hide them but some of the soldiers made the Negro tell where they were hidden so they got them and came riding them in, in great glee. My old grandmother went to the general and begged him not to let them take the horses. The general had them put in the stable and a guard placed over them until the soldiers were all gone. They made their quarters in the house and placed a guard so nothing was taken. Our women cooked dinner for them and they ate at our old family table and they gave our folks a voucher on the United States for $300. We were true blue Rebels but some of our neighbors turned Union people. They came in to rejoice that the Yankees were there and feeding on what little we had but, behold, the officers treated our folks with much more respect than did those rejoicing Union folks."

Personal Reminiscences

Rear Admiral Robley D. Evans was born in Floyd County, Virginia, August 18, 1846, the oldest son of Dr. Samuel A. J. and Sallie Jackson Evans. His father owned a good farm near Spangler's Mill, at the south of Pine Creek on Little River, and here were spent the first five or six years of his life, where many lasting impressions were formed. The county was comparatively new, with much of its original forests yet intact. The streams were full of fish, native to the small mountain watercourses; and the hills and woods abounded in game. Farming was the chief occupation of the people. The manners and customs of the people were at a half-way place between the primitive backwoods settler and the educated and refined. The old superstitions, sayings and ghost stories were yet believed in by many. These were carried back by the pioneer, added to and "colored" by the old black mammy; and last, but not least, Floyd County was full of Pennsylvania Dutch, fresh from Pennsylvania and the "Black Woods" of river Rhine, with a superstition native to Germany. These blended stories are yet native to Floyd and may last as long as the credulity of man is a factor in their propagation.

Dr. Evans was an educated man of the old type, owning a large farm and a number of slaves; and here Dr. Evans did a wide-country practice. He was the only doctor in a circuit of twenty or thirty miles. Admiral Evans says of his father: "For pleasure he owned slaves and farmed, and when requested to do so, represented his county in the State Legislature. The life of the doctor under such conditions was a very hard one, particularly in the winter season. Frequently he had to be in the saddle all night, facing the storms of snow and rain, to help some sufferer who could only offer his thanks as pay, for most of the people were very poor. It was this exposure that finally cost my father his life in the prime of his manhood and usefulness."

In relating the story of his boyhood days on the farm, he says that at the age of six years he was "the happy possessor of a gun, a pony and a negro boy." He learned to handle the gun with "considerable skill," and early formed the hunting habit, to which he was much attached in after years. The pony, he must have possessed for several years, as he mentions riding from his home on Little River to the Jacksonville Brick Academy. He says: "the pony seemed bent on breaking my neck." However, "Bob" Evans never gave up. It was not in him to surrender easily. The Negro boy taught him to "smoke and chew tobacco," was his close companion, who impressed upon his young master's mind "many superstitions and dreadful ghost stories."

He describes his "black mammy" as a short, thickset, very black woman, much the shape of a flour barrel. She, the mother of eighteen children of her own, was never too busy or too tired to coddle her young master and comfort him in a way of her own. This old colored woman, he later cared for in the city of Washington, she living to the great age of one hundred and two years.

He relates the pleasure of the wheat harvest time on his

father's farm, when he followed the cradlers in quest of the nests of the Bob White. How he gathered one hundred and twenty eggs in one field, and set them under hens in the barn, and how they hatched out the queer, unchicken brood, so puzzling to the mother hen.

It was the custom of the well-to-do farmers of Floyd County, "before the war," to gather up the farm produce, of tobacco, apples, potatoes, turkeys, chickens, butter and eggs and make a trip in the fall of the year in a four- or six-horsewagon to Lynchburg, Virginia, then the southern trading point for this part of Virginia. Admiral Evans, in his book, **A Sailor's Log** describes a trip he took to Lynchburg with his father's wagoner. As usual, he rode his pony a part of the time, slept in the wagons at night, and had a varied and wonderful experience for a boy of five or six years of age--and came back home with his red-topped boots. Dr. Evans moved from his farm on Little River to Jacksonville, about the year 1852, and lived most of the time in the three-story brick residence on the south side of Main Street. This was later the residence of Dr. William Pendleton. Dr. Evans was an Elder in the Jacksonville Presbyterian Church at its organization up to the time of his death, and was an active supporter of the Brick Academy.

His children were: Sallie M., Robley Dunglinson, Samuel T. and William M. Sallie M. Evans was a popular schoolteacher of the county, who later became the wife of Dr. Brainard W. Hines, one of Floyd County's beloved physicians. Dr. Samuel T. Evans was a prominent physician of Tennessee. William M. Evans was a lawyer of ability and standing of Portland, Oregon.

After the death of Dr. Evans, in the year 1856, the family broke up their home in Floyd County and went to live in eastern Virginia in the county of Fairfax, near Alexandria. Later Mrs. Evans married Captain Joel Pepper, an Englishman, and lived for a time during the Civil War, on the top of Pilot Mountain in Montgomery County, Virginia.

Soon after his father's death, Robley D. Evans went to live with his uncle, Mr. A. H. Evans, in the city of Washington. Mr. Evans was a lawyer, a busy newspaperman and in some way was connected with the government in the claims department. Here young "Bob" continued his schoolwork, spent much time about the legislative halls of the House and Senate. He frequented the river side and spent considerable time with the men engaged in boating, and got a touch of the "tar" which was so much to influence his future life and career.

He was offered an appointment to the Naval Academy at Annapolis, by the Congressman from Utah, a close personal friend of his uncle. This with the provision that he go to Utah and live long enough to be able to claim that territory as his home.

His experience in crossing the plains in the old emigrant wagon train; the large number of buffalo and elk he saw on the plains--especially the buffalo, the half savage bands of western Indians; the capture of their entire wagon train by one of these bands of Indians, with the loss of all their horses together with all of their supplies and camping outfit; his stay of a week or ten days at the wigwam of a friendly Indian chief, when he was the only white man in a company of a thousand or more; his experiences with the Mormons and residence in Salt Lake City, form a most interesting chapter. All of this at the tender age of thirteen years, out in the world alone, with no relative or friend of long acquaintance near.

Then his experiences at Annapolis with the coming on of the war. When the war began, he was in a quandary to know what to do. He decided that he was a ward of the government of the United States and that his duty was to remain at Annapolis. His mother, however, without his knowledge signed his resignation and forwarded it to the War Department, where it was accepted. Thus finding himself officially out of the Navy and free to return home, he re-enlisted within twenty-four hours, and continued his studies at the Naval Academy, and as he says, "allowing his domestic affairs to take care of themselves, or to be adjusted later."

But doubtlessly this breach in the family was never completely healed. There is a sketch of Dr. Brainard W. Hines and his family, in **Hardesty's Historical and Geographical Encyclopedia** evidently written by Mrs. Sallie M. Evans Hines. She gives a short sketch of her father's family, in with the Hines write-up, mentioning all of the members of the Evans family, with the striking exception of her brother, Robley Dunglinson Evans. His omission is the outstanding feature of the sketch.

He tells of meeting with his brother, an officer in the Confederate service. This took place late one evening when he had gone to a famous oyster house in Washington City. The young Confederate officer had slipped across the Potomac from the Virginia side and entered the city in disguise in order to get a mess of oysters. As "Bob" entered the restaurant the young Confederate officer was coming out. They recognized each other, when the officer from the Virginia side dashed around the corner and made a quick get-away. Our subject entered the restaurant and ordered oysters, ate and ordered more and kept this up until the waiter asked him if he were going to eat all in the shop. After leaving the restaurant, he sought an officer and reported that he thought he had seen a Confederate officer in the city. A quick and hurried search was made, with the result that they found where the fleeing officer had secreted his boat while in the city, but who had made good his escape upon being recognized. Young Evans was undergoing a gruelling examination, when he requested to see the commanding general. He took the latter aside and told him that the Confederate officer was his brother.

One of his best stories, told in his book, **A Soldier's Log,** is of his experiences while on a sail boat, or small vessel in the New York harbor. These vessels were sail boats, impressed by the Government of the United States to do duty about the harbor and along the coast. The young Annapolis midshipmen were put to work on these vessels with a number of experienced common seamen.

On this vessel was an experienced seaman of about forty years of age, with his brother. The latter, a large, awkward youth of about the age of nineteen. This young man, while manning the ropes and sails in the top of the rigging, lost his balance and fell to the deck, killing himself instantly. They had smallpox on the boat, were in quarantine and were not allowed to land. A coffin was made for the unfortunate sailor out of rough, green lumber. They had no screws and had to nail on the lid of the coffin. After all was done, the remains were carried out on deck, where all of the men gathered around while the captain read the burial service. While this solemn service was being enacted the lid of the coffin, with a harsh, rasping noise, ripped off some three or four inches over the breast and shoulders of the body. He tells how the knees of these hardened men of the sea, quaked and shook under the excitement of this sudden, unexpected and uncanny occurrence. After the first few moments of near panic was over, it was evident that the young, heavy body of the sailor, dying in the full bloom of health, had rapidly swollen after being placed in a closely fitting coffin, had exerted such force that the lid suddenly gave way, as described above. The burial service over, young Evans was put in command of a squad of seamen to take the body in a row-boat, out beyond the break-water, there to commit it to the sea. They sadly rowed out for about two miles, with the twilight and darkness rapidly coming on. They solemnly lifted their fellow sailor and slid the coffin into the water and turned about and were rowing rapidly back, when one of the men looked back and remarked: "Yonder he comes, Sir!" They stoppepd rowing and looked back, when the coffin was seen standing on end, bobbing up and down, and apparently riding the waves after them. After overcoming their temporary, near-fright, they rowed back, and with a hammer knocked open one end of the coffin, to let the water in and sink the casket. It was both air and water-tight and would not sink, being lighter than the water.

In the year 1891, when we were having strained relations with Chile, Robley D. Evans was sent with the battleship, "Yorktown," into Chilean waters. His handling this delicate affair with so much firmness and diplomacy won for him, through the American press, the name of "Fighting Bob."

Carried back by the spirit of reminiscence, engendered by the many hours spent over the old records of the first settlers of our native heath, the days of adolescence slip away and I am a boy again—at the old home. Father and mother are there. The time of year such that the old-time hickory-log fire is glow-

ing in the old-time wide fireplace. Bless them. Father is asked
to tell us a "War-Story." Nothing could please those old-timers
more than to have an opportunity of recounting the old days
spent in arms, and it is said the story often grows with the telling.

Well! father's little, grey eyes would kindle with a kindly
pleasure as he took on the spirit of reminiscence, told of his
Western campaign, the days spent scouting and guarding along
New River. "Should have been 'Woods River', of course it
should." His first little fight or skirmish at Pearisburg, Giles
County, Virginia, his coming by the way of, and through the
present site of Bluefield, on to Princeton, county seat of Mercer
County, saw old-man John Scott and wife, father and mother of
his townsman, Mathew Scott, heard them complaining that the
Confederate soldiers were burning their fence rails for fuel at
their campfires. On and across New River, lower down among
the hills of Greenbrier, at Big and Little Suel Mountains, on to
Lewisburg under General Floyd, formed on the hill a good position, but through error of faulty judgment, the curse of battle,
gave it up and marched down into the lower fields nearer the
town, leveling the fences as they went. Where to their surprise
an overwhelming force of Union soldiers under the command of
General Cox drove them pell-mell back over the level fields and
with such momentum that it was impossible, with such a rout
to stop and reform again on the crest of the ridge. Once an
almost impregnable position, the battle lost, and General Floyd
almost heart-broken, on farther west with the losing forces of
the Confederacy against the Master Spirit of the Grant of the
West, camp life—sickness and almost death—fever at Memphis, etc.

The hickory logs were burning low, throwing a dull-red
glow far back into the room, but not strong enough to shut out
the shadows. I grew faint, or slightly dozing, when who should
stalk across the meadow and into the house, but the ghost of
John Banks, and have the audacity to tell father that his little
Civil War experiences were mere child's play. That he aroused
by the frequent and oft-told tale of our war between the states,
had come to tell a story of a "Real War," as he called it. He

then proceeded to tell us of the "Crossing of Washington's army over the Delaware River," that he was one of them, of the intense cold that in these later times, we do not have winters so severe, snows so deep, ice so thick nor weather so cold as in his days. His march with the army to Princeton the next day; how they surprised those happy, beer-drinking Hessian-Germans; sent them helter-skelter to cover and gained a glowing victory, which so heartened Washington's army, that they were enabled to withstand the intense cold and near starvation in the winter at Valley Forge.

Oh! I was interested and wanted him to go on—when who should step in but the ghost of Mathew Cox, of the west end of the county, who taking up the story of reminiscence, said he could go him one further back. He proceeded to tell the story of his services for the "Colony of Virginia," as he called it, under Colonel George Washington; that his fellow-soldiers were: John West, George and John Mercer, Peter Hog, Dr. James Craik, Andrew Wagoner, John Wilson, Christian Bumgardner, James Givin, William Jenkins, Robert Jones, John Smith, Richard Smith, Nathan Chapman, Henry Bailey—and spoke of George Washington like I might speak of Col. Joseph Howard, so well did he know him. He narrated to us the march of the Virginia Militia under Colonel Washington along with the gaily dressed officers and soldiers under the grand old, and famous General Braddock, hero of many battles, fought in the Old World, where war was a study and a science, and the ambition and hope of all the then-young-bloods of England. He was in the ever-famous battle, now known as "Braddock's Defeat," assisted in carrying the dying General off the field. The General crying out "Colonel Washington what shall we do?" Washington answered, "For God's sake, General, retreat." Cox had heard the Colonel request that he be permitted to take his little band of back-woods trained Virginia Militia and fight the Indians from cover—in Indian fashion—and in the Indian ways of war. That the General had replied, "It is high time when a 'Virginia Buckskin' attempts to teach a British General how to fight."

Attracted by this rather loud, and enthusiastic recounting,

Major Thomas Goodson, two miles away, came up and joined in. Told of his experiences in the war for independence with General Washington. But he was a lover always, and had to be allowed to tell about stopping over on Roanoke River, on his return from the war, at the residence of a man by the name of Poag. How, he, a dirty, filthy and ragged soldier had been put to bed in spotless linen, fed food good enough for Kings. That when he left, the daughter and mother of the family gave him a large pone of light-bread, so large that he had no way of carrying it. Finally passing a string through the center of the pone, he swung it, suspended around his neck, and started on his way home, over the Bent Mountain to his home at Turtle Rock. Where he remained only a short while to clean up his cabin, get new clothes, shave and return to the Poag residence, marry the daughter and bring her to Turtle Rock.

"We came here for War Stories, so cut that out," cried a group of new arrivals, who on being introduced were: Hy Bishop, Elijah Dickerson, Benjamin Edwards, John Head, David Howell, Sr., John King and Thomas Trail. Such a greeting of old acquaintances and recounting of old stories and telling old anecdotes you never heard.

James Cannaday of Runnet Bag was introduced, and told of his services under General Greene, along the southern border of Virginia and into North Carolina, chasing and being chased. "Mostly being chased," put in John Banks with a laugh, "What we did for that fellow, Tarlton, confound him, was a plenty," continued James Cannaday. They all laughed and called him, "The father of Patrick Billy," now famous for his twenty-four children.

Joseph Cole was introduced, when taking off his war canteen of cypress wood, which he had carried all through the war. Told the assembled old soldiers that he lived in the northeastern part of the county, not far from Vause's Fort. When some of the company wanted to know where the Vause Fort was, and also where Fort Lewis was situated, said they knew about where they were. Both had been made so famous, the latter by General Andrew Lewis, the hero of Point Pleasant and the former as a more western fort, useful and famous for its notable experiences and Indian massacre, prior to the Revolutionary War. That General Washington had visited both of these forts in Colonial days.

Joseph Cole said Vause's Fort was on the headwaters of Roanoke River, about where our modern village of Shawsville is now located. That it was not so very far from his home on Laurel Ridge and that he had been there often, as well as to Fort Lewis, which according to Cole's narrative was near the present town of Salem, Virginia. Asked why the Vause Fort was so often beset by the Indians and had so much fighting with them, he said it was because of its prominent and strategic position. That it was situated on the main trail from the Kanawaha, to the Roanoke and Staunton rivers, that from the course of the mountains all travel east had to pass this fort. He recounted that Joseph Hicks, Lieutenant John Smith, John Tracey and John English lost their lives there. Was not certain about John English; knew he was killed by the Indians, but could not recall for sure that his death occurred at the fort. Those wounded here, said Cole, were William Robinson, Samuel Robinson, Robert Pepper, John Robinson and John Walker, and a much larger number were made prisoners when the Indians captured and burnt the fort. They were as recalled by Joseph Cole, "A man by the name of Cole, a distant kinsman of mine," together with a man by the name of Graham, Morris Griffith and his wife, Captain John Smith, Peter Looney, William Bratton, Joseph Smith, William Pepper, Mrs. Vause and her two daughters, a Negro servant and two young Indians, Ivan Medley and two daughters, James Bell, Benjamin Daries and Mrs. Mary English. "Quite a number, I should say!" remarked Captain Robert Wade, a new arrival from Mayo Fort in Patrick County, who interestingly related the story of a range taken by a company of thirty-five soldiers under him, in August of 1758, from Mayo Fort at the east end of Bull Mountain, up to and through Floyd County, crossing the Blue Ridge Mountains. "Blue Ledge," as he called it, at the Shooting Creek Gap, striking and following down Pine Creek to its junction with Little River. Here they found Francis Eason's plantation, and later on down to Richard Ratcliffe's on Meadow Creek, and after resting and killing sufficient deer, marched on toward Draper's Meadows, now the site of the town of Blacksburg, Virginia.

He told in vivid manner how they captured a band of five thieving and murderous Indians, who had five head of horses and scalps that appeared to be those of white men; how they kept them prisoners overnight, set them at liberty, and how the company became mutinous for not being allowed to kill the Indians, seeing that they had fresh whitemen's scalps. That it was finally agreed that a part of the company was to follow, and kill the Indians if they could overtake them. That four were known to have been killed by his Rangers and that the fifth, though desperately wounded, succeeded in eluding them.

Cole's description of Fort Vause and Captain Wade's Indian stories worked the company up to such a pitch, that Captain Benjajmin Weddle came down from West Fork to tell of the battle of Point Pleasant with his Company of Militia under General Andrew Lewis. General Lewis told Captain Weddle to take his company and ambush at the extreme northwestern end of the fort. He now re-enacted that memorable battle of grapple and death with the savages, the winning of which, according to Weddle, finally broke the backbone of Indian resistance to colonization along the Ohio and further on into the west. Told how the Indians, who were so enraged at him because he was one of Lewis' men at Point Pleasant, that they burnt his home at "Horse Shoe Bend" on New River the night after he fled with his family to Bent Mountain in Montgomery County, now Floyd. That after stopping there awhile he removed to West Fork in the west end of the county where he has since made his home.

Following Captain Weddle, came Captain Daniel Shelor with his grandson, Col. William B. Shelor, the latter modestly took his seat, when Captain Daniel Shelor, formerly of Maryland, told of his enlistment and services under General Thomas Johnston and Col. James Johnston in New Jersey, and of his services later in Maryland under Major Bailey. His description of the struggle of the Continental Army in New Jersey in the beginning of the war was very vivid. Told of the dire straits of Washington's army when the fortunes of the United Colonies hung in the balances and seemingly were almost despaired of.

A noise at the door was heard and promptly responded to by Major Tom Banks, son of John Banks, builder and once owner of this house where this very unusual meeting was being held. Who on hearing his father's retelling his familiar war story had, through parental affection, left the shades and come to the meeting, which too, was being held in his old home and in his father's yard. Responding to the knock at the door, was heard to say, "Your name, Sir?" (This is a rather private and to some extent a family meeting of old Floyd County men, or rather Montgomery men, and these old fellows are rather chary of being interrupted by idle and *disinterested* strangers.) "Why, Sir, I never saw you before, never saw you at my father's table, never saw you in my life." "You talk, Sir, like a youth, a mere boy, Sir." "I am, Sir, the father of your so-called Floyd County. I care not for your new names. We, Edward Bland and I, called it NEW BRITTAINE."

Well sir, such a shrinking back of those Old War Dogs, those Revolutionary fighters, you never saw, such deference, his very mien and appearance commanded respect, even from those war-grown heroes. John Banks advanced to meet him and with great deference asked the honor of his name and bid him welcome to this his home, as he called it.

"Sirs and Gentlemen, I am the Commander of Fort Henry at the falls of the Appamattuck River. My name, Sirs, is Abraham Wood, member of the Governor's Council and the explorer and owner of New Brittaine, including your so-called Floyd or Montgomery County. I was a member of the House of Burgesses prior to my appointment by the Crown to the Governor's Council. My home, Sirs, is at the mouth of the Appamattuck, where your modern City of Petersburg was later built. There I shall be honored to have you gentlemen visit me, and I promise to have a rather royal reception in your honor, by having a number of the independent Indian chiefs there on this occasion as my honored guests to meet you gentlemen." He then proceeded to tell the assembled worthies that while a member of the House of Burgesses and following as a member of the Governor's Council, he and Edward Bland had gotten an act, or

"Order," as he called it whereby an hundred men would be sufficient to constitute a county. That he and Bland, as he called him, had secured from the Governor and Council with the concurrence of the House of Burgesses, an order of authority, called an "Act of Encouragement" (and we needed encouragement too), to go far back among the enemy Indians, to discover a River of Unknown lands, beyond the mountains, where no Englishman had been--and if possible, a way, a route or pass to or leading to the South Sea, and on to India (Columbus' idea, we called it).

"Well, Sirs, and Honorable Assembly," (he talked as if addressing the Governor and Council, or the Assembly of the Burgesses) I came especially to tell you of this 'New Brittiane', your so-called Floyd County. This America is a wonderful land for a man of parts, a man of far-vision. Bland and I conceived the idea of colonizing this part of Virginia—and so made explorations, some of which were made by my men from the Falls of the Appamattuck, after Bland lost interest in the scheme, I then heading and financing the business alone. My lines of explorations were leading westward from 'Wood', or Fort Henry, many of my men persisted in calling my place, 'Wood', but I always wrote and spoke of it as 'Fort Henry'. As I was saying, my lines of exploration and adventure were in two diverging lines, starting from Fort Henry, the first leading to the southwest, back and along the Virginia and Carolina line, and on to the Catawba, but nearing the mountains, which you moderners call 'Blue Ridge', these as you know run in a northeast and a southwestern course.

"We followed their border for some distance, my men sometime alone, crossing the mountains if need be to trade with the Indians. And by the way, there is still a Pass over this mountain, Blue Ridge, bearing my name. Well, then I sent out another expedition, perhaps known to you Sirs, by the name of 'Batts and Fallam's Expedition'. Thomas Wood accompanied them—(here his eyes filled with tears, and I wanted to ask him if Thomas Wood was his son, but through timidity let the opportunity pass). To proceed, this expedition passed westward, on to the waters of the Staunton, the Roanoke and on to a 'River of Unknown Lands', which ran in a western course. It was described by the natives as a 'River of Long Extent'. These, my men cut their names, or initials, and those of mine on trees, and for many, many years this 'River of Long Extent', the first that runneth west, bore my name and was called 'Woods River'. Dr. Mitchell spoke of this river before the Royal Society calling it by the name of 'Woods River'.

"Bland and I had a little tract, or booklet printed, let me see, by a man by the name of Harper, Thomas Harper, Esq., Sir, for John Stephenson, one of our men in London. This was at the Sun below Ludgate, and there this little booklet was on sale, to induce settlement in this Floyd County of yours, our 'New Brittiane', a pleasant Country, of temperate Ayre, and fertile Soyle, as we so described it in our booklet, and it is so, a dear, dear country, tell you, Sir, indeed. If I had not so much land around Fort Henry, a matter of six thousand acres and upwards, and not Commander of the fort, which position together with that of Member of the Governor's Council, which I shall retain to the day of my death, which I say, if I did not have, I would make my home on the headwaters of 'Woods River', where there is no finer spot on earth." He stopped off suddenly, looking at the sundial, which with his poor eyesight, and it at night too, he misread, and saying he had to be present at a meeting of the Governor and Council, was gone in a jiffy.

After Col. Wood left there was an embarassing pause for sometime, none feeling equal to take his place. At last Major Tom Banks, who feeling perhaps more at home than any of the rest, seeing that he was in his father's yard and actually in the first dwelling house he ever built (and a fine one too, for that early day), came to the center, rapped on the table and called for something to drink—something to treat his guests, as he called them, seemingly to take on ownership of the place. My father looked at me, when I had to tell them that we had nothing but a little "Moon-shine," and that it was not lawful to have even that. Well! I wish you could have heard those old-timers laugh; they would say "Moon-shine," and laugh fit to bursting their sides. Bless them! They called it contraband—but "Contraband" or "Moon-shine"— they said bring it out.

Such conviviality, their old tongues were loosened up and the old days gone over, and over, each vying with the other in telling a more thrilling story. When something was said about "Tories," partly from an innate hatred for them and partly from the drinking of the "Contraband," they decided to go and catch old man Stocker, Thomas Ogle and the Terry family on Terry's Creek. Nothing could stop them, but off they must go.

The house grew deathly quiet after they were gone. I do not know how long I sat there hoping they would return. When I was suddenly aroused by the loud and persistent ringing of my telephone. It was my wife, wanting to know if I were going to stay at my office all night; that it was now three o'clock in the morning.

[Written by Dr. Amos D. Wood]

REMINISCENCES of DR. GEORGE MILTON WELLS

I was born on my father's farm, on Little River, in Floyd County, Virginia, on the 5th day of February, 1837. My father, Job Wells, was born of Quaker parents, in the State of Pennsylvania, and reared in Ohio, in the village of Zanesville, Saint Clairsville and Mt. Gilead, and learned the trade of a cooper. At that time the cooperage business was flourishing as such products were in demand in towns on the Ohio and Mississippi rivers. His brothers were: Hugh Wells, Eli Wells, Richard Wells and John Wells. The first two early emigrated to the West and were lost track of in the wide stretches of that open country which was just then beginning to open up and draw settlers to that magnificent domain. Richard Wells sought domicile in the umbragious hillsides of Southwest Virginia, while John Wells emigrated to the State of Missouri. Uncle Richard Wells lived on his farm of something like one thousand broad acres, in what was then Montgomery County, Virginia, with his wife, Jean Wells, and a few slaves, whom he treated with such kindness and with whom he was as lenient as many persons are with their children. As an evidence of Uncle Richard's care and sympathy for his slaves, it is well known that he taught them to read and write, and, to one who had been remarkably faithful, he gave his liberty, including as well, his wife, also, giving them one hundred dollars in money and one hundred acres of land. Lott, the liberated slave, was allowed to make choice of his surname; and, as he knew of Thomas Jefferson, then towering in popularity for his great political achievements, chose to be named Lott Jefferson.

My mother's maiden name was Elizabeth Shelor, daughter of William Shelor and Polly (Mary) Goodson. (Major Goodson, an officer in the Revolutionary War, was her brother.) One of my uncles, Rev. Thomas G. Shelor was a minister of the Christian Church.

In 1825 (or thereabouts), my father visited his uncle, in a spirit of adventure, and finding him childless, an attachment soon sprang up between them and his uncle offered him a good farm if he would remain there with him for life. The proposition was finally accepted and soon thereafter my father married and settled down to the business of farming. In a few years his wife died. Father then determined to return to the State of Ohio but his uncle proposed that they go to the far West, in Kentucky, and that he would give my father a fine western farm if he would remain with him. My father again accepted this second proposition. They got together several hundred dollars and placed it in concealed apartments about the body of their vehicle so that no one would suspect its presence and started on their way through the western wilds. In an attempt to get out of the conveyance the uncle injured his leg (he was a large fleshly man) so severely that he was forced to return to Virginia, without purchasing any lands. Shortly thereafter my father married my mother and continued to live with his uncle until the time of the uncle's death, during all of which time father and mother took care of the old gentleman; and at the death of his uncle, father fell heir to the old homeplace and resided thereon until the time of his death. By each of father's marriages he came into possession of one or more slaves and at the death of his uncle he came into the possession of other slaves and in this way he became a slave owner.

One of the earliest recollections of my boyhood is the impression made upon my mind of the bitter controversy, between a relative (of father's) and his wife, who had come over to visit father from Ohio, on the subject of slavery and of their denunciation of father in most violent terms. I also recall that others of my father's relatives were so abusive in their letters that all correspondence between them was broken off. This occurrence most likely took place about the time of the enactment of the Missouri Compromise measure in the Congress of the United States, at which period discussions of slavery were very common and also very bitter; yet, we of the South, failed to understand the intensity of the feeling in opposition to slavery, until years after, when it welled out in every conceivable way, until the limit was reached in the endorsement of the bloody and fanatical methods of John Brown, met well nigh universal endorsement all over the North.

CHAPTER II—Childhood Recollections

One of the pleasant memories of my childhood, is the many visits to "UNCLE LOTT" and "AUNT ALCIE" in their snug home and of their unfailing kindness to the young, "they being childless" and of also frequent calls of Lott to my father's as he would return from the county seat where he regularly sold his "gingerbread and cider," as well as his own brand of shoe blacking.

Lott would listen to political or religious controversy with great interest; and, although he was opposed to universal freedom of the slaves (he regarded them as not qualified for full liberties), he believed in some character of freedom for some few of them who might be qualified. Lott was a consistent Christian and a member of the Primitive Baptist Church, in which his rare vocal endowment was often in requisition in starting the hymns and at wakes (for both white and black) and at which times he would modulate his voice to suit the proprieties of the occasion; and, when he sang "Hark from the tombs," tears would well from the eyes of many.

The Ironside Baptist did not believe in prohibition nor enforce it upon their members and Lott enjoyed this liberty, in moderation, and as such was regarded as a good judge of liquors.

Lott continued his visits to our home while the war was going on; and, on one occasion, when I was at home and had failed to secure leave of absence, he preferred the explanation "that the doctor was such a fine person and such a good soldier, that the Generals could not spare him."

Lott was endowed with the faculty of genuine politeness; so much so, that he was said to be the politest person in the county. Upon one occasion, on a courtday, when a great number of citizens of the county was present, a wager was made among some of them, that a certain Captain Howell--who was an acknowledged Chesterfieldian--was the superior of any man in the county and Lott's friends pitted him against Captain Howell. The test was made before chosen referees, by the introduction of various strangers to each of the contestants at different places, neither of them being aware of the wager. After repeated tests, the wager was decided in favor of Lott.

It was Lott's invariable custom, on being introduced to any person of note, to bow very low or courtesy, quite similar to the custom prevailing with the Japanese, and, as soon as admissible began to compliment the person and during the conversation, to bow frequently, holding his hat in his hand, all the while. As time passed, "Aunt Alcie," enfeebled by age, was no longer to prepare her popular brand of gingerbread and cider or administer to their simple wants, and it was not long until she sickened and died; and, Lott, left to his own enfeebled efforts, aggravated by failing sight and pinched with poverty, became an object of charity, both to white and black; when, finally, the lamp of life was extinguished and Lott passed to his reward, receiving, I doubt not the plaudit "Well done, thou good and faithful servant, enter thou into the joys of thy Lord."

CHAPTER III—Oldfield Schools

There were no public schools in Virginia, prior to the War, but common school education was provided for by the cooperation of communities. Citizens, having children of school age, would meet together; appoint the necessary committees and these committees provided the schoolhouses and the teachers, who were supposed to be competent to carry on the schools. I well remember when the schoolhouse in our neighborhood was built, prior to which time schools were held in vacant houses, prepared for the purpose. This was called "Moore's School House," for the reasons that Isaac Moore gave the land on which to erect the schoolbuilding. A subscription was then circulated; patrons assembled; trees were felled; logs hewn; other materials assembled, as donated, and a "House-raising Bee" soon saw the schoolhouse ready for occupancy. Such schoolhouses were used for religious worship and other meetings in the neighborhood.

While the "Three R's—Reading, 'Righting and 'Rithmetic"—had constituted the principal curriculum, from this time on, there was an extension of the course so as to include English Grammer, Natural Uhilosophy, Rhetoric, Astronomy and the like I remember that half-brother had attended a school several miles away and one day brought home with him a strange looking book, called "Green's English Grammer." One particular thing I remember about the book was the "Conjugation of Verbs," and it was a puzzle to me, why it was reiterated "I love," "You love," "He loves," but never SHE LOVES: so, I was driven to the conclusion that the verb "To love," was too much for my comprehension; nor, was it many years until I began to experience even more difficulty in extricating myself from the meshes of the subtle little god's fabrications than it had been to comprehend the conjugation of the verb. Prior to this school, Pike's Arithmetic, Reckoning in Pounds, Shillings and Pence, had been the only textbook in arithmetic but was now superseded by "Smith's," but Webster's Elementary Spelling Book held its place in the esteem of patrons for some years longer, and, without doubt, imparted good training in orthography. The art of Penmanship was an esteemed accmplishment for a teacher, in the days of the Oldfield School, and the ability to make a good quill-pen, would take the place of the want of other accomplishments on the part of a teacher. The pens were introduced in the first sessions, at the new schoolhouse, but were more regarded as much inferior to the old reliable goose-quill, for the making of which, every pupil was expected to supply the quills. The school authorities learned of the success of a Mr. Payne, in a distant part of the county, in the management of young men and unruly boys, and secured him to take charge of the new

Moore's School House. A large and apprehensive (if not appreciative) class assembled to greet Mr. Payne, when his school opened.

Classes were formed in English Grammer, Natural Philosophy, Book-keeping, Surveying, Geography and other courses of study. Mr. Payne was a very successful teacher, curbing the recalcitrants; stimulating the laggards and satisfying the studious, as well as his patrons. During the Payne regime, an epidemic of scabes (itch) spread through the school and proved a fierce contestant with the textbooks for the attention of the classes; while, a little later, "pediculocis" (lice) was pittied against all enemies, with even honors. After the expiration of the Payne engagement, I was regarded as sufficiently advanced to Jacksonville Academy, at the county seat of that time, five miles distant from my home. At this time there was a Private Boarding School for young ladies, in the village, conducted by an experienced teacher from Baltimore, attending which were Miss Lizzie Goodwin, her sister, Miss Lucinda Goodwin, and their cousin, Miss Smith, from Roanoke County and who were destined to enact a most important role in the fortunes, happiness and life of myself and others of my immediate family; Miss Lizzie Goodwin becoming the wife of my boyhood friend, D. William Howard; Miss Lucinda, my own beloved wife; while a daughter of Mrs. J. W. Rible (nee Miss Lizzie Virginia Smith) became my daughter-in-law, the wife of my son, Dr. J. Hunter Wells; so, mysterious and phenomenal is the loomage of the warp and woof of human lives, when directed by Cupid's magic-working darts. All of these schools were simply preparatory and the young ladies attending them were soon enrolled in the splendid Southern Seminary at Hollins Institute a few miles from the prosperous city of Roanoke, Virginia. At the time I entered Jacksonville Academy, it was patronized by a large class of young men from Floyd and adjacent counties. The principal was a college-bred man, of fine personal and literary accomplishments and introduced better methods and more advanced training than had been previously enjoyed; hence, young men trained in that school, were stimulated to their best endeavors and became successful professional and businessmen. During my attendance at the Academy, one of the older students succeeded in getting up a fight between a tough from an adjacent county and myself, in which I was greatly out-classed, he being a wiry wild-cat of a fellow, who succeeded in getting my head underneath his arm and he made the hair and skin fly in a furious fashion, as he plied his long nails, in catamount-fashion over my face and head, with the result that I received such a fearful skinning, that when I reported to school next day, my face was so swollen and scarred as to be scarcely recognizable.

The older boys, who had instigated the melee, slipped away, leaving us to our fate;,and, in due time, after it was all over, I was much wiser, if not the better for the humiliating experience. The Academy continued to prosper, and a two-story brick building was erected, which was well-attended for many years.

CHAPTER IV—In Business

In the meantime, my uncle, Thomas G. Shelor (who had been associated with Dr. Samuel A. J. Evans, the father of the late Admiral Robley D. Evans, in the mercantile business), induced my father to join him in opening a General Merchandising business, in the village and take me in for business training. A stock of goods was purchased by my uncle, in Baltimore, and in due time, the store was opened for business. We had daily mails, connecting with the Virginia & Tennessee Railroad at Christiansburg, twenty-one miles away, and my uncle secured the appointment as Post Master, which added to the importance of our business.

There was a copper mine in operation some miles from the village and much prospecting for other minerals. The country was flushed with Tennessee money ("Shinplasters" as they were commonly called), which was of doubtless value and greatly obstructed business. In the meantime the copper mine was closed and everything sold out at auction or forced sale. Inasmuch as our store had done a large credit business, it was necessary to either increase the capitol stock or discontinue the business and my father decided on the latter course. During the time of my employment in the store, the Virginia & Tennessee Railroad was extended from Lynchburg, Virginia to Bristol.

CHAPTER V—Pleasure, Love Affairs, School and College

At Christmas-time, in the year 1856, I determined to take my first ride on the railroad; and, having laid up quite a little sum of money, as Deputy Post Master, I did not have to call on my father to finance the scheme, although he did not approve of my spending my money so lavishly, to so little profit(?). However, I boarded the hack; clad in a fine broadcloth overcoat, silkhat, fine boots, etc., I proceeded on my way to the depot. The turnpike road ran within a mile of my father's home. To my consternation, he was on the road, and I feared he would order me to abandon my trip but he did not, but allowed me to proceed and I had a most enjoyable and instructive trip, feasting my eyes on the busy little City of Lynchburg, in company with an old friend. My first ride on a railroad, proved, a most memorable trip, for the Misses Goodwin and their cousin, Miss Smith, were on the train, returning home from school, for the Holidays; and, so, I fell in with delightful companions and, possible for the first time, was thrown in company of Miss Lucinda P. Goodwin then, most likely, in short dresses; and, thinking little or nothing of preferences or society, yet, there was blooming in her beautiful face the charms, which a few years later, were to captivate and enhance my heart, not to whom, in the mysterious dispositions of human lives, was destined to link, not only my life, but that of a large family. Neither of us, at that time, had any idea that we were to travel the unknown paths of our future lives together; yet, as I review the events, then shaping our lives, I discern the existence of a feeble but genuine spark of affection.

While attending the store, I boarded at a hotel where there were three quite popular young ladies, one of whom was an acknowledged belle, whose attractions were so appealing, that few the susceptible class of young men were able to resist their allurements. You need not be skeptical of the foregoing statements: If a young man, under the pressure of a concatenation of circumstances, should yield and pay homage at the shrine of beauty, before which so many have paid obeisance. Howbeit, that affair ran a very brief course under the adroit handling of a past-mistress in disposing of the evanescent of too ardent admirers. I must confess that the next affair that I was involved in, had more significance, and that its ghost rose up before me many times to point the finger of confusion and serve to supply, even my unborn children, the data to turn the laugh on Pater Families. The wounds received in the encounter just referred to, were superficial. None of the red blood of the heart had been lost nor was its rhythm broken nor the nerves shattered and only the application of a little of the oil of sympathy was needed to restore the equilibrium and of that commodity, the younger sister I assure that uncle refers to his sister, Mary Jane Wells, my mother, (R.S.D.) had an adequate supply and with the tears and soothing emotions, offered a healing balm to the love-sick soul; and, not without its usual results; for, sympathy, rather than grace of person, often finds its way and influences our conduct, even though, in great measure uncalled for or over-wrought, it may go deeper than the surface and lead on to the development of tenderer emotions. Howbeit, village gossip was responsible for the current report that the relations between "Professor" (my cognomen) and Miss Henrie B. Williams were bordering on the serious. It is, at least, probable that my parents felt some anxiety on the subject for they readily fell into the plan to send me to an Academy, in an adjacent county, where an exceptionally good school for young men was in opera-tion, with a full attendance and, in a short time, I was outfitted for my first experience in school, some distance from home. My father accompanied me to the school, a ride of forty-five miles and there I met large classes of young men, preparing for college or business training. As I recall my impressions received at that country Academy, I recognize the great importance of good school opportunities for young men, in the formative period of life; the stimulus imparted by the study of mathematics, the languages, composition and rhetoric, to say nothing of the riv-alry and stimulus of mind on mind in debate. My desire for knowledge was greatly developed by the start at that school and one of my regrets is that circumstances overruled my am-bition. I am also led to admit that it is particularly unfortunate for a student to become too much involved in social affairs, which tend, inevitably, to distract the mind and displace the attention, so that the mind is not capable of the necessary con-centration to the acquirement of knowledge.

In other words, if a young man becomes involved in love affairs, his capacity to concentrate his mind on study is greatly impaired. Therefore, there is wisdom in the requirement that the sexes as a rule, should be kept separate, during the years when the emotions are apt to be subservient to the judgment, and at such times or periods, the judgment is often not well-grounded. Howbeit, human nature is the same now and always will be, and how often do we see the fond desires of parents thwarted by the inroads of the subtle little god of love, when the whole tenor of a life is altered by the unseemly machinations of the genius who presides over the realm of the heart!

IN MEMORIAM

Richard Wood, 1769-1859

One purpose, and one impelling thought inspires our hearts and minds. For five successive years we have met to honor our ancestral hero; and each year as we meet to mingle our words of devotion, the life and name of our great-grandfather assume larger, still larger proportions. We dedicate in his honor today this memorial, so fitting to the life he lived. Of the facts and incidents of his life it is unfortunate we know so little. But I invite you, fellow descendants, to scan some pages of the book of memory and vision, and glean therein, if you will, some sure indications of the life he must have lived.

O Muse, who dids't so oft for the Greeks of old lead them into the paths of wisdom, so lead us into the paths of human record and achievement. With thy magic key unlock for us a gold-embossed volume entitled "Richard Wood, 1769-1859." Enrich our impressions as we read the book and choose our words as we speak of the hero of our story.

Richard Wood, 1769-1859. A full life spanning ninety stirring years in American history! Wonderful years those, and they must have made their lasting impression on the life of Richard Wood. Let us open here this book of memory and vision and turn back its pages to 1769 in fair Virginia land, then an English colony. A new human record began that year in Lunenburg County, Virginia. In 1769, a boy was born named Richard Wood, son of John, grandson of Stephen Wood, his known ancestors going back to 1700, two hundred and thirty-nine years before this year of grace 1939. Great deeds were then being done, and great thoughts behind those deeds. And Richard Wood in his early boyhood must have pondered those thoughts and deeds. At that time Patrick Henry in Virginia and Samuel Adams in Massachusetts were stirring men's hearts and souls and teaching those lessons of liberty and equality, which were to culminate, before Richard Wood was twenty-one, in Jefferson's Declaration of Independence, Washington's victory at Yorktown, and Madison's Constitution of the United States. These are great names, and great things were then being done. Fortunate was Richard Wood that those things were being done while he was yet a youth. And fortunate are we, fellow descendants, that he passed on to us the impressions he then received.

Little Richard Wood at the time of the Battle of Bunker Hill in 1775, a boy of six years but much older in experience, was listening to his elders and to those accounts of patriotic courage and daring, which must have made a deep and lasting impression on his young, impressionable life. Accounts of hardships endured by patriots prepared him for the hardships to come into his life. Deprivations, which he saw men and women meet, were preparing Richard Wood to meet the deprivations certain to come in the days before him. He was just turning twenty when the Constitution became the supreme law of the land in 1789; his new country unfurled her flag of freedom to the breeze; and General Washington became the first President of the United States.

By that time a new vision was dawning in the minds of young Americans. The land to the west, these mountains and beyond, the great Ohio country, and the land of Boone, were saying to Richard Wood and others, as Greely said in later days, "Go west, young man, go west!" Then came Jefferson and the purchase of Louisiana in 1803, when Richard Wood was thirty-four. Jefferson's purchase of Louisiana in 1803, when Richard

Wood was thirty-four. Jefferson's purchase of Louisiana Territory, negotiated by James Monroe, another Virginian, more than doubled the area of the new country. Men's minds were fired with enthusiasm in contemplation of that great western country. And Richard Wood in his early thirties must have heard the call. It was between the years of 1789 and 1803, no doubt, that he left the place of his birth in Lunenburg County, Virginia, and came to the top of the Blue Ridge Mountain. "Why did he stop here and go no further?" you ask. The answer is brief and simple. Lack of funds necessary to such an undertaking; hostile Indian bands then roamed the unsettled country; roads had to be made, such paths as they were, through the primeval forests; making a substantial living for himself and family became paramount. So Richard Wood settled here at the top of Woods Gap, named for his ancestor, that illustrious pioneer and explorer, Colonel Abraham Wood.

In the War from 1812 to 1814, when Richard Wood was forty-three, his country gained her second independence. Freedom and independence became more cherished than ever; and the soul of Richard Wood was strengthened and his heart rejoiced in loyalty to his state and country.

The years from 1789 to 1846, in the life of Richard Wood, were years of industry; and, considering the great handicaps in an inaccessible mountain country, they were also years of a measure of prosperity. Then came 1846 and his country was again in war, this time with Mexico. Two years ended that conflict, and again Richard Wood saw his country victorious.

By this time and earlier he viewed with alarm the growing dissension in the minds of his countrymen caused by slavery and states' rights. He visualized, no doubt, the wreckage such a conflict would bring to his beloved southland. We rejoice that he was spared the experience of witnessing the destruction caused by the Civil War. He passed to his reward in 1859 just two years before the Battle of Fort Sumpter.

Yes, Richard Wood, our beloved ancestor, your life was full. You saw the beginning of your country and witnessed her progress to 1859, second to none in power and influence. Your life in your ideals kept pace with that of your country. We rejoice that it is the privilege of this generation of your descendants to erect and dedicate this memorial in your honor. We rejoice that our generation can here and now place your life and name in their proper perspective. We dedicate this memorial, this "barrow" as called in other climes and ancient days. Had you lived in those ancient days, methinks your ashes would have been placed in a golden urn and deposited in your memorial "barrow," near some great highway, that through the years men might come to do you honor. Thus the ancient Greeks honored many a favorite son; thus they honored Achilles. Homer in his immortal **Odyssey** gives vivid description of honors thus conferred.

They bore the body of Achilles from the field of Troy where he was slain in battle, placed it on a bier, and washed his fair flesh with warm water and ointments. They clothed the body in raiment incorruptible; and all the nine Muses, one to the other replying with sweet voices, began the dirge. For seventeen days and nights continually they mourned Achilles, bravest of the Grecians, immortal gods and mortal men. On the eighteenth day, they burned the body and killed many a fatted sheep around the pyre. They gathered together his white bones sprinkled with wine and ointments. His mother gave a two-handled golden urn to receive the ashes of her god-like son. They built a great and goodly tomb, a "barrow" it was called, high on a jutting headland overlooking wide Hellespont, that it might be seen from off the sea, by men then living and those to come thereafter. These honors and more they did for Achilles, for dear he was to gods and men. Thus in death he did not lose his name, but received a fair renown in all succeeding generations.

Richard Wood, our beloved ancestor, you are our Achilles. We honor you, not as a victorious general; not as one whose fame has spread around the world; not as ruler of man and nation. But we honor you a man amongst men in the ranks, a private who answered the call of duty. We have no golden urn to receive your ashes; but better still, your memory is enshrined in human hearts. We place not your memorial "barrow" high above the seashore to be seen of men; but high on this mountain of ethereal blue, in a gap named for your illustrious ancestor. Toward this sacred place paved roads are already reaching. Hard-by your memorial "barrow" is Blue Ridge Parkway, extension of Skyline Drive. Strange to relate, the paved roads you needed so much in your day have paved the way for us to do you honor. Here you rest in peace in these eternal hills, God's altars. To your memorial "barrow," Richard Wood, your descendants yet unborn will come and at your tomb call you blessed. Here we dedicate in your honor this your memorial "barrow" and raise our requiem in parting salute. And until the sun has made his annual course again we say adieu, but not goodby. Richard Wood, adieu!

Sparrel A. Wood,
Great-Grandson

July 9, 1939

CHAPTER V

List of soldiers from Floyd County, Virginia, who served in the Confederate war.

COMPANY A. 24th VIRGINIA INFANTRY

C. M. Stigleman	Captain
J. W. Headen	1st Lieutenant, promoted to Captain Lost an eye at Gettysburg, July 3, 1863
Jas. E. Reynolds	2nd Lieutenant, wounded and died at Drewry's Bluff
George W. Helms	3rd Lieutenant, wounded at Drewry's Bluff
B. P. Elliott	1st Sergeant
Nelson M. Stimpson	2nd Sergeant. Wounded at Williamsburg
Abram D. Burnett	3rd Sergeant. Lost an arm at Frazier's Farm
Thomas M. Simmons	4th Sergeant. Killed at Hatcher's Run
Peter I. Fishburne	1st Corporal
Luther W. Bower	2nd Corporal. Died at home
G. W. Lancaster	3rd Corporal
Robert H. Bower	4th Corporal
Caleb Sowers	Drum Major. Captured at Five Forks, taken to Point Lookout, released June 14, 1865
Isaac Palmer	Fifer

PRIVATES

Levi G. Atkins	Captured and imprisoned at Point Lookout
William Bolen	
Robert S. Black	Killed August 30, 1962 at Manassas
Peter Bolen	
James W. Bolen	
John I. Brame	

Thomas H. Boyles
David Bowers
Joseph Bachrach — Killed at Drewry's Bluff, May 16, 1864
John W. Baber — Died at Camp Winder of measles, date unknown
Edward J. Clark
Andrew J. Castle — Mortally wounded at Drewry's Bluff, May, 1864
James E. Carter — Died near Manassas
Isaac Carter — Wounded at Williamsburg and died in prison
James C. Cunningham — Killed at Seven Pines, June 1, 1862
Champion C. Daniel
William F. DeHart — Killed at Drewry's Bluff, May 16, 1864
Jesse H. DeHart — Killed at Chafin's Farm, 1862
Henry C. DeHart
Thomas DeHart
James A. DeHart
Frazier O. Dobyns — Wounded at Williamsburg May 5, 1862, captured at Gettysburg, July 3, 1863, and imprisoned at Point Lookout. Paroled 1865.

Manassas C. Dodd
James M. Dillon — Died at home of smallpox
John P. Dillon — Died at Chimbrarazo Hospital, 1862
Tazwell B. Epperly
Larkin V. Edwards — Transferred to Cavalry
John Edwards — Killed time and place unknown
Henry H. Earles — Wounded at Drewry's Bluff, May 16, 1864

Gordon C. Earles
Malachi Earles
Lewis H. Finch — Wounded and died at Drewry's Bluff, May 16, 1864

George W. Frost
William Ferguson — Transferred to 21st Va. Cavalry
Preston Goad
Tazewell T. Graham
Micheal Greer — Died at Manassas
Elkanah B. Griffith
Daniel A. Griffith
Matthew B. Gillenwaters
George W. Goodykoontz — Wounded at Drewry's Bluff, May 16, 1864

William M. Goodykoontz	Wounded at Williamsburg May 5, 1862, and at Gettysburg, July 5, 1863
John H. Gardner	Wounded at Williamsburg, May 5, 1862; died in Washington, D.C., June 8, 1862
Mathias F. Hylton	
John H. Hylton	
Maston P. Hylton	
Solomon Hylton	
Ballard P. Hylton	Wounded at Seven Pines, June, 1862
Asa Howell	Died near Manassas
Joseph Howell	Wounded August 30, 1862, at Manassas
Mazarine Howell	Wounded at Williamsburg and died May 5, 1862
John J. Humphries	Died, time and place unknown
Jacob T. Helm	Lost arm at Drewry's Bluff, May 16, 1864
John W. Helms	Wounded at Plymouth, N.C.
Martin H. Holt	
Monroe Howard	
Ferdinand A. Huff	
Martin Harman	Died at Richmond, 1862
Sparrel A. Hylton	Wounded, time and place unknown
Levi W. Hylton	Captured near Farmville and imprisoned at Point Lookout until June 14, 1865
Riley H. Hylton	Captured near Farmville and imprisoned at Point Lookout until June 14, 1865
Thomas Howell	
Dillard C. Howell	
Rutherford Howell	
Jehu Howery	
William Jenkins	Died in Danville, Virginia, of smallpox
Joseph Johnson	
John Jones	
G. W. Kitterman	3rd Lieutenant, wounded at Gettysburg, July 3, 1863. Imprisoned at Fort Delaware
Levi Keith, Sr.	
Asa Keith	
Joseph P. Kelley	Killed at Seven Pines, June, 1862
Isaac P. Levacy	Died at Manassas, 1861
Wilson T. Lawson	Wounded, time and place unknown

Dudley Lester — Died at Hospital
John T. Lester — Captured at Williamsburg, May 5, 1862

George W. Lester
Gideon L. Lawrence — Captured at Stony Creek, March 3, 1865

Preston H. Martin
Joseph Mayberry — Killed at Drewry's Bluff
John P. Mayberry
Albert Matthews
Isaac N. Martin — Killed at Drewry's Bluff, May 16, 1864

Marshall Martin
Marshall E. F. Moore
Robert W. Mills
Isaac A. Perkins — Killed at Seven Pines
Booker P. McPeak — Captured at Five Forks, imprisoned at Point Lookout until June 14, 1865

Clark Pugh — Died, time and place unknown
Austin G. Proffit — Died at Christiansburg
Francis M. Payne — Transferred to 21st Va. Cavalry
James Palmer
Samuel Palmer — Captured at Five Forks, and taken to Point Lookout, released June, 1865

Ranson Quesenberry
George Quesenberry
William Richards
James H. Roberts
Isaac E. Rigney — Wounded, time and place unknown
John W. Shelton — Elected Captain, wounded August 30, 1862 at Manassas

Ira H. Slusher
Isham B. Shelor — Wounded at Williamsburg, May, 1863

Charles A. Simmons — Killed at Frazier's Farm, 1862
John Sweeney
William Sutphin — Died at Culpeper Court House, date unknown

William T. Shelor
George M. Switzer — Killed at Cold Harbor
Edmund Sweeney — Captured at Five Forks, taken to Point Lookout, released June, 1865

Jacob Smith — Captured at Five Forks, taken to Point Lookout, released June, 1865. Wounded three times, places unknown

John Smith	Captured at Five Forks taken to Point Lookout, released June, 1865
Richard L. Simpkins	Captured at Five Forks, taken to Point Lookout, released June, 1865
Henry Taylor	
James C. Turner	Killed August 30, 1862, at Manassas
Samuel Terry	Wounded and captured at Williamsburg, taken to Fortress Monroe, exchanged 1862, August 10th
William L. Underwood	Killed at Drewry's Bluff
William A. Underwood	Wounded at Drewry's Bluff, May 16, 1864
Creed Underwood	Captured at Williamsburg, May 5, 1862
Joseph Underwood	Killed at Drewry's Bluff, May 16, 1864
John E. Underwood	
Darius E. Williams	Killed at Plymouth, N.C., date unknown
George M. Wells	Transferred to 21st Va. Cavalry
Harvey D. Wells	
Harvey Weddle	
Charles C. Weeks	
Malachi Weddle	
Ahab Weddle	
Samuel J. Woods	Wounded and died, date and place unknown
Lindsay Walker	
Jacob Yearout	
George W. Young	Captured at Five Forks, taken to Point Lookout, released, June 14, 1865

Total   154

COMPANY B. 42nd INFANTRY

Officers

Henry Lane	Captain. Promoted to Major, killed August 9, 1862. Wounded at Winchester May 25, 1862

Abner Dobyns	1st Lieutenant. Promoted to Captaincy and Lieutenant Colonel. Wounded September 16, 1862, at Sharpsburg, Md., captured May 12, 1864 at Spottsylvania C. H., taken to Point Lookout, then to Fort Delaware; then to Charleston Harbor, S.C.; to Fort Pulaski, S.C.—one of the Mortal Six Hundred—under fire at Morris Island, promoted Major and Lieutenant Colonel
James M. Howard	2nd Lieutenant. Discharged at Manassas, September, 1862, killed by Stoneman's men April 2, 1865, in Floyd County
James L. Tompkins	3rd Lieutenant. Promoted to Captain, wounded at Spottsylvania C. H., May 10, 1862, at Fort Pulaski, Va., May 25, 1865, surrendered the regiment April 9, 1865, at Appomattox Court House
Jarrett J. Williams	1st Sergeant
John W. Dillon	2nd Sergeant. Promoted to 3rd Lieutenant, then to 2nd Lieutenant. Mortally wounded March 25, 1863, at Mine Run
James W. Helms	3rd Sergeant. Elected Captain, assigned to Company K., 42nd Va., same regiment. Captured May 12, 1864, taken to Point Lookout, Md., thence to Fort Delaware, to Charleston Harbor, to Fort Pulaski, paroled June 1, 1865—one of the immortal Six Hundred—under fire at Morris Island
Marion Clingenpeel	4th Sergeant
Nathaniel Akers	2nd Corporal
Benjamin Tice	1st Corporal. Mortally wounded at Chancellorsville, May 2, 1862
James R. Tice	3rd Corporal
John H. Conner	4th Corporal

PRIVATES

Jonathan Akers — Wounded at Dinwiddie C. H., captured and taken to Point Lookout, paroled June 12, 1865

George W. Akers

Meredith Aldridge

Stanton Aldridge

William P. Argabright — Died, time and place unknown

William D. Argabright

Elisha Argabright — Killed in battle, time and place unknown

Samuel Argabright

Levi Atkinson

Cyrus Able

Buford Able

John A. Barringer

Robert Brogan

Creed Brogan — Wounded and captured July 2, 1863, at Gettysburg

Jackson Brogan — Wounded, time and place unknown

Cornelius Boothe — Captured at Chancellorsville, May, 1863, died at Elmira, N.Y., 1864

Asa E. Boyd — Captured, time unknown, taken to Point Lookout, thence to Fort Delaware, thence to Elmira, N.Y.

Abram Beckleheimer

William Beckleheimer

James N. Clark — Wounded, time and place unknown

Edward J. Clark

Braxton Clark — Wounded at Bethseda Church, June 2, 1864

Dr. William Campbell — Wounded March 27, 1863

Charles W. Coon — Died May 8, at Greenbrier White, buried in Floyd

William T. Collins

Cary Crawford

Daniel Conner — Wounded and died at Caroline C. H., March, 1863

Nathan F. Conner

Asa H. Cannaday

Alonzo DeWese — Killed at Sharpsburg, September 17, 1862

Moyer C. DeWese

John Davis — Killed, place and time unknown

Andrew Gearhart

Daniel Gearhart — Killed August 9, 1862 at Cedar Run

Wiley Guthrie — Wounded, time and place unknown. Captured, imprisoned Elmira, N.Y. Was color bearer of brigade of skirmishers and scouts

Washington Gearhart

Peter Goad

Joseph V. Graham — Wounded, time and place unknown

Harvey Gray — Wounded, time and place not known

Jebu L. Greer

Jackson Gallaspie

Wiley Gallaspie

Joseph E. Gallaspie — Wounded and captured at Cedar Run, August 9, 1862. Paroled at Elmira, N.Y., 1865

Augustus Horn — Wounded and captured, taken to Point Lookout, to Fort Delaware, to Elmira, N.Y., and died

James H. Hamilton — Wounded December 13, 1862, at Fredericksburg, killed May 12, 1864, at Spottsylvania C. H.

John W. Howell

Harvey Hylton

Jeremiah Hylton — Died, time and place unknown

Charles D. Hall — Wounded August 9, 1862, at Cedar Run

John F. Helm

James B. Hutchinson — Killed at Gettysburg, July 2, 1863

Phillip Harris

Charles M. Holt

Alexander S. Humphries

Robert Jackson — Wounded several times, lost arm at Fort Steadman May 25, 1865, and discharged at Petersburg July 8, 1865. Was brigade skirmisher

Isaac Jackson — Captured time and place unknown, taken to Point Lookout, to Fort Delaware, to Elmira, N.Y., paroled May 16, 1865

James H. Jackson — Captured at Cedar Creek, October 19, 1864, never returned, supposed to have died in prison

Isham Jones — Killed at Shepherdstown, August 25, 1864

Shelor **Jones**
Robert W. Kropff
John H. Kennett — Wounded December 13, 1862, at Fredericksburg, captured and paroled from prison

James M. Kennett — Wounded and captured, time unknown, taken to Point Lookout, Fort Delaware, Elimra, N.Y., and died

John T. King
James A. King
Thomas King
George S. King
Reuben King
Micheal King
Micheal O. King
Richard Lovell
John W. Light
David Likens
Philip Likens — Killed May 9, 1863, at Chancellorsville

James Mannon — Wounded time and place unknown
William Manning — Wounded time and place unknown, taken to Point Lookout, Fort Delaware, Elmira, N.Y., paroled and discharged

Henry A. Moore — Wounded, time and place unknown
German Martin — Killed May 12, 1864, at Spottsylvania C. H.

William J. C. Munsey
Elijah Munsey
James H. Munsey
John Merritt
Jesse Otey — Wounded, time and place unknown
William B. Otey — Killed August 9, 1862, at Cedar Run
John Price
Peter H. Poff
Columbus W. Paul — Wounded, captured time and place unknown, and discharged from prison

Charles W. Paul
Aaron Phillips — Wounded May 25, 1862, at Winchester, Va., captured May 3, 1864, at Spottsylvania, taken to Point Lookout, discharged after surrender

Hezakiah Paul
James H. Payne   Killed at Kernstown, May 23, 1862
Otey T. Reed   Wounded May 23, 1862, at Kernstown

John Reed
Micheal Reed
Calvin C. Rakes   Wounded, time and place unknown
John Rakes
Hamilton Richards   Killed August 9, 1862, at Cedar Run
Robert E. Richards
Christopher Richards   Wounded, time and place unknown
William Richards   Died, time and place not known
Samuel Richards
Samuel R. Richards   Wounded, time and place not known
John Ridgeway
Aaron Sumner
Jonathan L. Smith   Wounded and died, time and place not remembered

Thomas Smith   Wounded and died, time and place not remembered

John Smith
John A. Smith
William P. Smith
William R. Smith
John L. Shillings
Aaron Shillings
Jeremiah Shillings   Wounded August 9, 1862, at Cedar Run, captured, taken to Washington, exchanged in 3 weeks, wounded at Chancellorsville 1863, wound- at Winchester 1864

Demoss K. Shillings   Died, time and place not remembered
James D. Shillings

Dr. John D. Stuart
James E. Sowers
James B. Stump
George T. Stump
Austin Shank   Wounded August 31, 1862, July 2, 1863, October 19, 1864 at Cedar Creek

William Sowder   Captured at Fort Stedman, March 25, 1865, taken to Point Lookout, discharged from prison in 2 months

Louis H. Thurman

William A. Thompson — Wounded September 17, 1863, at Sharpsburg, Md., captured and taken to prison

Joshua Thompson — Died at Greenbrier Bridge in November, 1861

John Thompson — Captured at Fort Stedman May 25, 1865, in prison 2 months

Bailey Thomas

Jesse Underwood — Died, time and place not remembered

Charles Vest

Joseph H. Wilson — Wounded and captured, time not remembered, died in prison at Elmira, N.Y.

Cary D. Wilson

Ambrose Weaver

Jacob Q. Weddle

James R. Whitenack — Wounded May 2, 1863, at Chancellorsville. Had a fragment of shell taken from his side weighing 12 ounces

William H. Whitenack — Wounded at Kernstown, May 23, 1862

Cephas L. Walton

Bolling G. Winfrey

Thomas E. Willis

Thomas Wimmer

Total   149

COMPANY A. 54th VIRGINIA
OFFICERS

Andrew Dickerson — Captain

Thomas P. Dobyns — 1st Lieutenant, elected captain of new organization. Killed at Blackwater in Virginia, 1863

Early Dickerson — 2nd Lieutenant

James F. Sowers — 3rd Lieutenant

D. W. Sowers — Orderly Sergeant. Was promoted to Captain

W. A. Lee — 2nd Sergeant. Promoted to 3rd Lieutenant

George Hungate — 3rd Sergeant. Wounded at Reseca, Ga., May, 1864

William M. Dickerson	4th Sergeant
Harvey Dickerson	1st Corporal. Wounded at Chickamauga, 1863, captured at Peach Tree Creek, July 22, 1864, taken to Camp Douglas. Discharged June 15, 1865
Abram Watkins	2nd Corporal. Killed at Bentonsville
Joseph Sumpter	3rd Corporal. Wounded at Missionary Ridge, June 23, 1863
Andy R. Wickham	4th Corporal. Wounded at Resaca, May 14, 1864. Captured and taken to Fort Douglas
Robert Hammit	Made captain, killed at Resaca, May 15, 1864

PRIVATES

W. H. Anderson	Died at Russell Court House, 1862
Charles Bradbury	Died, time and place unknown
James Bradbury	
Asa D. Burnett	Died at Christiansburg
T. C. Brammer	
George Bradbury	
James S. Black	Wounded on retreat at Tallahoma, sent to Camp Douglas
B. P. Bolen	Killed at Resaca, May 15, 1864
J. Mat Burton	
Wiley M. Boothe	Died in Georgia
Joshua M. Bishop	
W. J. Beckleheimer	
J. Floyd Caldwell	Captured at Peach Tree Creek, taken to Camp Douglas
Solomon Cronk	
William L. Clowers	
Andrew Dickerson, Jr.	Died in Georgia
George Riley Dickerson	Wounded June 22, 1864, at Mt. Zion, Ga.
Elijah Dickerson	Killed at Mt. Zion June, 1864
DeWit Dickerson	Captured at Peach Tree Creek, taken to Camp Douglas
Amos Dickerson	Drummer
John Dickerson, Jr.	Died in Georgia
Riley Dickerson, Sr.	
Burdine Dickerson	Promoted to captain, captured at Peach Tree Creek, July 23, 1864, taken to Sandy Hook
Isaac N. Epperly	

C. M. Epperly	Wounded, time and place not remembered
James Epperly	Drummer
William M. Epperly	
Henry Epperly	
Job Epperly	
Allen Epperly	
Calvin Epperly	
Jacob Fisher	Wounded, time and place unknown
Alexander Graham	
G. W. Gillenwaters	
Joel Harris	
Henderson H. Hylton	
Ananias Hylton	Captured at Peach Tree Creek, July 23, 1864, taken to Camp Douglas, Ohio, and died
John Holt	
Charles M. Holt	
Sparrel Holt	
Walter Holt	
Cornelius Hale	
Ira Hall	
James D. Iddings	Captured time and place not remembered
Fleming Janney	Lost an arm at Resaca, May 15, 1864
William H. King	Died, time and place not remembered
H. B. Moricle	Captured at Resaca, Ga., May 15, 1864
W. H. Kingrea	
Austin Lester	
Hornbarger Lester	
Caleb Lovell	
Henry F. Mitchell	
John W. Mitchell	
Sam C. Mitchell	
Charles Mitchell	
Sylvester Mills	
Crawford Moran	Lost arm at Marietta, June 23, 1864
Daniel O'Mara	
Charles M. Pugh	Captured at Blackwater, Va., June, 1863
Fleming H. Poff	Captured Peach Tree Creek, June 23, 1864, taken to Camp Douglas, Ohio, paroled June 10, 1865
Samuel R. Palmer	

Crockett Peterman
George Peterman   Died at Christiansburg, Va., in 1861
Floyd Roop
William Roop   Killed at Chickamauga, September 16, 1863

Henderson Roop   Died, time and place unknown
Giles H. Roop   Died, time and place unknown
J. A. Ratliff   Killed at Jonesboro, Ga.
John P. Ratliff   Died at Prestonsburg, Ky.
William Richards
Daniel R. Simmons   Captured July 20, 1864, near Atlanta, taken to Camp Douglas, paroled June 16, 1865

Tazewell Simmons   Died at home
James A. Simmons   Captured at Bentonville, N.C., taken to prison at Rock Island, June 10, 1865

Gideon Simmons
William Simmons
J. H. Sumner
Asa Sowers
William Sowers
William S. Sowers
Harvey D. Sowers
Asa D. Shortt   Captured at Missionary Ridge November 24, 1863, taken to Rock Island, Ill., paroled February, 1865

John P. Shortt   Captured at Missionary Ridge November 24, 1863, paroled after the war

Ira H. Shortt   Died at home
Harvey D. Spangler   Lost a leg at Mt. Zion, June 25, 1864
    Time and place not remembered when killed

Issac Spangler

Samuel Spangler
John H. Spangler
William T. Spangler
David Spangler
Baxter Simpkins
H. B. Showalter
Joseph Showalters
William Showalters
Shelburne A. Smith

Joshua Sumner
Asa Sumpter
Charles Thomas   Wounded at Resaca, Ga., May 16,
                                  1864
James J. Thomas   Died, time and place not remem-
                                  bered
Fleming Thomas   Died at Christiansburg, 1864
Archabald Thompson
Charlton Thompson   Wounded at Resaca, Ga., May 16,
W. A. Thompson   1864
John L. Teel
W. C. Turpin
William H. Vansel
Thomas B. Wingfield
David Williams   Wounded at Bentonville, March 19,
                                  1865
George M. D. Williams
B. O. Wickham
Joseph Wickham
Sylvatus Wickham   Died in Kentucky
Matthew Williams   Died in Rome, Ga.
Reuben Wickham   Died in Floyd County
Alfred Whitlock   Captured, taken to Fort Douglas and
                                  died
Lemuel R. Wickham
Daniel Winter
Louis S. Weeks
John P. Winter
General Weeks
Louis U. Weeks
James R. Weeks
Abram Woolwine
Matthew Woolwine
Marvel Young
James H. Young
Andrew L. Young   Wounded in Georgia
James A. Yearout

                                  Total   138

                COMPANY B., 54th REGIMENT INFANTRY

                      Officers Rank—1861

Jackson Godbey   Captain
William Campbell   1st Lieutenant

A. O. Dobyns	2nd Lieutenant
Allen F. Howery	3rd Lieutenant
James W. Silvers	1st Sergeant
James M. Boyd	2nd Sergeant
P. T. Howell	3rd Sergeant
J. W. Tice	4th Sergeant. Wounded at Missionary Ridge, Nov. 25, '63.
Fleming R. Quesenberry	1st Corporal. Died, date not known.
James M. Cassell	2nd Corporal. Captured at Bentonsville, N. C. Mar. 19, '65.
Tobias Phillips	3rd Corporal. Captured at Missionary Ridge, Mar. 25, '63.
W. H. H. Cassell	4th Corporal. Captured at Bentonsville, N. C. Mar. 19, '65.

Officers Rank—1862

A. O. Dobyns	Captain.
J. M. Boyd	1st Lieutenant, promoted to Captain
Allen F. Howery	2nd Lieutenant
James W. Silvers	3rd Lieutenant. Killed at Bentonsville, N. C. March 19, 1865
P. T. Howell	1st Sergeant, promoted to 3rd and 2nd Lieutenant
W. H. Manning	2nd Sergeant Color Bearer. Killed at Bentonsville, N. C. March 19, 1865
Tobias Phillips	3rd Sergeant. Captured at Missionary Ridge, March 19, 1865
J. W. Tice	4th Sergeant.
Fleming R. Quesenberry	1st Corporal
Hiram Cox	2nd Corporal
H. D. Carter	3rd Corporal. Wounded at Chickamauga, Sept. 19, 1863
G. A. Slusher	4th Corporal

PRIVATES

A. G. Austin	
James G. Alley	
Michael Akers	
James Boyd	
William H. Bartlett	Killed at Resaca while carrying colors Sept., 1863
William H. Bolt	
George R. Bartlett	
Robert C. Beasley	
Thomas L. Blackwell	

A. G. Blackwell
Barney Bolen
Benj. Boone
C. H. Boyd   Died, time and place unknown
Henderson Beckleheimer
Wesley Bishop
Frazier Carter
Jonathan Conner
Harvey Cropp
Jacob R. Conner
Luke Cox   Killed at Chickamauga, Sept., 1863
Maston Cox   Captured at Bentonsville, N. C., May
                                 19, 1865

Jackson Cox
Braxton Cox   Died at Petersburg, Va., date un-
                                 known

Daniel Correll
Francis Collins
David Collins
John Campbell   Died, date and place not known
John J. DeHart   Captured. time and place not known
Henry M. Duncan
Floyd Epperly
David H. Duncan
Alexander Gardner
C. W. Gardner
Jeremiah Goad
Timothy Goad
Samuel Gallimore
Oliver Hurmegan
Samuel Harris   Wounded in Georgia, time not known
Thomas Board   Died at Tazewell C. H., time unknown
M. L. D. Haynes   Captured, time and place not known,
                                 and taken to Rock Island, Ill.

B. T. Howell
Joseph Harris   Wounded in Georgia, time not known
John Hewitt   Wounded at Missionary Ridge, Nov.
                                 25, 1863
W. B. Howell   Wounded at Jonesboro in spring of
                                 1863

Jas. P. Howery
Iriah Haley
James E. Hale
William H. Jackson
Jesse D. Janney
William H. King

Solomon Kennett — Died at Petersburg, Va., in 1863

Samuel Light

Abner Lester — Died in hospital at Abingdon, Va. in 1862

Lindsay Lester
Cannaday Light
Lewis Lester
Harrison Lester
Lynch S. Lester
Moore Martin
John O. Mitchell
Wm. F. Mitchell
Josephus Mitchell
Jas. W. Murphy
J. N. Nester
Bryant Phillips
James Phillips
Enoch Phillips — Died at Bentonsville, N. C., May 19, 1865, taken to Point Lookout, Md., paroled June 16, 1865

John Phillips
Preston Phillips
Mahlon Phillips
Robert Phillips
Tobias D. Phillips
Noah Phillips
Flemon Phillips — Died, time and place unknown
James P. Phillips
Randolph Phillips
Lewis Poff
Peter R. Poff
Thomas Board — Died at Tazewell C.H., time unknown

Lloyd Quesenberry — Killed at Bentonsville, N. C., March 19, 1865

Milton Quesenberry
Frederick Quesenberry
Noah Quesenberry
William Quesenberry
Wesley G. Quesenberry — Killed at Chickamauga, Sept., 1863
Crocket Quesenberry
Stephen Richards
Fleming Richards
Wilkins P. Ray
Jacob Slusher
John Sumner

Wiley Sumner
Isaiah Spence
Wesley Sumner
Benjamin Turman   Wounded at Resaca, Ga., May 15, 1864

Mahlon Turman   Died, time and place not known
Jacob Turman
Peter R. Vest
Weaver Josepah
Wilson A. Weaver
George W. Weaver
Harvey Wilson
Isaac Whitlock
Elenas Whitlock
Joseph H. Whitlock
Eli M. Williams
Addison Whitaker
George W. Whitlock   Wounded, time and place not known
J. M. Webb
James B. Whitlow   Mortally wounded at Mt. Zion church, June 22, 1864

Benjamin Weddle
John M. Wright

Commissioned officers	4
Non-Commissioned officers	8
Privates	110
Total	122

COMPANY D. 54th VA. INFANTRY
OFFICERS

Henry Slusher   Captain
Austin Harman   1st Lieutenant, elected Captain and promoted Major, wounded at Mt. Zion Church, June 25, 1864

Jonas Harman   2nd Lieutenant
Samuel Slusher   3rd Lieutenant
Jabez Harman   1st Sergeant
John Harter   2nd Sergeant. Wounded at Chickamauga, Sept. 22, 1863

Philip Guthrie   3rd Sergeant
Eli Wade   4th Sergeant
S. P. Weddle   1st Corporal. Made sergeant and promoted to Lieutenant

Bennet Willis	2nd Corporal. Died at Dalton, Ga., date unknown
Allen Weddle	3rd Corporal
G. B. Sowers	4th Corporal

PRIVATES

Thomas Alderman	
Asa Boothe	Elected 1st Lieutenant, promoted Captain
W. T. Boyd	
N. G. Bolen	
John C. Burnett	
S. J. Burnett	
J. B. Burnett	
W. H. C. Burnett	
John A. Barringer	
William J. Caldwell	
Samuel Chafin	
Buck Clements	
Eli Cronk	Died, time and place not known
Griffith Dickerson	
Calvin DeLong	
Crockett Duncan	
Joel Duncan	
Henry Dick	
Thomas Dick	
J. Akin Epperly	
Ira Earles	
James H. Guthrie	
Francis Harter	Died at Knoxville, Tenn., time unknown
Samuel Harter	
George W. Harman	
Lana N. Harman	
Eli W. Harman	Killed at Missionary Ridge, Nov. 25, 1863
Christopher Harman	
Peter Harman	
Joseph Helms	
George W. Helms	
Peter Helms	Died in Lexington, Ky., in 1862
Bethiel Hylton	
F. M. Hylton	
Ira Hylton	
Erastus Hylton	
Dennis Hylton	

Clayborne Hylton
William A. Hylton
L. J. Hylton
William A. Hylton   2nd Corporal first year of war
Hiram Hylton
Lewis Hylton
Lankford Hylton
Joshua Hylton
Chesley Hylton   Wounded at Chicamauga, Sept. 30, 1963, captured at Muffresboro, Tenn., taken to Columbus, Ohio, 17 months.

Ira S. Hylton
L. D. Hylton   Promoted 1st Lieutenant, wounded at Missionary Ridge, and died, Nov. 25, 1963.

John W. Hylton
T. W. Hylton
Zackariah Hylton
James G. Harris
Abram Harris
Elijah Harris
William Ivey
Benjamin Keith   Died at Castle Wood, Va., in 1863
William J. Keith
Daniel Keith
John F. Keith
James Keith
William Keith   Captured at Lafayettesville, Ky., paroled Nov. 1, 1962

Zebrum Keith
James K. Lovell
Alfred McDaniel
Henry H. McPeak
Claiborne McPeak
Benjamin McPeak
Hezakiah McPeak
Jonathan McPeak   Promoted Sergeant
Fleming Moles
Isaac W. O'Neal
Silas Pratt   Died at Prestonsburg, Ky., date not known
James Pratt   Died in Georgia, date not known
Jesse Pratt
S. P. Phlegar
Gideon Phlegar   Killed at Mt. Zion church, June 22, 1864

E. M. Phlegar	Died at White Sulphur Springs, Va., date unknown
Harvey Phlegar	Died at home during the war
William Quesenberry	
Lewis Quesenberry	
Nathaniel Quesenberry	Wounded at Mt. Zion church, June 25, 1864, died, time and place not known
Archibald Quesenberry	
Preston Quesenberry	
Frederick Quesenberry	
James Quesenberry	Wounded at Stony Side, time not known
John Quesenberry	
George W. Slusher	Died, time and place not known
John Sowers	
Henderson Sutphin	
Rolen Sutphin	
Hendrick Sutphin	
John H. Sutphin	
Lafayette Sutphin	
Harrison Sutphin	
Asa L. Sutphin	Died at home during the war
H. H. Thomas	
Joseph Turman	
James M. Tatum	
David Willis	Promoted 3rd Lieutenant, wounded at Mt. Zion Church, June 22d, 1863
Thomas Willis	Died, time and place unknown
S. Peter Willis	
Andrew Weddle	
Elijah Weddle	
Harvey Weddle	
Alex Weddle	
Ira Weddle	
Caleb Weddle	
Joshua Weddle	
John Weeks	
P. A. Weeks	Wounded at Bentonsville, N.C., May 19, 1865
Washington Weeks	
Archibald Weeks	Died, time and place unknown
Augustus Weeks	Died, time and place unknown
F. M. Weeks	
Elijah Weeks	

434

Foster J. Woods

Commissioned officers	4
Non-Commissioned officers	8
Privates	117
Total	129

COMPANY H. 54th VA. INFANTRY
OFFICERS

Rank—1861

S. H. Griffith	Captain
Peter L. Howard	1st Lieutenant
William A. Cannaday	2nd Lieutenant
Thomas H. Mosley	3rd Lieutenant

Rank—1862

Joseph Scales	Captain
James Scales	1st Lieutenant, promoted to Captain
L. A. Buckingham	2nd Lieutenant
John H. King	3rd Lieutenant
Joseph Mosley	Orderly Sergeant
Wright Boothe	2nd Orderly Sergeant
Joseph Young	3rd Orderly Sergeant, killed May 15, 1864. at Resaca, Ga.
James H. Black	4th Orderly Sergeant, wounded May 15, 1864, at Resaca, Ga.
James L. Kelly	1st Corporal
Benjamin Bickett	2nd Corporal
Joseph Green	3rd Corporal
James Newberry	

PRIVATES

John Black	Wounded at Resaca, Ga., May 15, 1864, captured at Mt. Hope Church, date not known
Hyrum Boyd	
Washington Boyd	
Pleasant Cole	
Bird Cole	Died at White Sulphur Springs, date unknown
S. S. Collins	

A. R. Collins
F. P. Flene
William Graham
Nath. Gillenwaters
Caleb Howery
J. H. Huff
F. Huff
Isaac Howery   Captured at Franklin, Tenn., date unknown

Harden R. Hall
A. P. Hodges
P. Hash
Jas. O. Galaspie
William Gallaspie   Died in Kentucky, date unknown
Burwell Janney
Fleming Janney, Sr.
John W. Janney
Moses N. Janney   Wounded at Missionary Ridge, Nov. 25, 1863

Jesse Janney
Robert P. Janney
Walker W. Jones
William King
Landon T. Jones
Isaac King
Moses G. Kelly   Captured at Franklin, Tenn., date unknown

Jacob O. Kinzie
William D. Kelly   Captured at Franklin, Tenn., date unknown

W. T. Lawrence
William Likens
William Lemons   Died, time and place unknown
Richard Leffew
James B. Munsey
William Mosley
Reuben McDaniel
Lucian McDaniel
Harvey McDaniel
John McDaniel
James McDaniel
John Newberry
Flem Pugh, Sr.
Flem Pugh, Jr.
Elisha Proffit
James T. Radford

John F. Redmon	Died at Rocky Gap, Va., time unknown
Charles Rakes	
Benjamin Sweeney	
N. J. Shortt	
Harvey Shively	
John Turner	
Jordan Thomas	Died at Russell Old C. H. in 1863
Charles Turner	
Jefferson Turner	Died at Abingdon, Va., 1862
James Turner	
A. J. Thomas	
Charlie Thomas	
John Underwood	
Richard Underwood	
Larkin Via	
Josiah Via	
Joseph Via	
George Whorley	Killed at Missionary Ridge, date not known
Isaiah Whorley	
Frederick Wood	
Burdine Wood	
Joshua B. Young	Killed at Resaca, Ga., May 15, 1864

1861—Commissioned officers	4
1862—Commissioned officers	4
Non-Commissioned officers	8
Privates	71
Total	87

COMPANY I, 54th VIRGINIA INFANTRY
OFFICERS

Rank—1861

Burwell Akers	Captain
Philip Shoemaker	1st Lieutenant
George Kefauver	2nd Lieutenant
Henry L. Smith	3rd Lieutenant
T. H. Howard	1st Sergeant

Rank—1862

J. R. Hammet	Captain. Wounded at Chickamuaga, Sept., 1863

Philip Shoemaker	1st Lieutenant
H. L. Smith	5th Lieutenant
T. R. Hall	3rd Lieutenant
Caanan Lawrence	Promoted 1st Sergeant

PRIVATES

William Aldridge	
Samuel Anglin	Died, time and place not known
Solomon Akers	
David Akers	
Henry Ballinger	Died in Kentucky, time and place not known
Joseph Ballinger	Died, time and place not known
Lewis Bell	
Jacob Boyd	
Nathaniel Basham	Died in Rome, Ga., 1864
Jas. W. Basham	
H. P. Burgess	
Joseph H. Carr	
Joseph Carter	
Thomas Carter	Died at Princeton, W. Va., date not remembered
Jesse G. Carter	Wounded, time and place not known
Chas. H. Craghead	
Robert Craghead	
Lewis Craghead	
William T. Craghead	
Samuel R. Conner	
David R. Conner	
W. M. Conner	
William Conner	
W. T. Clowers	
Jacob Clowers	Died in Georgia in 1864
Daniel Clowers	
J. T. Clowers	Promoted Sergeant
Samuel Cooper	
Pleasant Cole	
John Cunningham	
William Cunningham	Captured at Bentonsville, N.C., March, 1865
John Earles	
A. J. Earles	
Calvin Epperly	
Micheal Edwards	Killed at Resaca, Ga., May 15, 1864
Benjamin Edwards	
James Edwards	Wounded in Georgia in 1864

William Farris
John F. Furrow   Killed at Resaca, Ga., May 15, 1864
Harvey Gearhart
Thomas W. Gleason
James M. Gray
Joseph M. Gray
A. J. Hoback   Promoted Sergeant
C. M. Hoback
James Henderson
Peter Huff
Isaac Huff   Captured, time and place not known,
                                 taken to Rock Island, Ill.

Thomas Hurd
Osborne Hutcherson
Ira Hall
J. J. Hall   Killed at Chickamauga, Sept. 20, 1864
Jacob P. Helms
Henry B. Iddings   Captured, time and place not known
John Janney
James Jarrett
John King   Killed in 1864 at Marietta, Ga.
James M. King
Monroe King
George King
Robert L. Kennett
John A. Kitterman   Captured at Resaca, Ga., May 15,
                                 1864

Ruffner Kennecay
George W. Kenneday
William A. Lovins
Thomas Lucas
James G. Lester
William S. Lester
James Light
Wilson F. Light   Died at Rocky Gap, Va., date not
                                 known

Simon Light
James Likens
David Lovell
William B. Lawrence   Died at Mt. Sterling, Ky., date not
                                 known

James E. Lawrence
Isaac B. Lawrence
John W. Lee
Samuel A. Lee   Died at Emory & Henry College,
                                 date unknown

German B. Lee
Granville Leftwich   Wounded at Atlanta, Ga., Aug. 18, 1864

Caleb Maxey
Chas. Manning
Isaac Martin   Wounded at Atlanta, Ga., Aug. 18, 1864

Thomas L. Nixon
Samuel J. Owens
I. M. Overstreet
Andrew Poff
John Poff   Captured, date and place not known
Joseph Palmer
Solomon Palmer
Charles Reed
Jacob W. Rutrough   Captured at Bentonsville, N.C., May, 1865

Humphrey Reed
Bird Richardson
John Ratliff
Peyton G. Richardson
Tazewell Ratliff
George Ratliff   Wounded in Georgia, time not known
Major Sowers
Henry T. Stump
Eli Smith   Wounded at Resaca, Ga., May 15, 1864

Fleming Smith   Wounded at Mt. Zion, June 25, 1864
James M. Sisson
David Sisson
Daniel Spangler
Fowell Simpson
G. W. Simpson
Harvey D. Simmons
Erasmus Simmons   Fifer
G. W. Simmons
George Siner   Killed at Resaca, May 15, 1864
William Siner
Giles R. Shanks
W. B. Shelor   Lieutenant-Colonel, 54th Va.
Joseph Turner
Stephen Turner
W. E. Tice   Promoted Orderly Sergeant
Llody Thompson
John Thomas   Mortally wounded at Resaca, Ga., May 15, 1864

Joseph Thomas	
William Trusler	Died, time and place not known
Smith Via	Killed at Chickamauga, Sept. 20, 1863
George W. Via	
William Via	Wounded on picket, time and place unknown
James M. Vest	Wounded at Chickamauga, Sept. 20, 1863
Charles D. Vest	Wounded at Marietta, time unknown
John E. Vest	
Valentine Wilson	
Peter R. Wilson	
Jonas Wilson	
James Wilson	
John T. Wilson	
Laban Wilson	
Fleming Wimmer	
John A. Wimmer	
George Winfrey	
Giles Wingrey	
George Whitlock	
Phalus Wingfield	
Jesse L. Walton	
James W. Walton	
James P. Wood	
John Walters	
Philip Walters	
Peter Walters	
J. A. Whitenack	

Rank—1861

| Commissioned officers | 4 |
| Non-Commissioned officers | 1 |

Rank—1862

Commissioned officers	4
Non-Commissioned officers	1
Privates	144
	154

COMPANY G. 21st VIRGINIA CAVALRY

OFFICERS

| A. O. Dobyns | Captain. Wounded at Leetown and near Petersburg |
| L. V. Edwards | 1st Lieutenant. Wounded at Leetown |

Aaron Kitterman — 2nd Lieutenant. Wounded at Bunker's Hill, captured Nov. 12, 1864, taken to Fort Delaware

Tazewell Helms — 3rd Lieutenant. Wounded at Berryville

John S. Woods — 1st Sergeant. Captured at Morefield, W.Va., taken to Camp Chase, Ohio

M. T. Lawson — 2nd Sergeant

S. F. Dobyns — 3rd Sergeant

Early Dickerson — 4th Sergeant

A. O. McCandless — 1st Corporal

Wm. I. Howard — 2nd Corporal

James Harman — 3rd Corporal, captured and imprisoned at Fort Douglas

Fleming Price — 4th Corporal, captured and died in prison at Camp Chase

PRIVATES

N. J. Agnew — Captured September 22, 1864, imprisoned at Point Lookout

W. O. Angel — Captured near Lynchburg, imprisoned at Camp Chase

W. J. Akers

A. S. Akers

A. B. Akers

J. L. Abshire

W. T. Allen — Captured and died in prison at Camp Chase

J. T. Adams — Captured Nov. 12, 1864, after being wounded, and imprisoned at Point Lookout

John Agee — Captured Nov. 12, 1864, after being wounded and imprisoned at Point Lookout

J. L. Aldridge

Lee Belile

W. R. Bowers — Color bearer for General B. T. Johnson

A. V. Burnett — Wounded at Leetown, June 3, 1864

William B. Boothe — Captured and died in prison at Camp Chase

Jeremiah Barber

Abner Beckner — Wounded and captured Nov. 12, 1864

George H. Boone

Howard Bennett	Captured Nov. 12, 1864, and imprisoned at Point Lookout
Burdine Bishop	Dispatch bearer for General B. T. Johnson
A. J. Bowles	
J. J. Barton	
Jackson Bryant	
S. H. Cannaday	Promoted to Sergeant
E. I. Cannaday	
Creed Conner	Died, date and place unknown
J. P. David	Captured and imprisoned at Camp Chase
Floyd Dickerson	
Wm. D. Dillon	Captured and died in prison at Camp Chase
Jackson L. Dillon	Captured and imprisoned at Point Lookout
Martin East	
William S. Epperly	
A. P. Ferguson	Captured and died in prison at Camp Chase
William Ferguson	
George H. Gregory	Captured 22nd September, 1864, imprisoned at Point Lookout
E. W. Graham	
J. R. Gilbert	
J. W. Helm	Promoted to Sergeant
E. S. Harman	Wounded Nov. 12, 1864, left on battlefield, thought to be dead. Shot through and hacked over head with sabre, but recovered
David Hale	Captured and imprisoned at Point Lookout
Thomas Howell	Captured and imprisoned at Camp Chase
L. S. Heckman	
William Hagwood	Wounded and captured Nov. 12, 1864, and imprisoned at Point Lookout
T. J. Hippinstall	
E. J. Harbor	
Zack Harber	
Ferd Hoback	Wounded Nov. 12, 1864, and left on battlefield for dead, but recovered
William Hawley	Captured, but do not know where imprisoned
Caleb Howery	
Griff Hill	

Ira Hurd	Died, time and place unknown
J. P. Halsey	Died, time and place unknown
V. S. Haynes	Died in prison at Point Lookout
German Hollingsworth	
John Jones	
Shelor Jones	
W. B. Jones	
John Jamison	Captured and died in prison at Camp Chase
Jacob Jamison	Wounded near Winchester
Thomas Jamison	
Burwell Janney	Died, time and place unknown
L. G. Joyce	Promoted Corporal, then to Color bearer
Joseph Kitterman	Killed at Lynchburg, June 17, 1864
William Lawson	
J. Lackey	Captured and died in prison at Camp Chase
R. A. Mitchell	
William A. Mills	Courier for Col. Peters
William R. Mills	
Daniel McAlexander	Wounded Nov. 12, 1864, and imprisoned at Point Lookout
S. A. Morris	
Clary McCandless	
J. J. Moran	
J. J. Martin	
Geo. M. D. Owens	
Mark O'Neal	
Matterson Otey	
Robert Pettit	
L. L. Poff	
Zackariah Peters	Lost a leg at Beam's Station, Tennessee
Philip Prilliman	
F. M. Payne	Killed at Moorefield, W.Va., June 5, 1864
A. G. Pedigo	
William Pilson	
Powhatan Richards	
Jehu M. Ratliff	
Jesse Radford	
Ferdinand Radford	
D. L. Ross	
G. R. Rodgers	
W. S. Sutphin	Transferred to 24th Va. Infantry
Lafayette Slusher	

Peter Spencer

B. F. Smith   Bugler, captured Sept. 22, 1864, and taken to Point Lookout

T. G. Shelor   Captured June 4, 1864, and imprisoned at Point Lookout

W. R. Sowder
F. L. Slusher
Jos. B. Sowers
W. T. Sowers   Courier
D. W. Sowers
William Stoops
Mike Scott   Captured and imprisoned at Camp Chase

A. N. Tice   Courier for Major Halsey
George J. Trail   Wounded Aug. 29, 1864, at Smithfield

John Trent
Thomas F. Trent
William Underwood
M. A. Underwood
Jos. Underwood   Transferred to Co. A. 24th Va. Infantry

James Via
John Via   Killed Sept. 19, 1864 at Winchester
Anderson Via
Walter N. Woodson   Captured No. 12, 1864, and imprisoned at Point Lookout

E. B. Wade
H. S. Wade
W. B. Wells
H. D. Wells   Captured Nov. 12, 1864, and imprisoned at Point Lookout

J. T. Wells   Promoted to Corporal
R. H. Wells
Burwell Wells
J. L. Walker
G. M. Whitlow   Wounded August 29, 1864, at Smithfield

J. T. Weaver
S. P. Weddle
Isaac Young
Anderson Newberry

No. 134

COL. R. L. PRESTON'S RESERVE CORPS

J. B. Headen	Captain
John Thomas	1st Lieutenant
E. W. Graham	2nd Lieutenant
W. T. Lester	3rd Lieutenant
G. H. Ridinger	1st Sergeant
Andrew Dickerson	2nd Sergeant
And. O. Vansel	3rd Sergeant
Jas. G. Butler	4th Sergeant
James Martin	1st Corporal
Wm. I. Gill	2nd Corporal
J. S.Thompson	3rd Corporal
Jacob Alderman	4th Corporal

PRIVATES

Joel R. Agnew
Samuel W. Agnew
George Argabright
W. H. Akers
John Altizer
George Akers
Lewis Bowers
Christopher Bowers
John Bowers
Philip Bowers
John Bryant
Leroy Bartlett
S. G. Conduff
John O. Conner
John A. Conner
G. M. Dobyns
Michael Dickerson
John Dickerson
Henry Epperly
David Epperly
Solomon Epperly
Philip Epperly
Geo. W. Goodson
Esau Gillispie
Wilson Huff
Edward Harrison
Sparrel Holt
S. M. Hylton
M. S. Helms
Samuel M. Helms

Benj. Helms
David Howell
John B. Hylton
Peyton Hudson
Stephen Hill
William R. Holland
Benj. Harman
Henry Harris
Bird Huff
W. Ed. Howery
William Jones
Ben Jones
Abram J. Jones
Burwell Janney
John Janney
Leonard Keith
Levi King
A. J. Kirby
G. Lawrence
Jacob B. Lawrence
William Lawrence
Silas B. Lawrence
Bird Lester
Jacob Moses
David Moore
Robert Moore
Anderson Mills
Elijah Manning
William B. Oaks
W. H. O'Bryan
Isaac Phlegar
E. A. Radford
James Radford
Lewis A. Radford
Samuel Radford
John Stuart
Jacob Sutphin
W. L. Sutphin
Matthew Scott
Peter Siner
O. T. Simmons
Milton W. Sutphin
William Slusher
B. G. Sowers
Jacob Sowers
Joel Sowers

R. D. Sumpter
Chas. L. Simmons
Isaac Smith
David Shirey
Samuel B. Terry
A. J. Terry
Nathaniel Thompson
J. B. Tinsley
James Underwood
John Williams
Hector Williams
J. T. Woodson
John C. Wade
John Walters
Peyton J. Wade
Hiram Walters
W. T. Williams
William Weeks
Benj. Weddle
George Weeks
James Willis
Sebastian Wagell
George Young
John Young
Isaac Young

Officers	4
Officers	8
Privates	103
Total	115

Disbanded by Gen. John Echols at Christiansburg, Va., after Gen. Lee surrendered.

COL. R. L. PRESTON'S RESERVE CORPS

A. J. Graham	Captain
Asbury B. Williams	1st Lieutenant
Jonathan R. Lee	2nd Lieutenant
F. P. Thomas	3rd Lieutenant
John J. Huff	1st Sergeant
John Wilson	2nd Sergeant
Crawford Lemons	3rd Sergeant
J. T. Agee	4th Sergeant
Isaac Poff	1st Corporal
James Siner	2nd Corporal
Samuel Oaks	3rd Corporal
David W. Tice	4th Corporal

PRIVATES

John W. Akers
J. Argabright
James Bryant
Abner Boothe
Albert Cox
J. F. DeHart
Crawford Goodson
Jas. M. Graham
Bethel Harman
Creed Harris
Jerry L. Hale
Ira J. Hatcher
Eli W. Hylton
J. Pled Howard
Geo. M. Ingram
Beverly Johns
B. Johns
Micheal King
Asbury Moricle
W. J. Moore
Samuel H. Metz
Jesse A. Oaks
James K. O'Bryan
Fleming Poff
Moses Peters
George Phlegar
M. T. Phlegar
W. H. Reed
Joshua Radford
Americus Radford
Geo. W. Ratliff
A. A. Sumner
F. M. Sumner
Eden Spangler
Jacob Sutphin
Gideon Sowers
S. T. Turner
Elijah Turner
James Vest
David Wilson
James Weaver
John C. Weddle
Elijah Weddle
Thos. Watkins
I. T. Williams

J. W. Walton
Isaac Young

Officers	12
Privates	46
	58

ROLL OF VETERANS WHO SERVED WITH STUART'S HORSE ARTILLERY

Pelham's Battery

J. W. Altizer
Anderson Alley
Ennis Altizer
Joel C. Anderson
M. Altizer
Staunton Aldridge
Jesse Altizer
W. L. Bird
John L. Burgess   Captured at Woodstock, 9-23-64, taken to Point Lookout and paroled May 12, 1865

Lewis Boothe
Noah R. Boothe
William Brown
Daniel Brown
Thomas Boothe
George Brown   Killed in 7-Days Battle around Richmond

Jacob Boone
H. H. Basham
J. W. Boothe
John Carr
Joseph Carr
William Conner
Jonathan Conner, Sr.
Daniel R. Conner
Albert Conner
William Dulaney
Wyatt Dulaney
Geo. R. Duncan
Addison Epperly
W. H. Epperly
Philip Epperly

James Gray

Thee Gibson

Madison Harman

Robert Huff
Darius W. Howard
Jesse W. Hall
Jacob B. Lawrence
Robert Lancaster
A. W. Lancaster
John H. Link
James Likens
George Mangus
Edward Nolley
Rufus Nolley
Jos. H. Phlegar

Lee Phlegar
Isaac Pugh
J. Pugh
Wm. H. Poff
Isaac Poff
Joshua Poff
Robert Reed
Wm. B. Reed
Isaac E. Robertson
Jesse Robertson
John Reed
A. J. Reed, Sr.
John Reed
Ferdinand Shillings
Valentine Shillings
James F. Shelor
Wm. M. Shelor
Ethelbert Sledd
Roley M. Simmons
L. H. Slusher
Josiah Smith
James W. Smith
Geo. F. Shelton
Henry L. Vest
Jacob Vest
Harvey L. Vest
Washington Vest
John Williams

Captured April 8, 1865, paroled April 15, 1865, at Farmville

Captured and taken to Fort Delaware May 6, 1865

Lost arm at Fredericksburg, Va., Dec. 13, 1862

Jas. R. Williams
John C. Wade
Wm. Watkins
Isaac Wimmer
Burwell Wimmer
Robt. H. Willis
F. A. Winston
Harvey Wimmer
Jacob Wimmer
William Walters   Killed May 3, 1863, at Chancellors-
                           ville
                                  Total   84

COMPANY E 27th BATTALION, Afterwards Changed To 25th VA. REGIMENT

George E. Junkins   Captain
Madison Mayberry
John Mayberry
John W. Lester
Ananias Spangler   Wounded at Smithfield, Va., Aug. 29,
                           1864, captured and taken to Point
                           Lookout, Md.

John T. Conduff
Philip Guthrie
Washington Goodykoontz
Alfred Goodykoontz
L. T. Howell
Henry Harman   Wounded, time and place unknown
Bethel Harman
Jonas Harman   2nd Lieutenant
David Harman
Lewis Hylton
Lafayette Phlegar
S. H. Reeder
Noah Simmons
Obediah Simmons
Joel Shanks   Wounded with sabre, and captured
                           at Moorefield, W.Va., Aug. 5, 1864

Floyd Slusher
Levi Thompson
G. M. Hall
                                  Total   22

COMPANY H 51st VIRGINIA INFANTRY

W. H. Price   Captain

PRIVATES

M. L. Brammer
James M. Hylton
J. B. Hylton
William A. Howell   Captured March 5, 1865, at Waynes-
                         boro, Va., taken to Fort Delaware,
                         patroled in June, 1865

Caleb Howell
Isaac Howell
Abram Hogan   Captured May 2, 1865, taken to Fort
                         Delaware, paroled in June, 1865
Philip Harris   Captured near Shepherdstown, date
                         unknown, paroled June, 1865
Thomas Hungate
Nathaniel Lancaster   Captured May 2, 1865, taken to Fort
                         Delaware, paroled June, 1865
Jacob S. Moore
Naaman Knowles   Captured May 30, 1865, taken to Fort
                         Delaware, paroled June, 1865
Amos Ridinger
Philip Ratliff   Captured May 2, 1865, at Waynes-
                         boro, Va., taken to Fort Delaware,
                         paroled June, 1865
Tazewell E. Sowers   Captured at Waynesboro, Va., taken
                         to Fort Delaware, paroled in June,
                         1865
Flemon Reed   Captured, time and place unknown
John Richardson   Killed at Fayetteville, W.Va., 1862
David A. Sowers
Hulen L. Sowers   Died in hospital at Staunton, Va.,
                         1864
Nathan N. Sumner
George Smith   Captured May 2, 1865, at Waynes-
                         boro, Va., taken to Fort Delaware
                         until June, 1865
Samuel Scott   Captured May 2, 1865, at Waynes-
                         boro, Va., taken to Fort Delaware
                         until June, 1865
Deskins Semones   Captured May 2, 1865, at Waynes-
                         boro, taken to Fort Delaware until
                         June, 1865
John A. Weeks

W. H. Weeks	Wounded at Winchester, Va., August, 1864
Henry Slusher	Captured May 5, 1865, at Waynesboro, taken to Fort Delaware until June, 1865
R. B. Williams	
Thos. P. Young	Captured March 2, 1865, at Waynesboro, paroled in June, 1865, at Fort Delaware
David Zentmeyer	
C. P. Vaughan	Captured at Winchester, Va., Sept. 19, 1864, taken to Point Lookout, paroled after surrender

COMPANY D. 51st VIRGINIA INFANTRY

| M. M. Shortt | Died at home |

COMPANY F 14th VIRGINIA CAVALRY

Bill Smith	Captain
Thos. H. Cannaday	
Jefferson Griffith	
W. A. Griffith	
James Griffith	
William Ingram	
Otey Ingram	
Harrison Thurman	
R. C. M. Thurman	
Isaac P. Williams	

Total   9

CLARK'S BATTALION, 30th VIRGINIA

Daniel Bowers
Lawyer Cox
Samuel Hurd
Cyrus Keith
Joseph Keith
O. P. Slusher
F. M. Slusher
Isaac Vest, Sr.
W. M. Via

Total   9

The following is a list of soldiers who served in various companies, and whose companies were not organized in Floyd County.

L. P. Lancaster	Co. K. 10th Va. Cavalry
Jesse Reed	Co. I, 1st Va. Bat. Infantry
Mathias Manning	Co. I. 1st Va. Bat. Infantry
Floyd Dickerson	Co. K. 50th Va. Infantry
Walter Richards	Co. A. 3rd Tenn. Cavalry
A. J. Stigleman	3rd Ark. Infantry
Woodley Thomas	3rd Ark. Infantry
Beauford Cox	Co. I. 17th Cavalry
H. C. Jones	Co. E. 47th Cavalry
V. G. Paul	Co. H. 42nd Infantry
George Quesenberry	3rd Ark. Infantry
Zack Graham	3rd Ark. Infantry
Sam McDaniel	3rd Ark. Infantry
M. M. Reed	Co. A. 45th W.C.
Eli Sumner	Co. K. 25th Cavalry
Thomas Semones	Edgar's Battalion
Hendrick Sutphin	Co. G. 54th Va. Infantry
Fleming Cole	McCauley's Pioneer Corps
R. Marion Ballinger	45th Virginia Regiment

Total   19

List of Soldiers from Floyd County who served in Confederate service and whose commands are unknown.

John Huff	(Brother of Hiriam)
John Hylton	Preacher
R. H. Anderson	
C. T. Wickham	
Flem Radford	
David - -	
Ira J. Dickerson	
Harvey Cole	
Ira Dickerson	

Total   9

Roll of Capt. D. Lee Ross' Company C. 51st. Va. Regt., Infantry, Capt. W. T. Akers, Co. D. 51st. Regt. Va. Infantry and Capt. R. J. Woolwine, Co. D. 51st. Regt. Va. Infantry.

Capt. Ross commanded this company the first year of the

war, and it was then Co. "C" when the company was reorganized in 1862, W. T. Akers was elected Captain and was then lettered Company D. and remained Co. D. until the end of the war.

D. Lee Ross	Capt. 1st. year of the war.
W. T. Akers	1st. Lieut. 1st. year of the war and elected Capt. in 1862, promoted to Major of the Regt. 1864
A. J. Harbour	2nd. Lieut. 1st. year of the war and did not re-enlist
C. F. Ross	3rd. Lieut. 1st. year of the war and did not re-enlist
J. M. Cruise	1st. Sergt. transferred to Co. H. 51st. Regt.
S. F. Shelor	2nd. Sergt. then promoted to 1st Sergt. Co. D. then to Lieut. Co. D
Isaac A. Nolen	3rd. Sergt. 1st. year of the war and did not re-enlist
W. G. Price	Sergt. 1st. year off the war and then promoted Capt. of Co. H. 51st. Va. Infantry
John E. Lackey	5th. Sergt. Captured and died in prison
Wm. D. Via	1st. Corporal
C. C. Rakes	2nd Corporal
B. R. Hall	3rd. Corporal
R. J. Woolwine	4th Corporal promoted to orderly sergeant in 1861 and elected Lieut. in 1862 and promoted to Capt. in 1864
Akers, John A.	Elected Lieut.
Akers, Nathaniel C.	
Akers, W. Tyler	
Adams, N. P.	
Akers, Isaac N.	
Agee, G. M.	
Agee, John T.	
Akers, Sam'l. R.	Promoted to Sergt.

Anthony, J. V.
Adams, J. I.
Allen, Creed G.
Akers, E. A.
Branch, Joshua
Brammer, Jonathan S.
Burnett, Jeremiah
Balisles, Geo. W.
Burnett, John
Boyd, Isaac
Belcher, Costley
Brammer, M. S.
Belcher, Peter
Belcher, Daniel
Burnett, J. A.   Promoted to Sergt.
Bryant, Alex N.
Bryant, A. J.
Brammer, T. P.
Bradley, M. W.
Bowers, Jacob
Bryant, Wm.
Bowling, John W.
Bowling, Henry T.
Boyd, Sam'l. S.
Boyd, Wm.
Conner, Alexander
Canady, Randolph
Canady, Marshall P.
Canady, Pleasant
Canady, Constant
Clark, J. R.
Clark, Jackson
Cheely, R. G.
Cheely, Graves W.   Promoted to Lieut.
Conner, Geo. W.
Cockram, Charles
Cannaday, S. H.
Carter, Jno. P.   Promoted to Corp.
Cockram, Wm. H.

Corn, Peter
Craddock, James
Cox, Elijah
Cockram, David
DeHart, Pleasant
DeHart, John W.
DeHart, Eli
DeHart, Joseph C.
Dodson, F. W.
DeHart, Eleazer
DeHart, Thos. T.
DeHart, Aaron
DeHart, Robert
Duggins, Edward C.
French, G. C.
Foley, Peyton
Foley, James W.
Farley, C. P.
Foster, Peyton M.
Foley, Reed
Foley, Fleming
Foley, Wm. S.
Griffith, Perry
Graham, James
Griffith, M. H.
Hodges, Robert
Houchins, A. W.
Hubbard, S. W.
Hubbard, Jonathan W.
Hopkins, H. D.
Harriss, W. T.
Harriss, Geo. L.
Hall, David
Holley, James R.
Hall, James F.
Hall, David T.
Hylton, Ira A.
Harbour, J. T.
Harbour, C. J.

Hatcher, Elkanah
Hatcher, Edin T.
Hollensworth, T. L.
Hall, Wm. C.
Hall, John C.
Hall, Jasper R.
Horsley, Rubin C.
Hungate, Thomas
Hubbard, Thos. M.
Hancock, John T.
Hylton, Wm. B.
Holley, David
Harbour, A. J. (Hick)
Hanks, Pugh H.
Janey, John
Jefferson, William
Jefferson, John P.
Justice, John
Keaton, Hiram
Keaton, James M.
Lackey, James M.
Leary, Wm.
Lawson, James M.
Lawson, Lafayette
McAlexander, James
McAlexander, Jeremiah
Martin, Wm. G.
McAlexander, John
Moore, W. T.
McAlexander, Samuel
McAlexander, David
McAlexander, Daniel
McAlexander, Darius
Morrison, David J.
McAlexander, James C.
McGee, John P.
William McGee
McDonald, Hiram F.
Morrison, Thomas C.

Martin, David H.
Morrison, James T.
Martin, Larkin T.
Morrison, John T.
Martin, E. N.
Martin, Crawford
McGee, Green
Moore, Jacob S.
Manan, Wm.
Mize, W. B.
Nolen, C. M.
Nolen, Ephram S.
Nolen, John
Nolen, David
Pendleton, John
Price, B. M.
Roberson, Abram
Ross, James
Ross, Samuel
Roberson, Landon
Ratliff, L. G.
Rorrer, W. R.
Ray, Joseph
Reynolds, Geo. W.
Reynolds, Wm. A.
Ross, Chas. P.
Rakes, John D.
Ross, James W.
Ratliff, Phillip
Rakes, R. R.
Rakes, Alex
Ross, Wm.
Reynolds, Wm.
John T. Ross
Ross, Joseph W.
Rakes, Chas. J.
Rakes, S. J.
Shelton, R. L.
Spencer, James M.

Sowder, Emanuel
Stovall, Quincy A.
Shelor, James F.
Smith, George
Salmons, Jonathan
Shelton, Wm. A.
Smith, C. B.
Salmons, John
Turner, James R.
Turner, E. B.
Thomas, Pleasant
Thomas, W. H.
Thomas, Chas. T.
Thomas, N. A.
Thomas, Lewis T.
Thomas, Tazewell P.
Thomas, Peter J.
Turner, Creed O.
Thomas, J. R.
Turner, Geo. T.
Turner, Bruce L.
Vaughn, C. P.
Vaughn, James P.
Vaughn, E. D.
Vaughn, John J.
Via, D. G.
Via, William C.
Via, James R.
Via, J. E.
Washburn, Jno. T.
Whaling, James
Wood, German
Wood, John
Washington, David
Wood, Richard J.
Wright, C. J.
Willard, James
Wood, Levi
Washburn, J. P.

Young, Pleasant
Zentmeyer, David F.

We hereby certify that the foregoing roster is as near correct as we can make it.

> R. J. Woolwine, Capt. Co. D., 51st. Va. Regt.
> Infy. Wharton's Brigade, Breckenridge Division Early's Corps.
> S. T. Shelor, Lieut. Co. D., 51st. Va. Regt.

Approved
W. T. Akers, Major,
51st. Va. Regt.

A COPY:-

TESTE:

Clerk Circuit Court
J. S. TAYLOR

INCOMPLETE ROSTER OF COMPANY B, 21st VIRGINIA CAVALRY—COMPOSED OF FLOYD AND MONTGOMERY COUNTY MEN

Colonel William E. Peters, Smythe County, Virginia
Lieutenant Col. David Edmondson, Montgomery County
Captain Charles H. Burke, Botetourt County
First Lieutenant Jack Moore, Floyd County
Second Lieutenant J. W. Crockett, Montgomery and Floyd
Third Lieutenant Watt Moore, Floyd County
First Sergeant Jack Akers, Floyd County
Second Sergeant T. T. Turnell, Blacksburg, Montgomery Co.
Third Sergeant Robert Mills, Floyd County
Fourth Sergeant Wilson Howery, Floyd County

Privates

Robert Crockett, Montgomery County
Caleb Maxie, Floyd County
David Likens, Floyd County
M. P. Light, Floyd County
John Mills, Floyd County

John King, Floyd County
Charles Thomas, Floyd County
Robert Linkenhoker, Floyd County
Buck Richards, Floyd County
Thomas Garlic, Montgomery County
Charles Poff, Floyd County
Thomas Hall, Montgomery County
Thomas Sublett, Montgomery County
Larchas Wood, Choctaw Indian Tribe
Berry Vest, Floyd County
John Maddox, Floyd County

A list of Floyd County boys who served in the World War.

Agee, Murray V.   Enlisted in Navy
Agee, Cloyd
Akers, Madison P.
Akers, Howard
Agnew, Calvin W.
Akers, Roy A.
Akers, Waitman J.
Akers, Quinter B.
Akers, Martin McK.
Akers, Harvey E.
Akers, Isaac L.
Akers, Fred
Akers, Andrew J.
Akers, Woodie I.
Alderman, Lank
Alderman, Frederick Lee   Killed in France
Argabright, Fowler H.
Agnew, Benj. Kent
Angle, William Riley
Aldridge, Herman Willard
Ayers, Charley
Austin, George Moses

Board, Alvin Trigg
Barton, Moscoe John   Died in camp
Bower, William Wallace
Bower, Jabe Letcher
Bower, Posy

Barnhart, Courtland
Basham, Amherst S.
Bishop, John S.
Bishop, Staple
Bishop, John Frank
Bishop, James C.
Bolt, Clark G.
Bowman, Peter C.
Bowman, William Henry
Bowman, Carlie D.
Bowman, William F.
Boone, John A.
Boyd, Dewey H.
Burnett, Horace Greeley
Bowman, Charles T.

Claytor, Archa A.   (Colored)
Claytor, William R.   (Colored)
Claytor, Hunter McG.   (Colored)
Conner, John Clarence   (Colored)
Conner, John C.
Conner, William Ira
Conner, Martin T.
Conner, James Robert
Conner, Troy
Conner, Doctor H.
Conner, Curtis
Conner, Ernest V.
Conner, Troy
Conner, John Posy
Conner, Elmer C.

Cox, Warren C.
Cox, Eugene E.
Cox, Walter A.
Cox, Ezra
Cox, James P.
Craghead, Isaac E.
Craghead, Elliott
Conduff, Miles Glen
Clemmons, Amos
Criner, Ray E.
Criner, Everett S.
Carr, Posy Lee
Collins, James

Cannaday, Claude S.
Cannaday, Virgil H.
Cannaday, Arthur   (Colored)
Correll, Ernest
Carr, McKinley
Compton, Buford E.
Cooper, Willie A.   Enlisted in Navy

Dalton, Jet
Dalton, Cosley Hill
Dalton, Ernest V.
Dalton, Ernest
Davis, Fred L.   (Colored)
Dickerson, William Ernest
Dickerson, Dock
Dickerson, Clayton,
Dickerson, George T.
Dickerson, Ollie Brown
Dickerson, Griffith H.
Dickerson, Percy H.
Dickekrson, Emmett
Dickerson, Posy   Died in France
DeHart, Harman J.
Dulaney, Albert M.
Duncan, Walter E.
Duncan, Lewis A.
Dobyns, Joseph F.
Dulaney, Fred William

Edwards, Ellis E.   (Colored)
Epperly, Thos. Leonard
Epperly, Tezzie E.
Epperly, Trigg M.
Epperly, Minnis C.
Emberson, Ophus B.

Finney, Miles G.   (Colored)
Ferris, Posy J.

Goodson, Fred V.
Goad, Lawrence E.
Goad, Maury K.
Goad, Lerty G.
Graham, Charles T.
Gardner, Joseph A.

Hylton, Henry J.
Hylton, Tasker T.   (Colored)

Hylton, Jabe D.
Hylton, Luther G.
Hylton, Cephas A.
Hylton, Simmons
Hylton, Henry Howard
Huff, Thomas F.
Huff, Henry H.
Hale, Herman E.
Hale, Sim
Hatcher, David C.
Hatcher, Wayne F.
Hall, Curtis
Hall, Noah L.
Hall, Leslie W.
Hall, William D.
Harris, Roscoe C.
Harris, Jerry E.
Harris, Lorenza W.
Harris, Isaiah G.
Hawley, Hezzie W.
Houchins, Diamond
Houchins, Elbert   (Colored)
Hopkins, William Harvey
Hopkins, Claude E.
Hayden, William Albert   (Colored)
Harter, Henry Francis   Died in France
Harter, Luther Eldridge   Died in camp
Holt, William B.
Hancock, John Mac
Harman, Waitman
Harman, Pithus J.
Harman, Fonie L.
Harman, Herbert N.
Harman, Dayton F.
Harman, Leonard L.
Harman, Grover C.
Harman, Russell A.   Went to Fort Meyer
Horton, Lewis E.
Hollandsworth, Earley E.
Hollandsworth, James F.
Harvey, Irvin A.
Hurt, Shirley S.
Hungate, Hugh L.
Hungate, Jay Gold
Hill, Willis,
Howard, Glen W.

Howard, William J.
Howard, Joseph   Fort Meyer
Hundley, Willis G.
Hart, James W.

Ingram, William A.
Iddings, George W.
Iddings, Castille B.   Killed in France

Jones, Jessie B.
Jones, George L.
Jones, William Harvey B.
James, Walter
Johnson, Joseph D.   (Colored)
Jett, James William   Enlisted in Navy
Johnson, Hobart

King, Daniel E.
Kenley, Loring R.
Kenley, Grover Cleveland   Killed in France
Keaton, Jesse J.
Knowles, Walter R.   Died in France
Kenley, Joshua C.
Kelly, Joseph Wilson
Kersey, Burnett
Kingrea, Dewey S.
Kingrea, Clayton T.
Keith, Darus R.
Keith, George A.
Keith, Una Ray
Keith, McKinley G.

Link, Hubert
Lovins, William Martin
Lester, Lathie W.
Lester, Zachariah T.
Lawrence, Hubert L.
Lawrence, Hatten
Lawrence, Agie Frazier
Lawrence, James Ernest
Lawrence, Ernest L.
Lester, Casper H.
Lemon, Walter C.
Layman, Henry H.
Light, James G.
Lovell, Burdine

Martin, Peter W.
Martin, Graden Lee
Martin, Noah L.
Moore, Flournoy   (Colored)
Moore, Norman
Moore, William H.
Mangus, George H.
Mangus, William Everett
Meadows, Terry L.
Montgomery, John B.
Marshall, Edgar T.
Moran, Phalus   Killed in France
Moran, Killian
Mills, Claude
Maxey, Raymond L.
Mayberry, Roy C.
Mayberry, Henry C.
Mayberry, Brown C.   In Hospital Corp (Enlisted)
Moles, Wyatt
McPeak, Benjamin H.
McPeak, Samuel
McPeak, Reece
McPeak, Bob
McPeak, Robert W.
McNeil, Bernard S.   Enlisted in Navy

Nester, Sollie
Nester, Robert G.   Enlisted in Navy
Nixon, General P.
Nichols, Leonard T.
Nichols, James L.

Poff, Roy J.
Poff, Joseph B.
Poff, Albert H.
Poff, Lemmy I.
Poff, William R.
Poff, William A.   Enlisted in Navy
Poff, Murray J.
Poff, Alvin
Puckett, Cleveland T.
Phillips, William B.
Phillips, Charley Ross
Phillips, Harley E.
Phillips, Eli
Phillips, Everett C.
Phillips, William Wyatt

Phillips, Mount
Phillips, Glen E.
Phillips, William L.
Phillips, Jethro
Phillips, Roy Angle
Pratt, Lorenza B.
Pratt, Aubra V.
Pratt, George E.
Perdue, Cromer F.
Pugh, Halsie O.
Pugh, Everett R.
Pugh, Henry H.
Prilliman, Jacob G.
Peters, Cloyd H.
Peters, Hansford R.
Pendleton, Isaac E.
Penn, Lewis   (Colored)
Pogue, William R.
Proffit, Floyd P.

Quesenberry, Blane O.
Quesenberry, Charley
Quesenberry, Frederick C.
Quesenberry, Walter A.
Quesenberry, Samuel W.   Died in camp
Quesenberry, Talmage D.   Enlisted in Navy
Quesenberry, Collie R.
Quesenberry, Early C.
Quesenberry, Lonnie Ray

Reed, Enoch
Reed, Raymond R.
Reed, William A.
Reed, Homer M.
Reed, Henry E.
Reed, Oakley T.
Reed, Roscoe Q. E.
Reed, Archie
Reed, Samuel Q.   Enlisted in Navy
Reed, Oscar L.
Reed, Walter S.
Reed, Carl S.
Reed, Griffith L.
Reed, Vernon
Reed, William K.
Reed, Dennis W.

Reed, Jesse M.
Reed, Daniel W.
Reed, Lonnie M.
Ridinger, Thornton
Ridinger, Coy R.
Ridinger, Otto K.
Roop, Harley
Roop, Roscoe E.
Rakes, Palmer C.
Rakes, Roscoe
Rakes, Daniel G.
Reece, Peyton
Richardson, Gradon P.
Reynolds, Clarence C.   (Colored)
Rignery, Isaac
Roop, Herman
Rierson, Cluber K.
Robertson, I. Edward
Radcliffe, Grover M.

Shank, Noah
Shank, Tansaroyoo
Sutphin, Earl W.
Sutphin, Samuel L.   Died in France
Sutphin, Lonnie L.
Sowers, George L.
Sowers, Everett
Sowers, Otho T.
Sowers, Ballard P.
Sowers, Henry Cline
Shelor, Bruster B.
Shelor, Waitman T.
Shelor, Charles L.
Shelor, Harman B.
Smith, Matthew D.
Smith, Posy L.
Smith, Elza E.
Smith, Floyd P.
Stuart, Archa   (Colored)
Spangler, Herman W.
Spangler, Charles B.
Spangler, William McKinley Died in camp
Slusher, Charles A.
Slusher, Samuel C.
Slusher, Wyatt
Slusher, Luther W.   Enlisted in Navy
Slusher, Henry L.

Stump, Joseph	Killed in France
Stump, Demoss	
Stump, James	
Stump, J. Ernest	Enlisted in Navy
Shockey, Herman P.	
Sumpter, John S.	
Sumpter, Bernice A.	
Sumpter, Martin L.	
Stump, Cassell	
Sumner, Graydon O.	
Scott, E. J.	Enlisted in Navy
Semones, Ezra C.	
Sisson, Erastus	
Sowder, Claude E.	
Simmons, Hosea G.	
Slaughter, Henry A.	
Stovall, Sherman W.	(Colored)
Sweeney, Frank C. W.	Died in camp
Sweeney, Oscar R.	
Shortt, Eera	
Shelton, Kyle E.	
Stump, Lewis B.	

Thompson, James M.
Thompson, William J.
Turman, James M.
Tice, Isaac E.
Turpin, Charley
Turpin, Edward H.
Trusler, Posy G.
Thomas, Swanson
Trail, John

Underwood, Taz
Underwood, Arthur
Underwood, Stanton
Underwood, Isaac J.
Underwood, Pled

Vaughan, Arnold C.
Vest, Robert P.
Vest, Shirley E.
Via, Sylvester A.

Whitenack, Henry T.
Whitlock, June O.
Wade, Martin L.
Wade, Guy Mosby

Wade, Kyle J.
Wade, Hiley J.
Wade, Harvey W.
Wade, Wyatt W.
Wade, Henry C.
Weeks, Elmer
Weeks, Joseph L.
Weeks, Herbert G.
Weeks, Kyle M.   Fort Meyer
Weddle, Edgar   Killed in France
Weddle, Jonas L.
Weddle, William McK.
Wurzburger, Lawrence
Wilson, Walter H.
Wilson, Noah D.
Walter, Alonzo
Wimmer, Joseph E.
Willis, Peter A.
West, John G.
Williams, Ora D.
Weaver, Daniel E.   Hospital Corps
Yates, Abner C.
Young, Radford T.   Enlisted in Navy
Young, Claude S.
Young, Charlie C.
Young, Albert D.

EPILOGUE

In concluding these sketches of the dear old relatives of by-gone years, two little poems are presented, written on an imaginary visit to the old home of childhood days, after the lapse of many years. An effort has been made to recall the little incidents of childhood, especially the childhood days peculiar to the compiler.

---

by A. DeRussia Wood
July 14, 1921

Last night I couldn't sleep,
But lay awake,
And a trip back home,
With you did make.

We visited the old orchard,
Where the "gourdsour" apples grew,
Ate "horse apples," "sheepnoses,"
And Baldwins and "thinskins," too.

Then up the hill,
To the "rocky hollow,"
You would lead,
And I would follow.

We climbed the old mulberry tree,
And stained our mouths black,
And rounded our stomachs out,
Before we came back.

We went to the blackheart cherry tree,
Which grew in the orchard by the stable-lot,
And ate the winesap cherries too,
Then lay in the shade, it was so hot.

We went a'fishing in the crooked creek,
Below the "hollow field,"
And "hornyheads" and minnows,
It unto us did yield.

We washed our fish in a little pond,
The little branch made,
　　By the "horn ewe" cowhouse,
Under the cool shade.

We took the road to "Old Tom Barton,"
Crossed the ridge by "stingy lane,"
　　Went by Jake Bower's, and Jim Martin's,
And then walked back home again.

In we came by the old big gate,
Up the hill by the cellar hut,
　　My! we were so tired,
A walking in the wagon rut.

The real pleasure and fun,
We enjoyed it so,
　　In recalling the happy days,
Of the long, long ago.

You made me a little wagon,
All gratis and free,
　　When I asked for my bill, said,
You wouldn't charge me.

I have a little boy,
Whose name is "Little Dick,"
　　He isn't very tall,
And he isn't very thick,

He has often heard me tell,
The things you could make,
　　He wants to come to see you,
And him I must take.

Make thrashing machines, popguns,
And bows and arrows,
　　Wagons and wallbrackets,
And one-wheeled barrows.

How you could paint birds,
Write poetry and declaim,
　　And in his estimation,
You are not without fame.

He has often been told,
How good you were to boys,
  The pains you would take,
To make them nice toys.

  Cousin Sparrel, too,
Was a genius, very able,
  Could make wooden Arabs,
On little wooden tables.

  And little wooden monkeys,
With little wooden tails,
  And little bits of Jonas,
Swallowing down the whales.

  Taken all in all then,
With the ups and downs of life,
  Mine isn't worth living,
Without you count in my wife.

  Her first name is Annie,
Which is not quite Ann,
  But what I can't do,
She usually can.

  You live in the country,
I live in the town,
  We have had a good time,
A rambling around.

  You go to your own home,
I will go back to mine,
  I bid you good-night,
We have had a good time.

RESPONSE
by Daniel Hillsman Wood,
July 19, 1921, Dodson, Va.

I read your letter with mingled thoughts,
And lived again each act,
  I hardly knew within my soul,
Those scenes were yet intact.

Am glad you took that trip with me,
To the old homestead in Floyd,
And brought to life those golden memories,
That naught has yet destroyed.

We went through the old cottage house,
Lingered in each room,
Saw father with his book and pipe,
And mother in the loom.

We went through the orchard,
Ate to a finished fill,
Then took a cool refreshing drink,
From the spring below the hill.

Yes, then we went to the "rocky hollow,"
And climbed a mulberry tree,
And told a hundred foolish yarns,
Filled the air with untamed glee.

Yes, did we ride the cherry trees,
The ground was strewn with leaves,
Then wallowed in their cooling shades,
Like scrubby, stall-fed beaves.

Then we galloped to the "Clifton field,"
And to the winding creek,
Caught minnows, "hornyheads" and eels,
Till we were wet and sleek.

Came back by the "horn ewe" cow house,
Threw our fish in a muddy run,
Then took a flying sunset course,
In quest of a little more fun.

We saw Tom Barton's "razor backs,"
Come down the "stingy lane,"
And saw him lead across the field,
"Old Rachel" by the mane.

And as he took from 'round her neck,
A leather strap and bell,
I chafed him about his roguish sow,
He said to go to hell.

We met up with Uncle Flem,
And told him hardly half,
He pinned up his empty sleeve,
And took a hearty laugh.

Then 'round by Granddad Short's old place,
And out by Jacob Bower's,
We chased some muddy ganders home,
Plucked a few wildflowers.

We lifted our caps to "Aunt" Edith Ann,
She was mad enough to fight,
Across that sunny porch she ran,
And swore by G--d she was white.

The homeward bound we struck a trot,
With laughing shouts galore,
And landed on that much loved spot,
The old granary door.

We manufactured guns and sleds,
Sawed out wagon wheels,
And felt that independent stuff,
That every boy feels.

And now our perfect day is o'er,
Good by to creeks, fields and glen,
We'll live those happy scenes no more,
We are old grey-headed men.

Present these lines to little Dick,
Some day 'twill make him glad,
To read again those funny stunts,
Enacted by his dad.

Bibliography

Agnew, N. Johnson, Comp. **Floyd County Roll of Confederate Soldiers.**

Alvord, Clarence Walworth. **The First Explorations of the trans-Allegheny Region by the Virginians, 1650-1674.** Cleveland: Arthur H. Clark Co., 1912.

Baird, Charles Washington. **History of the Huguenot Emigration to America.** New York, Dodd, Mead & Company, c[1885].

Brock, R. A., ed. **Hardesty's Historical and Geographical Encyclopedia,** Richmond, H. H. Hardesty & Co., 1884.

Brock, R. A., ed. & comp. . . **Huguenot Emigration to America** . . . Richmond, 1886.

Chalkley, Lyman. **Chronicles of the Scotch-Irish Settlement in Virginia.** Rosslyn, VA: Commonwealth Printing Co., Vols. 1-3, 1912.

(Complier Unknown). **Colonel Buford's Detachment of Lewis's Records.**

Cox, Dr. Aras B. **Footprints on the Sands of Time; A History of Southwestern Virginia and Northwestern North Carolina.** Sparta, N. C.: Star Pub. Co. Printers, 1900.

Douglass, William. **The Douglas Register, being a Detailed Record of Births, Marriages and Deaths Together with Other Interesting Notes, . . . 1750 to 1797.** Richmond, VA., 1928.

Douthat, Rudenz Sharp. **Douthet Family Record, with Much Data Concerning the Wells Family, Salmon Family and Blake Family.** Huntington, W. VA., 1933.

Draper, Lyman Copeland. . . . **The Preston and Virginia Papers of the Draper Collection of Manuscripts.** Madison, Wisconsin, State Historical Society, 1915.

Evans, Rear-Admiral Robley D. **A Sailor's Log: Recollections of Forty Years of Naval Life.** New York: D. Appleton and Co., 1901.

Hale, John Peter. **Trans-Allegheny Pioneers;** . . . Cincinnati: Graphic, 1886.

Harman, John Newton. **Harman Genealogy (southern branch) with Biographical Sketches, 1700-1924.** Richmond: W. C. Hill Printing Co., 1925.

Hening, William Waller. **The Statutes at Large;** . . . Richmond, 1809-23.

Howe, Henry. **Historical Collections of Virginia.** Charleston, S. C.: Babcock & Co., 1845.

Hudman, Nita Ann. **History of the Lester Family.**

The Huguenot Society. **Records.**

Johnston, David Emmons. **A History of Middle New River Settlements and Contiguous Territory.** Huntington, W. VA.: Standard Printing and Publishing Co., 1906.

Kirkpatrick, Anne (Ogle). **A Short History of the Ogle Family.** Morrison, Ill.: Shawver Pub. Co., 1927.

Lee, Charles Carter. **The Maid of the Doe;** . . . (poems), Washington Peter Force, Printer, 1842.

McAllister, Joseph Thompson. **Virginia Militia in the Revolutionary War.** Hot Springs, VA., 1927.

Morgan, William Henry. **Personal Reminiscences of the War of 1861-5;** . . . Lynchburg, VA.: J. P. Bell Co., Inc., 1911.

Nuckolls, B. F. **Pioneer Settlers of Grayson County, Virginia.** Bristol, Tenn. The King Printing Co., 1914.

Pendleton, William Cecil. **History of Tazewell County and Southwest Virginia, 1748-1820.** Richmond, VA.: W. C. Hill Printing Co., 1920.

Ross, Captain D. Lee. **Muster Roll.**

Rupp, Israel Daniel. **A Collection of Upwards of Thirty Thousand Names of German, Swiss, Dutch, French and Other Immigrants in Pennsylvania from 1727-1776** . . . Philadelphia: I. Kohler, 1876.

Saffell, William Thomas Roberts. **Records of the Revolutionary War:** . . . New York: Pudney & Russell, 1858.

Salley, Alexander Samuel. **Narratives of Early Carolina, 1650-1708.** New York: Barnes & Noble, 1911.

Shearer, James William. **The Shearer-Akers Family,** . . . [Somerville, N. J., Press of the Somerset Messenger], 1915.

Sowder, Valentine M. **Jewels of Paste.** (short stories) n.d.

Stigleman, Dr. C. M. Newspaper accounts and letters.

Strickler, Harry M. **Forerunners: A History or Genealogy of the Strickler Families, Their Kith and Kin.** Harrisonburg: Ruebuch-Kieffer Co., 1925.

Summers, Lewis Preston. **Annals of Southwest Virginia, 1769-1800.** Abingdon, VA., 1929.

Taylor, Joseph Judson. **Daniel G. Taylor: A Country Preacher.** Louisville, KY.: Baptist Book Concern, 1893.

Taylor, William Carson. **John Lee Taylor: Minister and Missionary.** Nashville: Cokesbury Press, 1925.

Via, George W. **Partial Genealogy of the Via, DeHart and Other Families.** Floyd, VA.: Floyd Press Print, 1926.

Virginia State Library. Selected State Papers and Documents.

Watson, Thomas Leonard. **Mineral Resources of Virginia.** Lynchburg, VA., J. P. Bell Co., c. 1907.

Wingfield, Marshall. **Marriage Bonds of Franklin County, VA., 1786-1858.** Memphis: West Tennessee Historical Society, 1939.

Withers, Alexander Scott. **Chronicles of Border Warfare;** . . . Cincinnati: R. Clarke, 1895.

Zigler, David H. **History of the Brethren in Virginia.** Elgin, Ill.: Brethren Pub. House, 1914.

INDEX

Generally, the index covers names of the early settlers and their children (second generation) and spouses. There are 120 families so listed. Personal names in the index may apply to more than one family member. A name may appear several times on a page but have only one entry in the index. Separate lists have been compiled of churches, mills, minerals, schools, soldiers, land surveys and watercourses.